Judy Ferguson

BLUE HILLS

ALASKA'S PROMISED LAND

Voice of Alaska Press

Blue Hills

Voice of Alaska Press, formerly Glas Publishing
P.O. Box 130, Big Delta, Alaska, 99737

Front Cover: Ben, Sarah and Reb Ferguson, Maclaren Sevenmile
Lake Trail, Denali Highway, 1995.

Back cover: Ben and Reb Ferguson on Black with ptarmigan,
Maclaren Sevenmile Lake Trail, Denali Highway, 1995.

The photos in this book are from numerous private and institu-
tional collections. Photo credits are listed on page 246.

Graphic layout artist: Dragan Miskovic.
Printer: Publikum Printing, Belgrade, Serbia-Montenegro.
Publisher: Voice of Alaska Press, Box 130, Delta Junction, Alaska
99737, USA; 1 907 895 4101.
Email: outpost@wildak.net
Website: http://alaska-highway.org/delta/outpost/

First Printing: April 2003. Heleta Printing Company, Belgrade,
Serbia-Montenegro.
Second Printing: April 2004, Publikum, Belgrade,
Serbia-Montenegro.
Third Printing: 2005, Publikum, Belgrade, Serbia.
Fourth Printing, May 2010, Publikum, Belgrade, Serbia.

Library of Congress Cataloguing-in-Publication Data:
Ferguson, Judy.
Blue Hills, Alaska's Promised Land
By Judy Ferguson

Includes bibliographical references
ISBN 0-9716044-1-X (paper)

For my dedicated sister,
Marian Eskridge Sexton, my
editor, archivist and researcher,
who made *Blue Hills* a reality.

In memory of a singular
human being, and a very dear
friend, Charles Anderson
Boyd.

For Patricia Watts, of the Fairbanks
Daily News-Miner Heartland magazine whose work is reflected in the
seven years of published articles that
ultimately shaped...Blue Hills...

For the women who taught me how to be
a wilderness wife and mother:

Verna Lee Canter

Carol Dufendach

For my Icelandic-American friend,
Daniel Newby, who taught me
how to use a computer

Carol Studebaker Walters

Jeanette Brasier.

Special thanks to assistant editors: Joyce McCombs, Jonathan Riche, Diana Harper, Judi Fouse,
Nancy Porter, Walter Eskridge, Irene Mead, Suli Nee, Dave and Patty Davenport.

Table of Contents

Brooks Range

Deadh◦

★ Bowhunt

Noatak River

Pipeline

Kotzebue   Kiana   ★Ambler   Wiseman★

Kobuk   ★Shungnak   Chandal◦

River   P◦

Kobuk   Arctic Circle

Nome   Yuk◦n Crossing

Yukon River

Nulato ★ Koyukuk   Tanana

Kaltag   Kokrines   5

Unalakleet   Melozi   Ruby   Tanana River   ★ Fairb◦

★Holikachuk

Grayling ★   Delta Junction

Anvik★ ★Shageluk   Alaska Range 4

Holy Cross★ Innoko River   Denali Highway   1

Richardson
Highway

Stony River

Kuskokwim River

Anchorage

ALASKA   V◦

Kodiak   **MA**

1 Maclaren's Se
2 Castner
3 Fergus◦
4 M
5 CosJacket

Map place names are limited to t

ALASKA YUKON NORTHW

NORTHWEST TERRITORY

Tuktoyaktuk
★Inuvik
Tsiigehtchic
Old Crow
★Fort McPherson
MacKenzie River
★Fort Good Hope
★Norman Wells
★Tulita

...on
...rroll
...e
Eagle River

...le
...r
Dempster Highway

...ver
...le
...cken
Dawson

★Wrigley
Yellowknife
★

Tok
Northway

YUKON NORTHWEST TERRITORY BORDER

Ft. Simpson

...SKA YUKON BORDER

YUKON

★ Whitehorse

River

e Lake Trail
, Mt Si
tpost

, nearby

luded in the Blue Hills text.

T TERRITORY

Preface

Blue Hills, a longed-for place where life was visionary was a dream that Judy Eskridge, a young, midwestern woman, couldn't let go. Judy reached for a simplicity beyond the polarized world of the 1960s. Once a raw frontier, America had evolved into a competitive superpower, convulsed by deep rifts. Before the 1968 Chicago Democratic Convention, the boiling point of the revolution, Judy left Oklahoma for Alaska. As she journeyed up the Alcan Highway, Senator Robert Kennedy was shot, a signal to Judy that the world and the life she desired might never again exist in the Lower 48. A secret door opened for her into The Great Land: Alaska, a fresh country of opportunity, the epitome of America's frontier origins. Blue Hills is the story of Judy and her family. It is also the story of the Native people, and the Caucasian trappers and traders. Together the trappers, traders, and Natives are Alaska's grass-roots people who were Old Alaska. Reb and Judy met in Alaska six years before the Trans-Alaska Oil Pipeline began its transformation of classical Alaska. Carrying on the legacy of the old pioneers, Reb and Judy typified the Bush network; their lives were a window into the charm of a rapidly vanishing Alaska. Blue Hills covers the breadth of the North, and those who made it: from the Copper, Tanana, Yukon, and Kobuk River Valleys, to the Northwest and Yukon Territories in Canada. It is Alaska's personal story: the evolution from old to new, from the ice box to global neighborhood, the very human story of the woman and her family who lived it.

Introduction
Where Paths Cross

A soft wind ruffled the leaves; parts of an old trail showed near Rika's Roadhouse. Athabascan trails, later used by prospectors, became footpaths for my husband and our family. Early pioneers left cabins, which became our shelters. Like the lives of our trailblazers, our lives were also dictated by the Tanana River's freeze-up and by current fur prices, not by alarm clocks or by the schedules of others.

When Reb came to Big Delta in 1962, the community's founders, John Hajdukovich and Rika Wallen, were still living. Fort Greely was twenty years old. The local trappers were former soldiers, who like the civilian population, depended on military issue Arctic clothing. The Bush population subsisted on moose meat and anything they could jury-rig. Their caches were bursting with "stuff that might be handy." The contrast between America and Alaska caused local soldiers to call the Lower 48, "back in the World." This is Alaska's transition from Bush to global village.

Before Leaving…

In 1968, in Oklahoma's Turner Falls State Park, I stared at the beaded moccasins on my feet. The boulders under me felt natural in a way that the pavement of city streets did not. A waterfall spilled over the nearby rocks. Overhead, an eagle glided on a wind current. I'd been looking for my life's course. As I stared at the eagle, the simple reality of the out-of-doors orchestra filled my senses and the answer presented itself. A friend later called my dream, "Blue Hills." He taunted me, trying to teach me, "Blue Hills aren't real. They don't exist." However, in 1965, I had already seen Alaska. I had seen something others had not. I would pursue.

Alaska…

During the Great Depression of the 1930s, a poor prospector, trying to survive, had built the tiny cabin we found at McCoy Creek. The hovel was so small; a person could not stand up straight. I had to sit on the pole bunk made of spruce saplings to feed the stove. Hidden by a rocky, babbling creek, McCoy did not lack for beauty, but the shelter kept a person just from freezing.

During my first experience of spring beaver trapping, Reb hiked McCoy Creek checking his traps and snares. While he was gone, I perched on the bed sewing our ripped, canvas, Army mukluks in the light of a tiny portal, feeding the small stove as needed.

A Grizzly was out of hibernation, breaking into cabins. Alone in my small cell, I remembered my mother's 99-foot house, where I had daily cavorted, landing finally for breakfast in her sunsplashed kitchen.

Chapter One
STATE OF THE STATE

13. Martha Eskridge, mother, and Judy, at Eskridge home, Tulsa, 1966.

I n Oklahoma, in the spring of 1968, my father and I went fishing. We caught a mess of crappie. He didn't want to clean them, and insisted we throw them back. But I didn't want to. "Do you know what a mess cleaning fish makes?!" he declared. But, I was not to be deterred. We took the fish home, set up an elaborate cleaning operation in the backyard, and I got my only preparation for Alaskan Bush life: cleaning fish.

I had grown up in 1950s-early 60s' Oklahoma, the daughter of a lawyer in suburbia. From the beginning, I was drawn to trees. I lived in their limbs. While sitting under a tree, I told stories to my sister; I hid in trees, and read poetry in trees. A honeysuckle hedge surrounded my family's home. Within that wall, my family had our life.

Both lawyers, my grandfather and my father solved global problems while charcoaling steaks on a dime store grill, catching the meat's drip with a refrigerator drip pan wedged underneath.

In Comanche, Oklahoma, Granddaddy's small town, he groomed his clientele by rubbing elbows with the Ku Klux Klan or with the Masons. He was not happy when the Democratic Party ran Senator John Fitzgerald Kennedy for President of the United States. Granddaddy felt Kennedy was a betrayer of the original Jeffersonian Democrat ideology. Granddaddy, a retired U.S. Army Colonel, was a veteran of both World Wars, and subscribed to the ideals of General George S. Patton and President Harry S. Truman.

With Kennedy's administration, there came involvement in Viet Nam. The arrival of the Kennedy family signified a social liberalism, a critical thinking. Kennedy's policies were supported on U.S. campuses. After JFK's assassination, a student uprising that pushed for free speech and for a greater involvement in their universities, hit the front pages of the newspapers. In the spring of 1964, a young man thumped the newspaper headlines in front of me, "Students Demonstrate Free Speech, Student Control, Berkeley campus," and challenged me, "Do you understand the significance?! This will only be the beginning. It will spread like wildfire."

That spring, I was invited by my church to go to France and afterward, I visited Yugoslavia. Not realizing how dramatic my departure was, that summer of 1964, I left behind my grandfather's Oklahoma, and entered Tito's Yugoslavia. Eighteen years old, I boarded a student ship for Le Havre, France and left behind a mold in which I would never again fit. I entered Le Chambon Sur Lignon, Haute Loire, France, a town that had once been a World War II Nazi resistance, protective zone for Jews. I met people during the Cold War era who were very different to a girl from Oklahoma.

When I returned to the United States in the fall of 1964, revolution was stirring. The Freedom Riders in the Deep South were registering Colored People to vote. Social awareness was building on the East Coast. Folk singers and Beat poets in Greenwich Village were singing and speaking loudly of this coming revolution.

Chapter Two

1965-68: REVOLUTION

As the revolution rolled like a tidal wave from East to West Coast, I left Oklahoma, in the summer of 1965, to study art at Colorado College. Ibram Lassaw, an American sculptor of Russian-Jewish background, a founder of abstract art and open space sculpture in the United States, was my art professor. His daughter, Denise, had grown up in Greenwich Village, and visited in France. Her stories of adventures in France far outstripped mine.

In the fall of 1965, I moved to California to study at the University of California at Los Angeles, just as the social tidal wave hit full force. The Pied Piper was Bob Dylan, with Frank Zappa's Mothers of Invention adding a new twist.

San Francisco's Golden Gate Park was the paisley-decorated, concert hall. Haight-Ashbury was birthing communes. There was a pilgrimage to return to roots, to a simpler, tribal, natural life,

14. Work camp, College Cevenol, Le Chambon-sur-Lignon, France, 1964:
Judy, center; Misha David, Yugoslav friend, in corner foreground.

reverting to the ways of our ancestors. A Human Be-In called the tribes to gather at Golden Gate Park. Day and night Haight-Ashbury's streets echoed with the words of Bob Dylan, "Come mothers and fathers Throughout the land And don't criticize What you can't understand Your sons and your daughters Are beyond your command Your old road is Rapidly agin' Please get out of the new one If you can't lend a hand For the times they are a'changin'." The 1960s' answer to Senator Joseph McCarthy of the 1950s' was coming in spades. Zappa mocked, "Miss America, walk on by..." and girls from Oklahoma were what Zappa called, "Suzy Creamcheese." The cat was out of the bag.

In January 1967, in the Haight, I ran into Denise again. She took me home to her apartment where she pulled some hot, zucchini bread fresh from the oven for me to taste. We rejoiced over the celebration of life that surrounded us as youth everywhere were exploring their concept of freedom.

Throughout winter and spring of 1967, I worked my way across the United States: Berkeley; Yellow Springs, Ohio; and finally, New York City. My goal was experience and the money for the return fare to France and Yugoslavia. I kicked my father's World War II footlocker onto the baggage scale, and flew to Paris. There, I met my Yugoslav friends, but everyone had changed; we were passing through individual rites of passage. I had come intending to live my life in Yugoslavia, but it was not possible. After a month on the Croatian coastline, I hitchhiked back toward the West. As I waited in the Mediterranean air for a car to pick me up, I thought, rejected, and clarified to myself what I most wanted for my life. The result was: a horse, a cabin, and a good man. Like my beaded moccasins that had felt so natural to me in Turner Falls, Oklahoma, it was a simple need, and it fit, as my young, supple limbs had once wrapped around the trees of Oklahoma.

After my last year at the University of Oklahoma, I suddenly decided to leave for Alaska, where I had visited in 1965. As I left in June 1968, I suspected I was leaving Oklahoma, permanently, but it was still not known. I would miss the political "Be-In" at the July 1968, Chicago Democratic Convention.

In June, I entered the Sub-Arctic; behind me, a door clicked shut. Thirty-one years of a different color lay ahead of me. The door to Yugoslavia closed, and Oklahoma receded, far away. Within those years, unknown to me at the time, there was the matrix of a plan: an intra-connection. But for me, it was far too soon...to know any of that. My Iron-Woman time lay ahead, a gauntlet, reminiscent of my part Cherokee great-grandmother, who, in 1880, left her familial home, and crossed from Kentucky to Texas, in a Conestoga wagon.

15. Reb on Klondike, 1968.

Chapter Three
ENTERING THE NORTH

I n 1968, I watched the geese, in V-formation, flock to the North. I climbed into a friend's World War II jeep, and we drove the 1442 miles up the graveled Alcan Highway. In the Yukon Territory, we picked up a hitchhiker, Verna Canter. She had woods' experience, and promised to teach me. After we heard in a cafe that Bobby Kennedy had been shot, we continued north, as the door to the cities of the south closed behind us. We entered Alaska, the Land of the Midnight Sun.

We left behind the Lower 48 states' ordinary daylight. The sunlight began to intensify, coming at a different angle, forming deep, rarified hues. In Fairbanks, I gazed at the houses around me, bathed in midnight gold. It was a timeless zone: the magic world of Shakepeare's fairy, Puck, and of Queen Titania. An evening reverie washed the intensely emerald-green grass, the yellow-hued sky, and us. I knew I had arrived, and I was home. A few days later, Verna met Thom Nee, a woodsman. We agreed to meet Thom at Reb's, a trapper's cabin, 100 miles south on the Richardson Highway, near Big Delta, 10 miles north of Delta Junction.

Hitchhiking to Big Delta, Verna and I got into the bed of a pickup truck. I sang my rendition of a folk song, "It's a lesson in time for the learning…" I told Verna that while I was in Yugoslavia I had decided I wanted a horse, a good man, and a cabin, open to the sky.

As we stepped out of the truck, we left behind life as we had known it. We stepped into a for-est, deep in moss. As we entered the ancient quiet, we sidled down a deep moose rut. Warm sunshine filtered through the tree canopy, and a cabin sat, as natural as any mushroom. A spruce tree was growing out of the moss on the cabin's roof. Next to the house, a sorrel horse was chewing con-tentedly. Verna smiled at me, "There's the horse; there's the cabin. Let's go inside, and meet the man." We pushed the screen door open. Sitting next to the window, and amused to see us, Reb Ferguson, with slicked back hair, seemed to us like a benevolent father. Verna, adept at talking with men, charmed him while I walked outside, more comfortable with the trapper's horse, Klondike, and the wildflowers

16. Judy on Campbell's hill, August 1968.

17. *Verna and Judy hauling moss for MonteChristo Creek cabin, August 1968.*

in the forest. When I re-entered the cabin, holding a flower, Reb asked — like a line from *Beauty and the Beast*: "Who's been picking my flowers?" I tucked the flower behind his ear.

Thom Nee was living on a hill overlooking Quartz Lake, in a cabin that had once belonged to Charlie Glatfelder. Thom asked Verna to move in, to be "his old lady." Verna, agreeing, shouldered her pack, and I tagged along with my day-pack. Thom carried a chainsaw on his back.

Verna sometimes had asthma, but she would try. The road was a raw trail with no gravel bottom, a swamp of mud. I labored through the mud in my vinyl boots brought from southside Tulsa. Verna began to have problems breathing, so I took her load. My boots plunged into the sucking mud, and the morass hobbled me. I took off my boots, and plunged my bare feet into the permafrost, cold mud, laced with hidden, sharp sticks.

For two hours, we hiked the four miles to Quartz Lake. When my bludgeoned feet were throbbing, Thom turned left onto a hidden trail over the mountain. With no explanation forthcoming from Thom, we climbed the winding woodland path. Finally, the lake appeared, and then, a low cabin.

We walked under the roof's shed-like extension, and stepped over the threshold into the unusual cabin. The vaulted ceiling consisted of logs crossed in concentric, ever-shrinking squares, ending in a flat roof. In the dim cabin, Thom heated and cooked with a small wood stove, using a narrow countertop for his kitchen. There were only two cabins on the lake: Thom's and John Larrabees'. Looking out the windows of the cabin, Quartz Lake was a teardrop shape, set among low-lying hills, and bursting with Great Northern Pike.

The next day, Thom and Verna walked back out to the highway, and invited the trapper, Reb, to dinner. While they were gone, I took a bath in the lake, and hanging my head upside down over the water, I washed my hair. Verna had left me some fresh cotton pedal pusher pants. I slipped on a clean long john top, and started dinner. The trapper, wearing a black leather shirt, wide-brim hat, and sporting a .44 Magnum pistol arrived, riding in a saddle studded with nickel-plating on the Spanish tapaderos. Wearing hip boots, he dropped down off his horse to go fishing.

Reb and Thom caught some fish before Verna had dinner ready. I took the Pike to the lake, and using the skill my father had given me, cleaned the fish. As I climbed the hill to the cabin, Reb stood tall against the sun, watching me with pride. He never missed a detail.

After dinner and Verna's pie, she suggested, "We're going to pitch a little tent for Judy by the root cellar." Reb replied in kind, "I have a place fixed up for her."

18. *Judy mushing in burned MonteChristo Valley, November 1969.*

A couple of days later, Reb came for me on Klondike. I began organizing the house. He had a cupboard full of dirty dishes and I found a galvanized washtub in which to wash them. He put the packsaddle on Klondike, and from the saddle horn, he suspended 5-gallon, water cans. He led Diker to the gravel pit across the road, and got water to heat on the wood stove outside. I laid clean dishes to dry on every available surface.

Reb's friend, John Schulz, had a *Woman's Home Companion Cookbook*, which, through the understanding among friends, I pilfered. I opened it on Reb's Army cot, and studied how to cook. We had few of the book's stipulated ingredients. We did not even have an oven. Undeterred, I made my mother's macaroni casserole, and put it on the wood stove's coals to bake. Reb called it smoked macaroni. The joke sailed over my head; I could not be offended. One day at a time, one page at a time, I would learn.

Reb and I talked long into every night, until the morning came. He told me the story of how he had come to Alaska.

The son of an Italian mother, Reb, born Rowe, had grown up in inner-city Trenton, New Jersey, 10 miles from a patch of trees, his boreal woods, a block from Thermoid's Rubber Factory.

Both of Reb's parents worked and had little time for sport. Reb was not curtailed, however, by the conveyer belt existence. He learned to trap, and, in 1957, when he was 14 years old, he was given a 45-pound, Fred Bear hunting bow. In search of some woods, he hitchhiked to some property on Route 1 that was posted "Keep Out." He scrambled up a tree and balanced precariously on a branch, leaning against the trunk.

In the darkness under the trees, a flick of white caught his eye. Just below, 40 yards away from him, a little "button" buck, with budding horns, passed under the tree. Reb pulled his arrow back and sank it into the animal.

Tearing his pants trying to get to earth, he excitedly pulled out of his jeans pocket an *Outdoor Life* manual on "How to Field Dress." Improvising the deer itself into a field rucksack (also from on-the-spot directions), he skinned the deer's legs, tied them into makeshift straps, and hoisted the meat against his back.

For the rest of his school years, Reb and Bill Chmura, his best friend, hunted the New Jersey farmland.

When they were 19 years old, Reb and Bill hitchhiked to the Last Frontier, loaded with bow and arrows. Reb stayed, and Bill returned to New Jersey. Local trappers: John Schulz, frequently tagged "Schulz;" Charlie Boyd, often called "Charlie" or "Boyd;" and Bill Arrington taught Reb the lay of the land, and the basics of trapping. Six years later, I met Reb.

Every day, we got to know each other better. Two weeks later, Reb repeatedly walked into the cabin, pacing. He would start to talk, and then, he would leave the cabin. Finally, he asked me if I would marry him. A few days later, like two children, we sat in a friend's backyard and began discussing our lives, imagining every detail. I asked him to promise me we would always have a dime to mail a letter home and, occasionally, a couple of dollars for a public shower. He was good to his word.

At the Quartz Lake cabin, Verna and I sewed my simple wedding dress. One day while we were working, Verna's dogs began barking. A stranger was approaching. The door swung open, and an apparition poked her head into the dark cabin. "Denise!" I yelled with recognition. Denise Lassaw, whom I had last seen in Haight-Ashbury, entered Verna's cabin. She was a little exasperated. I, the Tulsa suburbanite, had beaten her to Alaska. Denise had come to Alaska to find a cabin where she might live alone, making all she might require with her own hands, discovering what she was as a human being not as a pre-defined woman or under any other convenient, societal label. She wanted to be quiet and to listen carefully to the wilderness. Hers was a mystical research. After we had caught up with each other, we found a cabin on the highway where Denise could live for the winter. Meantime, Reb and I planned a fall trapline trip. Reb did not think I would last two weeks. He was sure the country would test me beyond my limits, and then, I would change my mind. I assured him I would not. I had come a long way, looking for Blue Hills…

A Wedding for Just Us

When Reb and I had only known each other a couple of weeks, we were together in a cabin while others milled around us. He opened a Robert Service book of poetry, and said to me, "I'd like you to know how I feel." Slowly, he read me the poetry of the North's early days:

"The Lure of Little Voices

"There's a cry from out the loneliness — oh, listen, Honey, listen!
Do you hear it, do you fear it, you're a-holding of me so?
You're a-sobbing in your sleep, dear, and your lashes, how they glisten —
Do you hear the Little Voices all a-begging me to go?

"All a-begging me to leave you. Day and night they're pleading, praying,
On the North-wind, on the West-wind, from the peak and from the plain;
Night and day they never leave me — do you know what they are saying? 'He was ours
before you got him, and we want him once again.'

"Yes, they're wanting me, they're haunting me, the awful lonely places;
They're whining and they're whimpering as if each had a soul;
They're calling from the wilderness, the vast and God-like spaces,
The stark and sullen solitudes that sentinel the Pole."

Smiling, Reb said, "This is my favorite,"

"They miss my little camp-fires, ever brightly, bravely gleaming
In the womb of desolation, where was never man before;
As comradeless I sought them, lion–hearted, loving, dreaming,
And they hailed me as a comrade, and they loved me evermore.

"And now they're all a-crying, and it's no use me denying;
The spell of them is on me and I'm helpless as a child;
My heart is aching, aching, but I hear them, sleeping, waking;
It's the Lure of Little Voices, it's the mandate of the Wild.

"I'm afraid to tell you, Honey, I can take no bitter leaving;
But softly in the sleep-time from your love I'll steal away.
Oh, it's cruel, dearie, cruel, and it's God knows how I'm grieving;
But His loneliness is calling, and He knows I must obey."

While Thom and Verna were on their trapline, Reb and I married in Fairbanks' First Methodist Church. Though there were only four of us present when I walked down the aisle, Reb's eyes shone as he watched me approach. That night in Fairbanks, having no money, we slept on a friend's floor for our honeymoon.

In the fall, Reb brought two sleds into the cabin, and laid them on their sides. He began repairing them for the season's virgin trip, the most demanding, when every tree, every tussock was devoid of adequate snow cover. Guessing how tough it might be, I asked Reb, "Why do you bother taking me, a suburbanite, and teaching me…?"

He looked at me steadily, and said, "Because you have a heart to learn." Not Tulsa Edison High School, University of Oklahoma, U.C.L.A., not my dad, nor Yugoslavia had prepared me for what I would face. Perhaps the genes of my Depression-raised parents, and my part Native American grandmother, Ada Eskridge, helped give me steel.

19. Sox and Olie, with packs, trapline.

Chapter Four

TRIAL BY FIRE

Beaver, with a Side Dish of Rose Hips, Rice, the First Fall

In the fall, Reb and I, and Thom and Verna prepared to build Reb's third trap cabin at MonteChristo Creek. After the cabin was built, Thom and Verna planned to return to Quartz Lake, while Reb and I would explore McCoy Creek, called Flat Creek on later maps, looking for beaver sign. To aid in finding the lodges during the winter when they would be covered with snow and ice, we would blaze whichever tree was standing closest to the beaver lodges.

Reb had trapped the previous winter living in his

20. Judy at McCoy Creek Cabin with Reb's lead dog, King, August 1968.

Army tent at MonteChristo Creek. So, our needed shelter, stove and stovepipe were already up that valley, in place.

Reb had bought me my first Queen Knife and a pair of Red Wing boots. I had spent weeks sewing canvas dog packs for our pack dogs, Olie, King, and Sam. We strapped canvas saddle bags onto the dogs, and loaded them with dog food and grain for the horse. Reb slung our food and his chainsaw onto Klondike's back and secured the load with a diamond hitch knot.

None of us had a horse trailer, but Russ Trastek had a truck. From the corners of the pickup bed, Russ had an extended guard-rail, which was flush with the top of the truck cab. Reb and Russ loaded Klondike directly into the truck bed and tied his head from both sides to the bed's guard-rail. Russ drove very carefully to the trailhead behind Richardson Roadhouse where we off-loaded. From there, we packed over the narrow, wooded trail behind the roadhouse, over Buck Mountain, and the hills of Reb's first cabin, Campbell's. As Reb led the parade with the three of us trailing behind him, I imagined the trail would eventually become like my second home. Verna sampled mushrooms all along the trail. She claimed her tongue would tell her if a mushroom were poisonous, and she spat out whatever did not taste quite right.

As we scuttled toward Campbell's, our boots got soaked from the muskeg's swamp and our pants clung nastily to our ankles.

Reb described the history of the area as we passed through each drainage. "See that steam boiler," he said pointing to a heavy stove hidden in the wild grass. "Don't you ask yourself how it got out there? Fred Campbell, the trapper/prospector who built these cabins in the 1920s, had sledded the boiler in to thaw the ground for prospecting."

Like on the Ponderosa in the TV series, *Bonanza,* a tall rack for drying meat dominated the view of Campbell's Lake cabin. As we made each evening's meal, I learned the routine: haul water, make a wood stove fire, boil rice or macaroni; don't waste food.

The trail from Flat, or McCoy, Creek, Reb's second cabin, to MonteChristo was horrific. It took sixteen hours, and had three creek crossings through porous terrain that was littered with fallen trees and miles of muskeg. Those tussocks of grassy, rubbery earth grew, like two-foot high mushrooms, throughout the swamp water. They were impossible to walk on. In the tight space in between the tussocks, it was barely possible to walk, but very tight and always wet. I kicked into a strolling sailor's stride, reaching my leg from one open space to the other. For twelve hours, we crossed muskeg. Klondike packed the chainsaw, our food, and our gear. Reb stepped lively to avoid Klondike as he jumped each creek. Once, Reb wasn't quite fast enough. Diker landed on Reb's boot sole. When Reb picked up his boot, he had no sole. With some cord, he tied his sole to his boot, but he wrestled it all the way.

That evening in MonteChristo's narrow valley, we pitched the Army tent, and rolled out our military, chicken-feather-filled sleeping bags. As we curled up, Reb's eyes filled with tears, "To think," he murmured, "that Klondike would pack all that gear all this way, just for me."

The next morning, Reb and Thom made a table out of saplings, and Verna got her kitchen organized to begin doing all the cooking.

After Reb squared off the cabin's dimensions, we began chainsawing trees. He gave me a long leaning pole. To prevent the tree from popping back on us as he sawed, I braced the falling trees in the direction he wanted them to fall.

Because we were city kids, we did not realize Klondike could drag the logs to site. So, we were the mules and carried the logs next to the creek while Diker grazed contentedly on the wild grass.

When only a few logs were down, the chainsaw broke. All Reb needed was an Allen Wrench, but he did not have one. We tried to jury rig the chainsaw, but nothing worked. Every log for the MonteChristo cabin had to be felled with an ax.

Since it was August, the sap in the trees was no longer running, so we couldn't simply peel the bark off the trees. Reb and Thom had to blaze each log with an ax to help make the interior of the cabin brighter, and to prevent early decay. Verna and I gathered moss off the ground into burlap bags. As Reb notched each log, he laid the moss into the interlocking fitting and on top of each log. He then set each log snugly into place, fitting them together like a hand in glove.

When the walls were up, Reb pounded nine inch spikes through the sequentially, shorter logs,

21. Reb with Klondike at Campbell's cabin, September 1967.

22. Judy, Army tent, MonteChristo Creek, 1968.

forming two triangular roof gables, one on each end of the cabin. To brace the sides of the gables, we nailed two ridge logs across the top cabin logs. On top of the gables, he laid the main, crown log.

We cut forty slender poles, blazed them, and laid them perpendicular to the ridge logs. Reb covered the poles with moss, and spread polyethylene over the lichen bed. With a pulaski, a mattock and ax combination, he cut sod squares. He threw them onto the rooftop and snugged them into place. A layer of moss cover completed the roof.

To celebrate, we sat down for some salami and cheese. Arapahoe, Reb's lead dog, had just visited the latrine, and came over for a congratulatory kiss. We called him names and sent him packing.

With the work finished, Thom and Verna fairly ran down the valley, eager to get on with building their cabins for the winter. We would join them when we returned.

We were running very low on food and had to decide whether to push on exploring for beaver, or to return home right away. We had two scant meals worth of macaroni, and pancake flour for one and a half breakfasts. Reb gave me a choice if I wanted to cross the mountains. Somehow, I thought it would work out, and I answered, "Let's go over the hill, and the next one, and the next..."

The following morning, we crossed the mountain that separated MonteChristo and McCoy Creek valleys. It was covered with blueberries. I wanted to loll there, and enjoy the beautiful fall day, basking in the sun and feeding on the berries. I could see hill after hill, blue in the distance, to the north, south, east, and west. The land rolled on, wild and unknown, all the way to the Canadian border, and beyond. When he looked at the blue hills from any of the trapline's ridges, Reb said he could not believe that he, the guy from Trenton's Thermoid's Rubber Factory neighborhood, was living this life.

Chocolate Brown and Orange Delicious mushrooms poked their heads up through the fall leaves. Translucent-red, highbush cranberries dotted the Birch forest, spicing the air with their pungency. Wild grasses waved gently in the breeze. The poisonous Amanitas mushrooms lit up the woodland floor, displaying their red and white freckles. Branches grew across the trail like railroad ties. I scuttled through a tunnel of trees, careful not to trip on the in-grown roots.

Through the thicket of rose hips and spruce at the mountain's base, Klondike, Reb and I crashed toward the sound of a tumbling creek. Fresh water poured in a torrent over boulders and rocks. We had come out on McCoy Creek.

Reb set up the Army tent, and daily rode on Klondike up and down McCoy Creek, looking for beaver houses.

If I could make our scant food stretch, there was food stocked at the other cabins on our return home, our back trail. The first day, while Reb was scouting the creek, his lead dog, King, and I picked Rose Hips. King gently slipped the berries into his mouth. Even though he was pretty hungry, he was still, a gentleman. Reb returned to our simmering campfire on the creek that evening with the joy of a boy. He had found active beaver houses, and had marked the lodges. We celebrated with stewed rose hips and macaroni.

While I gathered berries the next day, Reb followed the winding creek downstream. He returned again at sunset, full of excitement, exclaiming he had found an old, tiny cabin, its roof covered with flattened Blazo cans. Reb explained that during the 1930s, old-timers freighted in 5-gallon, white gas cans, one at a time, flattened the cans, and fastened the metal sheets together, to protect the sod and moss roofs.

Inside the cabin, Reb had found an old crock, full of ancient sourdough starter. On a shelf above a pole bed, he found a tiny can of white rice. There was nothing wrong with the 25-year-old rice. We mixed it with our last noodles, stretched it with rose hips, and even shared some with King.

When our explorations were satisfied and the handful of rice was gone, we started for home on our back trail. Always prepared, Reb packed a Smith and Wesson .44 Magnum pistol in a shoulder holster.

Returning through MonteChristo Creek, King ducked into the brush. Suddenly, a bull moose came straight for us, at full charge. Reb whipped out his pistol, and hit him on his left shoulder, turning him just in time. Reb crashed after him through the brush, following the trail of blood on the dead leaves. I heard another blast, and the moose was down. Down the trail, I found a huge animal lying at Reb's feet. Reb directed me to use my new Queen knife to gut the moose for our winter supply. The musky smell of moose, spicy highbush cranberries, and decayed leaves filled my senses, as I locked me into the Alaskan life.

We butchered the moose, and then hung the quarters in our new cabin to wait for our return.

Chapter Five
THE PRINCESS' GAUNTLET

Many years later, I was handed a fairy tale, *The Princess Who Was Proud*. In the children's story, a jester captured the heart of a proud, and stubborn daughter of a king. The joker dragged her across the world, where she suffered, living from pillar to post.

In those early years, I knew nothing of the fairy tale; I had my own: I would be the pioneer queen. In the middle of the most remote wilderness, I would supply us with bread, cookies, and doughnuts. I was sure we would need some of the 50-pound sack of flour at MonteChristo Creek. Beyond that cabin, over the ridge, and down in McCoy Creek Valley, where we would spend half the winter, I was certain we would need the balance of the flour. Reb argued that we did not need that much flour, not on the first trip of the season. "But," I reasoned, "there might be only one trip in. I will get it in."

Starting from home, mushing across Shaw Creek Flats to Campbell's Cabin, we broke trail in the fresh snow. We alternated: one of us snowshoed ahead, while the other kept the two sleds on the trail, routinely righting any sled that slid off course. If Reb were up front, if there were dogfights, or if a sled slid off the trail, I had to deal with it alone. In my slippery, white canvas, Army mukluks, I waded into the soft snow, grabbed dogs, or fixed sleds. As long as daylight lasted, we broke trail. Then, with dusk, we returned on our back trail to the nearest cabin.

Typical Alaskan scene looking south from junction of the Alaska and Richardson Highways near Big Delta. Three-peaked Mt. Hayes, elevation 13740 ft on the right, and Mt. Deborah, with elevation of 12,000 ft on the left. Standing in the Big Delta River is "Old Bill" best known of the big buffalo herd in Big Delta.

23. Big Delta, Delta River, Mount Hayes, Alaska Range, U.S. Army Arctic Indoctrination
School Annual, 1947, Big Delta Allen Army Airfield.

It was dark by the time we reached each day's cabin, about 3 P.M. We chained and fed the dogs. One of us grabbed the empty, 5-gallon can, and headed for the open creek. The other always got a fire going, and lit the gas lantern. Once the chores were finished, we collapsed onto the pole bunks, twisted open the half-frozen peanut butter jar, gobbed some spoonfuls down our throats, and swilled it down with creek water. Dust particles glowed red, crackled and popped on the stove's top. When the stovepipe grew cherry red with trapped, burning creosote, Reb would holler, "Shut the stove down! Stovepipe fire!"

Resting in our cabin, we flipped on "God's Tower of Power," KJNP radio's fifty thousand watt station: the voice to the Bush, the Northern Hemisphere, and our cabin. The heat began to seep into our pores as we drifted off in its embrace, on our magnificent pole bunks. When the stove needed more wood, the chill woke us. Forcing myself up, scuttling between crude table and barrel stove, I cooked moose steaks, reconstituted mashed potatoes, cream corn gravy, and topped it all off with a dollop of jam for dessert.

When KJNP's Trapline Chatter came on, we stayed up to hear messages from the villages to the Bush. With that ritual completed, we turned off the lantern and scurried into our down bags, just as the lantern sputtered, and expired.

At that time, we had five cabins: Campbell's Lake, Flat Creek, MonteChristo, McCoy, and the Salcha. Each cabin was distinct from the other. Campbell's and Flat Creek had been built in the 1920s by Fred Campbell, a prospector who had come into the North in the first waves of white migration.

The previous fall we had built MonteChristo, snugged next to the head of a spring-fed creek in a narrow, alpine pass. MonteChristo meant to me what Heidi's Alm Uncle's cabin meant to her.

Down from McCoy Creek, and 60 miles up the Salcha River, we had found another old cabin. More centrally located, and a little larger, the Salcha cabin would be our headquarters during beaver trapping season. Two weeks of breaking trail were needed to reach the Salcha cabin from Campbell's Lake. Getting there was a marathon. If we were not fighting soft snow; underpowered dogs; trees; freight; muskeg; dark; and cold; then, it was overflow. Overflow struck terror to a musher's heart: water oozing under hydrostatic pressure, in the coldest of winter. In early winter, it was particularly bad, and also, in the spring. Several inches of icy water could be hidden underneath soft snow, ready to soak a musher in sub zero temperatures. During weeks of continued oozing, the ice mounded into slanty, bumpy stratifications. What may once have been a deep ravine-like creek crossing became a flat plain of ice due to repeated mounding.

I avoided thinking about the run from MonteChristo to McCoy. The sixteen-hour ascent into the muskeg valley was laced with creek crossings, and narrowed eventually into a moose rut. I had the 50 pounds of flour riding in front, pulled by three poor dogs over an unbroken trail. The sled continually overrode the trail, and repeatedly sank into pillow-soft snow. Walking forward, I sank, and dug desperately with my toes to lift the sled back onto the trail.

Most of the time, Reb traveled far ahead of me. If we were sledding a long, downhill slalom, my sled frequently missed a curve, overrode the trail, and wedged hard behind the far side of a tree. Frightened of abandonment, my dogs pulled insanely from the opposite side of the tree trying to catch up with Reb, far ahead. I could not pull backwards on three straining dogs to free my sled and follow Reb. Frustrated, I screamed, "REB!" but Reb just kept swishing over the snow. Blithely unaware, with his earflaps down, he could not hear my cries slicing the frozen air, and falling, unheard, to the ground. In the silence following my screams, my dogs panted. Like sap chunks on the blazed, wounded trees, my tears froze on my cheeks.

When I could finally get free, Reb was only two bends ahead of me, and up a rise. He would be leaning on his sled, waiting for me with smiling eyes. "Ready?" he would ask, and then off he would go again on his sled. The sled swished softly on the trail, punctuated by the dogs panting, and the pad-pad-padding, of their trotting feet. Birch seeds lay on the crystalline snow, and patterned sunlight filtered through the large spruce trees. Occasionally, a dog scooped snow with his mouth, while another, on the run, let their bowels fly.

Spring was our reward. By April, eighteen hours of sunshine made the trail punchy by noon. Our trail's concrete-like base thawed with the warming temperatures of early spring, causing our feet to sink through the trail up to our knees. Reb and I rose at 5 A.M., and sledded until late morning. By the time our legs were crunching through the crystallized surface up to our thighs, usually, we had arrived at a cabin. We chained the dogs, who slept with their noses securely protected by their tails. Reb threw off his Army parka, flopped a sleeping bag on the cabin's mossy roof, and listened while I read him a Louis L'Amour western. Reb dozed, stretched out in the miracle of spring's renewed warmth.

Chapter Six

ARMY ARCTIC TRAINING CENTER

A look back at the start of the military arctic survival school in the Delta area Many of Big Delta's trappers arrived through the military, and certainly the arctic clothing and equipment we used was U.S. Army issue. Alaska has been dubbed, "The House That Uncle Sam Built". After World War II, the military, more than all the previous gold rushes, pumped a billion dollars of equipment, money, roads, transportation, forts, and clothing, not to mention, young men into Alaska. In 1947, the Army sent Charles

24. Corporal C. A. Boyd, Big Delta Allen Army Airfield, 1947.

Anderson Boyd, formerly a young trapper from Oklahoma, to Alaska. In Delta, he began working with another soldier, Jess Taylor, to develop a classified military sled dog kennel. With their input and labor, Big Delta Army Air Force Base's new Army Arctic Training Center began a quality sled dog program that shipped canines to assist those fighting in the Korean Conflict.

Army Sergeant Jesse Taylor had just gotten his orders the summer of 1948. He tossed the question to soldiers at the Fort Richardson barracks, "Anybody ever heard of Big Delta?" No one had. But Taylor did not have to wait because right then a runner from the barracks announced the departure of his flight for Big Delta's Allen Army Airfield. In 1948, no one suspected Big Delta or Allen Army Airfield would become the future site of the twenty-first century's so-called Star Wars, the National Missile Defense Program's Ground-based Midcourse Defense. In 1948, Allen Army Airfield had not been joined to the future. Fort Greely, but served as a defense shield by being a landing strip for the Lend-Lease Program. Three years earlier, during World War II, when the Allies were supplying airplanes to the Russians fighting the Axis Forces in the U.S.S.R., Allen Army Airfield had been a landing strip for planes piloted by the Soviets through the Lend-Lease Program. By the time, Taylor arrived, the Army base had moved from World War II readiness into the Cold War era. During the previous war in Europe, American preparedness for cold weather warfare had been a weakness. With the Korean conflict anticipated, the base located near the Alaska Range was perfect for helping the Army strengthen its Achilles' heel.

When Jess Taylor landed at the air field, he arrived into an ideal training base. Delta's mountains, glaciers, rivers, swamps, lakes, tundra and muskeg were the grounds for the Arctic Indoctrination School, a forerunner of the Northern Warfare Training Center. Big Delta Air Force Base, a collection of Quonset huts, became the new training site. In November 1948, classes began in Jamesways, which were canvas-covered frames heated with a space heater.

Sergeant 1st Class John Callahan was a skiing and mountaineering instructor. Snow machines were not yet common and the Army relied on dogs for field support work. Sergeant Taylor was chosen to be an Army sled dog trainer with the help of Corporal C.A. Charlie Boyd, a young soldier from Muskogee, Oklahoma. Part of Taylor's task was to help build a sled dog kennel near the airstrip. Taylor knew gee and haw from driving horses as a boy with his dad in West Virginia, but as an Army dog trainer in Alaska, he needed some help, as well as dogs. Taylor found a sled dog transportation field manual from the War Department that showed detailed sled designs and fan and tandem rigging for dog teams.

Dogs were imported from the Nome Air Force Survival School, from Fort Rini in Colorado, and from Fort Drum in New York. A kennel of sixty dogs was established. The dogs were tattooed and records were kept; two of the dogs had been on Antarctic expeditions.

Dogs were trained for use in Korea. They could evacuate a wounded soldier more safely than a man could because they were dispensable; the dogs also ran lower than a man, below the ordinary bullet zone. Korea's cold was also hard on the men. The Arctic Indoctrination School conditioned the soldiers for the cold, and tested a new evacuation sled, the *ahkio*.

Local caribou trails were ideal for teaching the leaders to gee and haw, to turn left and right. However, wherever tanks had been, they left broken, sharp spears of ice, potentially savage on both musher and dog. For such potential accidents, Taylor carried suture supplies, and did vet work on the trail. Once, Taylor put forty stitches in one animal. He was not sure the animal would survive, but, in six weeks, the dog was able to work again.

In 1949, the Argentine military contacted the U.S. Army to purchase fifty dogs. Taylor's training assistant, Charlie Boyd, traveled across the state to find dogs to send to Argentina. In Nome, Boyd spotted an Eskimo boy, riding on sealskin around town, pulled by a big, black dog. The dog, Mike, was the only survivor, man or animal, after an Eskimo hunting party was lost on the frozen

25. Big Delta Allen Army Airfield, c. 1948.

26. *Sergeant Jess Taylor, U.S. Army Dogs, Army Arctic kennel.*

Bering Strait. Mike was an unusual dog and Boyd bought him for his personal dog team.

In Taylor's dog sled kennel, he had only trained enough animals to carry extra gear during campouts, and to accompany the soldiers. The soldiers were conditioned in the -65° F. temperatures to pull their own camping equipment. Taylor divided the soldiers into tent groups of six men each. As they broke trail, each group of men was harnessed to a 200-pound ahkio sled loaded with stove, tent, and supplies.

Originating from Finland, the *Ahkio* quickly became an Alaskan staple. When used by the Laplanders, *Ahkios* were a boat-shaped, wooden sled with a copper bottom, pulled by reindeer. The U.S. Army refashioned the Finnish design into a tough fiberglass body.

On Taylor's expeditions, he connected a string of loaded *ahkios*, spaced 5 inches apart. Taylor tested whether the dogs did better pulling one huge sled, or pulling a string of twelve *ahkios*. The dogs could budge a heavier load, more efficiently, in twelve connected units than they could when the load was concentrated in one unit.

"The sleds wouldn't turn over if the connecting lines were kept tight. Eight or nine dogs could pull 2400 pounds, in total," Taylor said.

Daily, the soldiers skied 20 miles, from early morning until late afternoon, no matter the weather. "We skiied and waited, sweat and froze, waiting for everyone to catch up. Duty in Korea might have been preferable," Taylor mused.

For overnight camping, the troops put up tents, built snow caves, or built brushy, lean-tos that faced each other and the fire. With parkas across their backs, the soldiers slept facing the fire, to catch the heat. The lean-tos were roofed with shingled spruce branches. To shield from possible melting snow, they made a sub-roof of ponchos.

Each tent group did its own cooking. They ate rats, C-Rations, or they combined rats with moose steaks or stew. For the steaks, Taylor always carried a 2-foot-wide skillet. The dogs ate dried fish. For drinking water, they melted snow, but the snow was littered with rabbit feces, so they strained the pellets with a shirt.

Taylor designed a harness for the dogs that allowed for minimal snow contact, reducing the accumulation of extra snow freezing into weighty globs on the harness' cotton webbing. The webbing looped from the leather collar, over the dog's shoulders and back, and then attached to the bellyband, above the snow's surface.

The soldiers traversed glaciers, mountains, and muskeg. Ski instructor John Callahan led troops across Black Rapids Glacier, testing the safety of the ice with his ax. For weeks, the soldiers camped and traversed. In the spring, Taylor dogsledded the refuse, left by the trainees, out of the area. The training camp for Callahan's skiers was the beginning of today's Black Rapids Army Training Site.

Taylor, Boyd, and Callahan developed an expertise for the military in Arctic travel. In the process, they also invented equipment: fuel oil, clothing, and sleds. The dogs wore collars that bore their classified credentials: "U.S. War Dog." In their off-hours, Boyd and Taylor hunted and trapped in the mountains.

Boyd traveled up the road to Black Rapids Roadhouse where he met the proprietors, Bert and Mary Hansen. To get ready cash, Boyd sold furs to Bert, making some good deals.

Black Rapids was not the Hansens' first roadhouse. They had originally come to Big Delta in 1939 to compete with Rika's Roadhouse located at the Delta and Tanana River confluence. Until the late 1940s, the Hansens operated Bert and Mary's across from Rika's on the Tanana River. To secure his investment, Bert filed on a homestead on land next to the Tanana and its adjacent

27. Double Tandem Hitch, War Department Field Manual
Manual, Figure 21, August 19th, 1944.

slough. Close, but hidden from view and snugged against a bluff, the protected homestead was dubbed "Hansen Hollow," or later dubbed, "The Holler."

In transition, Charlie Boyd was preparing to be discharged from the military. Wanting to remain in Alaska, he rode the military bus to the Hollow to see the land. Charlie asked Bert if it might be possible to trade some firewood for a couple of acres. Bert sealed the deal with Charlie.

Boyd's quiet spot on the Tanana slough, however, was interrupted in the early 1950s. Two other former soldiers, John Schulz and Russ Trastek, filed on two homesteads nearby. They purchased one lot that was contiguous to Boyd's land and the other was past his property. They moved a log home onto the second lot and immediately tagged it the Doll House, in hopes of transitory female companionship. Although they were friends in the beginning, Schulz and Charlie differed over the use of alcohol. Charlie Boyd never drank. He had more in common with Jess Taylor than with Schulz and Trastek, but after Jess' discharge from the military, he moved to Fairbanks.

In Fairbanks, Jess' new house typified classical Alaska. Jess used two propane burners coupled with a wood cookstove for cooking. He kept sled dogs, and until well into the 1990s, his kitchen shelving was made from Blazo boxes, the wooden crates that originally held white gas cans, a common sight in old time Alaskan trappers' cabins.

28. *U.S. Army ahkio with canvas cover on Tanana River banks.*

Base School

After 1944, the Army Arctic Center was also responsible for the education of the local children. In 1952, responsibility diverted to the Alaska On-Base School System, a territorial government division charged with servicing base schools.

In lieu of teachers, a string of Army sergeants proctored the school, using the Calvert Correspondence Course to instruct the children. The school included both military dependents and children of civilians from in and around the Delta area. "There were no grade levels. The thirty-three children were simply tested and given a textbook according to their individual skill level," former student Tom Theisen recalled.

One of the four original Big Delta students, and a 1959 graduate, Ray Woodruff remembered riding to school with classmates in a two-and-a-half-ton, four-wheel drive, military truck lined with benches. Covered with insulated canvas and warmed by a gasoline heater, the children were accompanied on the long, cold ride by a military policeman.

"School was held in four different facilities before Allen Army Airfield's Army Arctic Center transitioned into Fort Greely School, where in 1955 the current modern school was constructed," Woodruff said. "In 1948, the first school was a room in the G.I.'s Service Club. The winter of

1949-50, we moved into two rooms in the airplane hangar. By the fall of 1950-52, we shared the Quads with three families."

The Quads was military housing made up of four Quonset huts butted up against a frame washhouse. Strings of clothes hanging on lines, wringer washers, toilets, and showers filled the washhouse. Families lived in three of the four Quonsets while the school was in the remaining one.

"All the families as well as the school's thirty-three students shared the same toilet facilities," recalled Irene Hansen Mead, the daughter of Bert and Mary Hansen.

"Snow blew halfway down the front hall, and in between the floorboards," Velma Dickson, a former teacher at the school said. "Critters used to routinely visit the classroom."

This situation soon transitioned to private Quonset huts dedicated exclusively for school. The huts were built on the edge of the airfield, offering entertainment far superior to school.

"Because of the school's prime view, the class' attention span was easily diverted as students watched helicopters and airplanes taking off," said Theisen. "In 1953, the students got their own washhouse, facing away from the airstrip."

When the school originally was started, there was a required minimum head count needed, and the Delta school came up one short. Mary Hansen of Hansen's Hollow permitted her daughter, Irene, who was actually too young, to be figured into the count, thus authorizing the school's opening.

At the time that Irene Hansen was helping out the base school, Charlie Boyd was moving into his new home in Hansen's Hollow.

Chapter Seven
CHARLIE'S DOG TEAM

As a child, Charlie Boyd had built model airplanes and always wanted to fly. He used to joke, "I wanted to fly in the military, but I wound up looking at the hind end of a dog instead."

After he left the military, Charlie, having obtained sled dogs through his military connections, became a trapping partner with R.L. Bob Johnson. Bob had been reared in the Upper Goodpaster River area and had inherited the Upper Goody's (as the Goodpaster is sometimes called) trapping rights from his step father, Walter Johnson. Through Bob's step uncle, Lawrence Johnson, Charlie also obtained a trapline on the Lower Goodpaster. To these areas, he added the Goodpaster's South Fork and the Charley River, until the Charley River area became incorporated in the Wrangell-St Elias National Park and Preserve.

John Schulz met, and struck up a friendship, with old-timer, Slim Carroll, on the Lower Goodpaster. In exchange for helping the elderly Carroll, Schulz and Trastek obtained Carroll's trapping rights on Upper Shaw Creek.

Reb pointed out the difference in old Alaska in the decade preceding his arrival to the North, "The ten years' gap between 1952 and '62, when I first came to Alaska, made a big difference. In that window, Alaska changed a lot," Reb said. "Schulz and Trastek were very good trappers. In the spring, they brought in hundreds of beaver pelts from Shaw Creek." Reb went on to describe the many hides he had seen swinging in the breeze on the clothesline in front of the partners' cabin.

One spring, Charlie delayed his return from his Goodpaster trapline until May. By then, of

29. Charlie Boyd's sled with dried fish, and dog team: Toby, Kandik, Unknown, Cassandra and Mike, spring 1950.

course, he had to push the sled on the newly bare ground from one soft snow patch to another. After hours of pushing his five tired dogs that were lazy with the spring sunshine, Charlie, completely disgusted, left his team. He walked to Reb's cabin at Big Delta, and as he entered Reb's home, he jerked his thumb backwards and said, "If you want 'em, go get 'em." Reb, who had a small team, added four of Charlie's dogs to his string. Charlie kept his favorite leader, Who-Disser. Charlie, who was mechanically talented, had been looking for the opportunity to switch from dogs to his first love, airplanes. He also wanted to try out the new snowmachines.

For the non-mechanically-minded Reb, the early snowmachines were neither sufficiently dependable nor suited to Reb's mountainous trapline. From Charlie's team, one lead dog became Reb's soul mate: Arapahoe, called A'hoe or Hoe.

Arapahoe Returns

Reb trapped alone for several winters, with only the two favored dogs whom he brought into the cabin at night for company: A'hoe and his spotted bird dog, King. A'Hoe was wolfy-looking, and smart. Like Reb, he had dominant canine teeth. As the two sat by a Coleman lantern in the long evenings, Reb would urge Arapahoe to, "Smile, A'Hoe." On cue, Hoe would curl his upper lip, and bare his canines into a grin. The two of them sat, grinning like a trapline mirror, on the pole bed, "Smile, A'Hoe, smile."

In the spring of 1968, Reb took Fred Johnson, a G.I. friend, on a bear hunt on the trapline. They strapped a dog pack of grain for the horse on Arapahoe, and saddled two horses, and, like dudes, swung up into the seats for a proper hunt. Close to Campbell's Cabin, Arapahoe's back was breaking from the weight of the horse grain. When Reb, who was just learning animal husbandry, saw Hoe could hardly walk, he threw the grain onto the horse's neck. They continued to the cabin, but the next morning when the hunters were ready to depart, Hoe couldn't walk. Leaving Arapahoe there at Campbell's Cabin, Reb also left some food for the dog, figuring Hoe would follow later when he was strong enough.

In Rosa Pass that evening, two black bears scooted through the brush. Fred was thrilled to land them. When they had the meat packed on the horses, Reb left some for Arapahoe. After Reb had been home for a week, Arapahoe still had not returned.

Concerned, Reb asked Charlie Boyd, who borrowed an airplane, to fly him over the trapline. Reb leaned out the window of the small plane, and hollered, "Arapahoe, come home!!" while he scanned the terrain for his lead dog.

I met Reb the day after he flew with Boyd. To me, the dog seemed like only a vaporous myth. Two weeks later, when our dogs started barking, Reb went outside to investigate the commotion. Arapahoe was walking down the path. Tears started running down Reb's cheeks, and he embraced his wolfy friend, saying, "You came home, Ho…You came home."

One long, black night, Arapahoe blessed me with his intelligence. It was my second winter in Alaska and I had a poor team. The previous summer I had hitch-hiked to get George, one of my three dogs, from the dog pound in Fairbanks and then, I had hitched south to Tok to get my second dog. Both they and I were green; they were barely walking, let alone actually pulling the sled. So, I trudged until midnight pushing my mountain hotrod. To delay the agony of mushing the remaining ten miles home, we decided to look for a Shaw Creek cabin, Dahlman's, where Reb had been only once before, and that was in the summertime. Arapahoe had also been there with

Charlie Boyd, and even better – it had been on the winter trail. Reb was not certain he knew the way. In the moonless, dark night, he tried to remember, choosing trails by instinct. We came to a turn. Not knowing whether to go left or right, Reb saw, in the darkness, A'Hoe prick his head to the right. He followed the dog's lead. When we arrived at the cabin at 1 A.M., Reb concluded, "When I knew the correct turn, 'Hoe didn't, but when I wasn't sure, Arapahoe was!"

The Last Chapter in A'Hoe's Life

Reb was chainsawing trees for firewood in the spring of 1970 while his dog team waited nearby. The tree slipped, rotated, and fell directly on Arapahoe. At home, Reb could barely tell me the story. To others, he simply said, "A'Hoe had a heart attack." When he was alone, tears washed his face; he had lost his best friend who had shared his trails and his life.

30. Arapahoe with dog packs, June 1968.

31

Chapter Eight
NEST OF OUTLAWS

y the late 1960s, "Hansen Holler," the end of the road, quickly became Never Never Land for men who had resigned from mainstream society. John Schulz tinkered with snow machines in the winter, and fixed his outboards in the summer. His partner, Russ Trastek, a diesel mechanic, periodically worked on the North Slope. Trastek was everyone's sponsor; on his daily route to the Delta Post Office, he always bought drinks for the house at the bars along the Richardson Highway. He also grubstaked Schulz, stocking him with supplies for their mutual trapline.

Another resident of the Holler, reputedly once a school principal, Earl Miller, was affectionately dubbed, Jake the Snake and was a three time loser. Jake had managed to evade three wives, defaulting on alimony payments to all.

Routinely, during the summer, Jake would stride into a bar, throw a fur on the counter and demand of the clientele how much the fur was worth. Jake was adept at the role of mountain man, par excellence. Military wannabes plied Jake with Jack Daniels Whiskey to elicit the secret of his coveted life. Jake would sing about a valley of marten tracks, where he had snowshoed for miles, but somehow could not "get quite enough for a grubstake" to trap the valuable furs. Hours later, Jake had money, had obtained a partner, and could make it "just one more winter on the 'Line.'" That done, Jake would amble to the next bar, throw down his pack and begin the tale, again.

In the early 1960s, a 21-year-old muskrat trapper and his buddy, Bill, arrived in Big Delta from New Jersey, wanting to expand into Alaskan trapping and big game hunting. Jake promised to feed Reb Ferguson if Reb would just build him a cabin. John Schulz showed Reb how to handle

31. Russ Trastek, Bill Chmura, Reb Ferguson, Red Olivera, Jake Miller,
Bolio Lake, August 1966.

a chainsaw, and Russ Trastek introduced him to Delta's social life at three of Delta's nine bars: the Bay Hotel, the Buffalo, and Tom's Inn.

"By the time I arrived in the early 1960s, a lot of the Holler was wanted for something," Reb remembered. The law was after Jake for alimony. Edwards had reputedly been a pimp. Red Flaherty had a game going at the Buffalo Hotel. John Schulz and Russ Trastek's schedule mandated going to Delta daily for their mail, but it also included doing the bar circuit, both going to town and returning. Calamity Jane -- Lea -- Emerick Schulz, held her own, sometimes with a rifle. A sign noted, "Enter the Holler at your own risk."

I knew that. Once, when Reb and I were having coffee with John Schulz, Boomer, a barber friend of John's, accompanied by his young daughter, came to visit. John was inebriated, and felt like shooting his automatic rifle. He began peppering the road, right on the heels of Boomer. The child was terrified and crying. Boomer cried, "John! Not when my daughter's here!" The child eased her body along the car for protection, jumped in, and Boomer gunned the car out of the Holler.

When Klondike was new to Reb, he rode him over to the Holler. John did whatever moved him. When Reb arrived, John began rat-a-tat-tating around the young horse with bullets. Laconically, Reb suggested to John, who was afraid of horses, "John, now you get on, and I'll shoot."

This kind of gunplay was not uncommon. Lea was John's girlfriend. For a short time, she

32. Jake Miller and Red Olivera, Tanana River, September 1966.

lived in a guest cabin in the Holler next to John and Russ'. Russ Trastek did not appreciate his partner bringing a woman into the boars' nest. Fed up with Lea's presence, Russ approached her cabin one morning with a big spoon and skillet. He began banging it as if to waken the dead, "Okay. You've been here long enough! Time to go; time to get out! Let's go!!" Lea's presence suddenly filled the door. She pointed a rifle muzzle at the earth, and began firing near Russ' feet. Russ' spoon froze in mid-air. Silently, and oh, so efficiently, Russ put it in reverse.

After I arrived in Big Delta, Lea had established her quarters away from the Holler, two miles south in Big D. Reb and I often walked two miles to Probert's grocery store. On the way back home, we stopped at Lea's Quonset hut across the street from the grocery. Lea would stop everything and always served us hot coffee. In language that would make some people blush, Lea loved to talk about what she would do to Russ, if given half a chance.

Remembering Jake's means of survival, Reb recalled, "We lived pretty close to the starvation line in those days," Reb remembered, "We were doing well if we had groceries for a few days. When one of us got some food, Jake would suddenly show up. He moved from house to house, depending on the condition of the pantry. When the food ran out, Jake engineered an argument with his host, which gave him an excuse to move to where the larder looked better.

"Everyone was getting tired of Jake's free-loading lifestyle," Reb grinned. "One evening, I was watching John's place. John had a new sleeping bag from Recreational Equipment Incorporated:

the pretty blue, Mount McKinley, goose down bags, good to -50° F. John hadn't even slept in it yet. He told us all about it and had it on display, nicely fluffed up on his bed.

"That evening, Jake came in very drunk. He started arguing, and chopping dog chains with his ax. He squatted by a dog in the yard and defecated. But, he got tangled up in the dog chain. In his stupor, he tripped on his pants and fell backward in his own feces. Too intoxicated to realize, he simply made the situation worse.

"Jake was ready to pass out and headed for Schulz' bed. I said to him, 'Better not sleep in John's new bag!' 'Oh, hell with it,' Jake responded and passed out in Schulz' bag.

"The next morning, John, who had been at Lea's all night, came driving in rather early, pleasant, looking forward to the new day.

"'Uh, oh,' I thought, 'Here it comes…'

"John walked into his cabin, and said, 'I smell [expletive.]' Jake woke up, and agreed, 'Yeah, I smell it too,' and scratched his nose with a contaminated finger. 'And, it's…it's…me (?)!'

"Jake slammed his fist down on the table, and swore, 'I have done a lot of things in my life, but I have never, never [expletive] in my own bed.'" With that, Jake left the country. He was not heard from again for eight years…until the pantry again was well stocked with the boom of the construction of the Alyeska Pipeline.

When I came to Big Delta, Jake was only a legend. But in our trap cabins, he had left a legacy of his odor in our cabin's cache drums. Jake had trapped one winter with Reb, and left his long john tops in the 55-gallon cache drum. Consequently, all the stored food: the Oleomargarine, flour, and lard had a distinct flavor of Jake.

When Jake did return, it only gave entrance to new escapades. One day, when I walked into Schulz' cabin, Jake was present. To his great delight, I said, "Not the famous…mythological Jake…?!"

There was a new animal in Schulz' dog lot: a mongrel who bit the derrieres of anyone foolish enough to turn his back on the dog.

En route from the outhouse to the cabin, Jake got too close to the aggressive dog. On Jake's next trip to the Big D bar, despite that two lady schoolteachers were present, Jake, sans underwear, had to demonstrate to Moose, the bartender, just what the infamous dog had done to him. Everyone nodded seriously, offering his condolences until Jake exited the bar.

Schulz' friends were getting horses. Even though Schulz was afraid of getting off the ground, not to be outdone, he decided to get a young colt, Horser. One day when I visited, Horser was grazing on a tether in the Holler yard. Clint, our son, was with me. Jake bridled the horse, picked up my four-year-old son, slipped him on the colt's bareback and smacked the horse's rump, much to Clint's joy. I was aghast. Jake's eyes twinkled, and he said, "That's how you teach 'em to ride!" Clint handled the horse, a little like he had been *born to it.*

When Reb's mother came to visit us in 1975, she met Jake, who, like she, was from New Jersey. She smiled with great respect, and said to the man who greatly resembled Buffalo Bill, "Thank you, Jake, for taking care of my son!"

Chapter Nine
DIFFERENT CLOCK

The stopwatch has ruled our lives. The Iditarod, and the Yukon Quest, as well as our jobs – all have been timed; we compete to do each job quickly. John Schulz had a different understanding of time.

The last musher to reach Nome, John set the record for the longest time spent running the first – the 1973 – Iditarod dogsled race. Visiting John at his cabin in "The Holler" was to step back in time. Though the world around John changed from the 1950s to the 1990s, the "Holler" still had a 1950s, olive drab feel. The same snowmachine and outboard parts seemed to have been lying there forever on the banks of the Tanana River. Here, time moved like the slow river.

In every season, John had his own way of doing things. No matter what the temperature or the hour; if John felt like trapping, he hit the trail. If the price for boating too late in the fall was that he got frozen in up the Goodpaster River, he did not mind; he just walked back to the Holler.

Once, John was so slow that he won the Blue Lantern, set an enduring record for being the slowest driver ever, received two hundred dollars, a half-ounce of gold, and a lot of fun in Nome – all prizes for being last in the Iditarod Trail Sled Dog Race. But, on another occasion, his sense of timing almost cost John his life.

In the spring of 1984, breakup was almost over by May 5th, but John did not seem to notice. He was preoccupied with trap cabin repairs. When he got ready to go home, he mushed on what little snow remained.

33. John Schulz mushing in overflow on Shaw Creek, May 1966.

34. Quonset hut similar to one in which Lea lived. (Post Exchange at Big Delta's Allen Army Airfield, ca. 1948.)

On the trail, the dogs were accustomed to crossing a small, frozen lake. The problem was that this time there was water widening around the lake's perimeter. The lake was beginning to thaw. John intended to skirt the pothole. Out of habit, the lead dog stayed on course and jumped the water, taking the team, sled, and John out onto the disintegrating surface made up of crystalline needle-ice.

John committed to stay with the sled as he thought, "Oh, well, you gotta go sometime…". Suddenly, the first dog began to sink, then the second dog floundered, finally the sled was under water, and so was John. Then he thought, "Well, pretty soon, I'll hit bottom, and just push back off."

But in seconds, John was dog paddling, eyeball to eyeball with his team. Instead of screaming that he was drowning, he remarked to a dog how absurd all this was, despite the fact that the tug lines from the panicking dogs were entangling his limbs. The cold was starting to affect his mind and his body. Dogs climbed on top of him, fought to get onto the ice, stepped on his head, and then, fell back into the water. A harnessed dog had lunged onto the ice, and his tug line pulled tightly across John's belly, driving him into the ice, and ramming the sled into his back. John was pinned; his body had become useless with the cold. "This is it," John thought, "This is IT."

Suddenly, the dog changed directions, dug his claws into the solid ice, and the rope which had been a noose on John, became a lifeline. John grabbed the rope, and was jerked out onto the ice, followed by all the rest of his dogs. Lying on the ice like a frozen log, the hot May sun began to heat John's skin. But still, he could not even roll over. "If I can get rid of this shoulder gun, I could roll," he thought, and he threw his .44 magnum gun, which spun across the ice, the water, the mud, and into the swamp grass. Somehow, he opened his waterproof match case, but he thought the match would not ignite the grass.

He said, "What the heck," scratched the match in one swoop on a driftwood log, and threw it into the three-foot-tall grass. Soon, swaths of standing grass were burning. After the first fuel burned off, John rolled in the hot earth and stubble, gradually warming up enough, so that he could walk. His feet were only in socks. Knowing before that the lake could be a potential hazard, John suddenly remembered that he had previously cached a pair of leather boots, nearby, under a tree. He found the boots, slipped into them, and returned for his harnessed dogs.

He got the sled out of the water, and let his dogs loose. Thinking the fire would burn out, he left for his cabin, a quarter of a mile away. Back home, an hour later, he heard a sound approaching, "Whack-whack-whack-whack…"

"Uh, oh," John said. He knew it was the blade of Delta Forestry's helicopter, and it was hovering, overhead.

Looking out from the helicopter, Reb, quite familiar with John's trapline, assessed the tracks leading across the barren flats, onto the rotten ice, up to the hole, the deserted sled, and now, five acres of flaming grass. Apparently, it took a prairie fire to warm John Schulz back to life.

Chapter Ten

LEA SCHULZ

35. Lea, 1979.

I met Lea only days after I moved to Delta. She had black hair and lively brown eyes. An Alaskan gypsy, she and her two children, Dan and Megan Emerick, were living in a Quonset Hut on the Richardson Highway, next to the old Big Delta Post Office. The children's father, Red Emerick, had left several years earlier. Some called Lea "Calamity Jane," but she was a rare friend to me, one who offered warm companionship and stories.

During the early 1960s, she drew a buffalo permit in the lottery. John Schulz had told her to shoot the biggest bull she could. So, she did. No big deal. It did not matter that she had a broken leg mending in a cast. Somehow, she crawled within 100 feet of a massive bull. She dropped it with her old 30-30 rifle. Her son, Dan, said the animal was so big that it broke the axle of "Chuck" (Charlie) Boyd's 1948 Chevy truck right in half. "The meat was so tough that we even had to gnaw the burger," Dan chuckled.

Lea was raised in an urban home, but loved Alaska and the freedom it gave her to be herself. She did not believe in fancy and chose to drive a Herc, a no-automatic-anything truck into Delta. She always drove slowly, hugging the road's apron.

Dan patched up everything on her '57 Chevy pickup, from fenders to transmission, until she had what she wanted, a truck as strong as Hercules.

For adventure, but with no maps, she, John Schulz, Dan, and Megan riverboated from Dawson to Fairbanks. Until Lea was fifty, she played lots of tricks. She had sudden ailments, for whatever reason, which vanished as quickly as they had appeared. No one ever asked her why. It was common for Lea to suddenly appear to have a heart attack. Reb was worried the first time, but a wink from John cued him to wait. Soon, she was up, and around again.

Lea spent her energy mushing to her trap cabins: Spruce Tree and Double Cabin in Shaw Creek Flats, where she and Dan exercised their dog teams.

Lea required only the simple basics of life: wearing a plaid shirt, Army field pants and mukluks. All by herself, she had created the Alaskan Trappers Association to try to organize her independent trapper friends. Periodically, she wrote an official newsletter on her manual typewriter in her Quonset hut, pushing for registered traplines within the state, and advertising her association in magazines. It was in one of these magazines that Larry Dorshorst, then of Wisconsin, saw the ad. When he wrote her inquiring about trapping in Delta, she wrote back, "Welcome!! Another dead trapper...!" Lea did not want cheechakos, greenhorn newcomers, to blindly come north, so she figured, "weed 'em out early!" by scaring them into not coming at all.

Larry came to Alaska, anyway, and over the years, Lea adopted Larry, and he became like another son to her. She adopted more people than Larry. For years, on a fixed income, Lea donated to orphans and handicapped veterans groups.

In the 1960s, Lea wrote a regular column in one of Delta's early newspapers, enlivening it with her Bush stories. Some of it was even true.

In 1968-9, when it was -50° F., a strange sickness hit the dog lots from the Interior to Old Crow, Yukon Territory. Lea lost forty, almost all, of her sled dogs. We would also have lost ours, but despite how sick they were, we brought them into the house, and force-fed them onions, an old trapper's remedy. Despite the mess and the illness of many, none of them died. Lea blamed the disaster to testing being done at Fort Greely. In 2002, when the U.S. Defense Department revealed, for the first time, the extensive bio-chemical testing that was done at Fort Greely through 1967; it appeared that Lea had correctly diagnosed our problems that winter of 1968-9.

Chapter Eleven

GRAND COINCIDENCE

B y 1966, Reb had established his own trapline, and like any permanent resident of Alaska, he got his moose every fall. Winter nights, he, Schulz, Trastek, and Jake planned to ratchet up the hunt beyond the norm and go after a variation of the Grand Slam of hunting. Rather than going after the world's four types of sheep: Stone, Desert, Big Horn, and Dall; their hunt would be an Alaskan grand slam: moose, caribou, bear, sheep, and goat.

By fall, Russ Trastek had gotten a big bear; Russ, John Schulz, and Reb had each gotten a Dall ram; Jake and Reb had each bagged a caribou; and the partners had a moose aging in the shade of the Holler.

36. Reb, John Schulz, Valdez goat hunt, 1966.

Schulz found an abandoned military riverboat in the Tanana River. The 24-foot riverboat had a V-shaped bottom, and quickly became their most seaworthy boat. In late October, all four opted for a Valdez mountain goat hunt, even though Valdez was still a mass of rubble following the 1964 Good Friday earthquake and subsequent tidal wave, and was still mostly deserted two years after the disaster.

Taking just enough fuel and food for a quick trip in

and out, the four rene- gades, in their military riverboat, ignored the stares of locals who only went out in high-sided, ocean-going vessels. From their unusual boat, the Holler gang began scanning the slopes for game.

In Prince William Sound's Sawmill Bay, they set crab pots. While their attention was diverted scoping some goats across the water, a whale swam dangerously close to them in Galena Bay, nearly upsetting their

37. Russ Trastek, Jake Miller, John Schulz during storm on mountain shelf, Valdez goat hunt, 1966.

boat. After landing on shore, Reb and John began an easy ascent of the slope, but soon, their feet were desperately grasping for a slippery foothold in the wet, icy moss. Their legs tightened up with the relentless ascent. Vertical cliffs forced them to climb trees that were growing parallel to the rock wall. Wearing hip boots, Reb's feet repeatedly slipped. To catch himself, he often grabbed a Devil's Club, a springy Ginseng with a very prickly stem. Each time his gun whacked against his back, he wondered, "Would it never end?"

But on top, the snow-crested spires penetrated the sky creating an amphitheatre. Where, just over a ridge, and up a few cliffs, the goats were lying down, basking in the sun and level with the hunters.

"I don't know how we'll get them down," Reb said as he approached John. "Hell, I don't know how we'll get down," John retorted. Reb noticed a gradual decline, and said, "Maybe over there…?" "Sure, might work…" John said.

After they shot and gutted two of the goats, the early winter dark began moving in. They cached Schulz' goat under some brush and hid Reb's in a snowbank. The climb down was not too strenuous, but the visibility was shrinking. They had been heading to a place called Silver Lake when Reb felt his foot suddenly slide into the water's edge. The lake was hedged by walls that forced them to wade through the water. Exhausted, they climbed up the mountainside. Just above a waterfall, they found a 4-foot-wide cliff. Taking turns all night guarding a smudge fire, they shivered each time the wind blew water spray on them, also dousing their fire.

When the sun rose, the panoramic display revealed where they were. In this immense amphitheater, John and Reb were like two bugs hugging a cliff, wondering how in the heck they got there.

They began to go desperately hand over foot up a goat trail, until they reached the creek where, the previous day, they had left Jake and Russ. As they finally re-entered camp, Russ and Jake demanded, "Where in heck have you guys been…?!". When they heard their successful report, they also wanted to hightail it after the goats.

"No way. Not ever," John and Reb replied, wanting only sleep, food, and to never again think about goats.

However twenty-four hours later, rested and fed, Reb and John eyed the cliffs, saying, "Well, maybe if we had ropes…"

By 2 P.M., they were again on top, this time with Russ and Jake as well. Reb's goat remained where they had left it, but the cached one was gone. As they quartered the goat, heavy, dark clouds pushed by a fierce north wind began to obscure the sky. The ensuing unabated gale ripped their clothes. Hurrying to get down, their hands and faces unprotected, they bowed their heads into the driving pellets of rain. Wet slick rocks covered the steep descent as they felt their way in the dark. Jake nervously slid his loaded pack down a ravine. It missed a ledge and kept on going. They sought refuge on a shelf, huddled next to their fire, roasting their faces, while freezing their backs. They ate a quarter of goat meat as they took turns watching the fire and napping.

As soon as they arrived at the riverboat the next morning, they loaded and started across the calm bay. When they left the narrows and hit the open water, towering waves were engulfing boats in their troughs. They turned against the waves, using the last of their gas to push back to the shore.

With no protection, they slept on the beach for the next two days, living on goat meat, and waiting for the wind to break. When the cigarettes and the food ran out, their tempers began to flare. While two of them got into a wrestling match, the other two walked the shore. On the sand, the beachcombers, amazingly, found 5 gallons of mixed gas, still sealed tightly in cans.

By the fifth day, the waves were a little smaller, and the group decided to chance an escape. Covering their outboard with rain pants, they set out. Almost immediately, they began to take on water and were nearly forced to turn back, but they kept bailing and eventually arrived safely within the Valdez Narrows.

As winter approached, the trappers did not care so much about the grand slam story, but rather preferred to tell about the 5 gallons of mixed gas that had been sitting in the surf, waiting for four Alaskan renegades.

38. Fred Campbell, 1944.

Chapter Twelve

ARRINGTON'S TRAPLINE

A logger who frequented the Holler was Bill Arrington, a fine woodsman who came to Alaska in 1958 from the Washington State logging camps. When Bill was young, he watched his father build saw mills using only scrap parts, which taught him early how to improvise. When he was only fifteen, he could operate heavy equipment. After doing a military hitch in Alaska during the mid 1950s, he purchased a homestead on Shaw Creek hill, 10 miles north of Big Delta.

Fred Campbell (1878-1958), a trapper from the Richardson-Tenderfoot area of Alaska, had died two months before Bill's arrival at Shaw Creek. Eager to get back into the woods, Bill, with his ax, removed the brush that had grown up in Fred Campbell's old trails, and replaced the rotting roof of the cabin at Campbell's Lake. He heard about the Hansen Hollow trappers, and drove down one day to meet them. When he arrived, the woodsmen were on a break from their efforts to remove a huge tree stump. Bill asked, "What's the problem?" and added, "I could

39. Bill Arrington building log home ca. 1967.

pull that out in just a minute." He went to his truck, got his block and tackle, hooked it to the stump, and popped it right out.

Felling and handling trees was second nature to Bill. He built two beautiful homes, sized the natural logs, pegged them, and laid them into a perfect fit. His notches melded like a hand in a glove. He finished it off with the first gambrel, a stylized barn roof in Delta.

Naturally, Bill met Reb at the Holler. He knew Reb wanted to trap, but other trappers had locked up all the surrounding land. Schulz and Trastek used Shaw Creek. Charlie Boyd was on the Goodpaster. Healy Lake and the Fortymile were Paul Kirsteatter's domain. Bill was based out of Fowler's Dairy Farm at Shaw Creek, Rosa Pass, and Campbell's Lake cabin. Road trapping was all that remained and no one could claim exclusive trapping rights to the land along the road. The highway was public domain; no trapper had invested personal time cutting trails or building cabins along the state's thoroughfares.

Bill offered to partner with Reb on his trapline. In November 1966, the two men drove Bill's pickup, carrying two sleds, and ten dogs. It was snowing so heavily that the truck was shooting up waves of powder as they plowed through 3 feet of snow. At Fowler's, they hooked up their dog teams and took off for Rosa Pass, heading for Campbell's cabin. It continued to snow, and was very slow going. When they could go no further, they si-washed, camped in the open, in Rosa Pass. Bill pitched a tarp, and laid his sleeping bag under it. Reb spread a tarp over his back sled bow and sled's sides. Then, he crawled underneath the tarp, and slid into his bag. Comfortable, he dozed off.

The wind blew all night long, howling with snow around them. Many hours later, Reb woke.

The tarp covering him was weighted heavily with snow. He knocked it off, and looked around. Nothing. It was solid white. There was no sign of any life. "Bill!" Reb called. "Bill!" Slowly, the snow cracked as the tarp rustled, and Bill arose from under the snow's weight. His invisible dogs shook themselves to life. "We gotta get out of here!" was Bill's first assessment. After a campfire and coffee, Bill wanted to backtrack to Fowler's Dairy Farm rather than press ahead to the cabin. They left their freight load, took their empty sleds, and the teams started downhill. "But after awhile," Reb said, "the dogs couldn't even pull the sleds empty on a downhill slope! We hooked two teams to one sled," Reb continued, "and left the other sled. They went a couple of miles, and still, they couldn't pull…even with us breaking the trail in front! I have never seen such a blizzard."

Bill slipped on his snowshoes and led the way with Reb following. But, each step was a plunge into three feet of soft snow. "I can't take this anymore!" Bill exclaimed after an hour. "You gotta take over. I'm getting too old for this." For the balance of nineteen hours, Reb led the way. When his head swam, and exhaustion oppressed him, Reb sat down, nodding, but in his head, he heard, "You go to sleep, you're going to die," and he was up again. On and on, he forced his legs to go, up and down. Dreams of ice cream, chocolate milk, and canned, cold peaches at Fowler's Dairy Farm kept him going. He could make it. The dogs quit on them entirely. Too tired to do anything with them; the men left them in their harnesses. "We figured they might come in later, on their own," Reb said. At midnight, when the men crossed Fowler's field the lights, of course, were out, and the family was asleep. The two crawled into Bill's pickup truck, and headed home. The next day, they would return for the dogs.

But the following day, Reb slept, ate a little, and got up only to feed the stove. For five days, he slept and recuperated. Bill never returned for him, so Reb got Russ to drive him to Fowler's. Bill's team had chewed through a tug line, broken loose, and had created havoc with Fowler's cattle. Reb's lead dog, King, was also there. Russ took Bill's team home while Reb buckled on his snowshoes, with King next to him.

The trail had set up, freezing crusty-hard, and the walking was easy. Reb was at Rosa Pass in good time. He had not brought in dog food, because he was sure that his dogs would be dead. He could see the back bow of his sled sticking out of the snow. "As I got closer and closer, up popped a head, and then, up popped another head!" Reb exclaimed. As if only an hour had passed, instead of six days, his dogs were still nested in their melted out places in the snow, their noses tucked under their tails. Nothing was disturbed. The dogs yelped with joy, and wiggled frantically to see Reb, who hooked them up, threw the snowshoes in the sled, and said, "Let's go!" "Those sons of a gun weren't tangled up or anything," Reb exclaimed. "They'd just stayed in their little holes the whole time. They took off like a bat outa hell, and we were at Fowler's in no time!" Then, they followed the Richardson Highway, ten miles to Reb's home cabin.

In those days, Reb had no car; his transportation was the dogs, whether he was going to the Holler, or to Probert's Grocery Store. After I met him, he taught me, "When you mush on the road, don't let the dogs fade into on-coming headlights. They get hypnotized. Just say, 'Get over, gee!'" However, traffic was so scarce in those days that in a day's dogsledding, a musher might be passed by only twelve cars.

When Reb next saw Bill, Bill who'd recently married, said, "I'm going to be focusing on my new family. If you want the trapline for $200 and a radio, it's yours." Although there were only two cabins, Fred Campbell's mountainous trapline was Reb's key into the country.

Chapter Thirteen
GRASS ROOTS

Hans Seppala

40. Hans Seppala, c. 1965.

Reb remembered, warmly, "When I mushed across Shaw Creek Flats, I visited Hans Seppala, the Swede, who lived up the creek, and trapped the Richardson-Clear.

"Hans had huge dogs, but he only weighed 105 pounds. When he got on his sled, whoosh, his dogs took off!

"Every summer, Hans illegally set a fish net real low in Shaw Creek, lower than the outboard motors sat. He caught big Grayling and canned them in oil, but flavored with a little mint.

"With a little glint in his eye, like, as if to say 'I'm still living off the land,' Hans relished going down in his basement, and retrieving a jar of fish!

"He liked such tricks. Once, he pulled a stunt on Rika by tying a knot in her oxen's tails. They couldn't get loose!"

Isolated up the creek, Hans had a stroke, followed by pneumonia. Unable to get word out, he set his dogs loose. They ran down to his neighbors, Billie and Eldon Harrild, who soon realized there was a problem. They got Hans to the hospital, but he did not live long.

Slim Carroll, Goodpaster's Slim and Jolly

Al and Lucille Probert's crackerbox-size, grocery store was the Bush headquarters. Annually, the Proberts ordered groceries for the trappers in the fall, based on what they expected the Bush residents might need for the winter.

Slim Carroll, a one-eyed trapper who lived five miles up the Goodpaster, also came in to Probert's store every fall for his winter supply of case lots. "Slim was funny," Reb smiled gently, "he had two pairs of overalls. Every Saturday, he washed the pair he didn't have on. When I came by, the other overalls were always hanging on his clothesline.

"Slim had reputedly been in a gunfight assisting Wyatt Earp. It was one of Earp's last assignments, and Slim had been there to back the famous lawman.

"Slim depended on John Schulz, who was trapping Lower Shaw Creek, to bring him his mail," Reb said, "and a few groceries when John was passing through." He added, "Slim had gotten too old to keep trapping Upper Shaw Creek. In return for Schulz' kindness, Slim gave John his cabins on Upper Shaw Creek at Corda, Eagle, Upper Shaw, Highline, and maybe Camp Creek drainages."

Slim had a trick to prevent sportsmen from stalking the lucrative fishing hole in front of his cabins. He maintained a target directly across the river. If someone began fishing in the deep hole near Slim's bank, he simply maintained that his rifle needed sighting in. He wasn't shooting at anyone; he just needed to keep his aim sharp.

Reputedly, Jolly died during the 1920s; only his name remained attached to his partner's Goodpaster cabins.

41. Slim and Jolly's homestead, Goodpaster River, ca. 1991.

Chapter Fourteen

KING OF THE WOLFERS

efore the Gold Rush and World War II introduced white men's diseases, there was a Native population in the upper Tanana River valley who subsisted off the land. In 1939, they needed a school at Healy Lake for their seventy-five children. By 1943, however, the Native population was so devastated by diphtheria that a school would have been pointless. Exposure to white soldiers building the Alcan Highway sparked the epidemic, invading every cabin, touching every person.

After many deaths, Chief John Healy took his remaining people, including his nieces, Margaret and Alice Jacob, from Healy Lake to the new Alcan Highway area. Here, near the road system and the new centers of population, he hoped the children would be able to go to school. Purchasing an old cabin at the Little Gerstle River, John and several others began a small community.

Chief Healy's people got to know some of the Alaska Road Commission men working near their new village. One of those men was Paul Kirsteatter, who was moving buildings used in the Alcan Highway's construction to sell in the new town of Delta Junction. While Paul was hauling buildings, he saw Margaret Jacob and her sister, Alice, at the Little Gerstle Bridge, and a bond was struck between Paul and Margaret. Able to speak only a few English words, Margaret began teaching Paul the Athabaskan language. Adapting quickly, Paul also began to learn from Margaret the ancient tricks of wolf trapping and snaring wolverine. Little by little, Margaret picked up English from the radio, and by listening to Paul.

After they married and moved into a cabin at Healy Lake, Paul began to develop as a master wolf trapper. At that time, there was a bounty on each wolf caught. Paul knew all the wolf dens.

He went into them, and got both mother and pups. He said, "The first time I brought them into Fish and Game to collect the bounty, they were surprised at my asking for the advertised bounty, even for the pups. 'But,' I explained, 'a wolf is a wolf.'"

"One time," he said with a wry smile, "I almost deafened myself. I crawled into a den, and shot the mother with a .22. Even the noise of the low caliber gun reverberated on the cave's walls so badly, I couldn't hear for a week."

Paul said, pointedly, "I was the first one to use the gang set. Previously, trappers had set single snares on the trail. But, I put bait out and encircled it with so many snares that I couldn't miss when a pack

42. Paul and Margaret Kirsteatter taking wolf hides to market ca. 1990, Tanana River.

approached. Once, I caught as many as ten wolves in a gang set; I routinely caught quite a few at a time. In the spring, my cabin wall was covered with dried wolf pelts.

"Once, I was surrounded by wolves. I'd left my dog team, and hiked a few yards when I saw wolves begin stalking my team. Having only limited ammunition, I made every bullet count. I nailed a few wolves and sent the rest of them running."

Paul headquartered his trapping out of the former Indian village of Joseph in the Fortymile River country, setting traps from Healy Lake east to the Canadian border.

"I was gone a lot," he explained. "I never told Margaret when I would return. Hell, I might start having some fun out there; I didn't want no search party coming out after me.

"Every year, Margaret and the kids got our moose meat for the winter. They butchered and dried it. Margaret also made her own snowshoes and fish nets. She'd been raised by her grandparents, and knew the old, subsistence ways."

While Paul was out trapping, Margaret drilled holes in the ice and submerged the weighted fishnets. "At 50 below, she still had to check the nets every day," Paul said. She once told her daughter, Josephine Beaver, "We flourish with the fish. And we diminish when they disappear."

Josephine added, "We were the mountain people. We crossed the ridges, following the valleys of the Upper Tanana's hidden trails. In that time," Josephine continued, "the only reference points were Volkmar, George Creek, the Crossing, Nabesna, Copper River, Chisana, Tetlin, and Big Delta. The only junction was between trails coming from the Copper River Valley, over the mountains into the great Tanana Valley.

"From the 1940s until recently," Paul added, "our family were the only ones at the (Healy) Lake. After the Alcan Highway through the Upper Tanana Valley put the fur traders out of business, and after so many Natives died, it became lonesome at the Lake. We had Josephine, Margaret's daughter by a previous marriage, and our three children, Linda, Fred, and Dorothy."

"My dad home-schooled us by gas lantern light," Fred Kirsteatter, 48, said from his Healy Lake home.

For the first 10 years of Fred's life, the family's subsistence life ran smoothly. However, in 1963, a large military maneuver hit the area. "Ten thousand GIs swarmed onto the frozen lake, converging from the Goodpaster River and George Lake at Healy," Fred said.

"They ran their tanks over the old Sam Hill Native Cemetery and bulldozed our trapping trails.

"Soldiers stole our equipment, and we couldn't trap," he said.

"The caribou were pushed out, and we were hungry.

"However, there was no protection for Native lands," Fred said. "The State's Division of Lands told us to cease and desist our use of public domain property." The prospect of the Alaska pipeline forced the settlement of aboriginal claims.

Helping his aunt file for the Healy Lake's Native Land Claims, David Joe, a grandson of Billy Mitchell's guide, Chief Joe, worked many, long nights with Margaret. He and Margaret greatly facilitated the establishment of today's Healy Lake Village.

Paul concluded, "Margaret taught me how to survive," he said. "In her, I had the best of teachers -- my wife, Margaret."

Chapter *Fifteen*

43. Charlie coiling copper wire at McCarthy, 1967.

SCROUNGING COPPER

Charlie Boyd fulfilled a lifetime dream, becoming an Alaskan big game hunting guide. He had four big game guiding areas and had access to several others: moose and bear up the Wood and Goodpaster Rivers; sheep at the Johnson Glacier, and in the Wrangell Mountains; bear in the Admiralty-Baranof-Chichagof Islands, and also, fur seal before the Marine Mammal Protection Act of 1972.

The isolated Kennicott Copper Mine was located near Boyd's guiding area in the Wrangells. When the price of copper dropped in 1920, and the last train out of Kennicott was announced, residents left hurriedly, leaving meals untouched on dining tables, and reams of copper wire on the ground.

In Seward's Icebox, survival was often solved by necessity, the mother of invention. Scrounging was to Alaska what street survival was in the cities of the Lower 48. In Alaska, it was well understood that what might be one man's trash may be another man's treasure. The winter of 1966-7, Copper was worth $0.71 a pound. Boyd hired Reb, and chartered a plane to drop them near McCarthy Creek. They rode the ancient tram that spanned the creek, pulling its suspended chair and themselves hand over hand over the cable.

Boyd made a contraption for rolling the abandoned copper wire. Boyd anchored two intersecting boards with spikes pounded into a tree, and drove a handle into the intersection of the boards. With the handle, he rotated the the crossed members, coiling copper wire into 6-inch by 2 feet spools. Boyd planned on returning in the winter by snowmachine, when he would haul the wire out overland.

Boyd traveled light. He liked to survive on dehydrated potatoes. For two weeks, he and Reb lived on potato pancakes, mashed potatoes, and fried, mashed potatoes.

The coup came when Charlie shot a porcupine. He skinned and roasted it. Then, they poured gravy over their mashed potatoes, with meat on the side!

After fourteen days of such fare, a 3 foot high, 24 by 30 foot pile of copper wire covered the ground. Later in the winter, Boyd returned by truck, hauling a snowmachine. He used the latter to cross the frozen Copper River to retrieve the wire, then, trucked the spools into Anchorage. However, the price of copper had fallen $0.30, so Charlie did not make the killing he had planned. However, he saved what profit he made for his dream: a Super Cub to better launch his guiding business. Boyd did not know that in 1978, under President Jimmy Carter, Secretary of the Interior, Morris Udall, would crush his dreams by making the Wrangell-St. Elias wilderness off-limits to commercial big game guiding.

Chapter Sixsteen
MUSHING SPY

 ong lines of military vehicles lumbering down the Richardson Highway always signaled the onset of Delta's annual, grandiose Army maneuvers. The winter of 1966-'67, Reb encountered a similar Arctic exercise when he was out trapping, beyond the Tenderfoot Hills.

For many years, Alaska was an open field for military operations, and the maneuver of '66-'67 was much larger than those of the 1990s. That particular maneuver exercise began after Reb disappeared into the woods that fall.

Reb had been trapping alone for three months. He never saw another soul, except his five dogs. The radio was the only human voice he heard other than his own. At night in his cabin, while he played games with his two lead dogs trying to see who could outsmart the other, he sometimes heard and felt earth-shaking explosions and saw flashes of white in the velvet darkness outside the Visqueen window. He was not sure, but thought it might be the military playing their games of war.

At the end of January it was time for Reb to return home and sell his furs. Excited about heading back to civilization, even though it was -30° F., he got up while it was still dark, and loaded his sled. Without today's pipeline corridor access, he had to mush 10-12 hours over the mountains and across the flats.

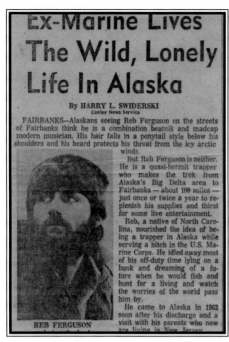

Ex-Marine Lives The Wild, Lonely Life In Alaska

By HARRY L. SWIDERSKI
Copley News Service

FAIRBANKS—Alaskans seeing Reb Ferguson on the streets of Fairbanks think he is a combination beatnik and madcap modern musician. His hair falls in a ponytail style below his shoulders and his beard protects his throat from the icy arctic winds.

But Reb Ferguson is neither. He is a quasi-hermit trapper who makes the trek from Alaska's Big Delta area to Fairbanks — about 100 miles — just once or twice a year to replenish his supplies and thirst for some live entertainment.

Reb, a native of North Carolina, nourished the idea of being a trapper in Alaska while serving a hitch in the U.S. Marine Corps. He idled away most of his off-duty time lying on a bunk and dreaming of a future when he would fish and hunt for a living and watch the worries of the world pass him by.

He came to Alaska in 1962 soon after his discharge and a visit with his parents who now are living in New Jersey.

REB FERGUSON

44. Copley News Service: Reb as "the spy," 1967.

He had not been back over the mountain in 90 days and he did not look forward to breaking the trail toward home. To his surprise, when he reached the summit, he saw the trail was already broken. With only the moon's reflective light off the snow, Reb trusted the dogs to follow the trail. The team suddenly picked up speed, zipping down the mountain, triggered by a scent, and ran straight into the door of a darkened Army tent.

"Wolves!" a G.I. yelled, "WOLVES!!" Dogs jumped on cots, and sniffed everywhere for food. Soldiers thrashed in their mummy bags, grabbing desperately for flashlights. Reb leapt for the harness tug lines, yanking them backwards. He snapped his lead dog's harness ring to a tree, and wedging his sled tightly behind a tree, he snapped it into a second chain.

The soldiers inside the tent lit a gas lantern. Before long, invader and guards were sitting on cots, sipping C-Ration coffee while Reb explained that he had been out trapping for months. The soldiers described the Army's large maneuver, Frontier Assault-1967. The sentries at this camp were holding the pass, securing Minton and Rosa drainages. Since Reb was wearing Army clothing, they thought he was in the maneuver. They could not imagine why someone besides a soldier would isolate himself in the Alaskan woods.

As daylight returned, Reb and his team went back to what had been a dog trail, but was now a broad, snow highway. As he flew down Rosa slope, he could see side roads, leading to unseen encampments. He glimpsed a foot soldier with a gun. The soldier ran and hid behind a berm pile, waiting to ambush the wild man in Army fatigues, riding a dog sled. The dogs faded over toward him, sniffed, and lifted a leg.

The guard popped up, shouting. "You're under arrest! Report to the major!"

"Do you want a ride?" Reb asked. The soldier snapped, "No." But, when Reb took off faster than the soldier could escort, he yelled, "Wait up!"

The soldier rode one runner, while Reb was on the other. The guard confided he had been sure Reb was a Canadian spy. He revealed the Army maneuver's passwords, so Reb would not be delayed by any more sentries. During all this, the weather was not getting any warmer.

After he dropped off the guard, Reb could not remember, "Was 'applesauce' the password for the Shaw Creek area and 'apple butter' for the flats, or the other way around?"

He snapped out of thought when jets began strafing the team, scaring his dogs. He discovered he was on a huge landing strip in Shaw Creek Flats; he had to remember the password to escape the guards. He tossed out a hopeful, "Applesauce" to a very serious guard. "You are a prisoner of war," the guard retorted.

Reb was cold, and losing time. The Army had trespassed his dog trail long enough. "There is

45. Soldiers in harness pulling sled during military maneuvers.

one thing I know about maneuvers. You guys use blanks," Reb told the guard, while he unzipped his parka, and pulled out his .44 Magnum, "But, I don't." Then he shouted to his lead dog, "Let's go, King!"

After only 5 more miles, two vehicles, once again, blocked his path. "Uh, oh," he thought as men started jumping out of cars, "I've had it now." To his astonishment, cameras started flashing and men gathered around with pencils poised over pads. The military press wanted to capture the wild Alaskan musher who was mistaken for a spy.

The story circulated throughout the syndicated military newspapers. Fan mail poured in, and Reb who had been just a cold trapper was now the spy who came in from the cold.

Chapter Seventeen
DOGNAPPING

had spent my first, impressionable years in Alaska listening to these wild men from the Holler.

At the same time, I was desperate for a dog team. In the summer, I hitchhiked to Tok, and bought a dog and a sled. I circulated the word, and stray dogs began appearing behind our cabin. But, they were not Huskies.

I had often heard Boyd and Schulz joke about dognapping to form a dog team. I was only twenty-three years old, and I thought it was an approved Alaskan technique.

After all, Reb had made friends with his dog, King, in a trailer court, and then, had simply had him jump into his truck.

One day, I saw a beautiful Husky at a gas station. She looked good to me. I unsnapped her chain, and invited her into my truck. But en route to the waiting vehicle, my conscience panged me; I turned around and returned the dog.

The next day, Boyd, who was a good friend of the gas station owner, Ed Crutchfield, laughed at me. Boyd chided, "Next time, you dognap, Judy, don't do it from the local magistrate."

Chapter Eighteen

CACHE-AND-CARRY

46. Franklin on the Fortymile River, c. 1905.

In our early years, we did not have a vehicle. Since dog mushing was impossible in the summer, I hitch-hiked wherever I went, even after Clint was born. Reb provided me with a derringer. The aim was so poor; I was not sure in what proximity it would be accurate.

Bayless and Roberts truck drivers, Andy and Bob Growden, always took care of me. Very trustworthy persons, they could be counted on to give me a ride. Pioneers themselves, they worked for a trucking company birthed in Alaska's gold mining creeks.

Howard Bayless was a big, hard-working man, born in 1911 and raised on Deadwood Creek, off the Old Steese Highway, the son of miner Otto Bayless. Otto had arrived to the Klondike as a 12-year-old and later hauled mail by horse team from Nenana to Circle.

Howard's wife, Alice Roberts Bayless, came from an equally historic family. Her father, John Roberts, a Welsh prospector, came to Dawson in 1897. When Roberts staked his claims, he decided it was time to marry. Forty-nine years old, he wrote to a 25-year-old woman, Ellen, in Wales, and asked her to join him.

"My mother crossed the ocean, traveling to meet a man she didn't know, and to a country she had never seen," Alice Bayless said. "Mother came by sternwheeler from Skagway to Eagle, and then was pole-boated up the Fortymile River to the old boom town of Franklin."

John Roberts ran a roadhouse and post office there, and Ellen worked the businesses as the children came along. Their sons, Bob, Dick, and Ellis grew up shoveling pay dirt into sluice boxes with their dad. The prospecting and roadhouse business supported the family.

Alice took a job cooking at a local mine after her father's death in the 1930s. There, she met Howard Bayless, a Caterpillar driver at the mine. "Mining was just transitioning from the old shovel work to heavy equipment," she said.

In 1938, the roots of two pioneer families merged with the marriage of Alice Roberts and Howard Bayless.

World War II scattered the town of Franklin's men and mining equipment. The government purchased the equipment as part of the war effort. When the war was over, Howard Bayless and the Roberts brothers returned to their Fortymile claims. Heavy equipment was becoming the new way of mining, so fuel to run the equipment had to be hauled to the remote sites. Starting up a cache-and-carry system, Howard and Ellis Roberts hustled fuel from Valdez before winter closed the road. Over a rough trail from Copper Center to Chicken, they hauled 50-gallon drums in a Ford, flatbed truck.

In the spring, Bob and Dick Roberts picked up the cached fuel in Chicken. Using sleds hooked to a Cat, they hauled 150 to 200 drums of fuel at a time over 35 miles of ice from Chicken to the mines at Franklin.

"Two mines required 600 drums, which took about three trips," Bob said from his Tok home.

In addition to miners needing fuel, there was a trucking boom, caused by massive military buildup and its construction. The Interior needed a lot of fuel. The Bayless and Roberts brothers installed bulk plants and fuel supply centers, first at Copper Center, and then in Tok and Delta Junction.

"Dick drove the 2500-gallon tanker to Valdez, where it was filled with fuel, and then off-

47. Howard Bayless, center, Bayless and Roberts Trucking, ca. 1957.

loaded fuel at Copper, Tok, and Delta. Ellis delivered to the Fortymile miners. Howard supervised the Copper plant while I took care of Tok," explained Bob Roberts. Additionally, Jack Goddard oversaw the Delta operation of Bayless & Roberts.

As the business grew, more drivers were needed. In 1956, Andy Growden was hired to drive the new Kenworth truck. Standard Oil, the supplier for Bayless & Roberts, in anticipation of statehood, bought the bulk plants, but the Bayless and Roberts families stayed on to run the operations.

During the 1960s, Bayless & Roberts expanded to twenty-five trucks and as many drivers, supplying the Interior of Alaska and some places in Canada.

When the 1970s pipeline boom hit, a trucking company could make as much profit as it dared to expand. Bayless & Roberts leased forty owner/operator trucks as well as freighting with its own twenty-five rigs, hauling day and night out of the Fairbanks Alyeska yard for points along the pipeline corridor.

Andy Growden moved to Fairbanks to dispatch the operation, making sure everyone had his load, and got where he needed to go.

Although the individual plants were family-run, between the fuel distributor business, and supplying Alyeska at Prudhoe, it was a big operation with all responsibility ultimately resting on one man, Howard Bayless. As the balancing act became more unwieldy, Growden decided to return to the simpler life of truck driving.

"It was an era when truckers looked out for each other," Growden said. From this author's perspective, the drivers also looked out for trapper's wives hitchhiking with a baby on one hip.

Chapter Nineteen
BIG GAME GUIDING

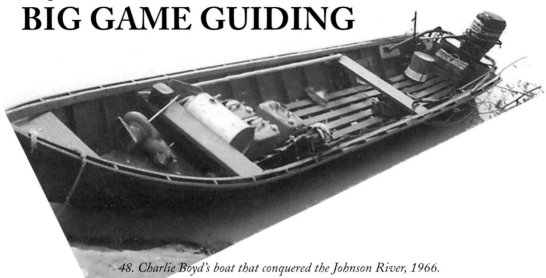

48. Charlie Boyd's boat that conquered the Johnson River, 1966.

Johnson River Trip

Before his death in 1982, Slim Moore was Alaska's most elderly, registered big game guide. His guiding colleague of many years, Charlie Boyd, although thirty years younger, died the very same day, April 1, 1982. Patty, Charlie's former companion, added, "They simply went sheep hunting together."

Reb worked as an assistant guide for Slim and Charlie in August 1966. Jet units for outboards were relatively new that year. Charlie needed one to stock his Goodpaster River trapline by boat. Slim needed freighting done for a scheduled hunt at the Johnson River Glacier. Since it would cost Slim the same to freight groceries by airplane as it would with Charlie's boat, Slim agreed to buy Charlie a new jet unit. Perhaps it was a fair exchange for the stunt of hazarding freight up the Johnson River.

Charlie's boat was a sea-worthy, wooden, strong, V-nose riverboat that could really plow upstream. With a new fifty-five horse, Mercury outboard, he and Reb, in high water, went all the way up the Johnson River. "I think we may have been the first, and maybe the only ones, to ever do it," Reb remarked. "I bailed so fast, as the water rushed over the prow, that I gouged the Styrofoam flotation unit Charlie had in the bottom of the boat. When I couldn't keep up, Charlie pulled over until we emptied the boat.

"There was a sharp curve in the river, walled by a steep rock face. The river appeared to dead-end there. I looked at the water rushing past that rock, and we appeared to be frozen in motion. 'Are we moving, Charlie?' Reb asked. 'Yeah, with the motor wide open, we are just keeping up with the water's speed,' Charlie replied."

When they arrived at the hunting camp, Slim's millionaire client looked at the boat in disbelief. "How did that get up here?!" he exclaimed. When Charlie told him, the client insisted that he absolutely had to join them on the return trip. "Noooo," they answered, but the client insisted.

"Going downstream was worse than going up," Reb said, "because the current increased our speed. We had to make snap and precise decisions about which channel to take.

"The client was laughing all the way downriver. He thought it was simply hilarious. He was having the time of his life!"

"Once," Reb said, "Charlie thought the motor wasn't working. He thought a rock got lodged in the jet unit, and hollered to me that somehow we had to pull over and stop. But, there was no way to land in that rushing water. We tried. I jumped out, and was trying to pull the boat over, but it was impossible. The boat was doing brodies, making circles, with me hanging on. The client was laughing his head off! Then, Charlie gestured to me to get back in. The motor had only been stuck in reverse, and was fine!"

49. Client with full curl ram.

Guiding for Robert Elliott: 1966-73

Reb remembered his guiding for Robert Elliott, "When I worked for Elliott, I went into the Mount Hayes camp in early August and didn't come out again until mid-October."

50. Reb packing clients' Dall sheep, 1970.

He reminded me, "Remember, we didn't have to hunt during those years. We had sheep, caribou, and moose from the clients. Our dogs ate the scraps from the local meat cutting business!" During the season, Reb met all different types of clients from all over the world.

I was alone for two months while Reb was in the mountains. Once, I got so lonely when I was cooking dog food down by the river, I just howled at the moon.

When Clint was 16 months old, I was determined to join Reb in camp. Elliott had agreed to fly me to base camp, but he did not want me and my infant going to spike camp (the higher camps whose supplies were stocked by backpack), where the men hunted seriously. Determined not to miss time with Reb, I sewed an Eskimo-like baby carrier on the foot-powered treadle sewing machine that had belonged to my grandmother. (There were no Snugli baby carriers back then.) I sewed a baby seat with connected leggings on the back of my shirt that would tie across my front. I could easily walk into the mountains then with Clint resting evenly on my hips. Before Clint was potty-trained, he made it to Trident Glacier on Mount Hayes.

Elliott offered clients hunting packages: sheep, caribou, moose, and/or bear. Reb had clients come for ten day sheep hunts. Hunters had to know sheep hunting was unpredictable. Reb had two Delta Airline pilots in top condition that hunted hard for ten days, but never got a thing. As they flew out, the pilots spotted some rams on a ledge just above camp and gestured to Elliot. On the return flight, Elliot brought in an obese man and his son. The next day, with the sheep already spotted, Reb took the flaccid hunter up the slope. On his first day, he had a prize ram.

Even when conditions are right, buck fever can mess it up. Reb had his hunter waiting and under cover, when forty outstanding rams raced by on the glacier, a rare sight. The most regal, full curl ram was within range. Reb cautioned the hunter, "I'll stay low. You pop up. Make sure you get that ram." The hunter did it perfectly, but he got so excited, he shot the wrong ram!

From the old photographs, I remembered the large flocks of sheep I had seen in Reb's slides. When I asked him if the numbers of sheep had diminished, Reb replied, "Those flocks were ewes and lambs. Fish and Game's permit system has probably saved the sheep population."

Chapter Twenty

51. Reb, 1948, Trenton Cowboy.

FIGHTING FIRE...

n 1953, a miniscule television screen flickered black and white images of a baby bear, Smokey, lost and bawling in the great, northern woods. In the background, the forest burned. Like a mantra, a deep voice intoned, "Only you can prevent forest fires." Children watching their TV sets saw the orphaned bear suddenly robbed of family and home. Reb Ferguson, a ten-year-old in Trenton, New Jersey's inner city, with his Hop-A-Long Cassidy bandana around his neck, followed the drama and dreamed of the Alaskan woods.

In 1962, when he was old enough, Reb caught a train west, and hitchhiked the rest of the way to the North. By 1968, Reb and his friend, Thom Nee, were standing in line at Fairbanks' unemployment office seeking work as Emergency Fire Fighters. They were dispatched to a few fires, and soon became regular E.F.F. employees at Delta Junction's Bureau of Land Management, under station manager, Wandell Eliot, and Crew Boss, Lynn "Curly" Brant.

Curly was a legend. He had come to Delta the same year that Reb watched the legend of Smokey as a child back home in Trenton. Curly was short and bald, and had the disposition of a U.S. Marine Drill Sergeant. Stories abounded of Curly and the other construction workers who founded Delta Junction. He was a ramrod.

In 1970, Curly and his buddies were shooting the breeze at Delta's Bay Hotel. Not far away, Reb Ferguson's wife and Thom Nee's lady were having coffee. When Curly was finished with his drinks, he hauled up his five feet six inches, shifted his belt, placed his hands on his hips, and announced to the young ladies, "Yeah, Reb and Thom are good firefighters, but they'll never be real ramrods!"

Reb never enjoyed office work, but when a fire was raging, stress was high, and men were low on sleep, Reb's stride shifted into his natural, fire-fighting equilibrium. The pressure daunted more conscientious, cerebral-type people.

During the summer fire fighting, Reb earned a grubstake: sufficient money for us to survive the winter. By fighting fire for the U.S. Bureau of Land Management, he bought groceries for us, hay for Klondike, and dry dog food for eight dogs to get through eight months of winter.

When he first fought fire in 1968, Fairbanks and the northern Interior were under a stifling blanket of smoke. The Alaska Employment Agency in Fairbanks hired the firefighters, untested and untrained. Men slept in sleeping bags on the sidewalk outside of the hiring office. Calls for emergency firefighters went out on the commercial radio stations. Reb and Thom Nee kept their ears strained to the radio for a job possibility. When the fire call came, they immediately hitchhiked to Fairbanks, and were gone for weeks on the Manley Hot Springs' fire, and, later, the Goodpaster fire.

52. Curly Brant, fire boss, 1967.

An Emergency Fire Fighter, Leigh Daniels, recalled meeting local trapper, John Schulz, during the Goodpaster Fire: "Standing in front of the Evergreen Bar and Restaurant, I decided to splurge on a cup of coffee. Once inside, I noticed fellows in yellow shirts, talking about a fire. One of them said a radio operator and logistician was needed at Rika's Landing. An hour later, I was running the operation at the boat landing. We built a two-bedroom Visqueen house where we set up a radio antenna. There, I met John Schulz, a river pilot, whom we hired to ship supplies upriver by boat. John stood out because he was wearing a hat with earflaps, which I found peculiar at that time of the year.

"I had heard of John and the other trappers, down in the 'Holler;' I had heard they didn't like strangers coming around. Of course, I heard the same thing about Reb. Someone said John was the King Of the River Rats.

"One evening, Schulz and his trapping partner, Russ Trastek, began telling me stories about how Schulz had run a boat from Delta to Dawson City, without a map. Not only was I impressed, but Schulz had obviously, also, had a nip or two.

"The EFF person in charge of the boat fleet announced it was time to haul the firefighting freight up the Goodpaster. John got into a boat, pushed off from shore, walked back to the engine, pulled a bottle out of his jacket, and took a swig. He grabbed the engine rope, and pulled hard. When the rope hit its end, the King of the River Rats tripped, and exited over the boat's side. No more was heard for awhile from Schulz about going to Dawson with or without a map."

In the fall, however, Schulz and Trastek redeemed themselves. They helped Reb as they always had. This time, they boated dog food to Reb's trapline for the winter, up the Salcha River to our beaver-trapping cabin. After a few rounds at the bars, Schulz and Trastek got Reb up the Salcha.

That same summer of 1969, a different project fire engulfed most of our trapline. Our friend and mentor, Charlie Boyd, warned us, "The marten won't be back in your lifetime. Their homes have been burned; their prey destroyed." We did not know if MonteChristo cabin had also burned. Lying on our Army cots that night, Reb wept. He said, "I built those cabins with my hands, and cut the trail…"

At the beginning of the season, Reb had figured his firefighting wages would supply us with the last things we needed for trapping: a riverboat, an outboard, another horse, a better sled, two more dogs, two good sleeping bags, and our winter's grubstake. He had been sure then, that we would be set for life. We could trap, full-time, and never again be obligated to work for someone, but now the trapline was damaged…In the winter, we would find out to what extent…

53. Joe Mead, horse trader.

Chapter Twenty One

"ALL A MAN NEEDS IS A HORSE, A DOG, AND A GUN…" *Reb Ferguson*

When I was sixteen years old in Oklahoma, my sister and I saved our allowances and bought a barrel-racing horse, Buddy. That Chesnut horse afforded me a space apart from my suburban life. Weekends and summers, I rode my horse, wandering the fields outside Tulsa, eating apples and singing at the top of my lungs. After I had later explored the world during my global wanderings, I had decided on only the simple things that I thought were necessary in life: a horse, a good man, and a cabin. Ironically, my future husband also concluded all a man needed was a horse, a dog, and a gun.

When we were twenty-five and twenty-three, Reb and I planned all winter for a second horse. By spring, Thom and Verna, Reb and I all agreed to cut fence posts for Clearwater rancher, Joe Mead, in exchange for three horses. Reb, Thom, and Verna had already gotten started while living at Mead's Clearwater ranch. In May 1969, I had just returned from a trip Outside, to Oklahoma. Wearing a beaded, smoke-tanned, moosehide jacket, I hitchhiked across Delta in the teeth of a roaring, dust-laden, chinook wind, typical of the spring season in Delta, to join them at Joe's.

For two weeks, we lived in one of Joe's bunkhouses, spending our days walking through felled timber, blackened from a forest fire. I carried a dried spruce pole, the exact length of the needed fence posts. With each charred timber, I laid the pole from butt to top, on the downed log. Reb's chainsaw cut into the timber like a knife cutting butter. Log after log, we sawed, and stacked. Eight hours later, Joe drove up with his flatbed truck. Thom and Verna, Reb and I hoisted the new fence posts into the truck's bed. Our reward was riding our prospective horses in the evenings: a sorrel and a dapple-gray for Thom and Verna, and a buckskin, Amigo, for me. Like children, with our hair blowing in the wind, we rode like Comanches, up and down Joe's fields. By nightfall, sooty black as the logs lying in the field, we sank into oblivion on the twin beds in the bunkhouse. No matter how little we had in those first years, we always maintained and wintered our horses. Like our dogs, they were part of us.

Chapter Twenty Two

THANKSGIVING STORY

was cold and bored as I shifted from one foot to the other trying to get warm in my canvas mukluks, as my husband baited yet another marten cubby, a baited trap cribbed in with branches, on our endless dog trail.

It was November and our first trapping trip of the season. Every half-mile we had to stop and set steel. I watched Reb pull out wire, gloves, lure, and bait from his homemade trapping box. It was a slow process; the marten cubbies had to be walled in with spruce branches, and then the No. 1 traps had to be set, baited, and scented.

That first trip was always a rough one. The snow was still shallow and the sleds bounced off every downed tree and hump in the trail. Our cabins had become dens for squirrels, porcupine, and bear throughout the summer. After miles of a rough, new trail, we pulled up to Campbell's Lake Cabin that almost blended into the woods in the early afternoon gloom. We jammed our sleds behind trees to prevent the dogs taking off and chained our lead dogs to the nearest trees. We looked cautiously at the snowy roof; the stovepipe was gone! The inside of the cabin was too shadowy and dark for us to find the stovepipe in the litter left behind by the summer bear. We lighted a candle that was wedged in a two-pound coffee can, a trapline flashlight, called a bug. We found the stovepipe in the dirt next to the barrel stove, but it was smashed flat.

Reb grabbed a hammer, beat the stovepipe open, and shoved it back into the collar of the stove. He retrieved the

54. Reb splitting wood at Peniel, 1982.

57

55. Putting a new roof on Campbell's Cabin as Clint is learning to whistle, 1976.

birchbark and spruce twigs we had gathered on the mountain, and got a fire going. Soon, the sweet smell of the bark filled the air. Reb took the 5-gallon, empty Blazo can by its wire bale handle, and scooped fresh snow off the roof. He settled the container onto the stove to melt for drinking water. Meanwhile, I lighted the Coleman lantern, flooding the dingy cabin with a yellow glow. From the cabin's food stock, we shoveled gobs of frozen peanut butter into our mouths, and then took care of our dog teams.

The snowy dogs were eager for attention. I pinned each one between my legs and slid the harness off, careful to keep one hand on the dog's collar. These guys were big, excited, and ready to eat. I gripped the ground with my feet, and led each of my four 80-pound dogs to a chain wrapped around a nearby tree. Reb finished with his seven dogs, while I hauled some of the baggage into the cabin. My last outside job was to turn my sled over, and bring my snowy harnesses in to dry. I unlaced my Bunny Boots, and slipped on some low-cut boots, called stags.

As I looked for the dinner I had brought, the heat of the wood stove unleashed the pungent smell of dog hair. Our damp parkas, gloves, and hats soon joined the harnesses hanging from the ridge log over the stove. Cooking would be a trick in this thicket of damp, hanging paraphernalia. I found the stew, and also some cranberry sauce. The sauce was not for now, but for Thanksgiving, a couple of weeks away.

In the cabin's dim light, I saw my tin plates, filled with dirt and mice droppings, scattered everywhere. Under the bed, my saucepans were half buried in the dirt floor. I needed dishwater, but the snow on the stove had only just begun to melt. Dish soap was frozen in the cache drum, behind the cabin. I washed a pot the best I could and set the stew on the flattened barrel stove for supper.

With the last bite of potatoes, we collapsed on our pole beds, and relaxed in the wood heat. A little after 9 P.M., we became conscious of two women reading Trapline Chatter messages, transmitting through our old, brown radio. It was too early for us to expect a message, but we enjoyed hearing the names of others out trapping. After listening to greetings, like "To Paul Kirsteatter at Healy Lake" and "To Thom Nee on the Goodpaster," we turned out the lantern, zipped up our bags, and hoped no shrews, a tiny rodent, would zip across our bunks in the dark. An outgrowth of the forest, our cabins provided four walls and a roof, but held no guarantees against such night-time visitors.

Traveling the mountain ridges for the next week, while breaking trail ultimately, to MonteChristo Creek, we watched for the quick flutter of grouse wings. Bagging a grouse would lend the *pièce de résistance* to a Thanksgiving meal of instant mashed potatoes, corn, cranberry sauce, and melted snow water. As Reb stopped his lead team on one of the birch-covered hills, there was a sudden whir of a bird overhead; it flushed, and crossed the trail. Quickly, Reb ripped his .22 out of the sled's scabbard and got a bead on the gray and brown Alaskan turkey. A light, frozen "Pop!" sounded in the air, and our trapline Thanksgiving was almost as good as cooked.

We kept the grouse frozen in a wooden box until the fourth Thursday of the month. Then, while there was still daylight, we ate our Thanksgiving meal by our little Visqueen window, perched on logs, by a raw board table set with chipped enamel, metal bowls of corn, mashed potatoes, cran-berries, and grouse. Outside the window, the snow quietly sifted down on MonteChristo Creek.

Chapter Twenty Three
BECOMING ADULTS

very fall, Reb and I were separated while he did big game guiding in the Alaska Range for two months, but the loneliest time was after I discovered I was pregnant. Waves of emotion swept through me; I felt marooned, morose, and bewildered. When Reb returned from guiding to go trapping for the winter, I only knew that I would not be left behind again.

I went to the library to get a book on natural childbirth, my only aide in the wilderness, but I was informed I could not check it out, because I was not a student. I had no money, and no child-birth guide. So, I lobbed the book out of the window, and went out-side and picked it up. It was my constant companion as my preg-nancy advanced throughout two months of trapping 30 miles up the Salcha River at McCoy Creek (listed on current maps as Flat Creek).

Dr. Dunlap, my obstetrician, supported my going. "Just take

56. Sledding a 55-gallon, cache drum down Flat Creek mountain, ca. 1972.

57. Reb wraps ropes around toboggan runners, roughlocking, to slow downhill descent, 1982.

your time; be careful not to fall on your abdomen," he cautioned. His support lent me credibility when my parents challenged me, understandably nervous about my plan. They tried to reason with me, but my mother agreed if she were in my position, she, too, would probably go. I told them I had a book, and I would return in January, long before the baby was due in March.

Reb had already boated the dog food and other supplies 60 miles up the Salcha to our furthest cabin. It was a good thing because with scant snow cover that year, it would have been very difficult to transport two months worth of supplies by dog sled.

When the muskeg was merely dusted with white, we started. Periodically, it snowed, but repeatedly, the ground was blown clean by Chinook winds. Frozen, naked mounds of muskeg lined the valley floors, continually jostling me between the trail's moose rut edges. My sled, pulled by three dogs, wobbled over the gauntlet course. Five months pregnant, I huffed and puffed up the mountains. Descending the other side, careening out of control, and dodging trees on the plunge downhill was the real hazard.

We tried to slow the maniacal speed of the descent by wrapping the sled runners with chains that would bite into the dirt and snow. It also helped to turn a dog or two loose to cut down on the power. I always dragged one leg behind me on the ground, using it as a rudder, while I rode the brake with my other foot. I popped up and down behind my vertical sled bow, ducking to miss low-hanging branches. Spruce trees whizzed by during the narrow, forty-five minute plunge off the mountain into McCoy Creek Valley. When the sled hit the sudden flatness of the valley floor, I was thrown onto my side into the soft muskeg. I got my awkward, pregnant body up and skidded the sled back onto the hard-packed trail, but then, I automatically hit another hummock, and was thrown again into the soft muskeg on the trail's other side. After repeated falls, I lay still for a while in the muskeg, imagining how other pregnant women were having baby showers, nibbling cookies, sipping tea, and opening gifts. What was I thinking and what was I doing here?

Once I got my sled to the flat-roofed McCoy Creek cabin, I told Reb I had to quit; I could not go any further. He sat while I paced the dirt floor in my mukluks. Slapping his mitts together, he decided we would return. Finally, with my emotions spent, I reasoned, "My doctor said the only thing for me to avoid was a direct blow to the abdomen." As a solution, Reb and I tied a pillow around my sled's back bow to protect me from impact with the sled handle. We then hooked up our sleds, and continued the six-day trip to our ultimate destination, the Salcha River cabin, overnighting at MonteChristo and McCoy Creek Cabins on the way.

When we arrived at the Salcha River cabin, there was wet, dirty garbage everywhere. I stayed with the dog teams while Reb, carrying his pistol, gingerly checked inside the cabin for a possible lingering guest. Finding nothing but wreckage, he circled the cabin to check our storage barrels. He returned, shortly, "Half the dry dog food we boated up is gone, as well as much of the white gas for the lantern! The bear got the ring off the barrel lid!" My heart sank.

58. Reb by Salcha slough and cabin, 1976.

We could not go back the way we had come to get dog food. The mountains were bare of snow; we did not have enough dogs, and it was too far. To feed two core dog teams, we had to cut back on dogs. To keep the dogs going as the winter progressed, we mixed our own rice and macaroni with their food, added beaver carcasses, and stretched the dry dog food as far as we could. To preserve body heat in our two shorthaired, lead dogs, Sam and King, I sewed capes for them from army blankets.

During the short, four and a half hour, winter days, Reb wandered the Salcha hills setting traps for marten, lynx, wolf, and wolverine: all land-based fur-bearers. He followed the river for water-based fur, setting steel for beaver, otter, and mink.

Sometimes, I walked with him. On a previous hike, Reb had chainsawed the ice holes to set the beaver sets. He cut and crossed two dead spruce logs at a 90° angle. After he had wired them tightly together, he laid them across the open hole. For bait, he cut a cottonwood log and slipped it in the center of the crossed spruce logs to the Salcha slough's bottom.

Beaver look for air pockets. In a layer of oxygen just under the ice, Reb set snares wired to the crossed logs at the height for a swimming beaver interested in both the oxygen zone and the bait. If the loop were too high, the rodent might swim under the snare, bumping it off to the side. If it were too low, he might swim over it. Gingerly, Reb set the snare's loop size, secured each one to the log, and eased each wire loop cautiously into the ice-choked water, careful to keep the snare facing the direction of an approaching beaver. This was Reb's still-water technique. In a faster current, he used a trap on a submerged platform.

On this excursion with Reb the holes had iced over, but he was prepared to check his sets with a four-foot metal handle welded to an ice chisel. While he tediously chiseled, I kept a fire going on land to warm his fingers. Reb painstakingly chipped around the beaver's snare wire. If he accidentally hit a wire, he could lose a snared beaver.

Like primitive peoples, we routinely scooped ice from the chiseled holes. Daily, jets would fly over our heads. We shook our heads as we scraped for a living while up in the sky people were reclining in their soft seats, sipping coffee. Overhead, the jets made vapor streams in the sky, while we, on the ground, made sled trails in the snow.

By this time, my army field pants were getting quite snug. I had brought a stretch, maternity panel along, which I stitched into the button-fly panel of my pants. A sweater covered the situation.

When Reb was out, I spent my days knitting socks for his Christmas present. I had to conserve our short supply of lantern fuel, so I frequently leaned toward a stubby candle for light.

One night when he did not return at the usual time, I got worried. I slid the globe onto the lantern, and went looking for him in the dark. When I met him in the night, he said some traps had needed special attention.

McCoy Creek was spring-fed, which helped make the ice weak in spots. Overflow, water oozing over the creek's surface, coupled with the effect of the spring, had made a rotten place in the ice under the thin snow cover. As Reb walked with me in the dark, suddenly, his legs punched all the way through the ice, and he went 4 feet down to the bottom, where he pushed off, and crawled back out on the fragile ice. A few nights before, he had had a nightmare of becoming entangled in a beaver snare under the ice. He was wet to his chest, and we hurried to the nearby cabin. While I prepared dinner, he quickly changed clothes.

While he relaxed and dinner bubbled on the barrel stove, I read him stories of northern explorers. He dragged a beaver over to a log, and began skinning its very resistant hide. (Beaver skinning was as tedious as the cold, slow process of trapping them.)

The hides were not worth much, but it was an added treat to our dinner. Beans had been simmering for a long time on the stove, flavored with a beaver's pork-like, fatty tail.

When Reb freed the beaver's dark glossy fur from the carcass, he tacked the round pelt onto a large, drying board. As he finished tapping nails, the lantern began to sputter. That was our signal to call it a night. We climbed into bed, drifting to sleep as we listened to the chorusing wolves on the bluff behind our cabin.

When Christmas neared, I daydreamed our trapper/pilot, friend, Charlie Boyd, might surprise us. On Christmas Eve, when a full, orange moon rose, I pictured Charlie bringing us gifts in his Super Cub airplane: our Bush Santa Claus.

Charlie did not come, but nonetheless I was prepared. I had baked pies in my gas can/oven that was sitting on my barrel stove. Then, with a one-burner gas stove, I had fried sweet dough, making my real coup: trapline doughnuts. Before Christmas Day, I stowed the goodies on our snowy roof, covered with pans. On our pole bed on December 25th we leaned against the wall, and listened to KFAR's Christmas Nostalgia shows, eating pie and doughnuts.

Before going to bed, just in case…I took one last look at the dark sky: Charlie Boyd might still stop in. In the starlight, our dogs merely wagged their tails. I threw them a few Christmas doughnuts, and turned out the light.

With the holidays over, there was no ignoring my state. I was seven months' pregnant; it was time to go home, and face our new world.

Amazingly, there was still hardly any snow cover. Reb warned me repeatedly, "You have to leave stuff behind, no matter how valuable. Not only is there no snow, but also we have fewer dogs. Our sleds must be light." When we loaded our sled boxes, we left behind a little home, where we would never again live.

The forest fire the previous summer had destroyed the marten habitat from Upper McCoy, or Flat, Creek, over Mt. Sam, around our MonteChristo cabin, and down its valley, just missing Flat Creek Valley. To compensate, we had based our winter's trapping operation out of the Salcha cabin, trapping the ridges on both sides of the river. But, that was not sufficient area for the future.

We had to build a completely new trapline, but first, we were having a child in the spring.

Reb's bigger dog team soon left me behind on the trail. As far as I could see, bare tops of naked muskeg stretched between the first mountain and me. A shear mountain face loomed in front of me. I despaired of ever getting my sled up it in my unwieldy condition. In the far distance, spidery figures were crawling up the mountain's face. Reb and his dogs were clawing their way up; the sight was overwhelming. As I trudged on, I suddenly saw Reb return, striding back to me across the muskeg bringing extra dogs for my underpowered team. He hooked his two dogs into my sled's tug line. As I ambled behind them across the muskeg, Reb pushed my sled up the mountain as the dogs clawed and strained to get the load to the top.

Once we crested, we were in the onslaught of a raw, raging, bitter cold wind. The valleys in between the peaks briefly protected us, but then, we continued up the other face right back into the bitter wind. My face and throat were exposed. I tried to shield them with my moosehide, mittened hand, but I needed today's wind-proof nylon hull/fleece facemask, and they did not exist. The wind ragged through my loosely knit hat. My face and throat became numb, and so did my sense of reality. Faintly, I remembered getting on my runners when we topped the mountain. As we topped the mountain, and careened into the timber on the downhill side, I was surprised, as if waking from a dream, that I was riding the sled. By the last descent I had warmed up slightly, but suddenly my mountain hot rod hit a tree, and became instant kindling. There was no solution but to throw my load into Reb's sled, hook my dogs into his team, and climb on his sled's runners alongside of him. We alternated pushing with our free foot, gripping one runner with the other foot, and holding each other to stay on.

Finally, back at Fowler's Farm, I waddled in my parka and field pants to the road to try to get a warm ride home, while Reb continued to mush across Shaw Creek Flats the 10 miles toward the house. From his picture window, George Fowler spotted me as I passed by. They had known I was out and that my delivery time was near; they had been looking for me. Instantly, George fired up his truck, picked me up, and took me home.

Chapter Twenty Four
CHILDBIRTH

y early April, as I lay in unimaginable pain, I knew the trapline's unending marches, the cold, and the fatigue, had prepared me for childbirth better than any book.

In Oklahoma, there is a statue of The Pioneer Woman, striding along in her skirt, with her child holding her hand. During the long hours in a St. Joseph's Hospital bed, in Fairbanks, I began to change from a girl into a woman.

Dr. Dunlap, my physician, was more than an excellent doctor; he was a healer, and he was my friend. He was the same for thousands of patients;

59. Reb, Judy and Clint in front of home cabin, 1970.

his love was its own communication. He dedicated his life to taking care of many patients like me, making each woman feel entirely protected. He paid for that dedication with sleepless nights, packs of cigarettes, and long hours away from his own home. Over the years, he continually upgraded his skills, mindful to give the best care possible in the Tanana Valley. After Dr Dunlap passed away in 1997, his son assured me that Dr. Dunlap had needed his patients as much as they needed him. In 1969, when I was pregnant with my first child, he supported my going on the trapline and like any good father, upon my return, he reproved me for having gone.

April 11, 1970, I was three weeks overdue. X-rays revealed possible complications impeding a normal delivery. But, to give me a fair chance, Dr. Dunlap jump-started my labor with intravenous Pitocin. Never leaving me through the long hours of labor, he played solitaire, smoked cigarettes, and waited. He was quick to see trouble when fetal distress set in. He pulled out the stops, and propelled me into the operating room for an emergency Caesarean section.

A week later, as I recovered at home on my army cot, I looked at the miracle of new life: our son, Clint, in his crib. I also wondered what I had done to myself. All indications implied life would never again be the same. Clint was the only baby among our circle of trapping friends.

Coining a nickname from ruckus and racket, they affectionately called him, "Funky Runky," and "Little Runkus," but he was Clint Abraham Ferguson.

Chapter Twenty Five
RIDING WITH THE GIRLS

Before Clint was born, Reb and I had begun making evening horseback rides with Charlie's companion, Patty Gooley, and with Diane Hansen. After Clint was born, I was the only one of our friends with a baby. Not to be a stay-at-home, I put one-year-old Clint in the saddle with me, and tied him securely to my body. But, while the others trotted, I continually had to rein in my horse to protect my child. My horse was snorting and pawing to keep up with the others. Diane, Patty, and Reb raced each other down straightaways and around curves; they were Apaches, set to get someone killed. They were young, with not a care in the world.

When Reb was at the Bureau of Land Management during the day, fighting fire, the girls and I rode together. One day, there were five of us riding. As usual, they clicked into a fast canter. Tired of feeling staid and conservative, I let Klondike have

60. Judy, Clint on Amigo, 1971.

his head a little. But, with the other horses enticing him, he stretched his neck out, and immediately went into high overdrive. A shallow place in the road opened up under us. Klondike went down into it, breaking his form at the high speed. I lost my leg grip, and Clint and I went flying. To protect Clint, tied on my front, I landed hard on my side. I sensed serious damage had been done. As I writhed in pain, suspecting I had broken my hip socket, I began praying with all my focus. The girls ran back to me. I could not open my eyes. I said, "The baby. Clint…is he okay; is he okay?" They untied him from me, and said he'd had a sudden bowel movement, but he was fine. That was all I cared about. I got up slowly. Charlie approached us, and said later. "As I watched that accident, it wasn't possible anyone could've come out alive."

Chapter Twenty Six

BREAKING TRAIL

61. Judy at Schist, 1971.

In 1969, massive fires burned our trapline. We had to relocate and start over, building as many cabins in a new area as the short summer season allowed. Starting at Campbell's Lake Cabin, we angled to the northeast toward Schulz' line. John and Reb's traplines would unite to make a mutual fortress, to protect both our lines. As we explored and cut trail, our goal became to descend Gilles Creek, and angle north to the South Fork of the Salcha River. We could follow the South Fork to the Upper Salcha and connect our line into a circle. In 1970, however, we took a year off from the trapline for Clint to grow past infancy. In 1971, we built Schist Creek cabin. Before today's versatile tents, modern rain gear, and Pampers, we explored, cut trail, and built cabins. Returning into the wilderness with an infant, however, was more difficult. I pretended it was okay, but when we left the road system for the wilderness, an invisible door silently clicked shut behind us. No backup; no phones; no helicopters; no doctors.

Clint had already been on two wilderness trips. Before Snugli baby carriers were available, Clint rode in a homemade one, snugged against me, under my leather poncho. Before he was 2 months old, we took two horse trips. On the first trip, I ran out of water for mixing formula, and on the second, I couldn't get to a jar for mixing his cereal and milk. During that first trip, Clint, strapped to me, started screaming for milk while my horse scrambled to keep up with Reb on Klondike, riding as if he were alone in the universe. Lacking water, I did for Clint what Reb and I did for

62. Judy, Clint on Amigo; Reb, Klondike, Sox, 1971.

ourselves. I strained water from a marsh, mixed it with powdered formula and fed my baby. On the second trip, as my horse bolted after Reb's, I put the baby cereal in my mouth, added some milk, sloshed it around, and spooned it slowly into his mouth. In a few minutes, he was content.

When he was 13 months old, when we had to replace our fire-destroyed trapline, there were no rainsuits for toddlers. Using a lightweight, coated nylon, I stitched a thin rain outfit for Clint. He could now sit in front of me in the saddle, but tied to me in case of jostling. As we rode, I sang to him, and kept his pacifier pinned to my shirt, with his bottle in my pocket.

As we cut trails through the deep woods of our new trapline, I threw chainsawed brush out of the path. Clint stayed in the saddle while Reb carved funny faces for him on the tree burls: Mr. Happy, and Mr. Rabbit. When we returned later on sleds, we always waved to Reb's tree characters.

Breathing in chainsaw exhaust, bug bitten, and dirty, we claimed about two miles of trail a day. Clint wiggled in the spaces between the trail's tree roots, playing car.

We spent many days up on the ridge cutting trail to what would become our Schist Creek cabin. Raindrops slid off the alder leaves and onto our heads as we plowed through the ridge's endless ups and downs. My army poncho only slowed the water down before it seeped onto my neck, arms, and back. Clint napped under my raincape. While he napped, I tried to stay as still as possible to keep from waking him. When he woke, I was stiff with cold from not moving. As soon as possible, I dismounted, and led the horse just to warm up.

Halfway to the new Schist Creek valley, we camped on the ridge's crest for a few days while Reb cut trail, and returned to our tiny tent at night. During the day, I prayed for a break in the weather to try to dry cotton diapers, and ever-dampening sleeping bags. Reb worked every day as rain poured off his hat brim, and sweat formed on his forehead. He never complained, but punched his hat up from the inside to help it drain. In the mornings, he sang to Clint and me, "There's a beaver in the woods," or when we saddled up all our gear, to move on, he intoned, "It's a movin' concern, a movin' concern, in the mornin'." Every night, he descended the ridge to a spring he had found, and brought us canteens full of precious drinking water.

Reb had cached boards at Campbell's that he would need for the new trap cabin. It was planned that after we began building, I would ride back alone to the lake cabin, pick up the load, and return with them. We knew that I was directionally impaired, so I scrutinized every aspect of the trail to make sure it was etched in my mind.

When we estimated we had gone about as far as we could go in one six-hour winter day of travel, we needed to build a cabin. We began to scan the steep, forested drop-offs, trying to find a descent into the valley. The location we were seeking needed grass for the horses, drinking water for all, as well as non-marshy, valley ground with logs for a trap cabin. When we could find no gradual descent, we tried pushing on to the next ridge, but it was worse. Finally, we simply crashed, downhill, through the trees. I kept looking backward to try to remember the silhouetted pattern of the ridges against the sky, so that I might be able to find the right ones when I had to return on my own. With no moose trail, and on porous, marshy ground, we squeezed between spruce trees, ripping our canvas panniers, which were huge, homemade saddlebags. As we plunged through swamp, the horses leap-frogged from island to island, looking for solid footing. When Klondike's thighs sank up to his buttocks in swamp, we had an emergency. Reb cut branches for better footing, unloaded the horse, and smacked incentive into him, so he would not give in to the sucking earth. With a huge lunge, Klondike ripped his front legs forward. It would not be the last time he had to perform that stunt. As we bounced from one thin, witch-hair draped, scrub spruce to the next, Reb was lost. We ducked our heads under branches, and scraped our legs, leading and scrambling just ahead of the horses. Then, there it was: an island, washed in sunshine, a low ridge in this valley of swamp and porcupines. It had trees. A fresh creek ran at the bottom, with meadows of wild grasses peppering the lower ground surrounding the island's base. It was suddenly home. The little creek ran with flecks of yellow mica schist, so we named it Schist Creek.

The next day, Reb walked off the dimensions of the cabin, and we laid the first rounds. When we had ten trees down, we backed the harnessed horse to the downed timbers. (After the building of our MonteChristo cabin, we had learned from cowboys, Joe Mead and Ray Dougherty, how to work horses.) Reb wrapped a chain around each tree, then hooked the chain into the rope "single-tree," which was connected to traces running through the saddle's D Rings and then, around the saddle itself. Reb slapped Klondike's rump. I led the horse, skidding the logs along the ground to the cabin site, where I peeled the bark off of them.

Clint waddled and sucked on his bottle, cribbed in by the cabin's first rounds. Olie Polie, our pack dog, was on the far side of the log playpen. Clint wanted to play with him. With his bottle in his mouth, he clumsily struggled over the cabin's base logs. But, he slipped on the slimy, sappy logs, and sank his only tooth deeply into his tongue. Suddenly, Clint was screaming and blood was flowing down his chin. Eventually, the bleeding stopped. Clint's tongue, like the blazes on the trees, is still marked today by that trip.

As we continued building the Schist Creek cabin, we were coming to the point when we needed the boards Reb had left at our Campbell's Lake trap cabin. If I returned with the horses to that cabin, and hauled the freight, Reb could continue working, and Clint would stay with him. As I began the return trip, I paid close attention; I did not want to miss the correct ascent out of the valley.

I rode Klondike back through the swamp, leading my horse, Amigo. My eyes were alert, watching for the blaze on each slender sapling, not wanting to move from one blaze until I saw the next. If I went up the wrong ridge, I could very easily become lost. With that in mind, I was suddenly in a swamp with no more markers in sight. I asked the Lord to show me the way. It began to rain; I had to get off my horse to untie my rain gear. As I leaned down, I saw one of the elastic bands from my braids, fallen during the previous trip and lying in the moss. Then I knew I was in the right place. Across the swamp, I spotted the blazes again and eventually arrived at Campbell's cabin. The next day, I started back from Campbell's with boards strapped to Amigo's sides. When I returned to the new Schist Creek cabin, Reb was building the pole bunks. We spent a few days cutting slender poles, smoothing them, and nailing them on cross-poles to make beds and a table. In an empty tin can next to the bed, we put a candle and matches. For mattresses, I cut, dried, and stuffed grass into burlap sacks. But unlike our other cabins, this one would have a third bed for the new person, Clint. For each pole that Reb nailed into place for Clint, the chubby toddler said, "Thank you. Thank you. Thank you."

After the roof had been put on, Reb chainsawed a hole for the stovepipe. He braced the weakened roof poles with four, 1-foot-long, crossed, nailed pieces of split wood. For fire protection, he slid a 5-gallon metal drum, open on both ends, through the roof hole for the stovejack. In the winter, he would fit the stovepipe into the stove and run it up through the stovejack.

Reb chainsawed openings in the logs walls for windows and a door. He covered the window holes with clear polyethylene, and stretched and framed it with thinner wood and nailed it into the window's opening. From the boards I had brought in, Reb made a door, framed the cabin's rectangular opening, and hung the door using hinges he had brought.

When we returned home in July, Reb made a fire in an empty, 55-gallon paint barrel to burn out the paint residue. On one end of the barrel, he bolted on a commercial stove door, and on the side, he bolted on a stovepipe collar, completing the stove for the Schist Creek cabin. However, to get the cumbersome, heavy load into Schist Creek, he had to have adequate snow cover for the trail.

On the trail-breaking, solo first trip in November, Reb, using a sled and dogs, bumped and cajoled the load to the Schist Creek cabin. On arriving, he squeezed the barrel in through the cabin door, set the stovepipe into the stove, and threaded the pipe up through the roof's stovejack hole. After splitting firewood, and further splitting kindling, he shaved fizz sticks with a sharp ax for quick ignition. He prepped more to be used upon his return. Should it be fifty below zero the next time he arrived, both heat and light had to be easy to ignite.

That night, the first smoke at Schist Creek curled up from the new barrel stove's stovepipe. Reb was sleeping on the new grass mattress in his army, chicken feather sleeping bag.

We had made a home where no person had ever been before.

Chapter Twenty Seven
FIRE SKETCHES

I n 1970, it was so dry that 6 inches of talcum-sized glacial dust hovered over the Clearwater Road, southwest of Delta.

One day at noon, I stepped outside of our log home curious about the eclipse-like light. I put our 3-month-old son, Clint, in the baby stroller, and pushed him up the forested path to the highway. As I walked, a huge, rolling black mass unfurled from the east. Mushrooming, its billows rolled toward Delta Junction. I could not hear the Bureau of Land Management's fire radio transmitting my husband's messages, but he was driving straight into the fire.

A farmer's berm pile, composed of masses of bulldozed topsoil and dry trees, had exploded into flame, which dominoed, catching more berms. Ignition after ignition blasted; the flames hungrily devoured an unbroken swath of forest, trapping some firefighters, and heading directly for Delta Junction.

Through the opaque dust and smoke, Reb drove

63. Firefighter waits for steak a la shovel and potatoes.

to help as the fire headed straight for the firefighters. As he traveled, retardant planes tried to drop liquid suppression bombs on the monster fire that threatened to destroy Delta. But like spitting from a moving car, the wind swept the red mass off course. The fire raged toward the Emergency Fire Fighters just as Reb got to the field and loaded the men into the open pickup bed. He covered the workers with burlap sacks and doused them with water from the truck's water tank. As burning trees fell and blocked the narrow road in front of them, fire also blocked them from behind. With nowhere else to go, Reb drove the truck into an open field. They watched as 60-foot flames topped the trees surrounding them.

Curly Brant radioed that he would send a helicopter to rescue the crew. Reb replied, saying that they would sit it out; the flames were too dangerous for the chopper. BLM waited, curtained off from Reb and the men by wind, dust, and fire.

As the fire roared by, Reb and the crew hosed the grass between them and the burning trees. As the fire moved on, they were dispatched to an area to try to angle the fire away from town. They worked around the clock. Finally, the fire stopped on a rise just behind the school, days after it first started.

In 1979, a similar incident happened when burning berm piles ignited huge tracts of agricultural land cleared for the Delta Barley Project. That fire began when a farmer, driving a Caterpillar, unknowingly began trailing a mile long wick of fire from the belly pan's broken hydraulic line. The farmer was oblivious, but when Reb and his pilot set the State Forestry helicopter down right in

64. Backburning to stop progress of Hell's Canyon fire.

front of him, the farmer stopped. However, due to Delta's drought and wind, fire was already crackling in the trees bordering the farmer's field.

Crews were sent in with Caterpillars to make firebreaks in front of the fire. As Reb supervised the four D-9 Cats, the firefighters seemed to be making progress, but suddenly the fire jumped the line and came straight toward them from behind, completing the wall of fire already in front of them. Quickly, the drivers cleared an 80-foot firebreak in a protective circle around them. They made a metal shield by parking the Cats in a semicircle with their blades toward the flames. Reb and the drivers got between the Cat blades and the Cats, and covered their faces from the suffo-cating smoke. In the whirling dark air, glowing cinders lighted on everything. The fire sounded like a roaring train; its heat was so intense and so close it heated the Cat blades up to a scalding temperature. Although it almost jumped their line, the fire finally roared past. The drivers revved the machines. To avoid catching the engines on fire, they ran the dozers backwards. The drivers lined up, staying in each other's view as they backed through the smoldering field. Like a high-speed military drill formation with a visibility of only 30 feet, the machines roared in reverse. The ground vibrated with their intense movement; countless burning sparks showered them in the dark, the smoke, and the dust. Finally, they backed safely out of the hot, dark side of the moon.

There was high stress in the late 1970s as the State of Alaska took over local fire control from B.L.M. At the same time that Delta's agricultural barley fires experienced several seasons of explo-sive fires. Throughout those summers, choppers flew overhead while retardant planes dive-bombed tracts and tracts of burning spruce. Borrowing firefighting resources from other areas, Delta Forestry had constant traffic of Caterpillars, trucks, and water tankers they were dispatching to

Delta's burning agricultural project. Yellow-shirted fire crews were imported from every corner of Alaska. In 1980, with the fire budget rolling like a slot machine out of control, the pressure was a lead weight on Delta State Forestry boss, George Fortier. The fires only abated when the summer rains finally arrived and the returning nights cooled the daytime temperatures. Finally the ag fires slowly evolved into a mere logo on a tee shirt that read: "I survived the Delta Barley Fire!"

About 1993, Reb was patrolling the Alaska Highway when he saw a suspiciously large plume of smoke. At home upriver, I could hear Reb on my radio's fire channel gasping, "Oh, my God. Oh, my God…" Right in front of Reb, the fire jumped the highway into the trees, heading straight for Dry Creek, a Christian community of 200 people, where many families' cabins were tucked into the timber belt.

Roads into the cabins were narrow; many families had no phones. Evacuation out of the tinderbox might be impossible. Before the fire mushroomed, Reb ordered the resources for a major fire: two retardant planes, Delta and Fairbanks helitack – helicopter crews – the State Troopers, trucks, and smokejumpers. Later, Steve Squires, a leader at Dry Creek, wrote in the local newspaper that because Reb saw the smoke early, immediately understood the danger, and called early for maximum resources, a potential holocaust was averted.

During 1993-94, the Gerstle River Fire became more complicated and more controversial as it spread into an old military test area where bio-chemicals had been stored and never cleaned up.

During one June-July lightning season, as I lay in bed, every gust of wind made the room shudder. Each surge seemed to press the room backward. Our wind generator tower outside the house squeaked and groaned against the log wall. Somewhere, Reb was fighting fire.

Days before, Reb had come home in between fires long enough to eat dinner. As he ate dinner on the porch overlooking the Tanana Valley and the mountains, his eyes had scanned the evening thunderheads. As he ate the last of his corn, the crackling static came over his Forestry radio: "Eighty-one reported lightning strikes. Ignition on the Goodpaster. Helicopter will arrive in 30 minutes for transport to Goodpaster fire. Expect a few days on location."

As I lay there listening to the wind, Reb had already been gone a week. The children and I were used to running the riverboat and the homestead alone.

In thirty-four years, the managing agencies for fire control, the official jargon, policy, and personnel have changed, but our domestic routine remained the same: "Kids, go feed the dogs. Dad's gone on a fire; who knows when he'll be home. The wind is still blowing."

Chapter Twenty Eight
RIDDLED SWAMP

When I had first wrangled Joe Mead, the local horse dealer, into trading me a green-broke – trained only to lead – buckskin horse, I felt triumphant. Even though Joe was the consummate horse trader, he had a tender heart. However his reputation for trading was so well-known that local poet, Ray Savela, penned,

I have a horse-lovin' friend by the name of Joseph Lyle Mead.
His pedigree dates back to a long-lost breed.
His father taught him all that he knew,
About swapping horses, none went for glue.
Horse trader Joe, as he's known far and wide,
His conscience is clear, he has nothing to hide.
Every horse in Big D has gone through his hands,
One time or another—it should have his brand.
A cheechako came by with horse flesh in mind,
So he looked up Joe Mead to see what he'd find.
Whatever the type that is to be bought
Joe has the knack to sell him what's sought.

65. Clint and spruce pole for bunk, 1971.

Considering I was up against a professional, I was pleased when Joe traded me a buckskin in 1969 for no extra boot, the money Joe had wanted in addition to exchanging the stumbling roan horse he had first sold me for wages earned when I worked cutting fence posts. After I rode the buckskin home from Joe's Clearwater ranch, I asked Verna what she thought I should call the buckskin. She answered, "Call him what you want him to become." I named him, Amigo, my friend. All during the summer of 1972, Amigo packed Clint and me -- as he had the previous summer -- as we built two new trapline cabins: Caribou, and Camp Comfort.

For days, we cut trail from Schist Creek along the leafy ridges, down Cannonball Run, and then slammed down into a forsaken valley riddled with swamp and creeks. The first night in the valley, we found a tiny island of high ground and few trees.

In Caribou valley, a gorge equally spongy to Schist Creek valley, we rode side-hills, thrashing between spruce trees, punching into moss-covered, swamp-perforated, hollow ground, crossing and re-crossing creeks, and over old beaver dams. At the last creek crossing, we felled poles, and covered them with brush to prevent the horses from breaking a leg. On the other side was an island of high ground; it was not quite as high as was Schist Creek, but it was solid and backed up to a mountain. However, the timber was scarce. We pitched our tent and began felling what timber there was. To compensate for the scarcity of logs, we dug 3 feet down into the dirt and then laid our ground logs on the top of the earthen walls to make a reasonably tall cabin.

Every morning, we staked the horses in the swamp grass to graze. As long as they could see or hear each other, they were consoled. My horse, Amigo, was hobbled by one leg, while Klondike was tethered on the other side of the creek. All morning, my buckskin whinnied to Diker, wanting to be closer. We thought he would settle down. Reb was working off the island's tip when he saw Amigo run and jump the creek. But his hobbled leg threw him off balance. He tripped and slid into a creek no wider than his body. Icy water washed up to his shoulders in the permafrost ground. Reb yelled for me. Clint was playing inside the cabin: a tall, wilderness playpen. Thinking I would only

66. Reb peeling log, Schist Creek, 1971.

be gone a minute, I ran to Reb. "Bring me a shovel!" Reb shouted. We dug with pick and shovel. Amigo was wedged in an ice canal coffin, which held him like a vise. Our digging was a slow-motion nightmare. Reb glanced at Klondike and said, "We'll rig a block and tackle!" He took the time to saddle Klondike. He saddled Klondike, then laced the picket rope up through the hole in the saddle, around the horn, and back through the D-rings. Then, he tried to thread the rope under Amigo's belly, but there was no way to slide it under him in the coffin-tight fit. Flakes of snow began to dust us. The cold tightened Amigo's face into a thin, facial mask. His breath became icy cold. I slipped on his bridle. Desperate, Reb slammed the horse with a board, beating his flank into action. Suddenly, Amigo lunged; his hoof pawed the side of the bank, groped for the top, lunged again, and he was out…for a second, then his hoof slipped on the icy ground, and he fell in backwards. Panicked, I held his head above water, holding the reins. Amigo thrashed wildly as he kicked me in the jaw. The reins broke, and Amigo's head sank beneath the surface.

From the unfinished cabin, I had been hearing Clint cry for a…long time. I had checked on him once; I felt desperate, trapped by the situation. With the battle for Amigo now lost, I walked like a wooden woman, numb with shock, and crossed the swamp to my desperate child.

Reb found some freeze-dried ice cream in our supplies. He made a little fire to warm our cold soaked bones, and added some water to the cardboard-dry ice cream. We tried to move toward normalcy. With one horse, we would finish our job, and eventually, work our way back toward home. Eventually.

We finished the walls and roof. Since it was nearly October, we kept warm by a little cooking fire next to the cabin. When Caribou Creek cabin was finished, I put Clint in the saddle and led Klondike in the snow back up the valley toward home. Reb led the way back over the mountains to one last, projected cabin site: to build Camp Comfort. Because this cabin would be closer to civilization, -- at the mouth of our trapline -- we built it on a camouflaged side-hill to protect the cabin from abuse.

During our winter's mushing, it took two and a half days to sled from our home cabin across Shaw Creek Flats and up Rosa Pass into Campbell's. To break it up, we used a cabin of Bill Arrington's, called Dahlman's, for overnighting on Shaw Creek. However, on the first trip of the season, from Dahlman's to Campbell's, it could take twelve hours. We needed an oasis: Camp Comfort.

As we built, the early snow melted away into Indian Summer, but the ice crystals stayed in the moss. By day, Clint prattled to me while I dug my gloved hands deep into the moss, stuffing it into burlap bags for roof and wall insulation. The balmy sun began to warm us at 11 A.M., and lasted until about 4 P.M. Then, the chill of the hills took over again. After the roof poles were in place and covered with sod, Clint and I wallowed on the roof in the fall sunshine, and put on the last insulating layer: fluffy moss.

When Clint's bedtime approached, I held him in my arms, sang a better version of "Rock-a-Bye, Baby," and tucked him into his down sleeping bag in our Eureka Draw-Tight Tent.

We had been out six weeks. At Camp Comfort, we were close enough to the highway that I could hear the eighteen-wheelers going through their gears as they climbed Shaw Creek Bluff. Lonesome for civilization, I began to sing, "Oh, I long to be on Shaw Creek Hill, grinding through the gears…"

Finally, we put Clint on our remaining horse, pushed shovels in the saddle's scabbards, and led Klondike, as we walked the long trek home. After a ten day rest at home, we would return to the trapline to get our winter's meat. Winter was coming.

Camp Comfort only served us two years. The construction of the new Trans-Alaska Oil Pipeline and its access road through Shaw Creek Flats made Camp Comfort unnecessary. By 1975, where we had often mushed for two and a half days, we could now drive in an hour.

Chapter Twenty Nine

67. Judy skinning bull moose, Campbell's, 1976.

MOOSE HUNTING

Before the Trans-Alaska Oil Pipeline corridor was built in the mid-1970s, affording easy access to the new man-made moose pasture, our trapline was rife with bull moose. Crazed by the rut, they haunted the quiet basins. They rubbed trees raw until the sap oozed. The grass was heavy with their musky scent glands. We always whispered when we hiked hoping to surprise one for our winter's larder. During those early years, many things were different. We drank freely from any swamp, lake or creek. Giardia, dubbed Beaver Fever, was a diarrhea-inducing parasite connected with animal feces that probably had not yet impacted the North. In any case, we had never heard of it. Most of our trapline trail was on the tops of mountain ridges where water was impossible to find. When we found it, we simply strained out the bugs and grass with a bandana, and all three of us drank it with no problems.

We filled our larder with case lots of canned vegetables and fruit, which we purchased at Probert's little grocery store. During the summer, before inflation greatly affected prices in 1973, we only had to earn two hundred dollars to purchase our winter supply of food, our grubstake. Every September, we marched into the only store in Big Delta and pointed to cases of green beans, peas, corn, tomatoes, canned peaches, fruit cocktail, and pears. We carefully selected several cases of Oleomargarine, a 25-pound can of MFB shortening, sacks of flour, cornmeal, oatmeal, sugar, baking powder, yeast, tea, and certainly, cans of dried potatoes.

From September until spring, a standard dinner was canned corn, moose steaks, re-hydrated mashed potatoes, and reconstituted milk, finished off with fruit cocktail. In the summer, we had no refrigeration, and generally, the meat was gone anyway; then, we resorted to Spam. I had not yet discovered gardening. When the more health conscious back-to-the-earth genre began arriving in the early 1970s, the notion of whole, unprocessed foods was introduced to us. Before that, we thought food was simply food: dehydrated, chemically preserved, and canned.

After building two trap cabins and then, returning home that summer of 1972, I was struck that my house was only a slight upgrade from the trapline cabins. Without plumbing and electricity, we filled Army issue, 5-gallon Jerry cans from the river in the winter and from the gravel pit in the summer. The Tanana, a glacial-fed river, is heavy with silt from May-September. Dishes washed in the water came out dirtier than they were before washing. Drinking water had to sit for an entire day to allow the gray muck content to settle. Gravel pit water was questionable, so when we got a truck, we hauled water from town. Coleman lanterns supplied our lights. Our heating system was a drafty, 55-gallon oil drum converted into a wood stove, blasting out warmth but hard to regulate. In the summer, the roof over one of our two rooms always leaked. In the winter, if the moss insulation between the logs fell out, we chinked the space with old socks until spring.

We did the same on the trapline. Home and the Line only differed by highway access. After building Caribou and Camp Comfort cabins, we stayed home for ten days before returning to Campbell's for a moose. After the long hike back into Campbell's, Reb, Clint, and I settled down for the night with Reb's .44 Magnum pistol safely in its holster by our bedpost.

Just before dawn, needing to relieve myself, I stepped outside into the dim light. The brush was alive with noise. Something was charging toward me. I yelled for Reb. In a flash, he was outside with the pistol. As the moose broke into the clearing, Reb brought him down.

The bull was laced with rich, white fat. The musky odor added to the scent of the Highbush Cranberries growing in the woods. We skinned the bull, made a high cache – a platform nailed to a tripod of trees – to store the meat for winter, and laced the hide as a tarp over the remaining meat to protect it until we returned.

While we were working, two bulls then suddenly broke into the clearing behind the cabin. Attracted to our camp reeking of moose scent, coupled with Klondike tethered near the cabin door, the bulls pawed the ground and bellowed. Sure that Klondike must be a cow; they were incensed that "she" would not come to meet them. They called and demanded. Undisturbed,

Klondike stayed on his rope. The bewildered moose resisted entering our questionable domain and ambled off into the brush.

We slung two quarters of the bull we had onto Klondike and scrambled up the mountain toward home. Clint and I camped in Rosa Pass with the moose quarters while Reb rode Klondike for a day to get the truck, back home.

Chapter Thirty

DELTA DERBY

68. Reb the jockey after Delta Derby, 1972.

n the summer of 1972, there was a drive in Palmer to legalize parimutuel horse racing. In Delta, Mike and Lorry Yates had just bought a pair of young quarter horses with the thought, "If Palmer can race, why not Delta?"

The Yateses, who had 160 acres next to Blue Creek and dreamed of having a racetrack, would host "The First Annual Delta Derby."

"How tough can it be?" Mike reasoned. The word went out to Blue Creek neighbors: "Come to a picnic/horse race July 4th, at Yates'."

In those days, Patty Gooley and Diane Hansen picketed their horses on the old military, grassy pipeline. Every evening, the women and their geldings met for a ramble. It was supposed to be a mere ramble until Patty baited Diane with, "You ready?" Anticipating it, Diane clicked her heels to Flapper Bar's flanks and cried, "Let's go!" Thundering hoofs pounded up the turf, leaving only dust behind. Diane's blonde head stretched over Flapper's long neck and Patty bent low over her more compactly built Rex.

Frequently, Reb joined Diane and Patty for the evening's ride. Klondike had two gears: lead foot and full out. When Flapper Bars, Rex, and Klondike contested, the horses got so lathered up it was a wonder they stopped before they hit Delta. With Diane on his back, Flapper had once cleared a 4-foot fence that was simply in his way. News of a race at Blue Creek reached our Tanana River neighborhood, and it looked like Reb, Diane, and Patty were in the running.

On the Fourth of July, Mike and Lorry returned from town with hot dogs for the few race spectators they were expecting. They were thunderstruck to see cars everywhere. "Two hundred people must have shown up and they all brought food along," Mike said.

The crowd gathered at the starting line and Reb, decked out in vest and spurs, sat on the fastest sorrel between mileposts 277-279. Patty followed, also in a leather vest, riding her muscled bay. Diane came in on Flapper Bars, the Morgan gelding who needed a furlong just to stretch out, prancing sideways.

Restlessly, several horses lined up, kicking and snorting. Lorry was stationed at the finish line as the timekeeper. She listened for the starting shot to begin her stopwatch, two sharp bends away and three-quarters of a mile up the silty road. Mike fired his .357 Magnum, not counting on that cannon sending the horses into orbit. The mounts reared and the riders fell. They climbed back into their saddles. Mike cocked his gun and the horses twitched. "Boom!" went the gun, and again, calamity broke out. However, with each disaster, the racers moved closer into Lorry's line of sight. Finally, Mike dispensed with the starting shot and just hollered, "Go!"

The chestnut, the bay, and the sorrel shot into the first sharp turn, but the riders didn't lean far enough to the outside. They lost their footing and fell like dominoes, right into each other. Patty's Rex tripped on his

69. Delta Derby, 1973.

unpredictable right rear leg, and Patty went flying over his head, bruised, but ready to go ten minutes later, when the race was restarted yet again.

The racers lined up, and this time Mike yelled, "OK!" But, the next corner was even worse than the first. It veered sharply, this time to the left. Klondike cut the turn hard, running into Flapper's path. Reb, not wanting to hurt Diane, pulled Diker hard to the right, but Klondike stumbled, throwing Reb, spur-side down, straight into the ground. The spur stopped, stuck into the ground, but Reb did not. Flying black hoofs pummeled Reb's body as Flapper ran across him, left the track, and with Diane still on his back, headed down the slash of the electrical line corridor. Reb, moaning and covered with silt, hugged his leg. Someone pulled up in a truck, and the gentleman jockey was helped off the ground and into the seat.

As I waited at the finish line, holding our baby on my hip, my stomach knotted as Klondike crossed the line with an empty saddle. We soon learned Reb was not seriously injured. Patty and Rex trotted in and were declared the winners by default. Diane's husband, John, retrieved Diane and Flapper, and the competitors finally collapsed on the grass. Patty brought her potato salad over and the picnic began.

"Two hours for a three-quarter-mile run!" Mike exclaimed, thinking back to that day. "Only a select few remember the First Annual Delta Derby," he said. "It was a simple kind of fun before work splintered us off in different directions."

Over the last quarter century, in our cache, our hombre's silver spurs have hung, just a little tarnished.

Chapter Thirty One
ELECTRIC DIANE

Diane Hansen wasn't born with normal wiring, or an average tempo. Energy snapped and crackled around her, and Beau, the son on her hip, was along for the ride. Because she bored easily, she made new curtains every week for their log home just to keep the atmosphere sparkling.

70. *John, Beau and Diane Hansen, 1972.*

Like me, Diane was best out-of-doors, unfettered, and roaming free. We spent our summers riding our horses; Beau sat in front of her and Clint, a year older than Beau, was wedged in front of me. We wandered fields and trails, talking, as we grew from girls into women.

In the limitless sunny hours of late March, when daylight was reaching its maximum and the spring snow sparkled like crystals, we decided to leave the boys with a girlfriend and ski across Shaw Creek Flats to the Arrington/Dahlman's cabin up Shaw Creek. The trail would be good because our husbands had just broken the trail to the trapline. We had planned to perhaps rendezvous with the men on the return, at a junction in the trail. I strapped on my surplus Army skis, wider and clunkier than Diane's civilian skis. However, my broader ones were reputed to float on unbroken snow better than her sleek, conventional skis.

Strong and slender, Diane effortlessly herringboned, keeping her heels inward, digging in with her instep and her tips out, up the Quartz Lake slope. When I imitated her, my knees locked together. Helplessly, I slid downhill on grease. Picking myself up, I plodded uphill, sidestepping until we were on the Flats riding Reb's dog trail to Shaw Creek.

The day was as if creation were a happy child and the sky remained blue until late in the evening. Diane and I stopped at every turn, talking and laughing, telling stories. In the woodland, tree roots grabbed our ski tips, until finally, I carried mine over my shoulder, but not Diane. She laughed and skied all the way up the creek.

When we pushed open the door to Bill Arrington's cabin – 10 miles up Shaw Creek – a mansion by trapline standards greeted us. The summer recreation bunkhouse was lined with eight G.I. cots, the essential stove, window, and countertop. Sweaty from our spring fever adventure, we gobbed peanut butter into our mouths, drank creek water, and slept until our moist bodies began to freeze in the chill. I pulled my abused body up from the prone position and made a fire, and Diane and I talked until the spring night was edging into morning.

We hit the trail for home the following day, as fresh as before. At the trail's junction, where we had planned to meet our guys, Diane scrawled with a stick in the fresh snow, "Gone home to the hot tub." Of course, the hot tub was a galvanized, hardware store variety in Diane's wood plank sauna. We would shampoo inside, rinse in the Tanana, and roll in the snow. By the time Reb and John returned from the hills, we would be refreshed.

Chapter Thirty Two
LAST MUSHER TO NOME

n the 1973 Iditarod, racing teams of two people were permitted. Casey Celusnick asked John Schulz if he wanted to go to Nome. After John agreed, Casey added, "By dog sled?" This was the beginning of the first Iditarod Trail Sled Dog Race for the man who took that year's longest recorded time of 32 days to arrive in Nome. Schulz won the blue lantern for a red lantern finish – the Nome hardware store had only one color in stock!

From start to finish, that first Iditarod race spontaneously invented itself. The race was almost cancelled when a sponsor backed out, taking the prize money. The mushers called a drivers' meeting and decided they wanted to go to Nome, with or without prize money. One encapsulated their feelings, "It sounds like a heck of a camping trip!" In the end, Muktuk Marston donated ten thousand dollars, which snowballed into almost sufficient prize money. The contenders were mostly trappers using heavier, bigger, freight dogs, not racing dogs.

On March 6, 1973, the dog teams pulled out, in intervals, from Anchorage's Tudor Road. Schulz and Celusnick drove their sled through private backyards, across railroad tracks, past Fort Richardson, over the bridge, and finally, across the tidal flats. The first Iditarod was described as "a reckless adventure in the wilds of Alaska," and Schulz said, "Heck, I was just having fun!"

Once Anchorage was behind them, they had to get past Cook Inlet's open water. Officials had marked the way with red paint, but falling snow had completely obliterated the paint. Schulz inched his way over an ice ledge, feeling his way in the dark. After having crossed the inlet, Schulz and Celusnick waded through fresh snow, arriving at Knik Lake at two in the morning.

The Army was preparing for a military maneuver and they had broken trail as far as McGrath. This helped, but the soldiers were not dog mushers. The crooked trail wasted needless miles, and an abrupt turn obscured a deep ravine. Going into this turn, Schulz, on one runner, grabbed a Devil's Club plant for a hand up. Celusnick, riding their mutual sled's other runner, fell back hard. The opposing forces broke Celusnick's

71. John Schulz at first Iditarod's starting line, 1973.

runner off at the back stanchion. The trail then dropped abruptly, 40 yards down into Happy River. The sled just missed the dogs, but slammed into Celusnick's knee. Climbing into the sled basket, Casey rode in the mangled sled while John pushed, walked, and rode into Rainy Pass Roadhouse south of Rainy Pass.

After a break at the roadhouse, the bad conditions only worsened. Thick brush and deep snow in Rainy Pass had hindered the military's efforts at trail breaking. Joe Redington, Sr., the Father of the Iditarod Race, acknowledged that this section and the upcoming Kuskokwim glare ice were the nightmare sections of the race.

72. *Toby, Kandik, Mike, and Cassandra.*

Schulz and Celusnick detoured Rainy Pass by crossing through Ptarmigan Valley, but Celusnick's knee had doubled in size. At Styx Lake in the valley, they found a heated wall tent sheltering another musher waiting for an Air Force helicopter evacuation. Both the waiting musher and Celusnick were flown to Anchorage's Providence Hospital, knocking Casey out of the race.

An Iditarod rule stipulated that if one member of a team scratched, both members of the team were out of the race. Schulz reasoned that his dog food was still waiting at the checkpoints. Whether he was disqualified or not, he decided to continue to Nome. Alone, he pressed on.

Schulz turned northwest, crossing through the mountains through Hellsgate Pass. Twenty caribou suddenly trotted into view. The dogs snapped the sled forward, and ran hard, stampeding after the smell of game. Schulz fought to brake as he and his team flew downhill toward the Kuskokwim River Valley.

The wind was howling. Schulz could see two men were already on the Kuskokwim's slick ice, being pushed by a wall of wind roaring down the valley. Cracks began splintering around the two mushers, and suddenly, the ice broke open and there was open water behind them. A hole the size of a small cabin waited to swallow Schulz's team. Running up to his lead dog and digging his toes into the glare ice, he yanked the frenzied animals off the trail and into the woods. The dense woods made for hard traveling and he soon found he had to return to the river.

Straight into the howling gale, Schulz pushed his dogs back onto the ice. The sled skidded sideways, and Schulz was along for the ride. The panicked team clawed to escape the sled, the wind, and the ice. There was no exit, no protection. Thirty-six hours of Kuskokwim ice lay ahead of them, and between them and the Farewell Lodge.

Many mushers had scratched. Without Celusnick, Schulz didn't know if he would be permitted to remain. Race Marshall, Dick Tozier, permitted Schulz to compete. But, as they left Farewell Lodge and crossed Farewell Lake, Schulz and Bruce Mitchell of Ester were on their own. Deep, falling snow had masked all markers except occasional dog scat.

Villages had their own competition, trying to out-do one another in musher hospitality. As each approaching musher was announced, villages prepared personalized banners to welcome them. Schulz had his own banner at McGrath, but to him it was only a blur. His team took off through town after loose dogs. After such trials, Schulz was delayed in McGrath for five days, repairing his crippled sled and relaxing at the local watering hole. Having originally checked in at McGrath in 16th place, Schulz chuckled later, "I could have been a contender."

From McGrath, the trail went overland, and out of Poorman, it scattered into confusion. In Ruby, on the Yukon River, Schulz took a bath in a No. 3, galvanized, aluminum washtub, while the village children took care of his dogs, hauling water and food.

When he was back on the trail on the Yukon, a villager called from Koyukuk's high riverbank, "Come on up for some moose nose stew!" Never one to turn down a party, Schulz joined an on-going carnival in the tiny village. Hours later, at midnight, Schulz plunged in the dark down the steep bank, to camp farther down the trail.

During the race, mushers were asked to share with local students, and at Kaltag, John squashed himself into a school desk, where he recounted his trail sagas. That night, he slept in the school's furnace room. When a Kaltag boy asked Schulz which village had treated him best, Schulz, ignorant of the villages' competition, undiplomatically answered, "Ruby was great!"

The trail out of Kaltag was poor. A blinding snow reduced visibility to 10 feet. Worse, John was aching with the flu. On the portage from Kaltag on the Yukon to Unalakleet on the coast, Schulz decided to wait it out and snuggled down in his sled. In the morning, he shook the blizzard's blanket off his sleeping bag, found a cabin, and slept for a week. When he was well, he followed the trail down the narrow Unalakleet River to the coast, foregoing sleep for days to make up lost time.

At the coast, the trail dropped off the land and onto the Norton Bay ice. The April sun was blinding Schulz as he squinted to see the path's willow markers. The dogs lapped the salt water at Shaktoolik and shook their heads in disgust. At Ungalik, overcome with fatigue, Schulz had to shake off hallucinations, imagining he was facing an uphill wall of ice.

He spent the next night in the National Guard Armory in Koyuk, but found out the hard way there was a curfew. During the night, he slipped outside in

73. John Schulz, Nome, 1973. Winner of the "Blue Lantern."

his long johns to check his dogs, but when he returned he found the armory locked. He managed to pry open an overhead window, climb in, and sink into his sleeping bag.

Schulz' dogs crossed cultural borders in the village of White Mountain. While John was bunked down for the night, his wheel dog, Clyde, got sick after gorging on seal blubber. Schulz had to carry the dog in the sled for the rest of the trip.

Schulz was far back from the front-runner, and only minutes away from Nome, when an Eskimo couple along the trail gestured to him to come up and have tea. They wanted to see a musher.

Four hours later, Schulz left for the last stretch into Nome. It was April, and snow had to be imported onto Front Street. Clyde, who had been lying like a corpse in the sled, woke up with all the cheering and clapping as the slowest musher on the Iditarod trail crossed the finish line. The sick dog sat straight up, as if he were ready for a party. A bystander ran to get Schulz a red lantern, but a blue lantern was the closest thing to the symbol of a last-place finish that could be found in Nome.

John Schulz, a veteran musher of many years, traveled across 1,063 miles in 32 days, 5 hours and 9 minutes, and finished in 22nd place. At the Losers' Banquet, he declared that he had come to see Nome and he had done it. Along with the blue lantern, the community of Nome collected two hundred dollars for Schulz, awarded him half an ounce of gold, and remembered for years the man who saw winter fade into summer on the Iditarod Trail.

Chapter Thirty Three
THE FIRST HOMESTEADERS

Fresh out of college, I knew nothing about dog mushing. My first winter trip on the trapline, Russ Trastek ferried our dogs, our sleds, and us to Fowler's Farm and dropped us off. We had not called first to ask if we might launch our sideshow from Fowlers' cattle pasture. Furious, Julian Fowler came out of his barn, yelling about how long they had been in the country, and about their own trapping rights. As in any friendship, this was only one aspect of the initial bond between the first, modern dairy farm and the local trappers. Until Trans-Alaska Oil Pipeline's construction in 1974 afforded us use of their gravel pad, we accessed our trapline from just outside Fowlers' farm.

74. Bobbie Fowler, Fowler's Dairy Farm, c.1968 at Shaw Creek.

The Yoke

In 1968, I saw Bobbie Fowler for the first time. She was in her large family garden on the knoll above Shaw Creek. Her husband, Julian, was carrying cartons of milk from the family's dairy, while the kids ferried milk crates to the truck.

"Julian Fowler was a 'Do-It-Yourself' man," his wife, Bobbie Fowler, remembered. "Whatever he couldn't invent, repair or build, he got a book and learned."

Coming to Alaska in 1947, just after the construction of the Alcan Highway, the Fowler family was, historically, the connection between Rika's farm and today's Clearwater agriculture.

In 1945, Julian's dad, George Fowler, returned home to his family in Nebraska after working on the Alcan Highway. He had seen homesteading in British Columbia and was eager to try it in Alaska.

George and his wife, Velma, Julian and his wife, Bobbie, spent many Nebraska winter evenings scrutinizing Alaskan maps, eventually picking out a forested knoll near a Shaw Creek, and naming it, The Garden Spot.

Two years later, they set up their small tent there, near the creek filled with grayling. Trying to get a roof over their heads, Julian cut cabin logs while his young wife kept an eye on their 2 year old and fed their infant son as well.

Grampa and Gramma Fowler put a garden in and planned to sell produce. Having only the cold creek water for scrubbing vegetables, Gramma Fowler plunged her hands into the icy water to prep the produce for the Fairbanks' co-op market. A few years later, without warning, the co-op abruptly dissolved, leaving the Fowlers with an entire summer's work, a wasted seven acres of vegetables.

"The Great Depression," Bobbie said, "was easier than homesteading. At least then we had running water and electricity."

In 1950, banding together, Grampa George Fowler, Julian, and the Salcha farmers, formed the Salcha-Big Delta Soil Conservation Subdistrict. They represented twenty-five cooperators and 3,525 acres, buying surplus government heavy equipment to rent to the struggling farmers.

However, the Fowlers had to pay rent on the machinery as soon as the machinery left Fairbanks, not when they actually received it. Additionally, a sheer bluff blocked them from access to the Richardson Highway, making it very difficult to get equipment in. Over the years, the rock was blasted down into a shelf, and equipment could then be moved easily to the farm.

Through working long hours and sacrificing at home, Julian and Bobbie bought their own heavy machinery. By 1953, Julian and his father had obtained two federal homestead patents.

"Mom and Gramma canned our moose and all the garden vegetables," daughter Julenne Fowler Herren remembered recently from her Fairbanks' home. "Grampa made a yoke to carry our water from the creek.

"Initially, Mom taught us our school work at home. Delta Junction was another world, 23 miles away, and it only amounted to ten buildings."

Remembering her later schooling at Fort Greely's Quonset hut, Julenne explained, "About 1957, the school buses ferried us to Greely."

"The community really began to become a town," Bobbie recalled, "when Julian and Bill Seitz, Delta's hardware store owner, convinced Golden Valley Electric Association to supply us with a central power station. Then, Julian felt confident enough to buy twenty cows and start a dairy.

"Additionally, Julian encouraged Golden Valley Electric Association, 'People are starting to homestead the Clearwater. If there's electricity there, more farmers will come as well.'"

"Dairying," Bobbie continued, "wasn't our idea, but the idea of the University of Alaska Cooperative Extension agents. The military had agreed to buy all the milk produced in Alaska and it was an open door for an Interior dairy.

"The pick up, processing, and marketing were all done by Matanuska Maid in Fairbanks, which was handling ten other local dairies.

"But, in 1965, an Anchorage processor, selling stateside milk, underbid Matanuska Maid, grabbing the Army's business and taking its revenue away from Alaska."

"Without telling us," Bobbie went on, "one day, Matanuska Maid just didn't pick up our milk. Their business had collapsed. Overnight, most of the Interior's dairies closed."

A former Marine drill sargent, Julian was not about to quit. Bobbie's motto, too, was "Forge ahead!" For the next three months, while they hurriedly built their own processing plant, they threw away milk and temporarily dried up the cows.

"Dad began delivering our milk," Julenne continued, "door-to-door in Delta.

"I was up at 4 A.M., milked sixty cows, went to school, did the afternoon milking, and fell into bed at 10 P.M."

While the kids were at school, Julian and Bobbie routinely started their 18-20 hour day.

In their free time, the children chopped frozen silage and ran the manure gutter system. "We knew if we didn't graduate from high school what we'd end up doing," Julenne grinned. "Without any time to study, we graduated with honors!

75. *Charlie Boyd and Julian Fowler, pilots discussing mechanics at Boyd's cabin, ca. 1968.*

"But with the dairy's success, more production was required. The deeper we got into the business, the more complicated it became. We were doing everything, from beginning to end: doctoring, an artificial insemination program, raising veal, growing most of the feed, and even calf replacement."

Remembering, Julenne said, "Dad always said, 'You only get out of a cow what you put into it.'"

"In 1973," Bobbie added, "we were voted the Farmers' Home Administration's National Farm Family of the Year. We flew to Washington D.C. to meet President Ford."

Bobbie continued, "By just working hard, we proved that a farming family could be successful without governmental assistance. We were beginning to operate in the black, but with our kids gone and having to pay employees and benefits, we just began to feel really worn out," Bobbie sighed.

"After fifteen years as a northern dairy/processing plant," Bobbie concluded, "we had to close in 1975."

About 1976, when their son, Preston, flew from Fairbanks to Shaw Creek, he checked on the lessee's handling of the dairy. To his horror, he saw the farm in chaos, and the family's dreams ruined.

However, more devastating was the drowning of Preston in 1983 at Chitina. Seven months later, Julian was killed in a small plane crash. "All the hard work seemed for nothing," Bobbie pondered. "However," she added, "if I had it all to do over, I would!" She added resiliently, "We did something with our lives, a very satisfying feeling. Our family worked together and we turned out some great kids."

As a testimony, Grampa's water yoke still hangs on Julenne's wall, a reminder of a family who paved the way for Delta's modern and successful Northern Lights Dairy.

The Wilderness of the Clearwater

In my first years in Alaska, Emily Keaster, homesteader and hardscrabble pioneer, always extended warmth, encouragement, and endurance to a young trapper just beginning her course. Emily was my hero.

In 1953, the Clearwater wilderness, southeast of Delta Junction, was penetrated by Al and Peggy Remington, Chuck Forck, and Walt and Emily Keaster. Until 1960, the only way to access the area, besides the Clearwater River, was over the Healy and Jarvis-Clearwater trails. The federal government, however, had opened it up for homesteading, even with the limited access.

Between 1935-42, Al Remington, the son of a Montana rancher, operated heavy equipment in the Flat mining district near the Iditarod River about 400 miles southwest of Fairbanks, and in the Ruby mining district on the Yukon River about 250 miles northwest of Fairbanks. Returning home to his father's ranch in Montana, a little homesick for the North, he researched the possibilities of homesteading in Alaska.

Delta's Clearwater River with its natural springs and flat ground seemed the ideal cattle country. The summer of 1952, Al set out to investigate and to stake a homestead on the Clearwater, temporarily leaving behind his family of seven.

May 1952, excited and full of blarney, Remington and nine Montana ranchers set out for the North, in a wagon train of trucks. Carrying seed, hay, farm implements, a sawmill, a light plant, a Caterpillar, tractor, building materials, and six months of groceries, Remington and the others who drove the seven-truck caravan had big plans.

Forty year old Al was interviewed by the Great Falls Tribune before leaving Montana. "Herds have been established near the Alaskan coast, but none are in the Interior," he said to the reporter. "All beef is trucked in or flown in."

"The Interior is a natural market waiting for a rancher with lots of grass and water for fattening beef."

A city boy, Charles "Chuck" Forck read this article in the Chicago public library. Chuck had been to Alaska in 1950 and was just looking for a way to return.

As soon as Chuck read the interview, he got on a bus and headed for Big Delta, Alaska. Nearing the northern end of the Alcan Highway, he noticed the same heavy equipment photographed in the Great Falls Tribune feature parked outside Delta's Dixieland Bar. Finding the expedition's leader, Al Remington, Chuck began hanging around these older, experienced ranchers, working odd jobs for them.

In his off time, Chuck searched for the perfect homestead. He found a high bank on the Clearwater River with a hidden, spring-fed pool and made plans to return the following spring.

He and Al both returned home to the Lower 48 for the winter. While in Montana, Al encountered an old friend, Walt Keaster, and induced his friend to return with him in the spring to homestead in Alaska.

The following March, Walt, the son of a pioneer cattle drover, filed for a homestead on 160 acres near Clearwater Creek.

One of the few ways to reach Al's and Walt's farms was an old trail that John Hajdukovich, a local prospector, walked from Jarvis Creek to the Clearwater. Widening the trail further, Al made a swath suitable for a dozer, but not smooth enough for a truck.

Into this wilderness, Al and Walt brought their families from Montana.

76. *Al Remington, Walt and Art Keaster en route to Alaska, 1953.*

Emily Keaster said later, "I never changed my lifestyle from the way I was raised to adulthood. I only went from one farm to another."

Al and Walt loaded Remington's fifty-six head of Angus and Hereford cattle into three stock trucks. Five horses were led into two horse trailers, each pulled by one of the two vehicles.

The Remington and Keaster families, plus four drivers, shared the school bus with "Clearwater Ranch" painted on the roof. For the next three weeks during the drive up the rough, gravel Alcan Highway, the bus served eighteen people as chuck wagon, bunk house, and dining room.

In Alberta, at Lesser Slave Lake, the trucks began breaking down. While the trucks were being fixed, snow fences were set up by the ranchers to corral the bawling cows.

A weary Emily finally arrived only 7 miles from her Clearwater ranch." Wondering where in the world she was going, Emily rode across the marsh in a truck, towed by Al's caterpillar. Her family's 16 foot tent was a welcome sight. "Just to get some quiet…," Emily remembered from her Clearwater cabin.

Thirty-seven rugged miles away, the George and Julian Fowlers were homesteading at Shaw Creek. That summer, the Keasters traded work with Gramma and Grampa Fowler, resulting in a small house for the Keasters to live in that first winter.

Getting the livestock through the cold months was the next ordeal. Every day, Walt and Al hauled feed from Fairbanks, no matter the temperature, and every day, Emily fed them.

"Al had his fingers in a lot of pies." Emily commented. "Also, there was no market for locally-raised meat. The market was undercut by those operating in high volume from Seattle. As it turned out, there was not much reason to raise them."

Emily shot rabbits, wintered chickens in her basement, and her older boys caught pike. "Mom held our family together," her son, Wes, said from the Keaster ranch. Cutting wood for exercise and shooting rabbits for dinner, Emily hoped those for whom she was working might pay them, so she could clothe her sons.

For two years, Emily was happy to stay in the Clearwater wilderness, seldom going to town.

But the cattle ranching dream began to fade, and in the spring of 1956, Al sold the surviving herd.

Always a cowboy though, Al began buying horses, introducing the Interior's first rodeos and taking over big game guide John Hajdukovich's hunting area on Granite Mountain.

"A hundred years too early, Dad's schemes for the Interior's cattle market were premature," Judy Gossack, Al's daughter, said from her home in Montana.

Emily said, "All we were trying to do was start a full circle, agricultural economy, growing grain and feeding beef."

"But no one could afford equipment in the 1950's to grow anything," Emily explained.

"Harvesting first with a hand scythe, Chuck Forck began to save for a tractor. Adding our money together, we bought an International tractor. In 1955, Chuck Forck and I cultivated the first crop of oats in the Clearwater," Emily smiled, triumphantly.

She explained, "It was hard even to cultivate the 20 acres required by the federal government for a 160-acre homestead. Getting the seed, the fertilizer, the storage space, and the equipment took time. So for cash money, everyone worked Civil Service at Fort Greely."

In 1960, the area was finally accessed by the L-shaped, Clearwater road. The coming of commercial electricity further accelerated homesteading on the Clearwater. Walt Keaster bought Al Remington's cattle and when Walt died in 1979, the Keasters owned a herd of a hundred cattle.

"A beef industry in Delta was my husband's dream," Emily said. "We cleared the ground, made the roads, and began Delta's Alaskan grown beef industry."

Whether the dreams of Al, Walt, and Chuck come true depends on marketing, the rest of the agricultural circle.

77. Remington Keaster Wagon Train, 1953.

Folding her hands, Emily said, "I'm just here to remember how things were done before: starting slow and making changes in little bites."

Partners Corralled Delta Beef Enterprises

In 1967, Joe Mead and Doug McCollum brought up a load of Montana horses. Among them was Klondike, a sorrel horse Doug had originally intended for himself, but let Reb purchase. Klondike was just the trapline partner Reb needed.

In the front yard of Joe Mead's Clearwater ranch, he and his friend, Al Remington, had GIs build pens for Delta's first rodeo in May 1968. Joe's partner, young Doug McCollum, was down the Alaska-Canada Highway, hauling up a string of Canadian range horses as potential buckers. Wes Keaster, only 16 years old, was working with the horses at the Mead Ranch. Joe Mead did all the horse-trading. He knew all the horses in the country and even took care of most of them during the winter.

Delta was not the same in the 1950s and 60s. The bars outnumbered the churches, and the unofficial unemployment agency was the Buffalo Lodge.

"Delta would have been different if all business could have been done on a bar stool at the Buffalo," McCollum, the owner of Delta Concrete Products, and Delta Meat and Sausage

87

78. Doug McCollum

Company, said as he and his wife, and business partner, Cathie McCollum, sat at their kitchen table. "Why, those guys were stumbling over more opportunities than you could shake a stick at," he laughed.

As a kid in Montana, one day in 1954, McCollum looked out his schoolhouse window at cattle being loaded on a truck bound for Alaska. Local rancher, Al Remington, was leading a caravan to Clearwater to homestead.

During the years, Remington traveled back and forth between Alaska and Montana to help his dad back home in Great Falls. While in Montana, Remington often talked to McCollum as the industrious teen-ager was growing up. Remington and his homesteading partner, Walt Keaster, repeatedly said to the young man, "Anyone who's not afraid to work oughta come to Alaska."

By the time he turned 24, McCollum had decided to "go north, get a stake, and someday…create cows." (Doug was referring to developing the Paulson Galloway steer, the species best suited for him both for northern survival and the market's palate.)

Teaming with Mead and Remington, McCollum observed that ranching, in 1967, was hard-scrabble.

"If Joe Mead ran out of feed for his horses," Wes Keaster said, "he just opened the gate, gave 'Betsy' a shove, saying, 'Get along, girl, the best you can.'"

However, one day, a passing motorist hit one of Mead's horses while it was scrounging on the Clearwater. The open range could no longer be tolerated.

"Today, I couldn't afford to have my beef forage like that," Keaster, a successful Angus grower, explained. "We run a cow/calf operation, trying to compete with the Lower 48 market. Everything has to be lock stepped: calf, grass finisher, and feed lot, to get a premium-grade meat. We're looking for consistency to please the restaurant clientele."

Rivaling with beef ranchers from Outside (from the Lower 48), Delta ranchers are tightening up into a local, full circle market. Keaster's cow/calf program, Scott Miller's commercial feedlot, and McCollum's slaughterhouse are working toward support-ing one another. Issues concerning breed

79. First harvested grain, Clearwater. Virgil Severns, Emily, 1955.

preference, use of steroids, and federal monies keep the dialogue lively.

In 1984, McCollum traveled to North Dakota, investigating the cold-weather-resistant Paulson Galloway steer.

Contending with McCollum's choice, Miller, a cross-Angus rancher, remarked, "Ah, a Galloway is practically a cross between a cow and a buffalo. They have a reputation of being hard to handle and slower to fatten, but I do have twenty-five I'm finishing up to butcher."

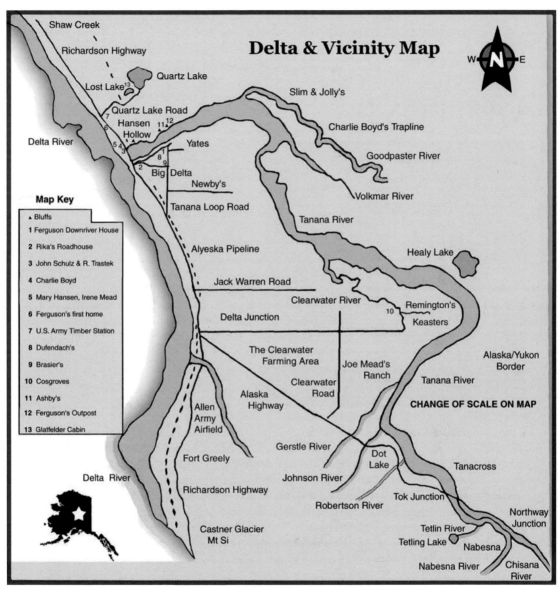

Delta & Vicinity Map

Shaw Creek

Richardson Highway

Quartz Lake

Lost Lake 13

Quartz Lake Road

Hansen 11 12

Hollow

Delta River

5 4 3

Yates

7

6

2

8 9

1

Big Delta

Newby's

Slim & Jolly's

Charlie Boyd's Trapline

Goodpaster River

Volkmar River

Tanana Loop Road

Tanana River

Map Key

▲ Bluffs

1 Ferguson Downriver House

2 Rika's Roadhouse

3 John Schulz & R. Trastek

4 Charlie Boyd

5 Mary Hansen, Irene Mead

6 Ferguson's first home

7 U.S. Army Timber Station

8 Dufendach's

9 Brasier's

10 Cosgroves

11 Ashby's

12 Ferguson's Outpost

13 Glatfelder Cabin

Alyeska Pipeline

Healy Lake

Jack Warren Road

Clearwater River

Delta Junction

Remington's

10

Keasters

The Clearwater
Farming Area

Joe Mead's
Ranch

Alaska/Yukon
Border

Clearwater
Road

Tanana River

Alaska
Highway

CHANGE OF SCALE ON MAP

Allen
Army
Airfield

Gerstle River

Dot
Lake

Tanacross

Fort Greely

Delta River

Johnson River

Tok Junction

Northway
Junction

Richardson Highway

Robertson River

Tetlin River

Castner Glacier
Mt Si

Tetling Lake

Nabesna

Nabesna River

Chisana
River

"I'm willing to try them if these work out," he added.

Starting with one bull and seventeen heifers, McCollum's herd today has increased to four hundred head that graze a 1,000-acre spread.

"My hobby kinda got outta hand," he said.

While he harvested hay, riding for hours on his tractor, McCollum dreamed up the Delta Meat and Sausage Company, a slaughterhouse converted from the Craig Taylor warehouse.

Today, the McCollums' son-in-law and daughter, Russ and Jeannie Pinkelman, operate the full-scale, state-inspected meat plant.

When asked what else might be in the hopper, Cathie said, "Just don't let Doug get on that tractor. I get worried when I see him out there, dreamin'. Lately, he's been talking about a silage bagging operation."

Chapter Thirty Four
OUTPOST

81. Reb packing 55-gallon, barrel stove uphill to new home, Outpost, 1973.

When Reb and I married in 1969, squatting on Alaska's public lands was quite common. According to Joe Vogler, the founder of the Alaskan Independence Party, at that time less than two percent of Alaska's land was privately owned. Very little federal or state-owned land was available to homestead or purchase. The Alaska Native Land Claims Act was not yet settled, which hamstrung the release of government-owned land. A Holler friend of Reb's, John Edwards, had allowed us to live on the land where Reb was living when I met him. However, I sensed it was the season to find our own property. In 1971, the state began to offer remote, 5-acre parcels, under the Open-to-Entry program.

Reb and I had maps with the available parcels marked. We rode our horses into Shaw Creek, then up the Tanana River, searching. We followed an old fire trail made once by a wayward earthmover, a Caterpillar, lost in the Quartz Lake hills. The trail opened up into an isolated area of land protected on either side by Tanana River bluffs. We wove our way around the thick woods, punched through deep moss, passed a small pond, and stumbled onto the river. We walked the land, noting a good drainage tilt, and a knoll at the back of the protected cove. We knew this was it, and we had our first meal – C-Rations – sitting in the warm sunshine by the pond. We walked our borders, stringing them with plastic ribbon, and left a jar on each of our eight corners. We claimed two, 5-acre parcels -- the maximum amount of land to which each of us was entitled. Our new location seemed very remote to us that day: a day's travel, but we would make the adjustment.In Fairbanks, we filed our claims at the State of Alaska's land office.

We began to take the land, adopting and domesticating it in stages. In November, Reb mushed over the Quartz Lake hills to see the new land. I was eager to hear the report. Reb said it was a long, rough mush, but doable.

The next summer, we hired R.L. Johnson to clear the scrub spruce off the 10 acres. His driver, Audey Sipes, walked a Caterpillar, driving it carefully over the precipitous hills to reach us. He pushed the spruce and moss into large piles – berms – that divided the now raw earth into three fields. With 2-year-old Clint, we camped for two weeks near the river. Reb flung fertilizer, brome, and oat seed with a pie plate, which later patterned the pastures with unique circles of grass. The oats were a nurse crop to prevent weeds while the slower, perennial, brome grass took root. What we did not realize was the previous moss cover had masked and insulated deep layers of permafrost – permanently frozen ground – notoriously bad for cabin foundations.

In 1973, we were ready to make our move. Clint was old enough to follow me in the fields. We three lived in a five-man Army tent. The oat hay that we had planted had died and the limp grass lay all around us, suffocating the brome from prospering. Having nothing but our arms for tools, I hand raked oat hay every day, roughed up the ground, and re-seeded more brome. Day after day I raked, wearing a halter-top and shorts, soaking up sunshine.

82. Outpost with wind generator, solar panels; barn; greenhouses and garden, 1980, southern exposure.

Our life, like desert tent-dwellers, had only the sky for a canopy.

Every morning, Reb pointed his boat downstream to his Bureau of Land Management firefighting job. As his boat disappeared, small against Mount Hayes' majesty, Clint and I turned to use Reb's new harrow. Reb had pounded spikes into a log creating a makeshift tiller. Clint and I rode Klondike, dragging the log behind, roughing up the ground for seeding. With the sun on our backs, we made circles in the fields while I planned next year's garden crops. I tried to think what crops might store well in the root cellar throughout the winter.

For two weeks, I chopped sod off our first garden using a Pulaski – a combination mattock and axe. I read the Alaska University Extension brochures, which said I should have equal parts: sand, loam, and dirt, with a little added manure. Reb had started digging a basement for our house; from that I dug and wheel-barrowed sand to my new garden plot. I dug organic matter from the berm piles, and mixed the sand and organic matter with the soil in my plot down to two feet. I planted some purchased vegetable starts, and was amazed daily to watch them grow. Under the open sky, I discovered my place in God's dynamic universe.

We turned to building the house. The cold would arrive in three months, whether we were

83. *Reb and Clint haul house logs with Klondike, 1973.*

ready or not. To ensure a tightly fitting home, Reb purchased logs matched for size from Dean Cummings, the local sawmill operator. Every night after work at BLM, Reb boated four house logs up the river. I hitched up Klondike and with him, I dragged one log at a time up a short hill and into the main field near the tent. The sweet, sticky sap covered my hands as I drew a knife blade over and over across each log, peeling the bark, racing to finish before the sap quit running -- around mid July. The resulting bare logs were a beautiful golden color.

Reb had begun a cellar in the main field, but each day as I rode the horse, I envisioned our golden log home up on the hill overlooking the 10 acres. Reb cautioned me that I could never have a well up there, and that every stove, each piece of furniture, all firewood, every load of groceries, all laundry, and each 5-gallon can of water would have to be carried up that hill. So even though I had already hauled the logs, and they were in position on the hill, I skidded them back to the cellar hole in the pasture. Nonetheless, I was held in a vision that the house should be on the hill.

One morning, we found melted ice water had back-filled our root cellar that Reb had dug. Our undulating fields were collapsing, one by one, revealing melted ice tunnels as thawing permafrost honeycombed our pastures. We abandoned the field site, and decided to build on the hill after all. Once again, I hooked up Klondike and hauled all the logs back up the hill.

In August, when Reb was laid off for the season from B.L.M., we quickly began to build. As Reb dug a dry, sandy root cellar on the hill, laid the foundation logs, and made the floor, 3-year-old Clint was his helper and handed him nails. The air echoed with our view of the crystalline, blue, unimpeded sight of the snowy Alaska Range, of Isabel Pass, Donnelly Dome, and the tilted sweep of the Tanana rushing past the backdrop of the Granite Mountains. At our feet, the fields had become an oasis in the forested wilderness, rising toward the cumulus clouds that rolled in every afternoon from Thompson Lake. I treasured the view, holding it in my mind even as the rising walls of the house gradually walled it out. Finally, the scene was reduced to the rectangles of the open windows and door. The reality dawned. The house must be enclosed; winter was coming.

As Reb placed logs one on top of the other, I placed the fiberglass in between them. Then, Reb spiked the logs together. Neighbors, Jon Dufendach and Brad McAllister from across the river, helped us raise the ridge logs onto the waiting gables.

Before the cold wind blew in the first sifting snow, and after just one short month of building, we were inside. Granted, we had a cardboard door, but the roof was over our heads. A rusty, 55-gallon stove was blasting heat into the empty interior. In the October quiet, our Coleman lanterns hissed out brightness, which was reflected off the spruce-gold walls. We had made it. The river was now coalescing with ice. Neighbors were no longer an option for company. We had no beds, and all of us bunked that evening in a half loft Reb had made for Clint's eventual bedroom.

Years later, we learned that far away neighbors could see the lights of the cabin on the hill being lit every evening – the only little eyes in the dark wilderness beyond the river, the cabin we came to call The Outpost. It was the beginning of a family home and of thirteen years of remote homesteading.

Chapter Thirty Five

84. Reb's fellow Laborers building Trans-Alaska Oil Pipeline at Shaw Creek, 1975.

THE PIPELINE

On March 13, 1968, three months before my arrival in Alaska, Atlantic Richfield Oil Company (later, ARCO), and Humble Oil and Refining Company (later, Exxon) announced the discovery of large deposits of oil on the North Slope of Alaska. They and several other companies began planning the Trans-Alaska Pipeline System to move oil from the north shore of Alaska 800 miles to the south to a seaport on the Gulf of Alaska. In 1970, the Alyeska Service Pipeline Company was formed to build and operate the system. First, however, agreements had to be reached that would settle the land rights of the aboriginal inhabitants. The resulting agreement was titled the Alaska Native Land Claims Act.

Christmas 1968, I hovered over a can of boiling water on a wood stove in MonteChristo, our remote trap cabin. Sweat poured down my face as I dropped red Rit Dye into the water, followed by military, wool socks. I had no money for Christmas gifts for my Oklahoma family, but I would sew letters from strips of moosehide, personalizing each Christmas sock with their names, and then fill them with gifts from the Great Land: hardened spruce sap and wild rabbit hides. My feet were cold on the packed dirt floor, and a couple of dogs lay under the pole bed. On KFAR radio, Disc Jockey Steve Agbaba kibitzed the question of the prospective oil pipeline and the Alaska Native Land Claims. They had been talking about it for a year. I did not take it seriously. I resigned myself to always mushing dogs and living on dirt floors. I saw us living a primitive lifestyle stretching on toward an endless horizon. The pipeline was just talk in 1969. I only knew two friends who were privileged to be construction workers earning union wages. By fighting fire, Reb earned four hundred dollars a month during the summer. At that time, the Laborers Union was not a significant means of employment; the Alaska enrollment only amounted to five hundred people, and was confined to the long-term construction workers.

However, by 1974, the Fairbanks' Laborers Union was opening their rolls, as the Trans-Alaska Pipeline became a reality. Being the early bird who got there first enhanced a man's number. Therefore, on January 1, 1974, at 6:00 A.M., a long line began to form in the −50° F. ice fog in front of the Laborers Union Hall on Noble Street. The freezing men under the street lamp shifted from one foot to another in their heavy, rubber, insulated Bunny Boots as they waited to get a good number when the Hall opened at 8 A.M. Reb was one of them.

By that spring, Reb had his first union job, and by summer, he was helping build the Delta Base Camp, near Rika's Roadhouse. The boom metamorphosed Delta, Fairbanks, and the Interior, just as the gold rushes had also dramatically shaped Alaska. Workers from Outside came up in droves. Bumper stickers read, "Happiness is a Texan With An Okie Under Each Arm, Heading South," and "Let the Bastards Freeze In the Dark." Long-standing Fairbanks families that had a background in the saloon trade brought in prostitution. It was said that law enforcement was on the take. Fairbanks was wide-open. Hippies lived in all of the abandoned, rotting outbuildings at Rika Roadhouse, collecting pipeline wages, and of course, paying no rent. Wives raised kids alone while husbands followed the work.

When the inevitable bust period followed the completion of the pipeline, new bumper stickers replaced the old, such as: "God, please send another pipeline. I promise, this time, not to piss it all away."

The Pipeline Widow

The pipeline years were an era of King Midas pouring out his treasure. For us, access to work in the summer was easy. Reb's job site was just a boat ride across the river from our Outpost home. After crossing the Tanana River, Reb only had to get to Delta Base Camp.

But after October's cold had begun, and before freeze-up – (that time when the river froze) Reb kept his outboard warm in a truck during work. One day, I had been in town, so after he got off work, and in the pitch-black, we took the motor out of the truck and mounted the motor on the riverboat. The river was choked with ice patties, coalescing into solid ice. The boat pushed ominously upstream, through the floating, slush ice, up and down, up and down. I laid on the bow of the boat scanning ahead with a flashlight, guiding Reb through the quiet trap of thickening ice.

On Halloween, 1974, the thermometer plunged to −35° F., and by morning, the Tanana River had frozen, two months prematurely.

Once the river was solid, I harnessed Reb's dog team every morning to help him with his daily commute. He stepped on his sled, slid down the fields, over the riverbank, and across the river ice to the mainland. An hour later, just outside the pipeline camp in the woods, he snapped his dogs into a gang line, a taut horizontal chain with intermittent snaps. With the dogs taken care of, he jumped the fence and went to work.

From 1974-77, our lives pivoted around the pipeline and the river conditions. In the dark of October, it became too precarious plowing through slush ice. Because of the dangerous conditions during freeze-up and spring breakup, we moved to a trap cabin we had on the road.

After the pipeline was completed, there continued to be construction work for Reb on the

85. Rosa Pass, the portal of our trapline, as pipe is both elevated and buried on our sled dog trail for the Trans-Alaska Oil Pipeline, looking south to the Alaska Range, 1976.

North Slope. Periodically, Reb left us for two-three months to work, leaving me alone with Clint, and later, with our new daughter, and finally, with a second son as well. Because our remote home had no road access, was without electricity, running water, telephone or other adults, having Reb gone for months seemed like a death sentence to me. In my isolation, my world shrank to having responsibility for chopping a hole in the Tanana River's ice; dipping water into 5-gallon cans; hauling water by sled up 10 acres; maintaining the wood stove and propane supply; cleaning our house; feeding, cleaning, clothing, and teaching our children; feeding and maintaining seventeen sled dogs; and sometimes, dealing with broken generators.

When Reb went to the North Slope again in 1981, I had had enough. We bought a house on the road in the Clearwater district and tried living like others. By spring, we were choking on suburbia's gas-powered flatlands and quickly returned upriver. As Reb told me when I was complaining of the hardships, "the Fergusons were not other people."

The next time Reb did another North Slope stint, the children, now three of them, and I stayed upriver. But, once a week for two days at a time, we stayed at my girlfriend, Yvonne Echo-Hawk's home. After each absence of two days -- when we returned home,   -- the log house was cold-soaked.

We had a large basement with a wood stove under our bedroom. When we returned from Yvonne's after two days, it was so cold in the house that we made a fire in the basement stove, and then, while the house was warming up, we lowered a sleeping Ben in his bassinet down into the basement. While it was warming, we made fires in three other stoves on the next two floors to knock out the deep ice. The house would not be comfortable, however, until the next day. After chaining up the dogs, we climbed back down the ladder into the basement, and as we sat with Ben around the warming stove, we ate peanut butter and crackers. In a couple of hours, the house was

86. Clint, a week after dog bite, hunting Easter eggs upriver, 1975.

tolerable. We climbed back up the basement ladder and crawled in between our chilly sheets in our bedrooms.

In the new millennium, Reb did one last round of North Slope work. But this time, we lived on the road system with its conveniences. There were no lanterns to fill, no stove to stoke, and we could talk every night with him on the telephone. However a look at our front porch covered with caribou racks, assorted traps, and perhaps a frozen fur-bearing carcass assured anyone "the Fergusons were not like other people" – even with running water and electricity.

Beware of Dogs

While Reb worked on the pipeline -- during the seasons when river access was so difficult -- we often lived in a small cabin we had on the road system. One Easter, when we had moved to it, Verna asked me to go with her to Schulz' in the Holler to get her chainsaw sharpened. As Clint, Verna, and I entered John's dog yard, I hollered to Clint, "Stay away from that white dog. She has pups. Don't go near her." We went into John's, had coffee, and were chatting when, to my horror, I saw a terrified Clint running for the cabin, holding his face, screaming, and sobbing. I threw open the door, and my child was holding his gaping cheek. His flesh hung open on his cheekbone, very near his eye.

Verna immediately took us in her car. Because it was Clint's face, I wanted an experienced Fairbanks surgeon to sew the wound. All the way to town, 100 miles, Clint lay on my lap with ice on his cheek. In the clinic, the nurse laid a cloth over his face with a hole exposing the area for suture. Clint lay bravely and quietly on the clinic table; we held hands while Dr. Earp carefully sewed.

Had it been a hair's breadth deeper, his facial muscle would have been cut. Or, had it been any closer to his eye, he would have lost his vision in that eye.

That evening, we returned to the tiny cabin to meet Reb who had just come in from his day's pipeline work. Shocked at Clint's face, he considered disposing of Schulz' dog, but she had had pups and Clint should not have gone near her.

Everyday, I cleaned Clint's stitches. By Easter, we were back upriver at home. I hid eggs in the grass. With a gaily-colored basket, my wounded, but gleeful son, hunted eggs. He wore a Confederate cowboy shirt with stars I had made for him.

Chapter Thirty Six
HOMESTEAD WIFE

Broken Generator

Work in Alaska is seasonal. When husbands work -- whether rigging machinery on the oil pipeline; fighting fires; trapping; or guiding for big game -- wives raise children alone, Subdivisions hardly existed in 1968. Less than two percent of Alaskan land was privately owned. Most people in the Bush lived on homesteads, home sites, in villages, or they squatted on public property. Families lived remote – isolated; when an emergency happened, the wife dealt with it. Once, when I was fuming over all the demands on me, my friend, Carol Dufendach, said, "Homestead wives are not like other wives." Carol did not simply teach me to accept my role; she modeled it. Additionally, through the C.B. radio, she was always available to me when I needed help.

Our home's 12-volt electrical system depended on solar power, wind power, and a Witte generator that I ran twice a week. When the Witte ran, we could even use the bright 110-current, incandescent lights instead of the duller 12-volt fluorescent lights. We could use the little black and white TV, the vacuum cleaner, and the tape deck! Late one night in 1984, during one of Reb's North Slope stints, as Clint, Sarah, and Ben slept in their beds, I puttered around the house. Suddenly, the house was plunged into darkness and an ominous silence filled the cabin. "Oh, my God…" I wondered…I grabbed jacket, hat, gloves, and flashlight and pushed the door open into the -50° F. temperatures. In the generator's cabin, oil was splashed over the floor, walls, and window. Horror filled my soul. "The wages Reb was working for would have to go to fix the generator! What did I do wrong?" I thought, desperately. I counted the hours until morning when I could call Carol's neighbor, Jim Moser, on the C.B. radio. Jim listened, laughing affectionately at Judy's "new crisis," and agreed to meet Clint in the Holler and ride in the dog sled to our homestead.

As Jim stomped into our house with the cold shimmering off his parka, I slipped into my coat to walk him to the generator shed. With a wrench, he twisted the oil filter off the machine. Jim diagnosed that Reb had torqued the filter on the generator with a maniacal twist. Pressure had built up, sending the oil flying and shutting the generator down. Jim simply twisted a new filter on and fired it back up. The generator had not seized up. After coffee, the friend who made house calls at -50° F. stepped back on Clint's dog sled before the short winter daylight hours limited travel.

A Mouthful

When the dogs in the yard started barking, chances were a tasty guest with barbs was wandering through. Inevitably, a dog broke loose and charged after the visiting porcupine. Unaware they cannot have a T-bone on four legs, the sled dog, for the fifth time in his life, took a big bite of the quilly land beaver. Enraged by the ensuing pain, he bit harder, tossing the varmint from side to side. By the time the howling dog got to me, there were quills down his throat, in the roof of his mouth, deep in his tongue, between his teeth, in his lips, ears, neck, and head. "Clint," I said, "give me your needle-nosed pliers and flashlight. I'll mix some vinegar and baking soda." I poured the liquid mix over the quills to open the wounds, and let it soak for a minute. Clint laid the dog on its back, gripped the dog's vise-like jaws apart, and stuck his knee in the dog's chest. Holding the light, I carefully reached down the dog's throat with the needle-nosed pliers and pulled each barbed needle out.

For years, Reb had cautioned, "Get every single quill. If one is left, it festers, or works to the dog's brain, eventually causing serious problems."

After an hour of surgery, the sore dog limped back to his chain. But, if the porcupine came through again that evening, the dog would again attempt a free lunch.

Landing a Riverboat in Merging Flashlights

One moonless, late September night, Reb and Bill Chmura drove up to the south side of the river, arriving late from a week of hunting. By the dark Tanana River, they turned on the car's Citizen's Band radio to reach our home on the north side. "Outpost, Outpost," Reb called, "Come in!"

I hollered at Clint to stop the wind generator, so the electrical interference would not muffle the message. "This is Outpost," I replied, "Over!" "We're home," Reb said. "Get a flashlight and meet us downriver with the boat." It was a dark night. I struggled into my moose hide jacket, laced up my L.L. Bean boots, and walked in the fall night to the boat. I pulled on the recoil of the 25 hp Evinrude and nosed the 24-foot riverboat away from the shore. I knew the shoreline, the shallow water, and the deadly trees overhanging the banks – the sweepers. I gentled the boat down the Tanana. To guide me, Reb had the car lights on. With my Magnum flashlight, I searched the bank until the beams converged; then, I eased the boat into shore. They had had a good hunt, and Reb walked back to the outboard and took over.

On a similar night, but in October after ice had begun to form, I managed to get children, packages, and packs upriver after a long shopping trip. Once home, I felt for my wallet and gasped, realizing I had left a pocketbook full of money on our car hood downriver. Apparently, I had loaded the boat, and then, simply gone home. When this hit me, I left Reb with the children, jumped in the canoe, pulled on the recoil of the 15 hp motor, and prayed all the way downriver. A neighbor on the south bank heard my lone motor in the dark, and pondered, "What fool is on the river tonight…?" I landed safely dowriver and got out where we left our Datsun pickup. There, in the beam of my flashlight, was my open wallet. I stuffed it in my pocket, and motored the thirty-five minutes back upriver, and to bed.

Chapter Thirty Seven

A MAN'S CUP OF COCOA

87. Clint and Reb, MonteChristo, 1974.

In the fall, after a summer season of pipeline work, Reb, 5-year-old Clint, and I had walked into Campbell's Cabin to cut firewood in preparation for the coming trapping season. Reb and Clint stacked firewood while I scooped frozen cranberries with a bear claw tool and rattled them into my bucket.

In 1969, a huge fire had burned the marten habitat for thousands of acres causing us to abandon the MonteChristo line, and build up a new trapline. Charlie Boyd had warned us that marten would perhaps not return in our lifetime.

The day the three of us hiked in a light dusting of

snow had fallen making it an ideal opportunity to easily walk our old trapline searching for marten tracks. On a whim, Reb and I asked Clint if he could walk that far. He said he could. Over dinner at Campbell's, we excitedly made plans to hike beyond Flat Creek, the next day's cabin, to MonteChristo, where we had not been in five years. Hoping Charlie might be wrong, we set out the next day for Flat Creek, and then the third day, for MonteChristo.

On the way, we passed chickadees fluttering on the snowy ridge. Spruce hens flushed to the treetops as we began the steep descent into the broad drainage below. We planned to pick up a Thanksgiving grouse on our return trip.

88. Clint and Reb, MonteChristo, 1974.

Overnighting at Flat Creek at Fred Campbell's former, second trapping cabin, I chinked the front wall with rags by candlelight. Reb bedded down on the dirt floor, leaving the single bunk for Clint and me.

Hiking the next day across miles of muskeg, we scanned the snow for the long striding tracks of a loping marten. Thick, falling snow began to obscure Reb's trail ahead of me. Little Clint's legs did not move quickly, and we worried about the snow deepening and the difficulty of getting him back. Deflated blueberries hung on the brush, and we grabbed them as we passed, enticing Clint to keep on walking.

We drifted along, telling stories of Pinocchio's Blue Fairy, as I recited every detail of Geppetto and his wooden puppet. Hours trickled by before we came to the burned area where we began to lose the trail in the confusion of charred trees. We paused while Reb warmed us with a campfire and we ate some cold, leftover pancakes. Then, Clint happily followed his dad up valleys that branched from one into another. The brush gave way to birch, and we entered the narrow, unscathed valley of MonteChristo Creek.

After nine and a half hours of walking, our cabin reached out to us like an old friend nestled on its mountain shelf next to a gurgling creek. The last time we had been here was two months before Clint was born. Now, we could show the cabin to our son.

Reb hauled water from the creek and heated it on the barrel stove. Finding a large enamel cup, he offered Clint, "a man-sized cup of cocoa suitable for a man's walk." Clint snuggled up to his dad on the dried grass mattress and pole bed. After dinner just before bed, I looked through the cabin's open door and studied the stars and MonteChristo's familiar ridges. I thanked God we were home again, shut the door, and turned out the lantern.

Returning the following day, it seemed Charlie was right because we saw no marten tracks as we pushed through 18 inches of snow. Along the way, I picked up a No. 1 trap of Fred Campbell's, hanging on a collapsed cabin wall, and showed it to Clint at the Flat Creek cabin. After dinner, and sitting in dried long johns, Reb showed Clint how to set the sensitive pan of the trap without catching his little fingers.

On the way back into Campbell's, we heard the whirr of wings. Reb had the .22 ready and bagged the wild chicken. At the lake cabin, I got my frozen cranberries and packed them over the mountain for home, ready to garnish our Thanksgiving grouse.

Chapter Thirty Eight
ALASKA'S SECRET DOOR
Following the Tanana and the Yukon, into the Bush...

89. Clint , Reb, Judy, 1975, Yukon River trip.

Our son Clint carried the cottonwood boat he had whittled as he walked with his dad to the Tanana Riverbank near our home.

"I want to let it drift, Dad," our 5-year-old said the summer of 1975, kneeling to release his boat into the current of the Tanana. "I'm sending a message to the people downstream, like the Indian boy did in my book."

Paddle to the Sea, a children's book by Holling Clancy Holling was a favorite of his at that time.

Reb smiled, "OK, but, Clint, why don't we put our big boat in and follow the river trail ourselves?" That evening, we decided to take a trip in our canoe from our Tanana River home near Delta, north to the Yukon River, and west on the Yukon toward the Bering Sea, a trip of 700 miles.

That night, Reb tossed and turned, unable to sleep as he pictured our loaded, 17-foot canoe. He finally decided it was not enough boat to make the trip to the coast. We delayed our trip for a day so we could go to Fairbanks to buy a 19-foot Grumman freighter canoe.

While we were in town, I contacted Charlie Wolf for some last-minute canoe instruction. Charlie, at 76, was an old student of the French-Canadian voyageurs, the boatmen who had freighted goods for the early fur companies. He knew some French, had a voyageur's hat, and had canoed both Canadian and Alaskan rivers many times.

Charlie showed me some oar strokes, explaining in both French and English, and I was all set. He cautioned about Squaw Crossing, an unprotected stretch of water, just above the confluence of the Tanana and Yukon Rivers. If the wind came up, the shallow water could quickly become boiling waves.

We were glad we had the longer boat and transferred the load from the shorter boat to the larger one.

June 21st, we fastened splash covers made from surplus Army canvas across the mid-section of the canoe to protect the food and bedding, and started out. Reb was near the outboard at the back of the canoe. Clint sat in his canvas porthole in front of his dad. Sitting in his camping chair, he could duck under the cloth skirt anytime, and escape the wind and spray.

In the bow, under my seat, I had slipped Lieutenant Castner's 1898 account of his Tanana-

Goodpaster river expedition as well as Archbishop Hudson Stuck's book, *Voyages on the Yukon and its Tributaries*. The archbishop had called the Tanana, "a bad river." "Oh, great," I thought as I saw Bates Rapids, a large, undulating water in front of us there where the Delta River tumbles into the Tanana.

We traveled up the white caps, and then down the 2-foot troughs, and up again. Our boat knifed through the swells powered by our 6-horsepower motor.

A shipwrecked steamboat, the *Nabesna*, lay up a side slough where Captain Clarence O'Flannigan had run it aground, many years ago: a testimony to the challenge of the Tanana.

In his early days, O'Flannigan had prospected near Tolovana Roadhouse, downstream from Fairbanks, Nenana, and Tanana.

90. Loaded to the gunnels, Yukon River trip.

We stopped at the original Tolovana Roadhouse on our fourth day out. It sat in a sea of grass, its floors covered with flood silt, but its log walls and ceiling were still beautiful and intact.

As we continued downriver, we passed a series of ghost towns, a reminder of the formerly busy Tanana, echoing now with emptiness. Gone from the river's edge were the Indian villages that had once saved the life of Lieutenant Allen, an Army explorer, in 1898. The buildings of Old Minto and Cos Jacket were shells of the once thriving river settlements.

In the 1950s, the era of the sternwheelers faded, taking with it a source of the Natives' income from cutting and stacking firewood to feed the ships' boilers. Up and down the river, the steamboats had loaded their piles of wood.

Cos Jacket, downstream from Old Minto, was an old relation to the village of Tanana. Exploring the Cosna (Cos Jacket) ruins, we found that all that was left were old brass beds, two Victrola phonographs, Edison records, a time sheet, and a 1939 National Guard album.

That night, as we pitched our tent in a bed of pungent Labrador Tea, I fussed about facing Squaw Crossing.

I was tense in the morning as we approached the bottleneck on the Tanana, doubled in width before its conjoining with the Yukon. Hidden sandbars divided the Tanana into a myriad of shallow channels. Wind could easily turn the rolling water into erratic white caps, but, thankfully, only a breeze stirred that day.

After Squaw Crossing, we reached the end of our home river. The mouth of the Tanana emptied into the vast arm of the mighty Yukon River, sweeping in from Canada. Broad, green mountains framed the endless sky of the river valley. We were in a different country now.

After the family was asleep, I sat in the moonlight and realized we had passed through an invisible door. The city with its man-made structures and schedules lay behind us. But on this side, the sky, water, and sand pulsated with fish, sunshine, and the Native way of life. Like a little boat set adrift into wide waters, we were filled with the anticipation of new things.

Calling the Old Names of the Yukon

Off in the distance, forest fires burned near Fairbanks. The air was still, and the smoke and heat oppressive. We began to see fish wheels – a device with two paddle-like spokes connected to two wire baskets, driven by the river, that scoop returning adult salmon from the river current.

Just past the village of Tanana, we hit the Tozitna River where it joins the Yukon. I jumped into the Tozitna's cold water to cool off. That night, the mosquitoes were thick. My clothes were caked with silt as I straddled a log on a sandbar frying Clint's grayling.

As a barge docked at Tanana, the Yukon's waves lapped at the shore, waking us at 7:30 in the morning. When we checked at the village's Northern Commercial Company to buy gas, we discovered the barge company had forgotten to off-load fuel. Leaving the flat lands for the aspen-covered mountains known as the Birches we saved fuel by running our outboard at half throttle.

At Big Eddy, just before Ruby, we found an old Delta friend, Mark Freshwaters, drying pike, sheefish, and salmon. We talked of the country long into the night.

The next day, rounding a quiet curve, we sighted the sloping hill of Ruby, looking as though it would slide into the water. A flock of little boys milled near the shore, and then, when we landed, led us to a man who would be our Ruby connection: Emmitt Peters, the 1975 Iditarod record-setter. As the rain fell softly outside his home, we shared sled dog stories. A nostalgic steamboat horn sounded in the evening air. I looked outside at the freshly docked barge, washed in the sun's setting rays, which colored the village in a shade to match its name: Ruby.

91. Emmitt Peters with lead dog, Nugget, record-setter for 1975 Iditarod, at Melozi.

Emmitt invited us to his parents' fish camp, where they spent each summer catching and drying their winter's salmon. The next day, we joined them, 30 minutes downstream at the old telegraph station, Melozi, now their fish camp. Greeting us at the shore, Emmitt's 65-year-old father, Paul Peters, received us with a warm and gentle smile. He led us past the sled dogs and the drying racks, then up hill to the cabin.

Inside the cabin, Mary Peters, Emmitt's mother, sat by the window on a pillow, -- girlishly -- with her long legs tucked under her. In her comely, homemade dress, the line of her back was straight and tall. Russian cheekbones accentuated her warm, brown eyes. Offset by silver hair and tan skin, her dark eyes were electrifying bullets.

Mary was knitting gloves. She picked up a moosehide money belt she had smoke-tanned and then, beaded with a pansy design. Slipping her feet into low boots, she took me out to her wall tent. She opened the canvas flaps and sweet alder smoke drifted out. Inside, some of the sixty-five moose hides Mary had tanned in her fifty years were hanging on the drying poles. Next to them were salmon strips, ready for hungry kids and wandering fishermen.

Selecting some half-dried fish, she called "eyuga," Mary carried the smoked salmon back to the house for lunch. She opened the oven, which was a compartmentalized unit in a Yukon stove's fire-box, and slipped in a pan of the eyuga. When the fish dripped like bacon rind, it was ready. I mashed potatoes while Mary told me of her life.

92. Peters family: Paul, Phillip, Mary, Nina and Timmy at Melozi fish camp, 1975.

In 1920, just after Mary turned 5, her father, Nehilyuh Torotenil, died of tuberculosis. Her uncle, John Minook; his sister, Erinia Pavaloff Cherosky Callahan; and brother, Pitka Pavaloff, then adopted her. John, Erinia, and Pitka were the children of Ivan Pavaloff, the Russian/Athabascan who was the last official manager of the Russian American (trading) Company in Nulato.

In 1896, Pavaloff's son, John Minook, discovered gold at Big and Little Minook Creeks. Minook, because of his Native blood, was never credited with this strike that began the village of Rampart, and also sparked the subsequent, international gold rushes.

Mary grew up with John, Erinia, and Pitka in Rampart; she also spent a lot of time in Nulato. During the summers, she traveled by boat above and below Ruby: between the Nowitna and Koyukuk Rivers. In the late 1800s-early 1900s, Native women and children began congregating for church and school near the new missions while their husbands stayed in the hills to run the family traplines. The Yukon River's chief decreed families should stay together. "So," Mary said, "the men came to town as well."

Looking thoughtfully out the door, Mary recited the old-time names for every slough, every landmark on the river.

When I asked her if she might recommend persons along the river for us to meet, she said with great finality, "The story is the same everywhere: alcohol."

Unexpectedly, Mary's sister, Madeleine Notti, and her husband, Emil Notti, the president of Doyon Native Corporation, arrived.

Before we left, I slipped Mary's landmark list into my pocket: "Birches, Mice Point, Novi, Kokrines, Hot Springs, Big Eddy, Cleaver fish camp, Deep Creek, Big Creek, Mukluk Slough, Red Allen camp, Yuriana, Melozi, and Ruby," all names that a daughter of the Russian-Athabascan Bush, born in 1915, knew well.

As we nosed our canoe into the current, Emmitt and his dad handed us a king salmon.

Gratefully, we then turned our boat, following Mary's landmarks for the next part of our trip downstream toward Galena: "Whiskey Creek, George Jimmy's, Jim Malemute, Old Louden, Bessie Slough, Beaver Creek, Campion Bluff, Galena, Old Roadhouse and Green Cup Mail's Dog Barns, Bishop Mountain, Koyukuk, Nulato, 6 Mile, Half Way, Koya Slough, Kaltag, 26 Mile, Eagle Island and Anvik." The shadows of the history of the Yukon River were waiting.

Paul and Mary Peters both died in the early 1990s.

In 1975, Emmitt Peters had set an Iditarod record that held for five years of 14 days, 14 hours, 43 minutes and 45 seconds. To celebrate the Millennium, Emmitt ran the Iditarod again in March 2000, but no longer a bachelor, this time, he was met at the finish line by his wife and two big sons.

Yukon's Villagers Share Sorrow and Bounty

The bluffs of the Koyukuk River came into view on our 10th day as our family ran our 6-hp kicker half throttle down the Yukon River. Hidden on its high banks, we could barely see the village of Koyukuk.

When we climbed the steep, dirt path to the village, we met a Koyukon-Athabascan woman, who suddenly buried her face in my neck, plaintively crying. A neighbor's son had drowned, Dorea Lolnitz confided, but a few days before that, her own son had been shot.

The next day, Dorea's sister, Pauline Peters, said, "There is so much death among the youngsters."

However, the day of the funeral in Koyukuk, another villager, Andrew Edwin, pushed away the sorrow. As we entered the village, he looked at my husband and exclaimed, "You look like something the cat dragged in!"

Then, glancing at Clint, our 5-year-old, Andrew chided us, "You got just one kid?" Promising to clue us in on the mysteries of life and help out the situation, Andrew was diverted when his dog came and begged to play with him. Throwing a stick as far as he could, Andrew grinned as the German shepherd repeatedly dived into the Yukon's icy, swift waters, fetching the stick just to get a pat.

The next day as we pulled up to Nulato, patches of ripe blueberries tempted us. High on the

93. Fish wheel scooping salmon on Tanana River.

cemetery's hill, the berries waved in the wind as Clint ate the half-green, half-purple fruit. Little girls giggled as we worked our way between the Moravian crosses and spirit houses, picking the fruit, and noting dates on the crosses – some as early as the late 1800s.

Below the cemetery's bluff, next to the Yukon's broad sweep, Emmitt's Uncle Arthur and Aunt Pauline Peters were cutting salmon freshly caught in their fish wheel. A man carrying a yoke across his shoulders bal-

94. Nulato's historical cemetery, 1975.

anced 10 gallons of water as he followed Nulato's wooden sidewalks home. The log cabin maze of caches, fish racks, and outhouses stretched toward the hills around Nulato.

On the boardwalk, we passed tents of drying salmon strips, alternating with dog yards.

Downtown, staring at a Lee Van Cleef poster on the side of a building, Frank Joe was startled to see visitors. Excitedly, he took me by the hand to introduce us to his wife, Martha, who had been visiting the home of the Alexies, Victor Sr. and Marsha. However, Martha Joe had stepped out, and as he searched for her, we began to get to know the Alexies. Victor briefly described the Nulato-Kaltag stick dance. A phenomenon unique to the area, the traditional dance centered around a wolverine skin, sacred to the Athabascans, held high on a stick.

An intersection for trading on the Yukon, Nulato was a traditional spot for exchanging Russian goods with the Kobuk River Inupiaq Eskimos, and the Koyukon Athabascan Indians.

The next day, as we drifted downstream, a grinning, 83-year-old John Deacon waved us over. Flapping a salmon at us from his fish wheel, John and his wife, Belle, signaled us to stop.

Handing us the freshly filleted fish, Belle deftly demonstrated cutting fish.

Pointing toward the Kuskokwim River's portage to the Yukon, John remembered the tram system that connected the Iditarod gold camps to the Yukon River's steamboats.

"English has only been spoken around here for the last fifty years, and the end of the steamboat era was only twenty years ago," he explained.

The Deacons waved goodbye as we regrettably left our new friends.

A few miles downstream, half hidden in the bank's overhanging trees, we spotted a familiar green-and-red canoe.

"Charlie's boat!" I cried.

"Come on up for supper!" the grinning Charlie Wolf called to us.

I had last seen Charlie, the 76-year-old, self-styled voyageur, earlier in Fairbanks when he gave me canoeing advice.

Traditionally, Charlie spent his winters studying the French-Canadian traders. During the summers, he acted out their lifestyle by canoeing the rivers in the Yukon and Northwest Territories, alternating with the drainages in north-central Alaska.

Charlie invited us into his kitchen. He offered me an air mattress seat next to his campfire. Wearing a wool cap and with a red bandana hanging from his neck, he shuffled around his fire in his moose hide moccasins, protected by his galoshes.

While I cooked the Deacons' salmon, we spoke of old portages. The nomadic Natives had used trails connecting drainages until they became more clustered for church and school around the six villages of Tanana, Ruby, Galena, Koyukuk, Nulato, and Kaltag.

While we talked, Clint busied himself building a cabin, smokehouse, and fish wheel out of twigs.

The next morning, Charlie, seated in his canoe, waved a farewell with his paddle. In his best voyageur's French, he smiled, "N'oubliez pas de m'ecrire." I agreed to write him.

That night, the moon was full and yellow. It was July 21st, my 30th birthday. Darkness was returning to the land, and we were edging closer to the communities of the Ingalik Indians and the Inupiaq Eskimos

Before There Was Grayling, There Was Holikachuk

July 22, 1975: we had been canoeing the Yukon from our home on the middle Tanana for 17 days. We now found ourselves at the buggiest camp on the river. I had hurriedly cooked a fish dinner and then tried to securely zip the tent's mesh door against the voracious gnats.

Backed up by huge ice jams that spring, the Yukon had flooded the surrounding bogs, providing the flat lands with prime mosquito nesting grounds.

Reb was in his sleeping bag and Clint was tucked into his cocoon when the zipper on the tent's netting jammed. I tried to safety pin the entrance, threatened anyone with a bladder problem, and hoped the droning horde would not penetrate the mesh door.

We broke camp next morning at a record pace. Loving the breeze, we ran our six-horse-power kicker toward Grayling. As we neared the town, we were startled to see a New England-styled town with surveyed streets and crowned with a brown, steepled church.

Before 1962, Grayling had had another life in a different place with a different name. Grayling had been a more remote village on the Innoko River, a tributary of the Yukon, with the distinctly more Athabascan name of Holikachuk. It shared traditions with its sister village, Shageluk, hidden by the Innoko reeds. Due to flooding and inaccessibility, the entire village of Holikachuk had moved to the Yukon River and become Grayling.

Shageluk and Holikachuk, like their upriver cousins, Nulato and Kaltag, came from mutual roots. While Nulato and Kaltag shared the

95. Judy cutting fish with ulu in Kaltag, 1975.

106

stick dance, Grayling and Shageluk had the same mask dances.

Elsie Maillelle described some local history after we began talking at her home in Grayling.

"In the winter, we make wooden, animal masks," she said, and then demonstrated the sweeping arm gestures of a village dance. "We hold woven roots, interlaced with feathers, so no evil spirits can slip in through our fingertips."

As Elsie's mother, Hannah, picked winter berries, or cranberries, behind her house, she told me this old story:

"Bury me under some sticks," a resourceful, Athabascan husband once told his wife. "I'll be under the tree, but afterward, don't you go there."

96. Mosquito blight at Holy Cross, 1975.

Later, the wife found the husband was not dead at all, but was enjoying himself with two other women.

The resourceful wife blew on some burning coals, found the two women, and offered them her fire. "Here is a pot of boiling water," she said, helpfully, "you can get oil from your fish for your dinner."

"But," she said, "if one of you grins at the pot while the other frowns at it, the oil will come out that much faster."

When there was enough oil, the woman quickly fried both their faces.

Then, she dressed herself in a brown bear's hide. Since the bear's skin was large, she filled the extra space with rocks. Finding her husband, she had her lover's revenge, but their subsequent children all became bear cubs.

"To this day," Hannah concluded, "bear meat is tough because of all those rocks."

Our stopover in Grayling was followed by a short visit to Anvik. While boarding our canoe to leave the former Episcopal mission, we met Luke Demientieff of Holy Cross. We sought his advice. We were trying to decide whether to take the old Yukon/Kuskokwim portage to the Kuskokwim River, or to go up the Innoko River to Shageluk. Demientieff told us the Kuskokwim portage was not nearly as pretty as going up the Innoko, but also warned us that crossing the Yukon to the Innoko could be tricky.

"It can be confusing," Demientieff pointed out, "because the Innoko has two mouths."

Still, we decided to risk it, cutting across squirrelly, 4 ½ -foot waves and spraying white caps that left us soaked. Finally, in the brownish-orange water of the Innoko River, we relaxed, riding its little chop up and down, past a grazing moose, and into the treeless hills of bear country. Reb spotted a black bear on Mount Albert and stopped to glass with his binoculars. Goose grass lined the river. Shimmering water, equal to Denali Park's Wonder Lake, appeared in the shadow of Mount Shageluk.

However, I was tired, as was little Clint. Around every curve of the winding Innoko we serenaded Reb, "I'm tired, hungry and cold, but my man, he just goes on and on…" Desperately, we added a verse, "Some go to Shangri-La, but we went to Shag-e-luk." Sandbar after sandbar, bend after bend, our song trailed in the air behind us until, finally, we pitched our tent for the night, 12 miles below Shageluk.

At the Yukon's Confluence of Athabaskan and Inupiaq

Episcopalian Missionary Archbishop Hudson Stuck had established a church on the Yukon River in Anvik when the twentieth century was barely more than a decade old. Familiar with stories of people turned into caribou, and babies kidnapped by bushmen, the archbishop reflected, "There is much truth in the primitive animism; it recognizes that the world and life are full of deep mysteries … it seeks, however crudely, if not to penetrate these mysteries, … at least to give glimpses that make men less forlorn. I have a tenderness," Stuck wrote, "and compassion for the infant gropings of mankind that will not let me treat them with harshness or contempt." In his *Voyages on the Yukon and Its Tributaries,* he finished, "I'd rather be a pagan suckled in a creed outworn, than go about this beautiful and mysterious world with no religion whatever."

Sixty-five years later, we had launched our canoe from our non-Native town of Delta Junction, floated down the Tanana to the Yukon, and into the deeply Native culture of the Alaska Interior.

97. Reb and Clint on the Innoko River to Shageluk, 1975.

Twenty-four days later, approaching the transition point between Athabascan and Inupiaq cultures, we landed at Holy Cross, once the largest mission school and church in the Territory of Alaska. In the early 1900s, ten nuns in long, muskrat-lined capes had supervised one hundred fifty uniformed, shorthaired, boys and girls. The supply point to the Interior's Iditarod mining camp, Holy Cross, was opposite the mouth of the Innoko River and its upriver village of Shageluk.

In his book, Stuck referred to Shageluk, emphasizing, "the old Chageluk Slough shaman exacts the old tribute from the people.

"Among the evidences of Eskimo influence is the kazheem, or communal sweat bath, a men's club house not found above this point on the river, the stronghold of the shaman." A common ritual in the kazheem was the Mask Dances, later discontinued in the early 1960s.

Taking the Innoko, a Yukon tributary, and leaving Holy Cross behind, we continued upstream to Shageluk where we quietly docked. The three of us waded through the tall grass, surounding silent houses, looking for people. In this remote site, faces peeked out from behind curtains, but no one appeared.

As a boat pulled up to the shore, gray-haired Bertha Dutchman grabbed my hand in a warm handshake, after handing her bowl of potent snuff to her husband.

Bertha directed us to old Shageluk and to Dale and Martha Swartzentruber, a Mennonite couple. Dale was working as a volunteer for the Episcopal Church.

Dale guided us through the ruins. There, buried in the river silt and tall, waving grass was the kazheem. With age, the roof had collapsed exposing the underground chambers of the men's fantastical club. Often hexagonal, the kazhem culminated in a four-sided skylight, and was the location for the mask dances celebrated during the cold weeks of January.

"These dances were elaborate with bird masks, putting the shaman in contact with the animal kingdom with whom early man had reputedly once had unbroken communication," Dale observed. "Shageluk," he added, "is a link geographically between the Interior Athabascan and coastal Inupiaq cultures."

Nearby, we met Lucy Andale Hamilton and her kinsman, Adolph Hamilton. Adolph talked about outboard motors with Reb, while Lucy and I discussed recipes.

98. Reb with historical church at Kaltag.

Adolph had never seen a lift, a ratcheted elevator for an outboard used to jack up the motor in shallow water. Reb, in turn, listened as Adolph described his trip, five years earlier, across the Yukon-Kuskokwim portage.

Lucy and I walked as she explained two recipes for Indian ice cream. "Wring out boiled fish," she said, "get rid of the bones, add three dips of bear fat or fluffy lard, also a little sugar and berries." "Or," she said, "you can use cotton snow off the shedding cottonwood trees, instead of oil."

That night, we slept at Dale and Martha's home. The next morning, Martha set a southern-style breakfast table. But, the meal did not include fried chicken livers, as in her native Virginia, but breaded whitefish eggs, sautéed and served stylishly on white porcelain.

The Mennonite couple had invited neighbors Riley and Irinia Matthews to join us. Riley held our interest with Native sayings such as: "If birchbark whistles in the stove, throw dried fish into the fire for luck."

After breakfast, we met Lucy and Adolph on their way to pick berries, and to picnic. As they pushed their boat off, flocks of geese zigzagged across the sky to the south. It was time to return home, harvest our garden and gather berries. Winter was coming.

We waved good-bye to Shageluk and left for Holy Cross, where we packed our goods. We sold our canoe and boarded a Bush plane, which used folding chairs for seats, and was bound for Aniak. As we flew out of Holy Cross, I pressed my eyes against the window of the airplane. I saw the Kuskokwim portage we had considered, but did not travel. Soon, flying from Aniak, we landed in Anchorage and from there, caught the train for the Interior and then, home.

Months after I arrived in Big Delta, I began a letter to Mary Peters in Ruby, "Dear Mary, I miss you …," and inside, I wondered why I lived so far from moose hides, elders, log cabin communities, fish racks …

Chapter Thirty Nine

PILOT OF THE YUKON RIVER

The Steese Highway ends at the Athabascan village of Circle on the Yukon River. It was there, in Circle, that I interviewed one of the last barge pilots of Old Alaska.

99. Albert Carroll piloting Brainstorm, 1975.

As Albert Carroll's loaded barge pulled out of Circle, one dark October night in 1979, it plowed through the Yukon River's slush ice, making one last run before freeze up. After the Yukon was behind him, he followed the Porcupine River up the Black River, hoping for at least 5 feet of water. Albert calculated the tight corners of the Black, as it wound east through the Yukon Flats. The cargo on that last trip was sewer pipe lashed to the 22-foot-wide craft. It was late in the season. The Yukon Navigation Barge should have been docked already for the winter, but the village of Chalkyitsik really needed the freight.

To prevent icing up during the cold, black night, Albert cabled the 600-horsepowered tug and its 110-foot barge in fast water to a cut bank. Throughout the night, he nursed the guiding mechanism with warm water to keep its oil running. Before dawn, he began pushing upstream, intent on keeping the *Brainstorm II* from being frozen into the Black River during the approaching six months of winter.

As one of the last of the barge pilots, Albert's life spanned from classical Alaska to the modern era. Carroll was born in 1933 when trappers and fish camps peopled the rivers of Alaska, offering an independent, subsistence-based, Bush economy. It was a time when the rivers were the arteries for trade, for missions, and for transportation. During the 1930s, missionaries like Episcopalian Bishop Bentley visited their parishioners using diesel tugs like the Bishop's *Pelican IV*.

In 1910, when wood camps lined the rivers to supply the sternwheeler ships' boilers, Albert's father, James Carroll, arrived at Circle City on the steamer, *Sarah*. In town, he outfitted himself to spend a winter in the Bush. As ice threatened the rivers, he boated up the Porcupine and the Sheenjek Rivers to trap for the winter. After he had a foothold in the country, in an Athabascan ceremony, he married Fanny Martin, a Fort Yukon girl. James continued to trap with Fanny at his side even when their first children began arriving. They then saved their fur money and established a trading post at Fort Yukon. In 1933, James and Fanny had their thirteenth child, Albert Bentley Carroll, named for his godfather, the Episcopalian bishop.

As young Albert grew up, he trapped the Porcupine and Black Rivers, using the fading portages. At seventeen, he mushed his dogs to Walter Roman's mining camp to look for work. While working there, Albert began to notice Chief Stanley Joseph's daughter, Alice, who was working there as the camp cook. Three years later, Roman lost his cook, but Albert gained a wife.

Steamships were coming to the end of their era. Alice's father, Chief Stanley Joseph, who had cut wood all his life for the steamers, began piloting for a Circle barge service. In turn, Stanley was a great help to his boss, barge owner, Bill Strack, showing him how to thread the tug through the confusing Yukon Flats. After the chief's daughter, Alice, and Albert were married in 1953, Strack hired Albert as a deckhand.

Fastening cables, Albert learned to connect the tug to the barge, making it one unit. Staying close to the pilothouse, he watched as his father-in-law loosened and tightened cables, then jack-knifed tug and barge around the sharp turns. If they hit a sandbar, Stanley untied the tug, ran it near the grounded barge, then using the engine's propulsion, he eroded the sandbar, washing out a new channel to free the craft.

"You gotta know that Yukon," Albert said with an intense sound in his staccato voice. He recalled a time when his father-in-law missed the channel leading to Fort Yukon, "That swift water, that timber. If you don't know that Yukon, you're outa luck!"

In the early 1950s, Jim and Mary Binkley ran freight and passengers from Circle to Fort Yukon using the *Pelican IV*. When a pilot ran the *Pelican* aground, Albert salvaged the boat, and in the process, got a job from the Binkleys. For the next three years, Albert's sharp eyes scanned the silty waters, feeling the channel, avoiding sandbars, and pushing freight onto the boat once owned by his godfather, Bishop Bentley.

"The Yukon Flats are tough and Albert is a good pilot," Jim Binkley said, adding, "Albert knows the channels."

Carrying a stick and a radio, sounding men kept Albert continually appraised of river conditions up ahead. In 1959, the Binkleys sold the operation to Weaver Brothers.

Inland Waterways, a river freight subsidiary of Weaver Brothers, hired Albert, who worked for them for ten summers before he began free-lancing during the 1970s. For Inland Waterways, Albert pushed loads upstream at 4 mph. Day after day, Albert sat in the pilothouse peering through his polarized sunglasses, while Alice cared for their ten children at home in Circle. Several times in his free time, Albert piloted for United States Congressman Don Young.

During the winters, Albert, Circle's traditional chief, trapped four major rivers and two creeks, switching in the late 1960's from dogs to snow machines.

The old Bush life was giving way to the modern age. In 1978, when the Dempster Highway penetrated the Yukon Territory, reducing Canada's need for barging, a Canadian company unloaded its tug, the *Brainstorm II*, and its barge, *Lucky*, to Roy and Sharon Smyth of Fort Yukon. The Smyths then went in search of a Yukon Flats pilot.

"I was the only one," Albert said. "The other pilots missed Fort Yukon's landing and wound up downriver near Beaver." In lieu of wages, he accepted the Smyths' offer of one-third ownership in their company, Yukon Navigation.

For the Smyths, Albert had to become licensed. Faced with taking the Coast Guard fuel tanker and captain's license exam, apprehensively Albert eyed the 2-inch stack of papers to study for the test. There was an option, he could draw the Yukon River, its risks and its tributaries from memory. For three days, he painstakingly labeled all his intended stops, and was only off by a half inch. Albert listed the route he knew by heart: Birch Creek, Black River, Chalkyitsik, Old Crow, Circle, Woodchopper, Coal Creek, Eagle, Dawson, and Stewart River.

In 1981, a mining resurgence spurred the need for more oil and machinery to be freighted to upriver gold mines. As he navigated, Albert continually updated his maps and noted channels, sandbars, and submerged boulders. When the wind came up, the water became difficult to read. "You can't be wrong when you're coming down a channel with 150 tons to guide," Albert wagged his head. "You could lose the contract."

"But you could do anything with the *Brainstorm's* steering," Albert said. Two of his sons remembered his reversing the engine at Fort Yukon's Forty Mile whirlpool. He swung away at just the right angle, 50 feet from the path of the vortex. Years before, the steamer, *Yukon*, had hit the same spinning water, which threw it against the bank and tore out its pilot housing. Albert lauded the *Brainstorm*. "That tug could turn on a dime and give you 15 cents change."

He never found himself in a situation desperate enough to cut the barge adrift. He assured me, "I always have the barge. Always got that one."

"You gotta know what you're doing," he concluded. "Sometimes you gotta think faster than your brain works, or you'll lose your whole outfit. The river keeps changing. If the water's running, you got it made."

But that was not enough in 1986. Yukon Navigation had a half-million-dollar contract riding on if Albert could get a tug and two adjoining barges down to St. Michael's hauling gravel. As the 600-horse tug pushed two 110-ton barges slowly out of the slough at Circle, Albert noticed its sluggish movement, but figured the flotilla would pick up when it hit the main current in the Yukon. Once into the sweeping river, the current hit the boats, but Albert had no power. The barges swung sideways out of control, and hit hard on a sandbar.

Upon inspection, Albert's suspicions were confirmed. A hurried mechanic had installed the propeller backward. When Albert had reinstalled it, he tried washing the sandbar's corner, as he had learned from his father-in-law, until smoke poured out of the Caterpillar engine. "Where in the heck is that extinguisher?" he exclaimed out loud. When he found it, he marveled, "The son-of-a-gun worked! The whole engine could have blown up."

But, the Yukon Navigation deal was still in danger of blowing up. For thirty-one days, the barges rocked on the sandbar while everyone in town tried to figure out how to save the contract. When it no longer mattered, and the contract was lost, the river rose one night, and the barges quickly lifted off.

Albert decided that his thirty-seven years of working twenty-four hours/seven days a week while piloting for others was enough. "How can a man do it?" he asked. He was tired of looking at the same old channel, so he sold his share in the barge company back to the Smyths.

Albert's father, James Carroll, wrote, in his book, *The First Ten Years in Alaska*, "The leader has the hardest time of it; he has to break the trail for the rear dogs to follow, just as the hardy men broke the trail for others in the Arctic Circle."

The old portages that Albert and his father crossed are no longer used. Crustily, Albert remarked, "They're not used because the old people got old. Young people don't know those portages. I can walk it, but I'm too old to do it."

Albert's son, Albert Jr., remembered running the barge, "You feel the river in the pitch black; you run on memory." Gesturing to his son, Albert III, he said, "We'd like to teach our kids to run a barge, but we got no boat." There is a small-business potential at Circle in hauling local freight, petroleum, and park service needs.

Albert is running the river with a different kind of boat these days. Alice recently bought her husband a fancy craft that goes 55 mph. "After four miles an hour, it's a heck of a change," Albert said.

No longer forced before freeze-up to push the boat one last time up the river, these days Albert comfortably watches fall's slush ice form thick pans, and float quietly down the Yukon.

Chapter Forty
PILGRIM, DOG MUSHERS

n 1976, while Reb and Clint were building our barn, I had a visitation. When Reb returned to the house for lunch, I told him I had remembered something important.

I explained that when I had been young, the Lord had been very real to me. I had walked several years in that relationship with Him.

However in 1964, when I had tried to share my knowledge of Him, often others had no idea how to relate to what I had said. Their heads were steeped in more cosmopolitan experiences, a world about which I knew nothing. It seemed to me I must unlock the mystery and learn what I did not know. To reach others, I had to understand the world in which they lived.

After several years and many mistakes, followed by marriage and life in a new land, I was now with my own family in Alaska. That day in October, the Lord again was near to me. He reminded me I had been created for one reason: to be one in whom He could live. As I explained this to Reb, he listened with quiet tears and softly replied, "I hope you can do that and still stay with me." I told him I did not know where I was going, but I had decided to walk downriver that night and find a church, wherever God might want me.

By evening, five inches of snow, cold, and dark had diluted my intention. But, Reb insisted I stick with my resolve. In my OshGoshB'Gosh Overalls and my heavy, felt lined shoepacs, I hiked along the Tanana River for ninety minutes to where we kept our Datsun truck. I gripped the cold steering wheel, waited a moment, and then drove.

Within the hour, I arrived on the steps of Alfred and Betty Fulkerson's home, where small, home services were held. When I appeared at the door, it was as if everyone was astonished, but also expected me to arrive. By the end of the service, I was baptized. I committed to hike to church every week. This commitment was the continental divide in my adult life.

For the next months, years…Clint and I mushed or walked at least once a week to attend service. During our weekly hikes, we sang, shared stories, and wished we could fly to arrive faster. For ninety minutes a week, my 6 year old and I walked in the snow under the stars…and sang, "Hark the herald angels sing…"

Chapter Forty One
THE KOBUK RIVER
The Ice Free Corridor into the Arctic

100. Charlie and Jack Horner in plank boat leaving us on Upper Kobuk, to return to Kiana, 1977.

As I dipped my kayak paddle into the winding Kobuk River, an Arctic strangeness settled over me. This was not Yukon River-Athabascan country, not the Tanana, the Copper, or the Kuskokwim. It was Inupiaq and it differed in every way. Small trees gave way to the tundra, whale muktuk - blubber - was common inland and the blue mountains to the northeast were a wall dividing the Alaskan Interior from the North Slope of the Brooks Range.

With the 1970s' pipeline wages, we purchased two Folbots - kayaks that could be folded into a box for transport - for our Kobuk River expedition. June 1977, we had flown into the village of Kobuk. Reb; 7-year-old, Clint; and I -- four months pregnant -- were in a nearly enclosed Brooks Range, mountain basin in the far north.

The Alaska Native Land Claims Settlement Act, ANCSA, had been finalized; Native corporations were newly born, and the Trans-Alaska Oil Pipeline had just been built.

There were no national parks that far north: as yet neither the Gates of the Arctic National Park and Preserve nor Kobuk Valley National Park existed. Kotzebue's Red Dog Mine did not yet exist.

The village of Kobuk, originally a miner's supply point, now with a population of eighty-six, was near the headwaters of the river.

Reb had wanted originally to fly to Walker Lake, the river's source. But, between the lake and the village of Kobuk, there were two canyons. Pregnant, inexperienced, and with a little boy, I was worried about possible white water.

Still, we wanted to see the prettier stretch of the river. We asked if anyone might take us up as far as the Reed River for hire. An old miner, Guy Moyers, directed us to Charlie Horner.

After Reb found Charlie, and his son, Jack, together they checked Charlie's 25-year-old boat, drydocked on the bank. There was lots of daylight showing between the boards of the plank craft. Not to be deterred, the Horners and Reb shoved the 17-foot boat into the water where, they said, its boards would swell and close the gaps. I left it to the men, and went to visit Charlie's wife. Snug on the sofa, Eva was weaving a fish net using a shuttle like a crochet hook, repeatedly passing it through the loops. Eva's soft face, her response to a hard life, bowed gently over her work. Besides surviving tuberculosis while raising her babies, Eva had suffered the loss of five of her ten children.

101. Clint and Judy on Upper Kobuk River sandbar, Brooks Range, 1977.

Remembering more pleasant times, Eva described staying in fish camp as a child with her sister, Olive Cleveland. They snared squirrels while the men went to the Noatak River to hunt caribou, sheep, and parka squirrel. They narrowed a natural canyon into a bottleneck and waited in ambush. When they had a good supply, they packed the meat home.

Before Charlie met Eva, he traveled the north extensively, working for freighters in mining camps. In 1945, he settled at Kobuk.

"Charlie was," according to his neighbor, Walker Nelson, "the best guide in the country."

The next day, the plank boat had indeed swelled out. The five of us climbed in with our gear; Jack started the motor; the two kayaks, tied to the back, trailed in our wake. Reb was in the bow; Clint, Charlie, and I were sandwiched in the middle, while 26-year-old Jack bailed water and steered the kicker.

Once the boat stabilized, we stopped in the sun for some fishing. The Kobuk swarmed with Grayling, Sheefish, Arctic Char, Whitefish, salmon, Ciscos, and big, bony fish like the Northern Pike that Jack had just caught.

When we were ready to go, the motor wouldn't start, but Jack calmly cleaned the threads of the spark plug with his pocketknife, and we were off!

As we plowed slowly up the river, Charlie told me his story, a history of the North.

Born at Point Barrow in 1910, Charlie had gone to the Wiseman strike on the Koyukuk River when he was only 8 years old. A freighter named Kelly was hauling goods to the Wiseman prospectors, using a string of nine horses and a launch, and Charlie assisted him.

As a young man, he trapped the Chandalar River, and in the summers, he operated the Nenana gold dredge.

Telling these stories just above the sound of the motor, Charlie pointed east to the archeological digs, west to the jade deposits, and south to the hot springs above Huslia.

He finished by saying, "The Athabascans and the Inupiaq once had a war at the Shelby River…just up stream …"

His learned hands pointed the way, guiding Jack, who continued steering and intermittently bailing the boat.

Every few hours, we stopped for tea … and finished with good fishing.

When the midnight sun was riding low at 3 A.M., stiff with fatigue and cold, we stopped for the night. Reb put up our tent; while Jack tied mesh netting to the brush, a mosquito bar that his mother had made him.

Charlie burned out a gas can, and then rinsed it thoroughly, making me a stew pot for the Northern Pike. In an hour, we were eating juicy, thick, white meat with boiled dried onions, wheat, and rice.

102. Daisy Ticket of Kobuk village making birchbark basket, 1977.

The next day, the wind was topping waves in front of us. Plowing slowly ahead, the loaded bow of the boat suddenly smacked down. To Reb's shock, a big wave suddenly hit him in the face, slopped over all of us, the gear, and then, tilted the boat.

We dried in the shore's cool breeze for the next few hours, and still, the waves were no better. The 55 gallons of precious gas we had bought was running low. Even though we were a little disappointed to stop short of our goal of getting to the Reed River, just below the head-waters of the Kobuk, we knew we had reached the end of our upstream travels.

Charlie and Jack zipped their coats against the north wind. We waved good-bye as they headed downstream. That night, as I crawled into my down sleeping bag, I wondered … "What was…so strange about this Kobuk River?"

I remembered that Charlie had said that there'd never been any glaciers here … and that it was an ancient corridor, connecting with the historical Land Bridge…"

"Oh, well …," I wondered drowsily … "Tomorrow's another day …"

Clues Found Ashore Along Corridor into the Past

The vigorous splashing of the river and the oven-like heat of our tent awakened us June 26th. As Reb crawled out of the tent, a magnificent bull moose was crossing the Kobuk. He paused with his rack framed against the blue hills of the distant Brooks Range to the north.

I lay in bed thinking about what Charlie had told us. The historic land bridge between Siberia and Alaska had stretched to the Kobuk River valley. Human remains had been found in this glacier-free river valley dating back 12,500 years. Trade between North American Natives and Siberian Eskimos had developed, relying on the Kobuk artery into the Interior, meeting later and trading at the great rock uplift, Sukakpak.

The morning of our first day alone, the wind picked up as we broke our large cargo into kayak-size loads. When both boats were loaded, Reb and Clint shoved off. In the distance, white caps were topping the waves as river silt blew into my eyes and mouth.

Far ahead, I could see Reb's back as he paddled with Clint in the bow of the two-man kayak. Being pregnant, I nervously balanced my weight as I eased into the small cockpit of the single-person kayak and pushed off into the wind.

The current was carrying us downstream, while the chop added a staccato rhythm. Boulders loomed ahead, but staying alert, I rode the water as it streamed by the timeworn rocks. As the wind began to still, we paused our paddling and were engulfed in clouds of mosquitoes.

103. Eva Horner, wearing traditional kuspuk, weaving fish net with shuttle, Kobuk village, 1977.

Nevertheless, a strange structure in the woods had caught our eyes and we wanted to take a look. I pulled on my military-issue, mosquito head-net, with a price tag still hanging in my vision. My sleeves were rolled down, my gloves were on, and my pants were tucked into my calf-high boots. Bugs were out of luck.

With Reb leading, we plunged through the woods. There, in a little clearing, was a conglomeration of turf piled up to make a flat-roofed, one-room house with an A-frame, Arctic entryway. A tiny, but high cache was nearby, still laden with nets, smoked fish, and trapping equipment.

We walked through the home's dark, earthen entryway, a traditional Inupiaq entrance. Peering into the shadows, our eyes gradually adjusted to the stream of light coming through a hole near the stovepipe in the roof. An urban wanderer of the late 1960s, wishing to re-create traditional Arctic lifestyle, had stretched caribou intestine across the open square in the roof.

He had also made a traditional sleeping bench around the walls of the home, serving as sofa, easy chair, and bed: all in one platform. In the Arctic, with its scarcity of trees, Inupiaq traditionally lived in tundra block homes.

As we continued kayaking, we found a similar structure at the mouth of the Pah River. Remains of tundra blocks lined the spruce pole walls, covered by a shredded Visqueen roof. Inside, three little stools still remained.

I began to grasp what marked this area. Not only was it ancient, but the Kobuk River was an unfamiliar, tundra Inupiaq culture. It was the easiest corridor between the southern swamp and the foothills of the Brooks Range, not far from the Chukchi Sea and Little Diomede Island, the dividing line between Alaska and Siberia.

Further downstream, propped against the shore, we saw an old handmade kayak with a narrow seat and a canvas bow. We were in a suspended time: ancient history, and yet, it wasn't so far past.

As we approached the village of Kobuk, our new friends met us. Again, we were with Charlie and Eva Horner, and their daughter, Bernice, who served us hot, savory caribou soup. I relished the wild flavor.

Bernice explained that the people of the lower villages, Shungnak and Ambler, had originally lived in Kobuk before 1923, but after repeated flooding in Kobuk two-thirds of the population relocated downstream at Shungnak, and then later migrated to Ambler.

"Shungnak was the original name of Eva's village of Kobuk," she continued. It was a corruption of "Issingnak," Inupiaq for "jade."

The next day, we would travel downriver and perhaps find some jade, but that night, we were tired. We had a dinner of Northern Pike caught by Clint, to which I added hot lentils, biscuits, and pudding. After dinner, we crawled into our beds with Arctic sunburns.

104. Mark Cleveland, elder and artist, Ambler village, 1977.

The Contradictions of the North.

The downriver village of Ambler was a study of contrasts. Here, many young Euro-American families embraced the historical Inupiaq lifestyle, while one of the Kobuk River people, had a home manicured like a Better Homes and Gardens example. Village children led us to their gated garden path, which were lined with wild iris.

Mark Cleveland, an Inupiaq elder, was more traditional: a craftsman and a storyteller. Mark told us a story about 12-year-old George Gray who was reported missing. The upstream village of Shungnak had emptied into boats to scour the river, while others searched the miles of tundra - treeless spongy ground - stretching between the two villages. A day later, when the boy appeared dry and 15 miles downstream, Cleveland explained, "the boy had turned into a caribou and flown across the tundra."

Enjoying his own stories, Mark then shared with us his handcrafted, caribou hide masks, and carved, wooden book ends.

By contrast, the lifestyles of three non-Native families near Ambler were both Scandinavian and Inupiaq. One home resembled an upside-down boat with squares of turf piled up for walls. Nearby, a non-enclosed, four-foot elevated, outhouse caused patrons to hope for no low-flying aircraft.

The Scandinavian, Ole Wik family served us an inventive Arctic dessert: boiled wild rhubarb, sweetened with dried apples and evaporated milk. For vitamin C, they boiled blueberry leaves and sweetened them with berries.

After dinner, we boated to their neighbor, Don Bucknell's, home. It was a small, round dwelling dug into the ground. With just enough room for us, Bucky sat on his curved bed, reached to the center of his hut for his homemade tools, and finished shaping a dried spruce root into a soup ladle. Bearded and smoking a pipe, he seemed comfortable as a hobbit in his Inupiaq Arctic den.

Next door, a neighbor, Dan Denslow, had found an archeological jewel he was not ready to publicize. While digging pylon holes for his wind generator tower, his shovel hit an ancient set of armor made from caribou ribs. The ribs were connected together with sinew strung through holes drilled in each bone, resulting in a covering for a warrior's chest.

By contrast, Naomi and John Topkocks' Happy Aspen Knoll sported a guest book, but more amazingly, hot water piped around the house from the wood stove heated the home's interior. Naomi, an Inupiaq woman raised in Kansas, showed us their greenhouse dug halfway into the earth. She explained that Ambler could get frost in June, July, or August, and that all vegetables were grown in a greenhouse.

In this land of contrasts, a different green stood out like a child's line drawing on the mountain. Serpentine, a mineral that is found with jade, was etched like a cartoon shape on a mountain. One spring, the river had unexpectedly jarred a jade boulder loose, and Issac Douglas had corralled it. We walked to his house where he sawed off a wedge weighing 6.5 pounds and sold it to us for $21.

105. Mark Cleveland's carved wooden, mask bookends, Ambler, 1977.

The wind was coming up as we left the high banks of Ambler. Pushing into 2-foot waves, we paddled against the incessant wind. Just above where the migrating caribou swim across the Kobuk, we rested for the night.

The next morning was calm as we paddled into the gracious, protected curve of Onion Portage, one of the north's traditional routes between river drainages. The purple-bristled tops of wild scallions blew in the gentle breeze. It was easy to imagine herds of caribou swimming to this, their ancient calving grounds.

At the portage site, ragged canvas flapped against old wall tent platforms, skeletons from a 1963 archaeological dig of this 12,500-year-old site. On July 4th, while we endured snow and rain, I tended two fires in my attempts to try to stay warm, as Reb and Clint made plans to hike the next day toward the Great Kobuk Sand Dunes, a strange deposit from the Ice Age's glaciers. I elected not to see Egypt in the Arctic, but Reb and Clint hiked toward it several miles and then shinnied up a tree to see the 25 miles of white sand in northern Alaska. They reported that it was very weird to see white, mounded dunes, mile after mile in the Arctic distance.

Each day as we paddled on, my mind drifted from jade, to sand dunes, and to sod igloos. "Kiana, Kiana, Kiana," Reb chanted ahead. He had heard it many times on his firefighter radio. The last village for us was just downstream. Dark was coming and the geese were flocking; we were ready for the last stretch toward home.

Site of Hermit's Fortune, Misfortune

"Kiana, Kiana, Kiana," Reb remembered having heard the word over his firefighter's radio as one Native crew called to another. The syllables had stuck in his mind; he did not know then that the Inupiaq village name had originally been "Katyaak" (KuhtYAAK) or that Katyaak meant "a place where three rivers meet," a traditional meeting place for the Kowagmiut Inupiaq Eskimos on the Kobuk River.

During the gold rush, Katyaak/Kiana was called Garbintown, and was named after Andrew Garbin, a miner whose daughter owned a store in the Kobuk River town of Kiana.

While we were unloading our kayaks at the town's riverfront in July 1977, Pauline Schuerch, Andrew's daughter, waited on her customers. We were dirty, our clothes were stiff with silt and fish scales, and we were in search of a shower.

106. Andrew Garbin and gold nugget watch chain, Kiana, ca. 1905.

The store was bustling with a celebrity in town. California Senator S.I. Hayakawa was researching the proposed Federal parks in the Kobuk area. A person who never met a stranger, Pauline thoroughly charmed the California senator at her store counter.

Later, after Pauline had shown us where to clean up, I talked with her. She enthralled me with her beadwork and then, told me the story of her immigrant father. Her broad smile lit the room as she described Andrew Garbin, her dad, whose gold strike transformed Kiana into a permanent settlement. Having a daughter whose smile filled her entire face, Andrew was ironically dubbed "the man who never smiled." A man who trusted no one, he was born about 1860 off the Dalmatian coast in Croatia.

His grandsons, Tony and Lorry, joined Pauline and me, and Tony described his grandfather as a street-wise peasant.

"Grandpa left the Balkans," Tony explained, "then knocked around South America, and finally came to San Francisco."

In 1900, the Nome gold strike electrified Seattle and San Francisco. Disliking crowds, Tony's hermit-like grandfather waited several years, but in the late fall, he boarded a ship for Nome. By then, all of Nome's promising gold ground was staked. Miners had gone up the Kobuk River to the Cosmos Hills.

Garbin had no Arctic experience, yet he loaded his sled with rice, dried beans, and tea to cross the Seward Peninsula, alone, in mid-winter. For weeks, he fed on rabbits he shot along the way, and finally, arrived at a little Inupiaq campsite just upstream from today's Kiana on the Kobuk River.

While resting, he asked the Natives if any white men had passed.

"Yes," they gestured, "many."

"Where did they go?" Garbin asked.

They indicated that a man had traveled up the Kobuk's right fork.

"Did anyone go up the other fork?" Garbin asked.

"No," they replied.

"That's where I'm going," Garbin concluded. Even after the isolation of his long hike, Garbin consistently preferred to be alone. The Inupiaq man guided him to Squirrel Creek and not long after, at nearby Klery Creek, Garbin struck it big.

His Inupiaq helper, Loren Black, remembered it was almost impossible to climb the valley wall out of Klery with 50-100 pounds of Garbin's gold on his back. They walked to the Kobuk and boarded a steamship for Kotzebue, and then crossed to Nome.

Unlike the Kobuk gold, the Nome ore was known to be fine grain. When Garbin deposited his coarse gold nuggets at the banker's window, the teller immediately became suspicious. He was sure Garbin had raided a sluice box. After an assay, the banker believed Garbin as to the origin of the nugget, bought them, and displayed them in his showcase window.

Miners gathered around the glass case stung with jealousy at the sight of the gold nuggets. Seeking Garbin, the men embraced him as a fellow miner, escorted him to the nearest bar, and began plying him with drinks, congratulating the hero.

"Soon, Grandpa's mouth got loose," Tony said, "and he told them everything."

"In days, three hundred miners headed out to Klery Creek," Tony shook his head. "By the time Grandpa arrived, it was too late. He had ruined it for himself."

Worse, there were claim jumpers who intimidated Garbin, saying he could not own a claim because he was not an American citizen.

"Dad never fought it," Pauline said. "He was already 45 years old. He moved down the creek, figuring he would always find more gold at another spot.

"After a while, he got too old. He stayed in Garbintown/Kiana, which sprang up around his gold strike."

"Grandpa didn't stay too long with my grandmother. They were culturally too different. The Eskimo's culture was to give everything away. That went completely against Grandpa's grain, but," Tony added, "he did take up with several other Native women."

As if to underscore the point of generosity, Pauline laid out exotic treats. Boiled white fish stomachs dipped in seal oil with blueberries, bear fat, raw, frozen grayling, dried white fish, muktuk rolled in oil, and salmonberries.

107. Gertrude Sheldon, Miss Kobuk, Kiana, 1977.

In the same tradition, a neighbor in town gave me a kus-puk, the traditional summer parka for Native women, which fit my pregnant body properly.

Kuspuk-wearing women lined a sandbar on the Kobuk that night as village people seined for Sheefish. Tony's brother, Lorry Schuerch, loaded our packed Folbots into an airplane. We prepared to leave the Inupiaq camp that had, in 1905, been forever changed by one hermit who just wanted to be alone. My mind turned from exotic places to preparing for the arrival of Sarah Ferguson, four months hence.

As we flew over the village once known once as Garbintown, the Arctic fell behind us and we entered the Alaska Interior bathed in the midnight sun.

108. Reb and Clint approach Kiana in Folbots, 1977.

Chapter Forty Two

SARAH REBEKAH FERGUSON

Clint's Snow Baby

We had been three for seven years, and now, I was expecting a baby. Not sure how Clint felt about it, I waited…

Meantime, Reb wanted to experiment with our fall moose hunt. Not wanting to take horses on the trapline when snow was due, he equipped a sled with wheels. Reb would go on the trapline on wheels, and when snow came, he would remove the tires, and revert to the sled's runners. The result was a wild ride. I tried but could not keep up with a sled bumping along on tussocks, pulled by four dogs over rough terrain. I walked with Clint while Reb trotted to keep up with the sled on wheels, bouncing off moose rut walls, but we did arrive at the first trap cabin.

The cabin roof at Campbell's was mildewing. Our job was to replace the roof's poles. When the first snow came, Clint made a Mama, a Poppa, and a child snowman. In the Snow Mama's arms, he made a snow baby. For me, that ushered in Sarah's arrival.

Sarah

We had known hardship before, but not the razor's edge of the tenuous grasp for our child's life. Before Sarah was born, I wanted a girl so badly my heart was laid bare before the Lord. As I lay, anesthetized for my second Caesarean section, I heard a voice say, "Judy, it's a girl!" Joy bells sounded deep inside my dark depths. I resounded to it; I had felt her closeness all along, and I had known she was a girl.

109. Three-year-old Sarah on porch near rain barrel, 1980.

She must have been born for the cold. It was -50° F. when she was born December 5, 1977. The sunrise glowed pink through the frozen air outside my window at Fairbanks Memorial Hospital the day Sarah came into our lives.

My joy was slightly eclipsed when I was told she was jaundiced, but in a few days, I was told, she would improve…

We drove to the Holler on December 12th, and while Sarah and I waited at a friend's, Reb mushed Clint upriver, and made a fire.

When Reb returned, he laid a soft laundry bag on the sled. I gingerly eased onto it, with Sarah riding in a Snugli on my front and inside my parka. "Huh! Let's go!" Reb commanded the team. I buried my face near Sarah's and listened for her quiet breathing. Arches of northern lights were dancing overhead, with the northern constellations quiet and stable in their place.

When we arrived at our remote home, we quickly brought Sarah into the house and I laid her in her new crib. Seven-year-old Clint drew near; "She sure is little," he said in awe.

Two weeks later, Sarah was still jaundiced. When I could get to a phone, I would call the clinic. Each time, I was assured they would let me know when they received her PKU/thyroid blood test report. When she was two weeks old, we went back to Fairbanks. Toward the end of that day, I caught a doctor's attention. "Excuse me," he said, "I have the flu; it's at the end of a long day, and you didn't have an appointment. There are many reasons for newborn jaundice. There are a hundred varied reasons; some are fatal. Excuse me," he said, "I need to go throw up."

The nurse looked at Sarah, and commented, "She is the most severely jaundiced baby I have ever seen." They sent us home with no direction, except saying they would call when the report arrived. I had heard sunshine could help. I laid Sarah in a beaded, birchbark baby carrier, and put her in the pathetic light of an Alaskan December, and prayed.

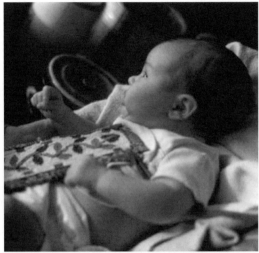

110. Three-week-old Sarah in beaded birchbark baby carrier-December sunshine.

When Sarah was a month old, I got a phone message from our pediatrician. Frantically, she confessed, "Sarah's blood report has been on my desk for two weeks. No one told me. This is very serious; Sarah is hypothroid. She either has no thyroid, or it isn't working properly. The thyroid influences human growth in almost every way - both the physical body and the nervous system. Every day an infant is without thyroxine - the substance secreted by the thyroid gland - is critical to the brain's development. Being without thyroxine in the womb is significant enough."

She urged, "Sarah must begin synthetic thyroxine treatment immediately. It will suppress the functioning of any thyroid she may have, but for whatever reason, it isn't functioning properly anyway." I was stunned; Sarah would have to be dependent on thyroxine all her life…I asked Reb to pray. He took five minutes, and said, "If it were my body, I might try alternative means, but this is Sarah's life. We have no choice; she must go on synthetic Thyroxine."

For the next four years, we watched and worked closely with Sarah. There were many struggles; hers was obviously a very valuable life.

Chapter Forty Three

PENIEL TO GILLES

111. Ferguson Family on Mount Gilles, cutting trail to Peniel and Gilles Creek, 1978.

n August, when Sarah was 8 months old, I lay in my bed listening to the wind howl and the rain beat on our attic roof. I lay in dread. For weeks, I had been trying to prepare myself to take Sarah, with our family, into the wilderness. She was fighting an ear infection. The pediatrician had given us her medication and promised us she would be fine.

We were long overdue to extend our trapline. Reb's work on the pipeline had kept us out of the woods for the past four years. We needed to go. But, when I went with a child, I always heard the door of security click shut behind me. However, nowhere else had I experienced the miracles I had experienced on the trapline, where I had no other options. Clint had once had an asthma attack, which stopped when I prayed. On this trip, although I did not know it, there would be more help when human options were not available…

The previous winter, Reb had sledded in a case of Pampers, food, boards, a stove, and tools that we would need for a six-week trip.

On a ridge beyond Caribou Creek, Reb had built a high cache in the trees and secured our goods there. To prevent bears from scaling the cache's trees, he wrapped the tree trunks with sheet metal flashing. For this August building trip, Klondike packed the chainsaw, axe, tools, and tent needed for cutting trail.

We rode the horses from our home upriver to Quartz Lake, followed the new pipeline corridor across Shaw Creek Flats, and turned into the mountains. The 800 mile corridor was maintained for easy maintenance of the line, and incidentally provided us a broad, easy trail. Once into the mountains, we climbed ridges and followed valleys. Leading out, Reb packed Sarah on his front, with only her bonnet and eyes peeking out. Clint kept up, walking in between us; I followed with the loaded horse in tow. We stopped periodically to change Sarah's diaper, dabble eardrops in her ear, and crush both her Synthroid and her antibiotic, mixed with juice, to give to her. Sarah clacked her tongue with delight, and talked with her dad as he trod for seventeen days over muskeg and ridges with her on his front. Sarah wagged her head from side to side, taking in the new sights and sounds.

We passed through Campbell's cabin, Schist Creek, and Caribou Creek. From there, Reb and Clint prepared to go alone, cutting the trail. Clint had a thin rain suit tied on the back of the horse; together, he and Reb set out through the tall grass leading Klondike, waving good-bye to Sarah and me waiting at Caribou Creek.

That night, I woke with an excruciating urinary infection. I had no antibiotics and no means of communication with the outside world.

Reb and Clint had their own problems. A howling wind was blowing an unrelenting rainstorm, lasting for two days. Clint, only 8 years old, had immediately lost his rain pants as they climbed the mountain. Step after step in the blowing rain, they cut trail. Out of fresh water up on the mountain where there was none, they strained water out of deep moose hoof prints, using a dirty sock to slack their thirst. They found a large spruce tree with sheltering branches. With the ax, they dug a

112. Reb packing Sarah on his front over hills as Clint leads Klondike to Peniel, 1978.

hole out at the tree's base for a fire pit. They sat under the tree, on the new dirt bench, and dangled their legs next to the fire, inhaling smoke. Drying socks on the low-hanging branches slightly scorched the fibers, crusting them yellow-brown, but when donned, they warmed their frigid toes. "Smoke-hole," we called that camp, which became a temporary overnight spot on the long ridge. They had gone the distance a sled should travel in winter, so they needed to find a cabin site. They cached the freight, and together, they rode ahead, looking for water, pasture, and a site. It seemed like a dead end. The trees were thick; there were only drop-offs into deep ravines, but Clint kept saying, "No, Dad, I think we're okay. Follow this way, go that way; I feel God in this place; let's just follow. I think we are being led." When they came to a turn in the path, Clint said, "Don't give up, just keep pushing that way…"

They turned right into a glade of trees, whose natural path led through a clean forest floor sprinkled with birch, high bush cranberries, and mushrooms. A natural pasture appeared, then a scrub spruce forest, and finally, a swath that opened up to an alpine lake. It was a paradise, hidden in the mountains. When I heard Clint and Reb's story, I suggested we call it Peniel. After Jacob wrestled with the angel, in Genesis 32:30, it was said, "So Jacob called the place Peniel, saying, 'For I have seen God face to face, and yet my life is preserved.'" Clint, an 8-year-old, had followed a leading into the unknown and I, stuck at Caribou Creek with an infection, had been healed. It seemed appropriate to call the jewel-like lake Peniel.

But, Clint and Reb were only halfway finished. They had cut trail on the ridge and found the new site, but still they had to hack brush and chainsaw spruce on past Peniel to clear the trail to our proposed furthest site at the head of Gilles Creek. Clint led Klondike, while Reb walked ahead, cutting trail. At one place, Clint squeezed through a narrow passage between two large trees, upsetting a hornet's nest. The big panniers (packs) on Diker's back hung up on the spruce trees. As Clint fought to get the panniers free, the hornets nosedived Klondike's flank. The horse

113. "Good morning, Sarah!" at Gilles Creek cabin site, 1978.

went berserk, kicking and throwing gear off, and getting free, he ran back a mile. Reb and Clint back-tracked until they finally found Diker calmly grazing on wild grass between the birch trees.

Retrieving the horse, they continued cutting trail until they arrived at the ravines and thick brush of the Gilles Creek drop off.

Meantime, at Caribou Creek, I had converted one bunk into a crib to keep Sarah safe. She played in her bed, while I agonized with my acute infection. I prayed hard, and remembered a bottle of Vitamin C we had once stashed in the stove's roof jack, the metal collar, in the ceiling. Treating them like gold, I took several pills. I hoisted Sarah on my back, and spent my days picking blueberries, crying to God for a helicopter. I hauled creek water, ate bowls of berries, and drank quarts of water, trying to acidify my system and flush the problem. One morning, when the pain was its worst, I remembered, "It's darkest before the dawn." It was the last attack. A week later, the pain returned for one, short siege. I remembered a story about a poisonous snake that could sting from its head and its tail. I figured this was the tail, flipping back on me, and that it would be the last. There was no more problem with the infection after that.

Peniel and Gilles Creek Cabins

Reb and Clint had been gone eight days. They had left their gear on the mountain, and reconnoitered down below on Gilles Creek. At the head of the creek, the valley floor was high. Further downstream at the creek's mouth, John Schulz had the second of his string of five trap cabins. Because a trapline is desired by many newcomers, Reb and John formed a barrier against trapping encroachment in the Upper Shaw Creek and the Gilles Creek drainage: a trapline Chinese Great Wall.

After Reb and Clint found a cabin site on Gilles, they returned past Peniel, the smoke hole, and down into Caribou Creek to get Sarah and me.

I heard the horse's hooves approaching Caribou Creek as Klondike brushed through the grass led by Reb and Clint. The

114. Smoke Hole above Peniel. Sarah in Johnny Jump-Up. Reb and Clint warm up by fire, 1978.

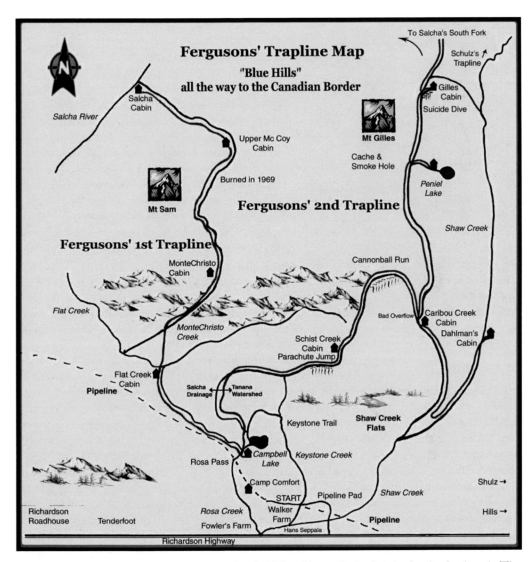

Fergusons' Trapline Map

"Blue Hills"
all the way to the Canadian Border

To Salcha's South Fork

Schulz's
Trapline

Gilles
Cabin

Suicide Dive

Salcha
Cabin

Salcha River

Mt Gilles

Upper Mc Coy
Cabin

Cache &
Smoke Hole

Peniel
Lake

Burned in 1969

Fergusons' 2nd Trapline

Mt Sam

Shaw Creek

Fergusons' 1st Trapline

MonteChristo
Cabin

Cannonball Run

Flat Creek

Bad Overflow

Caribou Creek
Cabin

Dahlman's
Cabin

MonteChristo
Creek

Schist Creek
Cabin
Parachute Jump

Flat Creek
Cabin
Pipeline

Salcha
Drainage

Tanana
Watershed

Shaw Creek
Flats

Keystone Trail

Rosa Pass

Campbell
Lake

Keystone Creek

Shulz →

Camp Comfort

START
Walker
Farm

Pipeline Pad

Shaw Creek

Hills →

Richardson
Roadhouse

Tenderfoot

Rosa Creek

Pipeline

Fowler's Farm

Hans Seppala

Richardson Highway

next morning, after an evening of stories, we loaded Klondike with the freight for the final push. The three of us climbed the ridges until we came to the midpoint, Reb's cache and the Smoke Hole. We had to sort the loads on the high cache for Diker to carry down the mountainside. To free our hands for work, we hung Sarah's Johnny Jump-Up on a tree of the cache where she could swing a few inches off the ground. With a small, smudge fire, we protected her from mosquitoes.

Sun streamed through the trees as we made our descent through the birches and into the wild grass meadow. A breeze rippled through the leaves of grass. We followed a moose path to the Peniel Cabin site where we set the wall tent up between timber stands back from the lake. We began our daily routine. Clint watched Sarah in her Johnny Jump-Up, while Reb and I cut and, with Klondike's help, dragged cabin logs. Cabin-size logs near the lake were scarce, and soon, we had a mud rut along

116. Ridge Mushing.

the lake's edge. Periodically, I returned to the tent to make lunch or to lay Sarah down for her nap.

Every morning, Reb broke the thin skin of ice off the lake and hauled drinking water to us. The beaver had two live houses they were currently using. Their fresh chewings shone tawny-golden in the fall sunshine. The marshy area around the lake's edge was laced with their canals, funneling the water where the beaver needed it. For thirty years, we drank wherever there was water, but today, better informed, we use a water filter.

Peniel was the first cabin we built for our larger family. The door had a high threshold. Inside, we built two wide, high beds with substantial bedposts on which to dry clothes. Under the small window, Reb built a table, fitted between the beds. We were snug in our cabin, still sticky with fresh spruce sap. In the lake, a moose was browsing in one corner, while a beaver was swimming, pushing saplings ahead of him as he swam. Geese and swans landed on this respite lake in the hills. The clearing was too small for bush airplanes. Peniel was a jewel hidden in the lap of the mountains.

We had another cabin to build. On the morning we were leaving to go to Gilles Creek, Reb had to break ice to get water from the lake. Leading Klondike, we climbed out of Peniel valley and hiked through mushroom-laden woods, past rock outcrops, mountains of spruce cone for squirrels' caches, and into the descent into Gilles Creek. At the bottom of every mountain, there seems to be hollow, marshy ground covered with a thin moss cover. We approached a large beaver dam that had backed up Gilles Creek, making it too deep to cross. Taking a horse across the beaver dam itself was an invitation for breaking Klondike's leg. Very carefully, Reb led Klondike across the beaver dam while Clint, Sarah, and I also followed the narrow corridor of piled logs. We cut across a peninsula that faced another bend of the creek. On high ground, protected by large trees, our new site was surrounded with meadow grass, had good timber, and overlooked the rocky stream. We dammed up a small pool in the icy creek to make a refrigerator for Sarah's milk bottle.

Nine months old, Sarah had begun to pull herself up on metal boxes, and then, hand over hand, she held onto a log and scooted along. While she passed milestones, I cooked over my kitchen fire, keeping the cabin building crew supplied in stews and soups. When Sarah was asleep in the afternoon, I gathered bags of moss for the roof and wall insulation.

Eight-year-old Clint was looking like a woods' waif. He was covered with spruce sap, one eye was swollen shut from an allergic reaction to a bug bite, and his shirt buttons were missing from survival on the trail.

As we were finishing the roof, the gubernatorial election returns were being broadcast on the radio. I lay basking in the sun on the insulating cushion of the moss, the roof's deep bed of green comfort, smiling, as the radio reported Governor Jay Hammond's landslide election.

To celebrate this Bush governor's successful election, I boiled up two jars of canned moose meat, garnished with Alaskan cranberries, served with pure, cold creek water, reconstituted powdered milk, and hot, re-hydrated mashed potatoes.

We worked on the interior of the cabin, carrying rocks for a hearth for the stove, and for our expanding family, we built four bunks and a picnic table to seat us. Gilles would be on the trapline's southern terminus what Campbell's was at the line's beginning: the headquarters. With spikes, poly-ethylene, a hammer, drill, chainsaw, fuel, and wrench, we went into the forest. When we left, homes had sprung up from the forest floor, ready to shelter us even at temperatures of -80° F.

Chapter Forty Four
JOE VOGLER

An institution even after his untimely death, Joe Vogler typified Old Alaska. A miner, Joe always dressed in the Miner's Tuxedo, a deep gray, working man's suit. Before the pipeline era, Joe visited communities throughout Alaska, encouraging the electorate to secede from the Union. "We are the treasure trove, the resource backdoor for the lower 48, a colony, the military's experimental playground. We could, like Kuwait, a much smaller country, become likewise, independent and sovereign, manage our own resources better, and certainly, if independent, profit more." Joe tried to hold back the dilution of Old Alaska, the metamorphosis into a domesticated population, inevitable with the advent of wealth. He knew the new Alaskans would bring an urban mentality, politically correct legislation, and finally, a used and tamed Last Frontier.

117. Joe Vogler, Alaskan.

One winter evening, we went to hear Joe speak at the Delta School. That meeting was followed by a winter involved with Delta Land Management Planning Committee meetings that Charlie Boyd talked me into attending. After the Native Land Claims Settlement Act, the land was in transition; it was being sectored, labeled, and planned.

The Alaska Tuxedo

Before World War II and the advent of military-issue Arctic clothing, the silicone-coated, water resistant, 100% virgin wool trousers and jacket, called Filson's Ripcords were coined the Alaska Tuxedo. Both practical, and yet slightly dressy, an Alaskan was dressed to go out for the evening wearing his warm, but expensive Ripcords. When the less expensive and still practical, Army Surplus clothing became available, Alaskans transitioned into wearing soldier garb. Traditionally, however-er, the Tuxedo was a symbol of classic, old Alaska: those who were independent and competent, ready to face any situation.

118. Ben in Russ Trastek's Alaska Tuxedo, 2003.

Chapter Forty Five
BUSH OUTINGS

119. Clint and Laddy, black Labrador friend, 1979.

W hen you get out in the woods, not a heck of a lot has changed over forty years," Bob Redding confided to me recently from his home in Sequim, Washington. Discussing the parallel between his Chatanika childhood of 1935, and the boyhood of our oldest son up the Tanana River in 1975, we concluded that not much was different in the Bush despite the forty-year passage of time.

We discussed the solitary life both he and our son, Clint, had known growing up. Cloistered in their respective log attics, and separated in time by four decades, both boys studied by a sputtering lantern, enthralled by Ulysses and his Trojan Wars as taught in their mutual Calvert's Correspondence Studies. Little differed between Bob's ramblings in the Chatanika woods and our son's explorations in the Tanana hills.

Two or three times a year, while growing up, Bob's Bush family had gotten a visitor from Fairbanks. Almost as infrequently, Clint sledded out to potlucks arranged by Dan Beck, Delta's correspondence studies' teacher. During the 1970s, Delta's fifty correspondence students looked forward to visits from Beck, who either snow machined, boated, or flew in to their remote cabins. Periodically, he planned field trips, bringing the children from the Goodpaster and the Tanana Rivers, from Healy Lake, and from pockets off the road system, all to a social at the Delta School.

In 1978, the gym of the Delta School rocked with laughing Bush children scaling the monkey bars and rolling around on mats at a Beck-hosted potluck. Beaver Schneider and Leon Marhanka climbed all over good-natured Beck while their mothers carried in hot dishes brought from their remote homesteads. The highlight of the evening was a 16-millimeter film that covered the wall with colorful entertainment.

Throughout the rest of the winter, other social events punctuated the school year, concluding with a home teachers' seminar in the spring in Fairbanks. But, the crown jewel of the field trips was in the fall of 1979, when the mining operation, the Mount Si Project, invited all of us to spend two days in their cabins in the Alaska Range.

Dr. and Mrs. Stoelting's granddaughter, Andrea, had invited her fellow correspondence students to embark from her home at their Mount Si mining camp and to be transported on a track vehicle deep into the mountains. Twenty-five children climbed the 30-foot-high, monster track vehicle driven by master welder Paul Marchuk. His rebuilt Juggernaut was adequate to carry fifty of us through the 5-foot deep Delta River, and then up into Rainy Creek.

Marchuk, part of the Mount Si staff, slowly ground his vehicle up the alpine valleys, driving the iron pack horse to cabins next to rolling streams. That evening, while correspondence mothers prepared hot dogs, Mike Bobo told a survival tale of almost dying on a December goat hunt high in the Wrangell Mountains.

Digging into the moss with walking sticks, the next day we climbed a steep slope to a plateau framed by the slate blue and orange of the nearby Rainbow Ridge. Munching blueberries as we strolled, Jack Stewart's girls took turns carrying my one-year-old, Sarah, while Clint ran with his new friend, Jonathan Marhanka, over the high tableland. Fall leaves twittered as we reluctantly said goodbye the following morning, and returned home, isolated from each other by the rivers and the miles.

Clint went back upriver, patted his best friend, his labrador, Laddie, and climbed the steps to his log attic to study for school. Just over his desk he had pinned a print of young Abe Lincoln reading by the firelight. Next to the picture, he had tacked up a snapshot of his new friend, Jonathan Marhanka. On a clear day, from our window, we could see Jonathan's neighborhood, the Clearwater, stretching to the Granite Mountains on the horizon. Clint counted the days until the next month's potluck at the Delta School gym.

Chapter Forty Six
MEDICAL EVACUATION

There were many of us who lived in the Bush without telephones during the 1970s and '80s. Our needs were radioed by citizens band to neighbors who kindly put up with radio static all day, just in case we might need their land line to pass along our messages.

New homesteaders across the Delta River, recreationalists and homesite owners up the Goodpaster River, as well as the Fergusons and Ashbys across the Tanana, all depended upon the Dufendachs and the Brasiers, who had both CBs and telephones.

Not only were we remote, but also access to our Tanana River homestead was difficult in the early winter. In October and November, strong, warming Chinook winds routinely thawed and blew out the shelf ice, our route around the river bluffs, crumbling it into the open river. The alternative route, the sloughs that paralleled the river, might, unpredictably, have two inches or two feet of overflow -

120. Western bluff obstructs access to our upriver home. The ice shelf has formed a narrow corridor.

standing water - a hurdle for getting to the road. Early winter was a season between decent sledding and the summer's boating. After the busy summer, a quiet season felt good; I was content, making Christmas gifts, waiting for the shelf ice to freeze into a sled trail.

One moonless November night, in 1979, when Sarah was nearly two, I had laid her down to sleep in her crib. Reb was on the other side of the wall from Sarah's room, watching our tiny, battery-powered, black and white TV. I was reading a magazine.

"Do you hear that?" he asked me. A strange, tiny sound was barely audible from our daughter's room. Only Reb heard the noise over the T.V., and peeked in Sarah's room. As he uncovered Sarah, lying in her crib, she was limp, turning blue, and laboring to breathe every few seconds. We were stupefied and shaken. Had she been poisoned, was she choking...? Reb gave her mouth-to-mouth resuscitation, and soon she began to breathe normally. But, she immediately went into a Grande Mal seizure that lasted over an hour, followed by convulsions. I called to her, but she was unable to respond. I screamed prayers, held her, talked, and coaxed her.

Reb got on the CB radio and called our neighbors, the Dufendachs, and pilot, Charlie Boyd. I had no medical training, but I kept praying as her small body continued to thrash, unendingly. I could hear Reb talking with Charlie, giving him the information needed for initiating a medical evacuation. Then, dimly in the background, I could hear Charlie and Danny Newby discussing the situation. Danny was very knowledgeable about radio transmission and had good CB contacts. He went over to single side band, a more powerful frequency, to try and raise Pat Moritz, who lived close to Fort Greely. Danny became the radio hub between Pat, Charlie, us, and the authorities. The Delta physician's assistant authorized a helicopter evacuation, approved through Fort Greely. Duck-like sounds came over the higher frequency as Danny and Pat continued the relay. The chain of contacts was activating the dispatch of the helicopter from Fort Wainwright to our Bush homestead.

As I focused my attention on Sarah, Pat reached the Fort Greely military police. Charlie supplied the VFR (visual flight rules) coordinates, so the Fort Wainwright personnel could find us.

Forty-five minutes passed before we heard the comforting chop-chop-chop approaching our dark fields. The helicopter crew was searching for our little cabin. Reb stood alone in the snowy field, waving a Coleman lantern, desperately trying to signal the pilot. He watched helplessly as the helicopter overshot our isolated cabin and headed southeast toward the Gerstle River. Then, Reb could see the aircraft turn abruptly, and return toward him. Guided by the Coleman's light, the pilot carefully set the chopper down in front of Reb.

Two young soldiers, dressed in olive drab, burst through our cabin door and came quickly over to Sarah. I hardly remembered getting into the chopper with my little girl. I stroked her, trying to calm her, as we huddled in a dim corner of that large aircraft on our way to Fairbanks Memorial Hospital. The big helicopter set down behind the hospital and we were taken into the emergency ward. Dr. MacFarlane admitted Sarah to the hospital and put her on an IV, anti seizure drip. During the night, I bathed her 104°-fevered body in a tepid bath. By the next day, with no further symptoms, there seemed no reason to remain. Clint had been looking forward to his correspondence school's monthly potluck held at the Delta school. Sarah had a normal temperature, so despite the doctor's hesitations, we took Clint to his party. Sarah, who had been sitting next to a friend at the party, suddenly fell over. We sat her up, and again, she fell over. We mushed home that night, hoping the incident was a one-time event. But at home, Sarah could no longer walk, pull herself up, and finally, she could not even crawl. Reb sat on the floor by my feet, with his head

121. October: the Tanana is choked with slush but the ice shelf around the bluff is not yet formed, preventing easy access. Sarah, Reb and Clint, 1980.

on my knees, weeping. My forehead furrowed, I waited for night to pass. I hardly slept, lying at the end of our bed closest to her crib. I lay, listening to her questionable breathing, and I rested on the razor's edge.

The next day, Sarah was chipper and happy, but unable to sit up and was still feverish. There was still no shelf ice to use to get around the bluff quickly, so we tucked her in the dog sled and mushed over the bluff, with no trail, bucking six inches of snow to get to the road. Ninety minutes later, we were on our way to Fairbanks in our truck. I entered the doctor's office at Tanana Valley Clinic holding a limp child. The doctor said, "Get her to the hospital. It looks like a brain tumor." The strength went out of my arms. We drove to Fairbanks Memorial Hospital and I carried her into Dr. MacFarlane's ward. Immediately, he said, "I can't guarantee you, but I am 90% sure this is temporary. She will get well. I think it is viral encephalitis." He laid Sarah onto the C.A.T. scan bed for a leaf-by-leaf picture of her brain. She had no tumor and no blot clot. I followed her to the room for a spinal test, checking for two types of meningitis and two kinds of encephalitis. In a few hours, we knew it was not the worst; it was, as Dr. MacFarlane had said, viral encephalitis, a flu the throat could not contain. It had attacked the brain's back, lower lobe. Sarah's fever continued. Doctors watched her behavior, monitoring, without telling me, if the disease might overtake her brain, putting her into a coma. Sarah was hot, but bursting with personality. When her dad and brother reentered the room, Sarah, who could only squirm, wiggled like a happy pup. That night, in the hospital's Meditation Room, Clint became feverish and hallucinated. As Reb also became sick with the flu, Dr. MacFarlane checked us all into Sarah's room, giving us each a bed. When Clint could be moved, he and Reb went to Delta and stayed in a friend's home while Clint healed.

Since the night of the potluck, Sarah had no longer been able to feed herself. I spooned food into her mouth, but she had no appetite. On December 5th, her second birthday, my parents ordered a special, Big Bird, birthday cake for her. She knotted her fists around the cake and tried to get it into her mouth. This was an improvement.

In the trauma, I never thought to eat at the cafeteria. I never left Sarah, and only ate what she could not eat on her hospital tray. Consequently, I began to notice a lack of interest in food - a fatigue - as I fought the flu; I thought it was only a part of my shocked, numbed senses. Food became as appealing as cardboard. One night, when Sarah was past danger, and sleeping, I walked downtown among the Christmas decorations. I walked for many blocks, hardly touched by the season, distant from the normal human flow. I was afraid to go home. Sarah could do nothing but lie on the floor. I felt helpless and frightened of another emergency.

We went to physical therapy, and the young nurse laid Sarah on a huge beach ball to exercise her trunk's coordination. The devastation of her young body made me nauseated and I wanted to run.

Just before leaving the hospital, I was holding Sarah's hands and walking, holding her, urging her to put one foot in front of the other. Dr. MacFarlane walked in and said, gently, "All it takes is just a little faith, and a little time." A tear rolled down my face onto the floor. His gentleness spoke to me, but what my shocked system did not realize was the absolute truth of his words.

At home, Clint made Sarah a doll for Christmas. He encouraged her, as she lay helpless on the floor, to reach for the new doll. He held her on his lap and played with her. As I worked around the kitchen, Reb and Clint took turns with her.

One day, I looked over, and Sarah was pulling herself up on the firewood box, and, as when she was 9 months old, scooting along holding onto the wood box. No greater miracle had I ever seen. Tears poured down my face, as joy sounded from one end of me to the other. We would be okay. In a month, Sarah's gross motor control had returned. She could climb onto Clint's bouncing horse. In two months, she could draw again.

Because of her thyroid deprivation in utero, Sarah had challenges later in school. The next few years, there were more skirmishes. By the time she was 15 years old, Sarah's grace and confidence began to blossom. I knew, finally, Someone bigger than I had handled things, and my part was subsiding...

Chapter Forty Seven
WASH AND DRY

Between 1968 and 1987, the Delta Laundry and Cleaners was my second home. I used to joke that anybody who was anyone met at the local laundromat.

Mothers fed their babies while their other children ran giggling and screaming around Theta Musgrove's Big Boy washers. Theta watched from behind her counter to make sure we did not overload the machines. She urged us to run hot water over our frozen diapers, so they didn't rat-a-tat-tat the washing machines' centrifuges.

Born in Cestos, Oklahoma, March 19, 1910, Theta taught school before moving to Alaska in 1941. In 1959, she began teaching school in Delta when classes still met in a canvas-covered Quonset hut called Mount Deborah School at Fort Greely's old post.

In 1990, her teaching colleagues, Judy Pease and Mary Madore, honored her on her 80th birthday, six years before she died.

Theta did everything from scratch. She was a veteran from the Alaska era in which every scrap was considered a potential spare part. She ran her laundromat single-handedly from above her basement home. She would frequently disappear into that mysterious basement, returning with a scoop of powdered bleach for the customer for fifty cents.

Once in a while, Clearwater homesteader Lois Cosgrove relieved Theta when she needed to run downstairs.

"But, Theta's wasn't the first laundromat," Lois joked with me recently. In 1955, Lois had hosted Delta's original laundromat in her tent home on the banks of Clearwater Creek. There was no winter access to the Clearwater; snow shut down the unmaintained Clearwater Trail. Five other equally isolated homesteaders depended on Lois' 5-kilowatt generator, and her wringer washer.

"Detergent wouldn't dissolve in that cold, creek water," Lois chuckled. "So, I carried my copper kettle to the creek, hauled and filled my wood stove's reservoir with ice water every afternoon to heat for whomever might be washing at my house the next day."

Lois added with a grin, "We were a close bunch."

In the 1970s, creek side washing on the trail gave way to Theta's laundromat on the Richardson Highway. In those days, I sat my son in a chair at the laundromat to do his correspondence math study. When his baby sister became too fussy to stay, I went into high gear. I stuffed wet clothes into duffle bags for the long mush home, planning to dry clothes on the inside lines there.

"I don't know how you do it," people said to me, shaking their heads.

"This is a luxury," I would reply, remembering the scrub board in a white gas can on the trapline, in a cabin barely lighted by a Coleman lantern. "Besides, I get caught up with the Delta news," I added as I smeared peanut butter on bread for my hungry child.

It was a ritual. Every Sunday for thirteen winters, I threw my two large, duffle bags of dirty clothes into my dog sled at our home up the Tanana River. I careened off our hill with a fresh team while my children placed bets if Mom could hang onto the sled, this time.

When Clint and Sarah became satellite students of Delta Christian Academy for one day a week, it was my ladies day out. I talked with Theta while the machines swirled my clothes. Theta recalled how the Federal Aviation Administration had originally moved her and her husband, Ed, from the Midwest to Talkeetna. A product of the 1930s Oklahoma dust bowl, Theta became a U.S. Commissioner serving from 1943 to 1956 in the Alaska Territory. Whenever a law was broken, Theta appointed an acting deputy to arrest the criminal.

Theta had many proverbs hanging on her austere walls. A particular one warned aggressive patrons, "Water automatically replaces an object when it is removed from a bucket. That's how much difference your passing from this world will make."

In 1987, I got a washing machine. At first, it did not synchronize with my generator-powered water pump. A helpful friend leaned over the agitator with a wrench and baited me, teasing, "Judy, you're destined to always wash your clothes at Theta's…"

But like my washboard at our dirt floor cabin at MonteChristo Creek, the laundromat has finally been replaced.

122. Clint, Laura and Sarah, 1979.

Chapter Forty Eight
HEIDI YEARS

hen I was young I told stories to myself, and to my sister, before drifting off to sleep. I escaped suburbia by imagining myself like Heidi among the alpine flowers running downhhill with my goats.

After Reb and I moved upriver and bought our ten acres, we began carving a farm out of the wilderness on a shoestring budget. I studied the University Cooperative Extension pamphlets and dreamed of filling a root cellar with beautiful vegetables. Our sled dogs were chained on the perimeter where the woods met our fields to protect us from bears; home was an island in the mountain wilderness. Within, the horses grazed contentedly. We raised pullets, ducks, geese, and turkeys in lantern-warmed, wooden boxes. I was horrified, more than once, to find, in the morning, a smoking holocaust when the lantern malfunctioned. We never had a cow because it meant being tied into a strict milking schedule.

One day in 1983, we boated to see our neighbor, George Probert, who had a homestead on an island across the Delta River. His goats enchanted me as they stood in their milking stanchion in his little barn. But Reb was not going to get a goat.

One evening, however, George pulled up to our place with a loaded boat. He rolled out bales of wire, a pre-fab barn, and led two beautiful, pregnant goats onto the bank: Laura and Lady. George announced, "Here's your dairy, Judy!" The two Sanaen goats produced a gray kid for Clint, which he named Princess, and one more - Snowflake.

I loved returning home in the evenings and being greeted by the goats. Sarah skipped; Clint stalked frogs; and the baby goats and nannies frolicked around us as we walked up the path.

First, I was the milker and then 10-year-old Clint took over. He did not enjoy, however, milking in the black, October night. He had a feeling a witch lived in the barn loft. He screwed up his nerve, though, and entered the cold barn, safely inside the warm circle of his Coleman lantern's light.

In the winter, as the nannies' milk diminished, I realized we needed a billy for Laura and Lady to continue producing, and lactating. A friend offered to sell me hers, B.G. His goatee dripped with his scent glands. He loved to rub his head on us when we passed him. Not only might he start butting us, but also he left his perfume on anyone who touched him. His smell was so strong that when I approached our land by riverboat, his pungency drifted down to me on the air current. But, our ladies kept producing.

One night on our sentinel hill, I was glancing out my kitchen window when I heard a blood-curdling scream from the lower field. I streaked out the door and, from our porch, peered into the pitch-black. Grabbing Reb's 0.44 Magnum pistol, I ran downhill into the darkest part of the field.

Clint lay on his back shrieking, holding the billy's horns away from his groin as it tried to ram him. His strength was waning. I grabbed the goat's horns and pulled him off.

I decided then to relieve us of B.G. Following the veterinarian's instructions, I tranquilized and neutered him, and waited six months to see if his smell might improve, which would make him a candidate for the larder. He did not improve much. But, set not to waste the meat, I persevered. At dinnertime, Clint always knew, when he approached the kitchen, if we were having a B.G. roast. He would sniff the air, and intone, "Hmmm, B.G.!"

As Clint grew, we decided to try life on the road system, to let him attend study with other children. Before school, he went to our new barn, a greenhouse, and amused himself, in between milking, by squirting milk on the greenhouse walls. By spring, we had dried, abstract paintings all over the walls.

The first time my parents, who live on the finer side of Tulsa, Oklahoma, visited us, I fussed to my friend, "I'm nervous about my mom's visit. She has never even seen a slop bucket." But, my mom had grown up in Dust Bowl, Depression-ridden Oklahoma and knew more than I thought. However, riding in a riverboat with a goat was a first for her.

That June, we were moving from the house on the road system back to our remote home on the hill. We had to get our goats back up the river. To protect her clothes from the spray and the dirt in the boat, Mother was dressed in my military-issue, baggy, yellow rain pants. I helped her into our 24-foot open Ouachita boat. To keep Lady and Laura in the boat, Clint snubbed them to the sides of the boat. Excited, they sprayed the boat with nuggets. Mother shrank. I revved up the 25-horsepower motor and we topped the waves. Tanana chop sprayed back on us. The goats finally calmed down and turned their tails to the wind. And somehow, Mother survived and can laugh about it, today.

123. Clint, Laura, Lady and B.G. walking on shelf ice around bluff, 1981.

I had high hopes for our dairy program. Both of the females were pregnant that spring, and Laura, who was already a good producer, was guaranteed to greatly increase our milk production. On a beautiful day, the goats got loose and cavorted through the dog yard. They flicked their tail just once too often at the sled dogs. The team ravaged them. I found both nannies stiff with their young kids, stillborn, inside their lifeless bodies.

After that, it seemed easier to simply buy powdered milk, but still, when I see "Heidi's goats" cavorting in someone else's yard, I long again to take one home.

Chapter Forty Nine
SMOKEY BEAR

124. Veteran firefighter Hell's Canyon Fire, Oregon, 1995.

In 1978, the summer after Sarah's birth, Reb was 35 years old and had long been fighting fire for the United States Bureau of Land Management. Laborer jobs also supplemented his trapping income. With nothing dependable, we kept our belts tightened. Reb needed a steady job beyond moonlighting.

In 1979, Reb became State Forestry's Fire Warden, Smokey the Bear's official job title. The new Delta Agricultural Project prompted farmers to make their freshly cleared land fully arable. Newly cleared land was still covered with bulldozed trees and vegetation, dumped into long rows, called berm piles. The fastest way to get rid of them was to torch them. The fires were generally lit in the spring while there was still snow on the ground. If they had not completely burned out by mid-May, the drying Delta winds could whip the smouldering organic matter into a frenzied forest fire. The resulting fires kept Delta Forestry racing throughout the 1980s.

From early May until late July, we hardly see Reb. If he is not on a fire in our local area, then he is on an assignment elsewhere in the state.

In the fall, Reb frequently may be assigned to fires in the Lower 48. He is skilled to fill many leadership positions, but he enjoys most taking Native crews Outside. At a moment's notice, he might find himself in either deserts or mountains. In tall, leather boots, with little sleep, he has hiked in 104° F. temperatures, up and down steep mountains.

One summer, when Reb had disappeared on an Alaskan fire, I needed him, and called Fairbanks Forestry. Reb had been dispatched off the Kuskokwim to Stony River. When I called, a villager answered the phone and I asked him, "Have you seen a six-foot tall man? You know, he wears a red bandana, boots to the knee, a leather vest, and a wide-brimmed hat?" Despite a crowd of two hundred Emergency Fire Fighters, EFF'ers, the villager found Reb in three minutes.

Frequently, Reb may be sent as a Liaison Officer escorting village crews to the Lower 48. August 13, 1997, the telephone rang.

Delta Forestry called, "Reb, orders just came in for a Liaison Officer to take a crew to the States. You'll be flown from Fairbanks to Galena [on the Yukon] to pick up Nulato I; Stanley Demonski is the Native crew boss. You'll pick up the crew in Galena and go on to the staging area at [Fort] Wainwright, and continue from there to Oregon."

Village crews, adept with a Pulaski - a mattock and ax combination - have earned a reputation as good firefighters, and this time, even for killing snakes!

That same day, one hundred Alaskan firefighters were flown into the base at Galena, west of Fairbanks on the Yukon River, and divided up into five crews to be sent Outside. Mike Trudeau, Jeff Yarman, Mike Sterling, George Coyle, and Reb Ferguson each acted as a crew representative for a group of nineteen men.

Reb was with the Nulato I crew; while Mike Trudeau and crew boss, Victor Alexie, led Nulato II. The crews were going into hot conditions and were admonished to continually drink lots of water, and to also watch out for snakes.

A teacher demonstrated the pop-up, aluminized, emergency fire shelter, affectionately called "shake and bake," by stepping into it and pinning the corners down with his four limbs spread eagle style.

The crews then jetted out to the record fire and drought conditions in Oregon. Reb and his Nulato I crew set up camp near Ukiah, Oregon, and were then bused out to the Tower Fire.

Arriving at night, Reb said the surrounding woods were bright with light from the monstrous fire. Stanley Demonski and squad leaders, Bergman Esmailka, Ralph Silas, and Bennett Madros climbed with Reb over the lip of the canyon and saw the entire valley engulfed in flame. Thousands of embers were blowing with a violent wind. The full moon was strangely red. Chunks of glowing ash the size of silver dollars whirled around them.

It was impossible to get in front of a fire this large and widespread to burn out the potential fuels. It moved too fast and the fire had too many heads, like locomotive engines consuming the woods. Putting a line around the fire was the objective.

125. Sarah and Smokey, Delta Parade, 1999.

Intricate plans were engineered after each evening's flight over the area, when, from the air, the rate and direction of spread could be seen.

Like a good army flanking the enemy, the firefighters tried to isolate the blaze with back burning, shovels, bulldozers, water, and chemicals. The fire just simmered under cloud cover, but when the weather cleared off, it was as if the dampers had been opened and the fire came alive. The red of the canyon glowed at night like a scene from hell.

A complex tent city became necessary to service the firefighting operation. The mess hall, commissary, finance, communication, and first aid tents served the crews who worked sixteen hours a day. Long lines for eating, showering, and for the telephone became a way of life for the personnel.

Every morning in the frosty, dark night, workers, sleeping in insulated paper bags, began to toss and turn, slowly waking. They could be heard coughing because of the oppressive smoke and dust.

Out of the dark, someone called, "Hey! Madros, get up!!"

Headlamps slowly clicked on in the 30° F. Oregon morning chill. Leather boots next to the paper sleeping bags lay stiff and cold. At 5:30 A.M., the mess hall lighted up and began to fill with men and women, waiting in line for the scrambled eggs, bacon, and oatmeal.

In each morning briefing, crew bosses met with fifty overhead personnel. Problems were addressed. The day's firefighting plans had been printed and were distributed among the personnel. In the field, Reb could multitask between the crews due to the high competency of the Nulato I's crew boss, Stanley Demonski.

Before back burning, fire crews dug into the dirt to make a wide stopgap between the forest and the back burn ignition point. The men used drip torches - a device for throwing a stream of flaming liquid - and fuses to burn dead trees, brush, and grass. When the project fire hit the stopgap strip, the fuels would be gone. At that point, the fire would not jump the gap and would begin to burn itself out. But often, intricate, strategies were foiled by afternoon temperatures and by shifts in wind direction. Firefighters working on uphill grades could become particularly vulnerable. A canyon fire could easily box them in.

When the crisis had subsided and moved into the mop-up phase, the Nulato I crew walked in the heat and dust, their eyes tearing from the smoke. As they used their pulaskis to open and extinguish pockets of burning coals, they covered their nose and mouth with bandanas to avoid inhaling the flying ash.

These same coal beds became little ovens where the crewmembers could push their barbecued beef packets into the embers, resulting in a good, warmed up lunch. While the MREs - Meals Ready to Eat - heated up, salmon strips were passed around. Reb's mouth watered over the fish's smoked, salty flavor.

After a hot lunch, they pumped water on the ash pits. In the final phase, fifteen men and four women walked abreast, gridding very slowly, looking for any remaining fire. They continued until they secured a 300-foot perimeter around the most aggressive point of the fire.

After many days of sixteen-hour shifts, muscles were tired, and each day was a little harder. Hunting season would arrive soon, and the snow would not be far behind. September 3rd, the Nulato I crew returned home up the Yukon River, and at our home, the annual Delta Fair was just beginning.

Festooned trucks, marching bands, and clowns filled Delta's main street with the annual parade. With my youngest son, Ben, towering over me, I remembered back to a parade that was typical of thirty years of Delta Fair openings, all of which I had witnessed. High on the yellow fire truck, all those years ago, an enormous Smokey Bear rode, waving to the crowds. Next to him, a boy, almost big enough for his wide-brimmed hat, sported a red bandana. Clint, grinned, throwing candy to the crowds, while his dad, in the hot, bear suit, also waved to the people on both sides of the street. Sarah caught some of the goodies thrown by her dad and brother, and saved some for Ben, the baby riding on my hip.

We drove to the fairgrounds, and at State Forestry's cabin, we saw Smokey giving out comics of the bear cub's story to the public, as well as showing videos of what carelessness can do.

Chapter Fifty
BEAR STORIES
Cubby

A female bear had consistently been robbing the dog food behind our house. Clint often fed the dogs, so Reb lay in wait for the bear, and shot it. He had no idea the bear had a cub. High over-head, near the tops of the trees, we heard an unnerving bawling. We craned our necks and saw a black clump clinging to a tall tree, sway-ing in the breeze. "Maaaaaaa…" the cub cried. "Maaaaaaaaaaaa." It wrenched us, and we knew, some-how, we had to get him down.

Reb donned heavy gloves that reached up to his mid-arm, put on an insulated jacket, and covered his face with a bug net. Careful to

126. Clint, Reb and bear that was raiding our dog yard, 1976.

cut the tree so it would not fall on the cub, he revved up the chainsaw. "Crash!" the tree hit the ground with the cub on the up side. When we approached, the cub hissed, baring his teeth. Reb slipped a collar around the cub's neck and snapped a chain onto it. While Reb secured the cub, Clint daydreamed of having a pet bear that followed him everywhere, like a dog, as in his book, Big Ben. When the cub reached out with an arm-amputating swipe, the fantasy of a pet bear dis-solved.

In Archbishop Hudson Stuck's book, *Voyages On the Yukon and Its Tributaries,* a prospector built a tree stand by sawing off the top of a tree and nailing on a platform. He chained his bear cub at the base so he could still exercise but yet be constrained. Reb duplicated the stand and secured the bear we named Cubby to it. At arm's length, we fed him milk-soaked dog food and sweet-talk. When we returned home from town one day, we found Cubby's chain empty. He had broken the snap and headed for the hills. I hoped he would not return as a grouchy adult, but he was very small, and needed a mother to help him survive.

The Beauty and the Beast

One summer morning, half asleep, I stumbled out of the house to walk down to the pasture to take our horses to water and then, stake them on grass. Reb, equally sleepy, followed me out the door, stood, and surveyed the ten acres from the top of our hill. "JUDY!" he screamed at me as I led two horses to the pond. "Bear!" I glanced and saw a bear loping across the field and disappear

127. Cubby

into the woods. As the horses lowered their heads to drink at the pond, across the water, I saw the head and shoulders of an elegant, silver tipped Grizzly simply watching me, like the beast in the fairy tale, quiet and regal, above the brush. He was gone when Reb returned with a rifle

Mirror Image

One summer, a black bear kept visiting our boat shed by the river. A sack of dog food was stored inside. As we hiked to the river one morning for Reb to leave for work, I suggested that he might need his Smith and Wesson, .44-Magnum pistol. Reb sent me to get it. With it in his hand, he slowly eased his head up the wall to the open eaves of the boat shed. At the same time, like a mirror image, the bear also eased his head up the wall. The bear and Reb were eye to eye. Reb took aim and fired.

If Reb believed in reincarnation, he would say he had been mountain man, Jim Bridger, in a previous life. When a bear became a threat to a fire or construction crew, Reb, like Bridger, was always the hired assassin on the job.

The Oreo-eating Bear

When Reb was working, building a remote, log home for a lawyer, a female bear and cub kept raiding the construction crew's kitchen tent. The sow loved Oreo cookies. Reb strung a trip wire across the kitchen's entrance with a hammer on the wire that, if triggered, would bang the propane tank. At 4 A.M., the alarm sounded. "Oh, no," Reb muttered, and wearing only his underwear, he struggled out into the mosquitoes with his gun. Spooked by the alarm, the bears ran out of the tent into the woods. Just as happy to return to bed, Reb snuggled back into his sleeping bag. An hour later, "Dongggg!" Once again, Reb braved the bugs. The cub ran out of the tent, but seeing Reb, he skedaddled up a tree and began bawling. The sow heard her baby and charged out of the tent, ears flattened. She tripped and rolled over the wire. Up, she sprang, and charged again; Reb stopped her with a bullet.

The baby could not survive alone in remote location, so Reb was also forced to shoot the cub.

Peaches and Gun Muzzles

"Bears aren't always dangerous," Reb said, "Simply remember that they are unpredictable." On a fire assignment near the Yukon River village of Beaver, the theory got tested.

In camp, many of the Hot Shot crew - a first strike, highly trained firefighting force - had been storing candy bars in their tents. A bear kept visiting one firefighter's tent, tearing up the canvas, and ransacking the food. The crew member said, "Hey, Reb, you gotta get this bear!"

Reb watched for the bear, but he eluded Reb. As the crew was packing up to permanently leave camp, the bear attacked the tent yet again. Reb sidled up toward the bear and yelled at him, "Get! Get outa here!!" The bear, who was eating peaches, was not the least effected. Reb beat pots together. Nothing. Finally, Reb stabbed his rifle in the 2-year-old bear's ribs. The bear continued slurping. "I can't shoot that bear; he's like a dog." Reb turned to the guys and they simply ran the bear off.

In a similar situation in another fire camp, a bear had been making the rounds, raiding tents. One night, Reb was pretending to sleep. He opened one eye to see the bear sidle past him to inspect the firefighter in the other bunk. The bear was too close to the open-mouthed sleeper for Reb to get a shot. The bear waited, and waited…puzzled at this comatose firefighter. Finally, he simply shook his head, turned around, and left the tent.

Chapter Fifty One

SANTA CLINT

One Christmas Eve when Santa would ordinarily have been flying in his sleigh, he was hiking around the Tanana River bluff. My upriver neighbor, Donna Ashby, and I wrote this account about one special Christmas night.

128. *Alicia and Golden Ashby, 1983.*

The Ferguson House, Christmas Week - Our family's sleds slid up the frozen Tanana in December 1983. Passing by the Ashbys' house, we waved at their children, 7-year-old Golden and 5-year-old Alicia, and continued on around the bluff to our cabin, farther upstream.

When we arrived home, 13-year-old Clint parked his sled behind our house, and then brought flour and spices into the kitchen for making a gingerbread Christmas tree. Enticed for years by a photo in my cookbook, Clint had wanted to go beyond a gingerbread house and make a cookie tree, lit with candles.

He began kneading a spicy mass of butter, molasses, and sugar, leaving a trail of the batter clinging to cupboard handles, and mashed into the well-worn floor. Rolling the dough out on the table, Clint cut stars in graduated sizes. First, stacking the larger star cookies and following them with the smaller stars, he skewered them together with toothpicks, and slathered the little tree with green icing.

Nothing distracted him from his grand moment. He fixed a tiny birthday candle to each of the tree's "spruce" tips, and left it under our regular Christmas tree in the corner.

A few days later, on Christmas Eve, we began getting ready for bed when I heard Clint rustling around upstairs. Looking through his loft door, I saw an apparition of Santa Claus. Clint's eyes twinkled above a fleecy white beard. On his head, he wore a red and gold shopping sack trailing a cotton ball attached on the tail. Wearing his dad's red, long john top, he had stuffed a pillow inside, and cinched his waist with a belt.

"What are you doing?" I exclaimed while horsey laughs shook his oversized belly.

"I'm going to surprise Golden and Alicia tonight, and convince them I'm Santa Claus," he chuckled.

"At this time of night?" I asked. "In the dark, and around the bluff?"

"Yeah, and I'm going to give them the gingerbread tree," he answered, and ho-ho-hoing out the front door, he slipped out into the Christmas Eve night.

129. Santa Clint.

The Ashby House, Christmas Eve - We had expected guests that Christmas Eve, but the weather kept them from coming. However, trusting that Santa Claus could come, our children, Golden and Alicia, had hung up their stockings, believing that all things magical were possible.

They scrambled into pop's lap for a story, when suddenly the sled dog alarm sounded. Intense howling and barking could only mean a late visitor.

"Who could it be?" We wondered.

Popping my head out the door, I heard a voice, "Ho, ho, ho! Thought I'd come by and bring you a little treat."

Ready for the fun, I replied, "Come on in, Santa," but I had no idea who he was. Santa looked a little strange wearing bunny boots, and Carhartts - the workingman's brown canvas pants - topped off with a beard that obscured his face.

Carrying a Christmas tree made of star-shaped cookies, he lowered the dessert for my children to see. On each star's tip, a candle glowed, and it matched the light in Golden and Alicia's eyes.

They chirped, "Hi, Santa," not surprised that he had come to their house. After a little chat, but growing tired from a long day of sledding, they climbed into bed where sugar plum fairies soon danced in their heads.

Meantime, I was trying to figure out who was playing this fun masquerade. Those jovial eyes peeking over the fluffy beard seemed so very familiar, but I just could not place them.

Finally Santa said, "Well, good night. I hope you enjoy your gifts in the morning."

Still trying to decide which of our friends this might be, I waved goodbye as he disappeared into the night when suddenly, it hit me.

This was the little boy I had given hot cocoa to in my kitchen for years, whenever he and his parents stopped here on their way home, upstream. I had known him since he was a baby, but somehow in the grind of daily life, I had not realized he had become a man.

"Good night, Santa Claus," I yelled to the disappearing back, "thank you for coming."

Christmas Day - "Guess who came last night, Reb?" Golden and Alicia called out when Clint's dad stopped by the Ashbys the following morning. "Santa Claus!" they confided.

Hearing this news, Clint was thrilled. His Christmas was complete; he had impersonated the Man from the North Pole with nothing but glued-on cotton, a red shopping bag, and a trailing, white tassel.

130. Clint's Christmas Cookie Tree.

144

Chapter Fifty Two
THE LONGEST MUSH HOME

In 1983, we had lived remote twelve years. The stove was going and winter was quietly settling its blanket of peace around us. Summer boating was over and the winter's sledding had not yet begun. It was the bad access time of year when overflow was the rule. With little means of communication, the world slipped away, and the citizens band radio was the only link to our friends: The Crazy Alaskan, Goofin' Off, Hey, You and Spud Farm. They, too, were tucked in, but they were across the Tanana, far away from us. Our harvested vegetables were in our root cellar, and the children's school curriculum lined the shelves.

Clint was starting seventh grade and Sarah was in the first. Once the sloughs were frozen, Clint and I mushed two teams into town with Sarah on one of the sleds. For a day, the children were satellite students, studying with their friends at Delta Christian Academy. We came in the previous night, and the Echo-Hawks always had a room for us.

When school was over late one afternoon, I felt tired and achy. But regardless of how I felt, I only wanted to get home. Using the CB landline network of friends, Reb had called the school and warned us not to sled around the base of the bluff; the ice shelf was gone and the river was open. He told us to go over the hill, which meant we had to break trail in the dark.

131. Frozen Tanana with moon; mushing east toward home.

After tutoring Academy students all day, I packed up my children and we drove to Hansen Hollow, and to our waiting sled dogs.

Leaving the warmth of our car, we shrugged off the outside chill and wrestled harnesses onto jumping huskies. Clint put a large, new battery charger onto his sled to freight home. The teams sped over the bridge that spanned the slough - the tributary, or backwater, to the main channel - from the mainland to Hansen's Island. Only a few boards remained of the bridge decking, and little Sarah dreaded the gaping holes of the bridge with the icy slough below. We bounced behind racing dogs, when suddenly in the dark, the next slough appeared strangely black. The surface had a gleam. It was spring-fed, and I was afraid the channel was open. I rolled my sled onto its side and chained the team to a tree, then I tapped the surface of the ice with an ax. It was skating rink-smooth, blown clean by the wind, and was only reflecting a little moonlight.

As we crossed the slough, Sarah rode in my sled, half asleep in a sleeping bag. A dark hole appeared where two sloughs met. I veered away, but the dogs trotted right into fresh overflow, plowing ice water up into the sled. Sarah, dampened before I realized it, stood up above the slush, but I heard Clint behind me, suddenly screaming at his dogs. The heavy battery charger had broken the brittle ice skirting the open hole. The charger and Clint were in a foot of open water. The dogs soon had him and his cargo back on the surface again, a little wetter and a little colder.

We were following the side slough, when my lead dogs abruptly melted into the dark. Was I dreaming? They weren't there. Just as quickly, they reappeared, climbing out of a hole that had thawed in the middle of the ice trail. A little shaken, our teams pulled the sleds, crunching over a layer of freshly frozen overflow.

Since we could not continue to the Tanana's edge, we turned and faced a less familiar and unbroken trail over the bluff. Straight up, the three of us trudged, pushing the sleds, stopping often for Sarah, who was slipping backward in the fresh snow. At the top, the old trail diffused into willows making it difficult in the dark to discern the direction. Off to the left, an opening to a haphazard swath appeared. But, below that was a gully. It did not seem right. Clint stayed with my team as I searched for the trail, maintaining voice contact with him. Suddenly, across several ravines, three shots rang out. Reb, alerted by the dogs at home, was on our porch on the hill looking for us. We plunged down the side of the ravine and ducked our heads as our dogs ran for home.

As we climbed up the slope to our homestead, our headlamps reflected off the glowing eyes of the dogs still at home. The warmth from the light in the living room windows reached out to us like a haven. Reb met us, holding a Coleman lantern above his head, embracing us with his help. I left the team to him and muttered, "I want a house on the road." My stomach ached, my muscles throbbed, and all I wanted was to sleep.

I had gotten a virus, but in a few days some symptoms were gone, but not others. I wanted only to lie on the sofa and for nothing to touch my midriff. It was soon clear that a new musher was on his way. A few weeks of hibernation were in order. Nine months later, when I was 39 years old, Benjamin Rowe Judah Ferguson was born.

132. Sam and Chaddie
Kelly, 1940.

Chapter Fifty Three
A LITTLE SOUTHEAST OF NOME

Everyone needs a friend. Yvonne was mine. When we were on the road system, not upriver, her family offered their home as my home. Due to her warmth, my children and I had a social life, enjoyed church, and the children had peers.

Yvonne had come to Delta as a child in 1953. I used to joke that newcomers should sign in with Yvonne before entering Delta. In a sense, it was true; Yvonne and her family owned a motel -- one with authentic Alaskan roots. Born in Alaska, Yvonne, who often minded the hotel desk, could shovel snow when necessary, even in a fur coat and heels. She learned it from her pioneer parents, Sam and Chaddie...

On a recent spring night, I gazed at Kelly's Country Inn twinkling with little, white lights, reflecting off the snow. It struck me how Kelly's had grown up with early Delta. When Sam and Chaddie Kelly moved to Delta Junction, few homes had electricity and there was no store. However, pioneering was not new to Sam and Chaddie who had spent the previous twenty years with the miners and settlers of territorial Alaska.

133. Chaddie and Yvonne Kelly Echo-Hawk, 2000.

The Alaskan Territory was an intimate society of Natives, miners, military, builders, and merchants who had their own ways of doing things. Leaving behind the Great Depression in Seattle, Sam Kelly came to the Alaskan gold fields in 1935.

In the old boomtown of Flat, Sam Kelly and his buddies, Russ Diehl and Al Remington, worked as mechanics. When fall arrived, most of the miners headed south for the winter. But, like Seattle's Big Sam in Johnny Horton's song, *North to Alaska*, Sam Kelly also headed further north.

Chaddie Byers arrived in Fairbanks in 1934. From Canada, her family had fallen on hard times in Saskatchewan. Chaddie's uncle, Hosea H. Ross, offered her father a job in Alaska - freighting lumber to Fairbanks for building homes.

"Times were pretty tough in Saskatchewan," Chaddie explained, "My father, Ernest Byers, was a farmer and a coal miner. When coal dropped to five cents a ton and a drought set in, farmers were forced to trade their butter and meat for coal."

Uncle Hosey, the lone Fairbanks undertaker and a real estate dealer, met the Byers family in Valdez, chauffeured them north where they rode Rika's ferry across the Tanana River, and then on into Fairbanks, the hub of mining activities in the Alaskan Interior.

Fairbanks was a town of only four thousand people, but it had its brush with celebrities. Ernest Byers, a great admirer of Will Rogers, spotted the inimitable cowboy diplomat shopping at the Co-op Drugstore on Second Avenue and politely introduced himself. Shortly after, it was Hosea Ross' duty to prepare the bodies of Will Rogers and Wiley Post after their fatal plane crash.

Chaddie was enjoying high school when Russ Diehl introduced her to Sam Kelly, the winter of 1939. She was captivated by the man who was twelve years her senior; they married January 1940.

Their first summer of marriage, Sam and Chaddie went to Rampart where Sam worked as a mechanic for the Reid/Crane gold mine on the Yukon River.

"Sam was never boring," Chaddie said.

One day, while he was resting in their sod-and-grass-roofed cabin, the stovepipe caught the dry grass of the roof on fire. Chaddie hollered, "Fire!" at her sleeping spouse who, though nude, ran outside, looked at the roof, shrugged, and said, "It'll go out," and returned to bed. He was right.

When winter came, the couple moved to a hotel in Flat, near the Iditarod River, 400 miles southwest of Fairbanks. Pete Miscovich, the father of Chaddie's Fairbanks' girlfriend, Eva, was mining outside the former boomtown of Iditarod. Chaddie remembered buckets of gold nuggets scattered around Pete's clean up - the refuse from the gold's initial separation from gravel. When Chaddie climbed the hotel's stairwell to the roof, she was amazed to see another kind of bucket: rows of frozen honey pots - chamber pots - waiting for spring to be carried away.

For more than thirteen years, Sam and Chaddie traveled from Nome to Colorado to Seattle, as Sam worked mechanic jobs. In March of 1941, they were returning north from a year's work in Colorado. Sam, who had signed on with the Canadian Oil (CANOL) Project preceded Chaddie, who soon followed the trail north with friends. Sam rode into the Northwest Territories with the first Cat train for CANOL, breaking trail up the Mackenzie River to Norman Wells. Twelve Caterpillars hauled wannigans - short, habitable trailers - from Edmondton, frightening Inuit as they went.

Chaddie headed north on a steamship, traveling straight into a March storm. When the vessel began to ice up, it became necessary to return to Juneau. Even after the weather cleared and the boat was again on its way, war priorities caused Chaddie and her friends, Tony and Liza, to get bumped from the boat at Skagway. They managed to book passage on the White Pass Railroad, riding over the Sawtooth Mountains, staying warm by means of wood stoves provided in each car. In Whitehorse, Tony sweet-talked a military pilot to take them all the way into Fairbanks.

Sam had to do his own hitchhiking. Once the CANOL Cat train arrived in Norman Wells, tired and dirty, Sam spotted a pilot warming up his engine. "I'm going with you!" he hailed the aviator, who replied, "But you don't know where I'm going …" "Anywhere, just outta here!" Sam retorted.

Finally, Sam and Chaddie were reunited in the North, where they flew to Sam's next job in Ruby, landing on the Yukon River's spring ice. They met Doc LaRue, the flying dentist, who invited them to socialize at the local dances. At some functions, they cut a rug to the dance melodies of an old Edison phonograph and at others, an old, sleeping, fiddle player would wake from his exhaustion and suddenly burst into, "The Old Rugged Cross." Then, he would fall into slumber again, only to wake up seconds later to plunge into the hymn again.

A problem common in the North was burial. Once, when Sam was sent into a Ruby root cellar to get vegetables for dinner, he was stunned to see, along with the family's larder, a solidly frozen relative laid out on the table, splitting open with the cold and waiting for spring burial.

There was no place like Nome though. Chaddie remembered both the driver and the horse of the local honey wagon detail. Daily, they wandered into the famous Board of Trade Saloon, sucked up suds and both wove their way down the street, carrying giggling Inupiaq children, and scraping cars as they went.

Chaddie arrived in this very colorful town in the late stages of her first pregnancy. She began labor in a cold, dark building. With chagrin, she remembered the ancient doctor who used outdated anesthetic methods. Just after their daughter, Susie, was born, a diphtheria epidemic broke out, delaying Chaddie and Susie's trip to Kodiak to join Sam at his new post.

Sam and Chaddie's second daughter, Yvonne, arrived in Kodiak, in February 1947, when it was necessary to use cleats or chains on this icy island in the Gulf of Alaska.

Moving from job to job with Sam did not bother Chaddie. "I loved it," she said.

The Kellys returned to Fairbanks where Sam, in 1950-51, acquired the U.S. Mail delivery contract between Fairbanks and the Canadian border. Fairbanks was a different town then. The Kellys' dentist, Doc LaRue, practiced dentistry out of his home. Yvonne remembers walking past wicker baskets of gold and silver dollars. "That's the way Alaska was in those days," Chaddie explained, "you could leave things lying about and nobody would bother them."

The Kellys arrived in Delta in 1953 when Sam was hired at Allen Air Field, the airstrip built for the World War II Lend Lease Program. The fall wind was blowing silt all around as the Kellys moved into a small house near a trailer park.

"The trailers were 8 by 16 feet," Chaddie said. "and the bed froze to the wall. When a wandering buffalo rubbed its backside on the trailer, it felt like an earthquake. The entire herd, originating from a 1928, buffalo transplant to Delta, routinely wandered through town."

While Sam worked at the base, he began to fulfill a dream. He built a family-run, hardware-lumber store. Chaddie was expecting their third baby, and in June 1953, Sam Kelly, Jr. arrived. With great expectations, the family invested everything in their new store. But, on New Year's Eve, after a severe cold snap, it burned to the ground. Sam watched helplessly as their uninsured business was engulfed in flames.

As the family considered their next step, Sam noticed that the town needed a hotel. Built on lessons learned, Kelly's Motel was constructed in 1963.

Business associated with Fort Greely provided the Kellys with a winter clientele. In the summer, tourists filled the parking lot. In the midst of the family's success, Sam began to get sick. He was diagnosed with a benign pituitary tumor.

Kelly's Motel switched gears to Sam's original vision, a business for the kids to run. It was a new era, the beginning of the Alyeska pipeline. Susie was at the helm, while her son, Todd, and her brother, Sammy, became acquainted with all the visitors, catering to the helicopter pilots and hoping for free rides. Pressed by the pipeline traffic, the family added more units. In 1981, Sam passed away at the Pioneers Home in Fairbanks.

As the children's lives diverged, Chaddie ran the motel for several years. Helped by family and friends, Kelly's was transformed into the new Kelly's Country Inn. Sam's dream of a family-operated business was realized when Susie, along with Howard and Yvonne Echo-Hawk's family assumed the operation.

At Chaddie's surprise 75th birthday party, Chaddie, ever the refined lady, expressed warm, demure astonishment at the one hundred fifty people gathered to honor her. Yvonne, who is every bit the showman that her father was, sang her version of North to Alaska: "Big Sam left Seattle in the year of '34… Said Sam, 'You're a'lookin' at a lonely, 'lonely man, 'lonely that is, until he met a Canadian-born gal, Chaddie Byers, 'just a little east of Nome.'"

Chapter Fifty Four
FRUIT CAKE

When I first arrived in Alaska, the dark, distance, and cold were especially felt at Christmastime. Reb and I were newly married. As yet, we had none of our own Christmas traditions. One evening, when our neighbors, Johnny and Diane Hansen, knocked on our door with big smiles, bringing a beautiful fruitcake, the gesture took on a special meaning.

The next Christmas, I scoured through the *Woman's Home Companion* cookbook I had obtained from John

134. Ben mixing fruit cake ingredients, 1990.

135. Judy mixing fruit cake by lantern glow,
upriver, 1981.

Schulz, looking for a fruitcake recipe. An imposing one and a half pages described, "Jewish Wedding Cake," a dark fruit delicacy, very moist, with little flour. The cakes were fruit and nuts, bound with butter, molasses, and preserves, steamed in a pressure cooker. Soaked in rum-soaked cloth, the cakes became a Ferguson tradition for thirty-five years.

I rarely got to Fairbanks and had little money for cakes. Nonetheless, in 1983, my friend, Yvonne Echo-Hawk, was kind enough to pick up the cherries, oranges, and pecans in Fairbanks for me. She delivered the groceries to us at the Holler as we prepared to go upriver. Dark had fallen as we harnessed the dogs by the light of our headlamps.

As we sped softly up the dark sloughs, we watched the ice carefully for ominous holes. We passed our neighbors' cheery lights just before hitting the frozen Tanana. In the dark, our headlamps poked through the ice fog. I held my lead dog's collar and led him carefully out onto a 4-foot-wide ice shelf around the bluff. Sarah got out of the sled in case the dogs should make a fatal mistake. Thirteen-year-old Clint rode the brake and one runner while 6-year-old Sarah rode the other runner, closest to the bluff. Safely past the bluff, we left the river behind. Sarah climbed back into the sled and we slid quietly up the hill into our lower pasture. The full moon had just risen and was washing our snowy, upper field with its light. On the hill, the cabin sat waiting, like a dark sentinel, dark because Reb was away on the trapline.

Clint and I made fires in the wood-burning Ben Franklin fireplace, the Fisher stove, and my Home Comfort cooking range. The lanterns were burning as I measured three pounds of raisins, two pounds of figs, and one pound of dates. I cut and sugared fresh oranges and lemons, and added the cherries and nuts. This old-fashioned wedding cake recipe called for just enough flour to bind the fruit, pecans, and walnuts together. The batter came up to my elbows as I added the molasses, eggs, sugar, and jam.

As I poured the wonderful goo into the pans, Clint did his correspondence school work by the open fire. Sarah licked the bowl and I set the bread pans into the pressure cooker to steam for one and a quarter hour, which would transform them into solid, colorful puddings of fruit and nuts.

As I unlocked the pressure cooker, I thought about my cousin, Ed Speer, who was planning to ski over the hills to celebrate Christmas with us on Saturday. The warm cloud of spices smelled inviting as I took each cake out to cool overnight.

The next morning, Clint and Sarah went out into our woods to cut a tree and brought it back on the dog sled. They had begun stringing cranberries and miniature marshmallows when we spotted Reb through the window, mushing seven dogs up the trail and bringing in the last load of gifts. With no time to spare, he had gone to the post office fresh from the trapline, and then hurried on home.

I made Christmas dinner and we all waited, hungrily: 7:00 P.M., 8:00, no cousin Ed, 9:00,

10:00, but he still had not come. I walked to the C.B. radio, wondering whether to bother anyone to try to find this wayward cousin. At 11:00 P.M. our roof began to shake and an awful racket erupted over our heads.

"Whoa, Dancer, whoa, Prancer," some lunatic yelled, "No, Donder and Blitzen!!" It could only be Santa - or Ed. We ran out into the dark to watch this crazy person stomping around on the snowy roof, wrestling with invisible reindeer. We told Santa to get off the roof and come in, and have some fruit cake!

Thirteen years later, the pages from *Woman's Home Companion Cookbook* are harder to pull apart from all the years of messy batter. In 1989, Sarah began cutting the fruit, battering the nuts, adding rum to her own steamed cakes. When they were ready, she took some of the fruitcake with her father and her when they left for the trapline. After a hard day on the trail, her delicious cake would put the glitter back in their tired eyes just before rolling up in their sleeping bags for the night.

Chapter Fifty Five
TANANA TRIALS

136. Judy with 24 ft riverboat, 35 hp outboard, 1997.

When Reb, Clint, and I began living upriver, Reb boated us in and out. If he were not available, I hiked to our car, beating along the brushy riverbank for an hour and a half until we arrived at the road. Every fall, Reb freighted supplies up the Tanana River to our home, just before the long winter. But it was Reb, not I, who drove the boat. The Tanana was glacial fed, grey with silt, clipped along at 4 and a half miles per hour, and hovered just above freezing. If a person fell into the water, even wearing a life jacket as we always did, the cold made it difficult to breathe, and clothes became heavy with silt.

In 1977, when we kayaked down the Kobuk River, I saw a woman in a red bandana, with a child and her laundry, driving a boat up to her home village of Ambler. I decided that when I got home, I would learn to run a boat. By August, I was sitting in the seat of power in the stern of our Grumman canoe, humming up the Tanana. The bow of the boat seemed like a precarious banana, skimming ahead of me in the beautiful sweep of the huge waters flowing around me. I felt free, and alone, with the wind blowing my braids and my maternity clothes. I was six months' pregnant with Sarah.

The next summer, Sarah was riding in her bassinet in the boat. Eight-year-old Clint made sure she had her pacifier while I got us down the Tanana, into a connecting slough, and to our parked car. It was a new world! However, new worlds have some scary times and I have had several.

It was deep dusk, and I was going home. I still did not have the confidence on the river that comes with experience. Sarah, my only passenger, was 3 years old. When I tried to nose our 24-foot boat into our shore, a cut-bank, the boat bounced off the abrupt cliff. With the boat rope in my hand, I tried to make the leap to the bank, but I fell into the icy water. Sarah sat there quietly, oblivious to her danger, as the boat began to rotate and drift downstream. Summoning up all my strength and disregarding the Tanana's icy shock, I hoisted all of my weight out of the river and onto the bow of the boat, and was soon able to regain control. Sarah was just fine; only her mother knew what had happened.

One evening, a few years ago, Reb wanted me to start the little 15-horsepower motor on the canoe. We needed the canoe, as well as the riverboat, taken home upriver. I had made up my mind that I would not start that motor. Several times before, I had pulled for an hour on the canoe's recoil cord, but to no avail. Now, Reb will not take "I can't," and certainly not, "I won't" for an answer. So, I started the motor, but as I drove the canoe upriver, I had an attitude.

Reb and the children were traveling up the river, side-by-side with me, in the other boat. The children were protected from the wind and the spray by a camper shell bolted onto the boat. There was no weight in the front of my canoe and the bow was riding dangerously high. Reb yelled at me to walk forward to level it. Thinking I had slowed my speed with the throttle, I let go of the motor's handle and walked forward. At top speed, my canoe immediately went into a curve, unbalancing me, and throwing me out of the boat. To my horror, the canoe was headed directly at the riverboat, straight at my husband and children.

Ben was in the camper shell, and Sarah shrank, screaming, into the protective hull with Ben. The canoe hit the camper shell, deflected and fell back, upside down, into the Tanana. The children had been crying, but started smiling when Reb pulled me out of the water. No one was hurt, and we recovered the canoe - even the motor worked.

Each summer, I had death-defying moments when the motor would lose power and we would stop going forward. The boat did circles in the rapidly moving current while Clint and I paddled to get to shore. I would hoist the motor, retrieve a shear pin from the tool kit, wade into the water, and extract the broken one. But, that was far better than when smoke blew out of the engine, and the head gasket was blown.

When driving our boats, I stand in the stern holding onto the outboard motor's long extension handle to steer and to change speed. The long handle is screwed to a shorter accelerator stem protruding from the motor.

Once, as I pushed off, Ben was my only passenger. We eased out of our slough and I began revving the engine to round the bluff ahead of us. My eyes were averted for a moment. When I looked up, we were heading straight for the bluff. I twisted the long extension handle to decelerate, but to my shock, the handle in my hand was no longer attached to the motor. I had two and a half seconds to grab the motor's short accelerator handle and twist down, which only slowed us slightly before we hit the bluff and climbed several feet up its base. Chagrined, I shoved the boat off the rocks, crunching the metal, and back into the water. We were fine except for a few ruffled nerves.

One summer, we decided to get a new kind of boat to transport us up and down the river and around the bluff. It was an inboard, jet boat with a rounded bottom and an upturned nose, and it could be driven at high speeds. I did not think I would haul goats in it, like in the older boat, but we thought that it would get us downriver much faster and would go into the north wind without risk. We had high hopes, but, in fact, Reb and I never could get used to sitting down low in the driver's seat, barely able to see over the bow, driving at break-neck speed. The $12,000 boat sat in our downriver yard for years, while we, happy in our familiar, Ouachita riverboat, continued to ply the waters at a reasonable speed, standing up.

Chapter Fifty Six
RETURN TO THE COPPER

137. Judy King Salmon, 1976.

Summer is exquisite, intense, and short in the Alaskan Interior. Getting the pantry full of poultry, produce, berries, fish, and game takes much of our abundant sunlit hours. A long winter is a given, and lavish summer wages are never guaranteed.

Near the town of Chitina, Wood Canyon is an historic fishing site for the Ahtna Copper River Indians. Where the river narrows, today's Alaskan residents cling to rocks, wade into the current, and fish the back eddies of the Copper River. If a stick is thrown into the Copper River, it disappears immediately in the silt-opaque boils, but pops up seconds later many yards downstream in the tumbling, locomotive-fast river. When the salmon swim upstream to spawn, they arrive in dense flotillas and may be caught along the shoreline in the back eddies where they seek momentary asylum from the turbulent Copper River. "Dip netting" is to stick a 2-foot-wide, hooped net on a 15-foot pole into a roaring river and somehow, incredibly… a fish swims into the open net and is miraculously netted.

Since 1976, we have dip netted for reds and kings from Wood Canyon's cliffs hoping for a big salmon run. Once again in 1989, we drove the dirt road that drops straight down into O'Brian Creek. We edged our truck, with no lateral clearance, across the narrow bridge over the creek. Then, we climbed the 70° ascent into Wood Canyon and began rounding the hairpin turns. The higher we climbed, the more the mountains pushed us to the edge of the cliffs where the Copper River twisted far below, roaring with boils. We went under the remnants of the relic train trestle, turned two 90° corners, and ascended steep, back-to-back switchbacks. A waterfall cascaded down the mountain, steadily eroding the road. We passed the long, rockslide where, the previous year, we had fished under the full moon. We began to look for a gap in the brush, the path to our fishing spot.

Reb stopped at our usual camping site, braced the tires of the truck with rocks, grabbed his dip net, and headed down to the river. He says a net should be in the water at all times. After setting up camp, the children and I crawled under branches, thrashing through the woodland trail, carrying our 15-foot long dip nets. We peered down through the trees at Reb, far below, on a nearly vertical rock ledge sitting just above the roiling Copper River. The rope that held him was tied securely around a large spruce tree in the thicket right next to us.

The sound of the wind and the turbulent river filled our ears, and we yelled down, "Did you get anything yet?!!"

"Four!" he hollered up. The desire to fish hit us and I had to restrain 5-year-old Ben from jumping down to his dad. My legs felt weak as I tied and roped each precious, life-jacketed soul very carefully to the big spruce. I eased down, past the dirt and the willows, to the 60° angled slab of rock with its footholds and hollows. Ben sat in the hole closest to the trees, and settled back, anchored, napping as he had the previous year.

We prefer a private place to fish. Many stand in the river, caked with silt, numbed by the wind, elbow to elbow with other fishermen sweeping the sandbars. However, I was once glad for a fellow fisherman. A 32-pound king hit my net, and above the boiling waters it bent my net pole down to the level of the river. I called for help, and together, my neighbor and I pivoted the heavy monster in. But this time, Reb was here, able to be away from his fire fighting, and it was good to be a family alone.

The water pulled at Reb and at 12-year-old Sarah's dip nets, turning the nets inside out, as they braced their poles into the rock. To catch a salmon, the net has to be submerged at a 90° angle and open, into the eddy. Our dip nets felt like tea strainers in the flow of the wide Copper River. Reb and Sarah waited patiently, hoping for a 7-9 pound Red salmon's subtle bump! into their nets.

138. *Judy Grapengeter, Judy and Ben. 1994.*

The water was so silty that one or one hundred could have slipped by without our knowing. We grew chilled as we watched the shadows crawl over the distant peaks across the Copper River. The sound of the wind and water filled our little cove and every turn in the canyon's walls. We wondered if we had come before the salmon had really begun running.

"Thump!" Reb felt it. He wondered, "Is the net caught again on another rock, or … is it … a fish?" We all watched, anxiously, as he pulled his net up, breaking the surface of the water. "It IS! It's a FISH!" he shouted. The big, silvery red flipped wildly to get free. "He's a BEAUTY!" Reb twisted the net safely over the salmon and slid it up the face of the rock to me. Eagerly, I grabbed the fish by the gills just as Sarah yelled, "I got one!" But, we were amazed to see it was not one, but two fish that were leaping in her net. The extra weight made her pole bow, but she held on. Reb got over to her, and helped her lever the fish up to me, to do my assassin's duty.

Ben called from his nest above me, "Dad, get a king!" Reb and Sarah kept me busy. The fish were on a run. Pushing her pole hand over hand up to me, Sarah thrust her net into my lap to empty it out again and again. We yelled out the fish count as each one was caught, "Fourteen!" Because the fishing was so much fun, I dreaded reaching the limit of thirty. When, in years past, only Clint and I had gone to Chitina, I was the one who limited out for the family but, now, Sarah was neck-and-neck with Dad, and I was the handler. They were keeping me running so much that I hardly had time to kill and bag the fish.

Reb yelled, "I'VE GOT A KING!"

"Great!" we shouted, and turned quickly as the net came up. Arched above the river's turbulence, the pole was bent with the weight of the prize. The 40-pound king bulged out of the net with its dorsal fin waving in the air. Reb turned with his load in his right hand, and bunched the rope, with his left hand, to scale the rock. He made sure to hold the struggling giant tightly. We crept over the shale to see the impressive king salmon.

Slowly, the run came to an end. The children and I went stumbling off toward the tent to get out of the cold wind and the bugs. Stiff with exhaustion, we zipped the tent netting shut and fell into our bags.

Reb sat fishing until 2 A.M., numb with cold and fatigue. Waiting for the last few salmon to be caught, he was barely able to hold his net in the Copper River. At 6 A.M., after only a four-hour break, he was out of the tent again. Hours later, we found him quietly sitting on his slab of rock where we brought him hot coffee and breakfast.

Sarah and I relieved him while he ate in the morning sun. Once we reached our limit, we divided the fish into packs and strapped the weight on our backs. Then, gripping our ropes, we pulled our loaded bodies up the dirt and willow cliff, resting momentarily in the grove of trees above.

Trip after trip, we loaded the silvery bodies into the old freezer, packed with homemade ice in the back of the truck, postponing the cleaning until we got home. When we were finished, we refreshed ourselves at the bottom of the waterfall, washing off slime, silt, and greasy bug dope.

While rinsing off, I remembered a much harder trip we made before the canyon could be driven, when 12-year-old Clint and I had done all the fishing. Another time, in 1990, I had eased my body on a rope down the vertical rock face just above the roaring Copper. Sarah had guarded me, watching in case of accident as I fished alone on the precipice. She had sat above me in the stand of trees, sometimes dozing.

Now, we try to watch for an opening on the calendar when Reb can be free from forest fires and go with us to be our chief fisherman at Chitina.

As I drove home, letting Reb sleep, I remembered a beautiful night of fishing the previous July. At 2 A.M., the Fergusons had all scrambled over the rocks from a protected bend where we had been dip netting in the canyon for hours. I looked back where we had been. The moon was full over the dark Copper River below. Higher up, the old railroad tracks emerged out of the mountain in the moonlight. Higher still, on the other side of the river, jagged, black peaks majestically cut this canyon off from the rest of Alaska.

Chitina is a sanctuary of cascading waterfalls, where the mountains push the river through a gauntlet of narrow turns. It is an ancient fishing spot and a river to respect. At home, by our gentler Tanana River, I smoked and canned salmon. Jars of smoked salmon would be ready for lunch salads and sandwiches during the long, cold winter.

Chapter Fifty Seven
BERRY PATCH

139. Vera Berezyuk picking blueberries like in Ukraine, ca. 1995.

Berry picking is more than scooping berries; it's gathering sunshine for long, winter months. In the fading sunlight, it's one of the last times on the warm mountainside before we go indoors for the winter.

The blueberries, raspberries, and cranberries we gather are little packages of solar energy from among the golden grasses of fall. It is also mothers' time-out. While the mothers gather, the children wrestle and roll through the berries, playing in bush forts. The women savor the peace and joy of being outside, away from chores, with nothing pressing. The jams and pies are extra dividends for later in the winter.

Carol Walter, whom I have known for thirty-five years, introduced me to the berry patch and taught me to make jams without commercial pectin. Carol lives deep in the Bush and only comes in once a year. In 1973, she flew in for her annual shopping trip. From our home upriver, we rode my horses to go berry picking over the mountains behind our homestead at Thompson Lake. Carol's 2-year-old son rode in front of her and my 3-year-old son was in front of me.

It was a long ride and the berries were past their prime. We picked blueberries around the lake, packed our berry buckets into the saddlebags, and then started back home. The last mountain we had to descend was long and steep. I turned to look back and to my fright, I saw Carol and her baby riding a horse that was leapfrogging, back and forth, across the face of that steep grade. I was horrified. "Get off, Carol, get off!!" I hollered. Quickly, they slid off, and we walked home, leading the horses and carrying our blueberries, trying to keep them from being ruined.

Later, over my two-burner stove, we cooked an experiment in my cast-iron pot. Rose hips and high bush cranberries simmered, as we added only sugar, cinnamon, cloves, and nutmeg. As we brewed up Alaskan apple butter, Carol had a hunch the rose hips could be substituted for the apples the recipe required. Her recipe did not call for pectin and it was wonderful as a condiment with meat or slathered on hot biscuits.

But, Carol lives several hundreds of miles away in the Bush, and it is not easy to find companions who like to get stickers in their knees, swat bugs, and pick berries in an all-day marathon. My friend, Judy, however is one who -- like I -- cherish it as one of the highlights of the year.

Additionally, Judy Grapengeter has six boys which considerably increases Ben's enthusiasm for berry picking. During the winter, we stretch our berries with rhubarb to make them last the season.

My Ukrainian friend, Vera, also loves to pack up and go berry picking. Vera has lived not only in Ukraine, but also in Estonia, while I was raised on the other side of the globe. When two people speak different languages, have been raised on opposite sides in the Cold War atmosphere, and yet, discover a fraternity that goes beyond culture, language, and political systems, it is a miracle. I grew up hearing the air raid siren during its weekly test, as we lived across the street from the Civil Defense System. Any day, it seemed, Russian bombs might drop from the sky. Vera's family had similar fears. Vera's oldest daughter, Antonina, had nightmares that the American bombers might invade their territory also at any moment. The political tactics of fear are effective.

As we became friends in the warmth and relaxation of the berry patch, we laughed with her daughters, Olga and Tamela. Vera was delighted to find a sea of berries in Alaska as plentiful as any back home in Ukraine.

Months later, Sarah, and her school friend, Christine Winston, made Christmas batches of jam. The assortment of preserves - the sparkling, dark red raspberry and deep purple blueberry - was sent to family members for Christmas. Jam was the mid-winter coup resulting from those last moments of sunshine, when women talk and children roll in the berries - a harvest from a time set apart.

Chapter Fifty Eight
CANNING IN THE BUSH

Canning Summer's Bounty Enriches Winter Mealtimes

Turnips, sauerkraut, tomatoes, and rhubarb; peppers, greens, squash, and celery: the garden cornucopia overflowed in the fall. There was enough work for every family member.

In 1973, our only refrigeration was our root cellar, and the freezer was a small rental locker in Delta, 14 miles by boat, then truck from our upriver home. I canned what I could not store in the dirt cellar under our floor.

140. Sarah canning peaches at downriver home, c. 1996.

I depended on a food preservation book, *Putting Foods By*, which talked to me; it did not simply dictate instructions.

Having grown up in the city, I knew nothing of canning, drying, salting or smoking, though my two grandmothers' musty cellars had always been full of sealed fruit jars. Moreover, my father's

141. Reb rototilling garden at Outpost home, ca. 1997.

mother, a widow, had raised seven children through the 1930s Depression in Dust Bowl Oklahoma. One of her tools was a pressure cooker that she passed on to me in 1970.

One morning, I told Reb I wanted to can moose stew. However, hours later, I was still sitting in my rocking chair, scrutinizing the *Ball Canning Book*, trying to understand basic canning principles and the golden rules of handling meat preserva-tion.The two small para-graphs of instructions really contained orders for two days worth of work.

At that time, all of our drinking water came from the rainwater we collected off the roof. Wastewater had to be carried outside. When I canned, I continually hauled fresh water in and refuse water out. I used my Home Comfort wood range and had ample burners for my canning needs, but I had to wear a sundress. Sweat rolled off my face from having the kitchen at melt down temperatures in the summertime. Once, after I had loaded all the zucchini and tomato sauce into seventeen jars, the pressure in the cooker just would not build. Perhaps there was a petcock leak or the gauge was broken. I did not know.

I showed pressure, even if the cooker did not. After slaving over that hot stove for hours, I sprinted out into the field and collapsed into the grass. My husband noticed I had a problem and kindly fixed it.

The lesson for that day: it is not a bad idea to thoroughly examine canning equipment before the critical moment.

Broccoli and cauliflower should only be frozen. When Ben was 7, he started helping us blanch broccoli to take to our freezer in town.

At first, Sarah helped with canning, but by the time she was 20, she did the greater portion of the canning program.

Drying vegetables was as easy as throwing celery leaves on top of window screens suspended from the ceiling. The thicker, chopped celery stalks had to be dried in the oven on the lowest heat. Some homesteaders dry cole crops - broccoli, cabbage, and cauliflower - but it is only a method to use when all other methods are unavailable.

Jeannette Brasier, a homesteader across the Tanana, taught me that a boiling water bath makes pickles soft. Instead, she recommended heating the pickle liquid and then pouring it over cucum-bers, letting them heat through for a few minutes. Next, she drains them (keeping the liquid), cov-ers the cucumbers, re-heats the solution, and pours it over the vegetables again. Then, she inverts the jar with its rubberized lid, and lets it cool. She says you do not need the boiling water bath because "nothing can live in all that vinegar."

Jams are a different matter. The University Extension Service says that some molds can be harmful, so I use a short boiling water bath on the jams. Ever since Carol and I experimented, our family makes spiced apple butter by juicing rose hips and high bush cranberries. At Christmas, we mail the tangy, fruit butter to relatives, along with jars of Alaskan blueberry and raspberry jam.

Smoking fish intrigued me when I saw it done during our trip on the Yukon River. Reb made a new smokehouse while Ben cut and peeled the sweet smelling, hardwood alders for smoking fish. I prepared a brown sugar brine with Christmas spices. After I took the filleted salmon out of the brine, I laid them on racks where a blowing fan sealed their flesh; then, they went into the hot smoke until they were sufficiently dehydrated that when they were bent, they snapped.

Cookbooks generally advise against canning fish. Stability of the pressure during canning is essential. For canning, in general, if the pressure in the cooker varies, liquid seeps out of the jars, making a bad seal. With fish, the heat must not fluctuate even a pound; if it does, the cook has to start the pressure-cooking all over again.

The Embarcadero Canning system was the end of canning stress for me! A wonderful genius improvised a propane burner connected with a rubber tube to the open petcock of a pressure cooker. The thermostatically controlled device gauges the flame relative to the pressure cooker's setting and then, regulates the burner accordingly. I need only look at my pressure gauge every fifteen minutes to assure myself that the pressure is maintaining at an even 10 pounds. For further information, contact: Embarcadero Home Cannery, 2026 Livingston, Oakland, Ct. 94606; (510) 535-2311.

Similar to fish, but not as delicate, canning game can also be tricky. When we took Sarah and Ben on our summer, family trapline trip cutting trail, we arrived at Gilles Creek cabin and had a wilderness feast. Bill Arrington had left several jars of rich moose meat, each containing an inch of fat. The hot meat was succulent garnished with low bush cranberry relish and macaroni. We ate in the evening under the trees overlooking Gilles Creek, happy as kings, listening to the wind and the water. Since we had been walking in the mountains for two weeks, we could afford the fat!

A high point in the growing season was the annual Delta Fair. Sarah and Ben got their peas and onions in the ground no later than May 11th. By the end of July, their vegetables were mature enough to take Grand Champion at the Delta Fair.

The children and I like rooting around in the soil during the summer: weeding, snacking, and listening to cassette tapes. The reward is looking at the root cellar, seeing the walls lined with jars of red tomatoes, yellow squash, turnip greens, and the rich brown of mincemeat. The storage bins exude the fresh smell of carrots and potatoes, heads of cabbage, and dried onions. It's the last ritual before snow.

Judy Ferguson and Carol Walters Highbush Cran-Apple Butter

(Using applesauce or rose hip puree)
8 cups, juiced high bush cranberries
1 cup of water (just enough to keep berries from burning)
4 cups applesauce or rose hip puree
6 cups of sugar (taste to maybe reduce sugar)
1 teaspoon cinnamon
½ teaspoon cloves
½ teaspoon salt
1 lemon, grated rind and juice

Prepare jar lids.

If a juicer is available, run the berries through a juicer, or if not, boil berries and water together until berries pop and are soft. Put through a sieve or food mill to remove seeds. Do the same with the rose hips.

Heat berry and rose hip pulp (or applesauce) together, adding sugar, cinnamon, cloves, and salt to taste. Simmer until thick. Remove from heat and add the lemon juice and grated rind. Spoon into hot jars, leaving ¼ -inch headspace. Wipe jar rims, and add prepared two-piece lids. Process for 15 minutes in boiling water canner.

Chapter Fifty Nine
SEASONS OF THE TANANA

142. The Tanana at confluence with Delta River, bluff, Alaska Range and Mount Hayes.

When we first built our home upriver, I remarked to my electrified friend, Diane Hansen, "Now, I can sit on my porch and watch the Tanana change from winter to spring and summer to fall." Not interested in such passivity at age 26, Diane remarked, "Oh, big deal." She was right, but for me sitting by the river was healing. For thirty-five years, I have lived close to the Tanana; I have come to know it well.

During a cold snap, our family watched a lone merganser flying over the Tanana's open waters. At -50° F., the only living thing in view, he searched, in the ice fog, for a fish. Mergansers, who habitually winter over in our area, are no longer the only waterfowl that do. Two hundred mallards have also discovered the warm springs of the river. During the winter, all of the Tanana River usually freezes solid, except for one area. Originating from the Nabesna and Chisana Rivers in far eastern Alaska, the Tanana, in its remaining 438 miles, only has significant open portions, free of solid ice, near Rika's Roadhouse at Big Delta.

According to Craig Mishler's book, *Born With the River*, early Athabascans called the Tanana, Tey Nda' or "trail river." The Delta's large salmon run spills over into the Tanana adding to its other fish varieties. Historically, it was a fish camp for the Tanana River Athabascans long before the Caucasians built Rika's Roadhouse, or today's Alyeska Pipeline bridge. Now, returning with the swans and geese, today's recreational fishermen have come to catch their grayling limit. They relax in the April sun, watching the eagles that ride the currents high above the ancient bluff.

In 1981, 4 miles upstream on another bluff, our family enjoyed the spring sun on our faces as Reb read to us. Four-year-old Sarah let her Dad lean his head against her shoulder as he told her of the first time she saw the new budding leaves of spring. After Sarah's first traumatic winter of life, we had been relieved when she could welcome spring like any 5-month-old baby. Just as she had fingered the unfurling buds then -- as she listened to her Dad now -- she handled the purple crocus with the little yellow centers growing from cracks in the rocky outcrop.

As the balmy spring breeze ruffled our clothes, Reb read to us from *Ten Thousand Miles with a Dog Sled*, a 1913 book by Hudson Stuck, an itinerant Episcopalian missionary. Stuck described the Tanana's open waters near Rika's: "A river difficult to navigate in summer is usually a river difficult to travel upon in winter, and the Upper Tanana is notoriously dangerous and treacherous … It is emphatically a 'bad river.' Therefore, as far as there is any travel to speak of, land trails parallel the river … past the mouth of the Big Delta [traveling from the northwest] with the great bluff on the opposite shore and the rushing black water at its foot that never entirely closes all the winter … we came at length to McCarty's, the last telegraph station on the river … and here we leave the government-made trail and take to the river surface and the wilderness."

As Reb finished reading, we looked down at the Tanana flowing below us in a sweeping S-shape, capriciously carrying ice around the base of the bluff between our home and our neighbor's, the Ashbys.

The open confluence of the Delta and Tanana rivers has historically been the site for the year's last chum salmon spawn within the Yukon drainage. As many as eleven to thirty thousand fish arrive well into December, leaving their spawned-out bodies in the shallow waters at the mouth of the Delta River. Their carcasses had once been our dog food. Today they were the food for the ravens and eagles that swooped down, crying over the Delta's braided channels.

The salmon eggs lured grayling, which migrated as far as 70 miles, preferring to over winter in large numbers in the spring-fed waters of the Tanana. In November, bald eagles sat quietly in the ice fog, poised on naked trees, scanning the waters for dinner. Mink tracks laced the snow along the Tanana's open shoreline. Fish and slithery otters squeezed out of the ice through tiny holes wherever there was open water.

When everything else was in deep freeze, this oasis was a haven for wildlife. Ice fog formed when the warmer water met the -50° F. air above. Farther upstream, nine tenths of the river froze, pushing the roiling current, now a torrent, against the riverbank of our downriver home. We lay awake nights unnerved by the roaring rapids --potentially erosive to our riverbank -- rolling over snarled, frozen trees. In January, the water level dropped once again and the tempest became a subdued channel, a companion.   In that quiet water, in April, thousands of salmon fry squirmed in the shallow pools just an inch from our bank.

For Ben, a sign of spring was setting a burbot line in a quiet eddy at the foot of a Tanana bluff. His weighted hook sank out of sight as he anchored its string to a nearby spruce tree, hoping for a lingcod the next morning. Boiled or fried, this eel-like delicacy melted in our mouths, like fresh Tanana lobster.

In May, the sandbars vibrated with hundreds of ducks and geese, resting from their marathon flight. Our boat disturbed them ... and their wings began to rustle. Soon, they glided to a safer sandbar, out of our reach. A beaver tail slapped the river just as Mount Hayes, Mount Deborah, and Mount Hess came into our view in the sun's slanting rays.

A mallard and his mate flew low. In June, they scooted wildly from our boat, with eight fuzzy ducklings propelling behind them. It is a season of transition, a time to travel Tey Nda', a spring-fed trail river, a home to Alaskan wildlife and its people.

Chapter Sixty
OVERFLOW

verflow!" The word strikes alarm to the musher's heart. Throughout the winter, sub-terranean water seeks release, oozing over the edges of the frozen waterways, creating stratifications of ice. Masked by fluffy snow, and appearing even in the extreme cold, the icy water lies beneath the snow and under thin ice, a nasty trap; ready to soak a musher in sub zero temperatures.

When Reb was still a bachelor, he was mushing on a -30° F. day up Keystone Creek to check his traps. He saw a half-inch of overflow snaking its way downstream. Reb's lead dog hated getting his paws wet, so the dog left the middle of the frozen creek and headed for the land. Suddenly, the dog was swimming in 18 inches of overflow. The trail quickly melted from beneath the dogs, and Reb was immediately in icy water over his canvas mukluks and up to his knees. Getting his soggy team out, he turned around and headed 7 miles back to his nearest cabin. The

chill of his ice-encrusted clothing began to seep into his feet and legs and rubbed uncomfortably as he noisily trudged up the slopes and down the mountains. When he approached the cabin, he was so cold that he mushed straight inside the cabin: team, sled, and all.

He fumbled with his freezing hands, anxiously making a fire in the wood stove. Then, desperately he pulled at his mukluks, but his frigid feet were held prisoner in the heavy, ice casts. He propped them up on the warming stove and watched as the ice began to dollop onto the floor. Finally freed from the

143. Caribou Creek overflowed into Caribou Cabin, filled 3/4ths of it with ice and jammed the door shut, 1997.

mukluks, his toes tingled with the delicious warmth as he massaged them near the open door of the wood stove.

In 1997, Ray Lewis, who lived on the Nowitna River, was not so fortunate. Snowshoeing across an overflowed creek, Ray gambled that his snowshoes would glide across the unstable surface. His crossing, however, was slowed down as he made several trips across piggybacking his wife and three young daughters. As he gambled, pushing to make one last trip, he sank through the soft layer up to his waist in water. On the bank, they made a small fire and wrung out Ray's mukluks. Then, they hurried to keep to their schedule. Ray had lost his snowshoe binding and had jury-rigged a cloth hitch for it instead, but it cinched down too tightly on his left foot. That night, at their line camp, Ray discovered that two of his toes were frozen solid. Miles away from professional help, he and his wife, Cindy, doctored the foot. His toes were salvaged and he is continuing to recover.

Light, canvas mukluks are easier for walking than heavy, clodhopper bunny boots. But since -- on a recent snow machining trip we would be riding -- Reb and I wore the heavier boots. As we traveled up Caribou Creek, open water began to appear and Reb walked ahead to see if this was the end of the line with the machines. But, we could splash our way on the snowmobiles through 8 inches of overflow, enjoying the sun-splashed spring day. Our machines crunched across the lacy ice that decorated the smooth folds of frozen overflow.

Abruptly, we came to our cabin, but it looked strange, stunted somehow, in a wasteland of white. In the summer, this was a trickling creek sunk in the valley's crooked gut, the melted ice vein, Caribou Creek. Usually, we walked across our log bridge to an elevated bench, a protected location for the cabin's site. That day, there was not even a dip in the crossing to the cabin, but only a flat, icy plane that flowed straight to and halfway up the cabin door. There was no getting in. A frozen ocean was against the door.

Lying on our bellies on the ice, we peered through the tiny window in our cabin and were stunned to see an inside skating rink. The stove was totally out of sight, encased under the ice, and the frozen pallet across our beds was not at all inviting to tired travelers. Only the table, the bedposts, and the stovepipe could be seen.

"The logs will insulate all that ice," Reb said, "and it will be August before it's entirely melted."

As we left, I thought how overflow is such a paradox. Valleys with muskeg and ornery creeks that make summer passage really difficult are smoothed out with the ice and snow of winter, making travel almost easy. On the other hand, I was grateful it was not the evening of a short December day arriving by dog sled to a cabin choked with ice, but a beautiful day in March and we were headed home by snow machine.

144. Clint's first Dall sheep ram, 1988

Chapter Sixty One
CLINT'S GRADUATION

Since Reb had guided Dall sheep hunters for many years, he knew there were no guarantees of getting a ram, and certainly, not on the first day.

Clint had just graduated from high school. For a gift, Reb chartered Harvey Wieler to fly the two of them to Mount Hayes in the Alaska Range where Reb had once guided. When they landed, two other hunters had a ram already, which further whet Clint's appetite for the hunt.

The next day, when Reb and Clint hiked up a valley, they spotted four rams. Because it was steep, Reb figured they might approach head-on. They had gotten fairly close when the sheep started to move. "Get on the ridge above them; I'll chase them toward you," Reb whispered. Clint ran around and up, and Reb chased the sheep to him. "Bang!" But, the ram rolled downhill and it was just before dark. They tracked it, finding nothing, when night forced them back to camp.

"The next day," Reb said, "when we returned, we glassed with binoculars, but saw nothing." Finally, on a little knoll, there was a little patch of white. When they reached it, they felt its warm belly and knew it had just died.

"Oh, Clint was so proud," Reb smiled. "I told him how hard it was to get a sheep the first day out.

"But then," he continued, "I had to get one. That took nine more days. We made a spike camp, a day's hike out from our base camp, and hunted from there."

Reb described, "One day, Clint returned to base camp to get some groceries. On the return, he shot us a mess of ptarmigan and brought them back to eat.

"With our larder replenished," Reb continued, "we followed a valley to the Wood River. And, there were three, gorgeous rams there, about 300 yards away, but it wasn't a good shot." Warming to the chase, Reb said, "As the rams lay there, I could see their heads and shoulders. I figured they'd get up pretty soon, so I just waited. I waited all day for that good shot. They never got up, so finally, I said, 'Let's go back to camp; it's getting dark.' We had a long way to go.

Pausing, he continued, "We started downhill, and oh, my gosh, there were three or four more rams there, right beneath me. With my heart racing, I ran down. A beautiful, full curl ram was right in front of me, 100 yards away; I just squeezed a shot off and down he went. It was just about dark. We gutted him. By the time we got the cape off, the night was pitch black. It was a long walk down, following a creek, to camp. The next day, we returned for the rest of the meat."

Using the Citizen's Band radio, Reb called me a few days later as they waited in the car by the Tanana. I left 11-year-old Sarah in charge of 4-year-old Ben, while I ran the boat downriver. Waiting on the shoreline, I saw two men with matching, ¾ curl rams: my 18-year-old son with his first Dall sheep, and alongside him, the old wolf, the veteran guide.

Chapter Sixty Two
THE BUFFALO
HUNT AND THE PREACHER

n 1928, John Hajdukovich helped bring a herd of bison - buffalo - to Delta to supplement the Natives' dwindling food supply. They flourished, and by the 1960s, it had become the largest, free-roaming herd in the United States that can be hunted. A decade later, as a member of the Delta Junction Fish and Game Advisory Committee, Charlie Boyd fought to protect the animals from competing agricultural and poaching interests. To regulate the harvest of the buffalo, State of Alaska Fish and Game holds an annual permit drawing in which 100-130 buffalo are selected annually for harvest.

In 1987-8, Reb was drawn for a buffalo permit. He drove out to the herd several times, but they had been hunted and they were spooky. Reb had to stalk them several times. On one trip, he asked our pastor, Bill, and a friend, Bob, to accompany him on a hunt.

Just off the road, Reb and Bob lay behind a snow-covered berm and began inching their way, on their bellies, toward the herd. Bill napped in the car and then wearing unlaced Bunny Boots, he got out to find the hunters. After stalking the herd for an hour, and just when

145. Reb and the buffalo, shot with borrowed rifle, 1988.

Reb and Bob were lying within shooting distance, Bill walked out to the field in full view shuffling through the snow, filling his unlaced boots with snow as he walked. Together, the three lay on the frozen ground for hours, watching the buffalo and waiting for some to drift close. With freezing feet, stiff, and out of patience, Bill goaded Reb, "You don't really want to shoot a buffalo!" With that, Bill trounced back to the car to warm up, but even the car's poor heater was no help. When Reb and Bob got to the car, Bill's feet had chilled his whole body. Reb said, "Hand me your boots, Bill." Reb poured hot tea into each rubber, heavily insulated boot, and said, "Now, try it, Bill." "Ahhhh," was the contented response.

Suddenly dubbed Buffalo Bill, Bill resumed his role as preacher while Reb and Bob returned the next day to the hunt. At the critical moment, Reb's gun froze up. He hissed, "Hey, Bob, can I use your rifle?" With another man's gun, Reb brought down his prize bull buffalo.

Chapter Sixty Three

IN THE MIDST
OF THE MIGHTY

When I met Reb Ferguson in 1968, he had Dall sheep horns on his wall, a definite coup of Alaska big game hunting. Whether Reb took clients, or later, our sons, he never returned from the field empty-handed.

In 1990, Reb wanted to increase his natural accuracy and purchased a .308 Stire, with set, double-triggers and a Redfield, Acu-Track scope. Not only did he have high precision sighting, but also he could set the triggers before shooting to lessen the jarring of his aim.

He asked Harvey Wieler to fly us into the Robertson River Valley. I entrusted Sarah and Ben to friends; left my domestic world, and climbed into Harvey's Super Cub. I was 45 years old, chilled easily, and worried about becoming lost in fog on a glacier.

As we flew low, the Robertson River, thirty miles west of Tok, unfolded before us. We set down on a sandbar below the glacier. As the plane left, and the sound disappeared into the waning light of September, the silence of the glacial valley enveloped us. We put up our tent in the protective brush and were lulled to sleep by the roar of the nearby river.

The next day, I packed dry gear in a heavy pack and struggled up the glacial moraine behind Reb.

The pea-sized gravel made walking hard; the moraine's rocks bruised my feet. The pack dug into my shoulders. When we saw some ewes on the slopes, we dug our feet into the steep turf and clawed our way uphill for a better view.

On the fifth day, Reb spotted three regal, full-curl rams. We climbed, crossing the loose shale of the steep mountainsides; scaling sheer, rock faces and crouched below the sheep, out of the reach of their keen eyesight. Within rifle range, we hoisted our packs, and finally eased ourselves up over the lip of an overhang, and then onto a shelf. Relying on his naked eye, Reb breathed in, and touched off the set triggers. "Zing!" The projectile hit high above the sentinel ram. The lower ram woke suddenly as a second bullet ricocheted to his left and then bounced like an insane pinball down the slope. In a flash, the white monarchs flew up the sheer face of the rock and disappeared as if they had never existed.

Leaning against the mountain to balance my load, I crumpled with fatigue and disappointment. The folly of scrambling up and down mountains, on a trip that cost as much as a ticket to Paris, only to get skunked in a wasteland seemed a bitter joke.

For the next few days, we stayed in a high spike camp on a mountain shelf overhanging the glacier, opposite where we had first spotted the rams. We euphorically hiked in the fall alpine vegetation, lifting our wings in the balmy winds that swept across the mountaintops.

Then, the rain began to pour. We were above the tree line, so it was impossible to make a fire because of a lack of fuel. To conserve body heat, we confined ourselves to our sleeping bags. Hourly, insidious moisture, like a threatening ghost, leaked its way from the tent walls into our only insulation, our down bags.

Adding to my anxiety, I heard the sound of airliners above me, hourly it seemed. I wondered how could so many jets be passing overhead? Under us, rumbling deep in the earth, the glacier talked. As the ice moved during the dark night, I fretted. The creek could be flooding. The mountains could

146. Judy pointing to missed Dall sheep ram, Robertson River Glacier, 1990.

be pouring waterfalls. The gush of sky and earth could have transformed the valley; locked inside these tent walls as I slept, I would never know. Under and around me, the planet had become an alien force.

On the fourth day, the earth was quiet. With difficulty, we unzipped the tent door, but found we were encased in snow and ice. We broke camp, and by evening we were at our base camp's tent.

But it was not over. Reb decided we could look for game on the far side of the river. A hunter had told us before we flew in that he had left an inflatable raft stashed under some rocks on this side of the river.

With my pack on, and feeling some apprehension, I followed Reb toward the river the next morning. The river looked shallow, not too wide, maybe a little swift. We blew up the raft, placed our cheap paddles and our packs inside, and then climbed in.

In a snap, the current tore us away and threw us into the watery torrent. We zipped from the stream into a new channel, bouncing from one bank to the other, going at break-neck speed to God-knows-where. Powerless, with a worthless paddle, I cried, "Reb! Save us!"

He clawed for a nearing shore, grasped it with one hand and dug his foot into the shifting riverbed against the raging water. Desperately holding the raft, he shouted, "My leg can't hold!"

But somehow, we grabbed a handhold and threw ourselves onto the shore. There was no explanation how Reb had done it; there must have been some extra help from above. We unloaded the raft, drydocked the dime store craft and lay, exhausted, and incredibly grateful, on the solid land.

In the warm sun, contemplating the living glacier and the severe, barren mountain heights, I thought of the scripture, "What is man that You are mindful of him?"

Days later, a plane returned us home - to domesticity. We left behind the mountains of the moon, where sheep, not men, are at home in the lap of a wild planet.

Chapter Sixty Four

FERGUSON DALL SHEEP OUTING

n 1996, Ben was lucky to draw a Dall sheep hunting permit. Fly-in areas were expensive to access, while walk-in drainages were over hunted. We wanted a family, fall hike, and did not have much time, so we opted to pack into Bear Creek in the Alaska Range. Ten-year-old Ben shouldered a 30-pound pack, while I had 35-pounds, and Reb and tall, strong, 18-year-old Sarah carried more. Reb gave Sarah a hand as she placed her foot on rocks, slippery with moss and running water. As the canyon narrowed, Ben dropped his pack and leapt up a moss wall to pick me a lavender Moss Campion flower.

Our feet flexed over miles of rocks, flattening under our loads. Around a bend, Sarah and Ben watched nannies and kids feed at a natural salt lick. We left the valley behind and searching for toeholds, we inched our way up a mountain. On top, the lichen, brush, and berries were a diffusion of wine and yellow colors. Running like incongruous patches of white, kids and nannies cavorted on the hidden tableland and down along valleys. We hunkered down on a rock shelf, and surveyed the valley and the river beyond.

As we followed the undulating plateau, Ben ran with the Dall kids. When we topped the exposed expanse of the mountain, the wind hit us like a cold wall, driving us backwards. Our eyes ran with tears and we pulled our hands into our sleeves. For lunch, we turtled in a shallow ravine, rolling up against the ground to keep our bodies barely warm. As Reb and Ben glassed the surrounding ridges with binoculars, they saw a ram, but he was across another valley.

As we took in the spectacular, 360-degree view of the Alaska Range, we reasoned it was still sufficiently early to catch the end of caribou hunting season. We had not seen enough rams to warrant camping for a week. When we awoke the following day, we were blanketed with snow. We returned home to get the horses and let them do the heavy work packing after caribou.

Chapter Sixty Five

HORSEBACK INTO SUMMER DAYS

had a horse before I knew Reb. When we met, our lives converged around a horse. During our early days of courting, we used to ride double at top speed around the old military pipeline Timber Station, shooting his .44 Magnum, running through the ditches, and then jumping into the gravel pit, still on the horse, as he began to swim in the deep water. We always found the money to have horses, whether we could afford doing laundry or not. We had our priorities. We went through a string of horses over thirty-five years: Klondike, Cimarron, Amigo, Rojo, Black, Clancy, Yahna, and Aussie. Klondike was with us twenty-four years. He helped us build our home and our trapping cabins. Today, our classiest horse is Clancy - a black, flashy, part Percheron horse.

147. Ben, Sarah and Judy upriver, returning horses to winter quarters at Brasiers', 1997.

Too lazy to feed and water the horses through the harsh winter, we farm them out to our dear neighbors, the Brasiers, who are farmers and are feeding and watering stock anyway. Every spring, we ride the horses upriver to their home pasture.

The spring of 1996, Sarah rode Clancy; Ben rode the gentle mare, Yahna; and I saddled up Black, Clint's horse. We rode through the tall, wild grass along the power line, singing my traditional song, "Back In the Saddle Again," followed by, "Head 'Em Up, Move 'Em Out, E'yah, Rawhide!" The old leather of the reins felt good in my hands, leaving its familiar greasy dirt, while our bodies swayed with the rhythmic glide of the horses' gait. Horseflies buzzed around the oozing, horsey sweat, and I scratched Black's mane as I rode.

Black gave me friendly side-glances between alternately flicking his ears back at me. He knew where we were going. It was the annual migration to the new feeding grounds.

We walked the horses over the Tanana Bridge, and then melted into the woods. Cares slid off my shoulders. I only sensed the drone of insects in the luxurious heat of the day.

In our saddlebags, we had packed precautionary raingear, along with critical bug dope, and snacks for lunch. Remembering once when I got caught in a thunderstorm, I had had to crouch down on my horse under a scrub spruce, thankful for my wide-brim hat as rain and hail beat down on me. But today, there was not a cloud in the sky.

When we built our early trap cabins, Clint was a baby. We had lived in in the saddle with Clint tied to me in case of jostling. I sang songs to him with his pacifier safely anchored to my shirt and his bottle in my pocket. We had lived in the saddle for weeks while we cut trails through the deep woods of our trapline. Now, on our spring trek, I still preferred the woodland trails, swamp and all, rather than ride a gravelled, car-infested road. The trails were also better on our horses' unshod feet.

That spring, we ducked through the woods onto a swampy trail made by a Caterpillar, paralleling Quartz Lake road, and turned right into the woods for home. We clutched the mane of our respective horses as they grunted up a series of 70° angle hills. On top, we stopped for lunch on the grassy, mountain Cat road. We broke out some C-Rations. For dessert, the kids wrestled over who got the M &M's. I laid back and listened to the gentle munching of the tired horses as they grazed. The woods were pungently sweet with Labrador Tea, Rosebay, and Wintergreen.

After lunch we swung onto the horses, and as we neared home, the dogs started barking, heralding our approach. The horses picked up speed, cutting close to the spruce and dangerously close to the scraggly branches. Zigging and zagging through the dense forest, we felt almost surprised as we broke into the clearing of our homestead.

The soothing breeze off the Tanana River blessed our tired eyes. The unsaddled horses shook off the memory of their burdens, and rolled in their old dirt circles, long ago rubbed free of grass. They were home. It was the beginning of a new summer.

Chapter Sixty Six

MIRACLE ON KODIAK

After he graduated from high school, Clint was living not too far from us. For a long time, he and Reb had wanted to go deer hunting on Kodiak Island. Although Clint had to work, he was able to get vacation. In October 1989, he, Reb, and Larry Dorshorst flew to Kodiak. They chartered a Widgeon - an airplane that could land on its belly in water - to deliver them into Ugak Bay, off Kodiak's south side. They carried their gear, wading through the water, and onto the island. Tall grasses on the hills were blowing in the sea breeze, backed by high mountains. Reb, Clint, and Larry had the use of a cabin, an important asset, due to Kodiak's frequent storms. They began what Reb called, "Many sheep hunts rolled into one." Day after day, they hiked mountains, looking for trophy deer.

A gunshot on Kodiak is an automatic dinner bell to the bears. Reb had just shot at a deer, and missed. Shortly after, a huge Kodiak bear reared up on its hind legs, peered at Clint, sniffed the air, and sidled back to his fishing stream.

Day after day, Reb, Larry, and Clint climbed the tussocky island, shooting animals, and packing meat back to camp. Every day, Clint had been wanting to follow a particular valley that was not as inviting to Reb. One evening, Clint wanted to pursue it. Reb agreed to wait where he was if Clint returned in a reasonable time. "But," he cautioned, "if you don't come back this way, and if you should need a shorter route back to camp, you can descend and go along the shoreline, but watch the tide. It comes right up to the rocks. You can only go that way if it's still light enough to see, and if you know the tide."

Clint stalked a nice buck, but shot him in the late evening. When he looked, the tide was in and it was almost dark. He decided to leave part of the deer, his jacket, and pistol. He shouldered some meat, hung his rifle off his pack frame, and made his way back to camp along the cliffs' rocks. Without a light, he was fighting blind, beating his way through a mass of Devil's Club plants, and feeling with his feet for good footing. A storm was coming in. In minutes, wearing no jacket, Clint was being pummeled by cold rain and a driving wind. His hands became raw, and the hours crawled by.

148. Reb and Clint, successful deer hunt on Kodiak, 1989.

Back at the cabin, Reb listened to the shrieking storm, and paced the floor, checking his watch. Several times he shot his gun as a signal, but there was no answer.

A friend at home, Howard Greenfield, suddenly felt the need to pray for Clint, as I also did. The sense lasted several hours.

Clint had crept across a rock with a hole it it. Suddenly, with no warning, his feet went out from under him; he fell through the hole, with the surf lapping far below. But, he was jerked to a halt when his rifle caught on the porous rock around him. The ends of Clint's gun hung up on either side of the rock outcrop and held him.

Once again, Reb shot his gun. Finally, at 10 P.M., in the sheeting rain and howling wind, muffled by the night, Reb heard one answering shot. Still, it was another hour before Clint returned. Finally, a haggard, drenched, young man appeared at the cabin door. Relieved to be safe, Clint began telling his story to a very thankful father, and to Larry.

The next day, despite a fierce storm, the three set out to find Clint's deer, pack, and pistol. Reb's knee had blown up to twice its normal size, suffering from the daily rigorous climbing. He waited as a landmark on the ridge, while Clint searched in the valley for his deer and pistol. Clint zigged and zagged; finally, he spotted it.

Several days later, the trio threw eleven gunnysacks of bloody, deer meat onto the baggage conveyor belt at the airport. "Don't worry," Reb assured the attendant, "it's deer meat." And with that, the heroes returned with bags of horns and provisions for the winter.

Chapter Sixty Six

REB FERGUSON LIVES

Mistakes made at 0° F. may be over-looked. The same errors made at -50° F. may be fatal. Traveling alone on our trapline, but without communication, if Reb were overdue, there was no way to know if he might need help.

On a trapline trip in the winter of 1989, Reb took a Motorola, two-way radio. The radiotelephone communicated off a radio repeater on a mountain, maintained, not by us, but by its owner. Reb and I agreed he would check in periodically.

The mercury plummeted to -50° F. I had heard from Reb once, but in the middle of a second transmission, he cut out, and I did not hear from him again. The radiotelephone owner swore to me, "If Reb were trying to call out, I absolutely would hear him making the

149. Reb flying down hill to Campbell's Cabin, 1981.

attempt. No question. I have heard nothing. Those batteries he has have thirty hours of life. There's no way that one call would've used up all of his supply. I don't think he has technological problems." I hung up the phone, contemplated sending 19-year-old Clint and a friend out looking for Reb, and dropped my head in my hands, and cried.

We decided to wait three more days to see if he showed up at Rosa Pass for us to pick him up as previously planned. But, I envisioned him with a broken leg, alone on the trail, freezing to death in only a few hours. The children and staff at my childrens' school, Whitestone, were praying.

A few days later, an ice-encrusted Reb Ferguson showed up on schedule at Rosa Pass. As his soft brown eyes looked out from frozen eyelashes, whiskers, and facemask, I kissed his snot-encrusted mouth; thankful to God he was okay.

To thank the children at Whitestone for their care and prayers, Reb wrote the following letter, which was later published in the school's newspaper.

Well, kids, I'm going to take you on an arctic adventure on the trapline. We can't just go out there. We've got to prepare: a 250-pound toboggan load of dog food, bait, snares, traps, gas, lantern fuel, sleeping bag, arctic clothing, chainsaw, food, and me. The dog harnesses are in good shape, but the toboggan needs a new brush bow - that is the front bumper.

November 2nd, we head out! I put all the dogs in the dog boxes that ride on the truck's pickup bed, and on top of that, I slid the toboggan onto the roof. We drive north, turn onto the pipeline corridor, and go as far as the road is maintained, a few miles from

150. Reb relaxing on pole bunk at Caribou Cabin, 1981.

Rosa Pass. I unload the sled from the top of the truck, load it with freight, and fasten it to the truck with a rope and a quick release snap. I lay out the tug line and harnesses, and secure the lead harness by a rope and snap to a tree. My dogs are raring to go. One by one, I hook them up to the sled. The taunt line helps to prevent tangling while they jump up and down in their harnesses. Judy waits by the lead dog. When I have harnessed the last dog, I pull the quick release snap that anchors the sled to the truck and nod to Judy. She releases the lead harness' tie-off line, and like a shot out of a cannon, I am gone.

Alone for two weeks! Just the seven huskies and me! I wonder what waits ahead.

I mush up the pipeline pad to Rosa Pass. I start to descend downhill, when I notice the pipeline gate is shut! I can't get under it without my back bow - the handle - hanging up on the pipeline's locked, steel pole. Deciding to quickly skirt it, I call to my lead dog, "Zeb! Hah!" He does what he's told, and heads to the left. Blocking our way, though, I see a boulder as huge as a car! I push, tug and grunt, and finally hoist the sled over the snowy boulder. Like a bat out of hell, my team wants to keep going downhill, but we have to make an abrupt, 90° turn. I holler to Zeb, "Gee!" We turn right and leave the pipeline corridor, but make the continued, and necessary, 180°, U turn onto my trail that breaks the dogs' direct pull on the sled. The sled quickly bottoms out in the deep snow and the dogs don't have the leverage to break it loose. Wading off the trail and over to the sled, I push and grunt, straightening up the sled until the dogs' line is once again tight and the sled is lined up, ready to go up the mountain again. The ascent is slow with lots of gut wrenching pushing and screaming at the dogs, "Let's go! Let's go!"

After an hour of maxing out, we finally glide easily onto the mountaintop. As we slide across the top, I can finally take time to notice there are some marten tracks near my old favorite set. My dogs wait. I open my sled box, dip a stick into the scent lure bottle, and grab some rotten meat. Like little houses in the woods, I make a cubby - walls of sticks running up against the base of the tree trunk with the meat and the trap at the base of the tree. I dip a stick into my marten lure bottle and smear some on the set. The marten will smell the strong meat and lure. He will investigate, but the walls of the cubby hedge in the meat. Trying to steal the meat, he will approach and

151. Lynx

place his foot on the pan of a steel trap. Marten feed on mice whose numbers vary greatly from year to year. When the mice population is high, the marten should be thinned to prevent the inevitable sickness and wasted death. When the numbers of mice are low, marten should be thinned to prevent their needless starvation. As I return to my sled, I hope that a marten will be there waiting for me when I return. Mushing up and down knolls, I intermittently set traps all over the top of the world.

As I ride the razorback of the ridge, to the south I can see Delta and Isabel Pass in the Alaska Range. To the north, I see the Salcha River drainage. Looking toward Fairbanks, I see a huge, ominous cloudbank moving in; it looks like lots of snow coming.

At the halfway point to Campbell's cabin, I pick up a sack of dog food, cached a few days earlier. Throwing it on the load, I start my descent through the fresh, unbroken trail, but at least I'm able to ride. On level ground, I steer by throwing my weight to the left, and then to the right. When going downhill, I ride the brake - two claws of steel attached to the underbelly of the sled - steering by varying where I dig in the brake. To stay on course, I drag my free foot like a rudder. The trail is riddled with low hanging branches; I hunker down below my sled bow through the low hanging arch of trees. Yelling "Whoa," I bump down at the bottom of the hill, and wind my way on an ancient moose trail to the cabin. The dogs pick up their pace when they wind a fresh moose scent. I see lots of fresh moose tracks in the snow. Rounding the bend of spruce, I see the cabin half buried in the snow.

I wonder if a bear has damaged the cabin, or may even still be inside. Ducking my head to get in the low doorway, I see a bear has gone through the Visqueen window in the back, but has left no serious damage. It's almost dark. I must get a fire going, chain up the dogs, haul the sled contents and harnesses into the cabin, grab a bucket of snow to melt, raid the cache drum for supper, put fresh Visqueen in the windows, light the Coleman lantern, and dry out my clothes. I settle in for a comfortable winter's night. For supper, Judy has packed me baked chicken and apple turnovers. I mix powdered milk with cold snow water. In the familiar, musty cabin atmosphere, I eat and turn in early at 8:00 P.M.

After sleeping for an hour, I realize I don't feel so good. I remembered talking to Jon Marhanka, the radioman, the day before and he complained of having 24-hour stomach flu, but I'm on the trapline! I can't have stomach flu! But still, I don't feel too good.

After a rough night's sleep, I get up about 7:00 A.M. I still feel rough. It's snowing pretty heavily out. I think, "If I lay over and pamper myself, it'll be much harder the next day on the trail because the snow will be deeper." So, I head out. I don't feel like eating, so I mix a half a cup of hot water with instant, dried oatmeal, and then drink melted snow water because I'm supposed to eat.

I snap the dogs' harnesses into their tug lines, get on the sled, and take off. We begin to climb the hills and the steep mountains again. Neither the dogs nor I have any strength. I push and strain, but I'm weakened by nausea. I know I've got to keep going. It's only 24-hour stomach flu and soon it should be over. After three hours of straining up the mountains, I finally crest out on

152. Caribou Cabin, 1981.

the ridge tops. Still feeling rough, I figure, at noon, I'll give the radiotelephone a test. I hear the voices of Judy, Sarah, Ben, and Mike and Joy Beebe! What a great comfort way out here in the hills to hear their voices. I start feeling better right away after talking to them. (Later, I found out they'd prayed for me.)

I continue slowly mushing and setting traps through the heavy snowfall. I keep mushing until the abruptly steep descent before Schist Creek: Parachute Jump we call it. It's so steep that I have to rough lock. I roll the sled onto one side, take two-inch rope, and weave it around the runners to create drag, hence slowing down the sled. I also unhook two dogs, temporarily letting them run free.

We plunge down Parachute Jump, with both of my feet riding on the brake. I'm yelling, "Whoa, easy! Whoa!" all the way, mashing my foot down on the brake to keep the sled from running over my wheel dog - the dog closest to the sled. Bumping and bouncing off trees, the sled careens from one side of the trail to the other. I finally screech onto the valley floor. I throw my sled over and take the ropes off the runners. Flipping my sled back upright, I realize the brake snapped under the strain. Thank God, it broke at the bottom and not at the top of the hill. I throw the sled back on its side, and with my Leatherman pliers, I thread number 9 wire through the brake, re-connecting it to the sled.

Down Schist Creek valley, I run into minimal overflow, and sled up the back of the knoll to the Schist Creek cabin. I chain up the dogs and carry in my freight. The flat, newly re-roofed cabin looks good. Before turning in, I look at the sky and wonder when it will stop snowing.

When I wake up the next morning, it's still snowing. All day, with snow falling on my head, I push through deep fluff as I climb the mountains. I get a break whenever I stop to set steel. At dusk, I encounter the last thrill of the day dodging trees va-rooming over three advanced ski

153. Marten

slopes, which twist, at the end, into the Chute.

The Chute is a straight-shot, narrow bob-sled run. As I fly down the drop, after rough locking the runners yet again, the sled hits first one side and then the other, bouncing from sapling to skinny spruce. Finally, I am in Caribou Creek valley and the ride slows, as the ground becomes more level. I take off the rough locks and tell the dogs, "Let's go!" Caribou Valley has a lot of wolf traffic, so I set a few snares. At the beaver dam, camouflaged by winter into an icy waterfall, I was leery. Because there have been no really cold temperatures before now, when I ride over the dam onto the icy surface below, the ice could break, plunging me into open, but shallow water. Sure enough, as I hit the ice, it cracks. Rusty brown water rushes around my sled, slowly sinking it and my survival gear with it. When I try to yank the sled upright, it's stuck in the gluck. Desperately, I urge the dogs, "Let's go!" I give the sled a good jerk and the dogs break it loose. The sled is freed like the Trident missile coming up out of the ocean, and I leap onto the back runners, praying the ice will be good. I reach the second beaver dam and test the thickness of the ice by hitting it with my ax; it's pretty thin. Very carefully, we creep across. The next hurdle is the crevasse, a narrow creek, 5-feet deep and 4-feet wide, covered only with hollow ice. Down I go, but the sled's front bow jams under the opposite bank, while the ice gives way underneath me. While my seven yammering huskies maintain the tension, I pull down and back to try to pry my 250-pound sled loose from the lip of the bank. I get the dogs calm while I loosen the sled. And, off we go up the bank.

Out of a feeling of duty, I set another wolf snare. But I'm too tired to be careful. I don't use my scentless gloves that are kept in a plastic bag just for setting snares.

The rest of the trail is okay and we make good time. Pulling up onto Caribou Cabin's long island, the shelter looks like a castle in the wilderness. I step down into the half-dugout cabin and see evidence that a bear has been there. The windows are out; the tables and stove are knocked down. I get the cabin livable, take care of the dogs, and try to takeoff my frozen parka. The snow hitting me all day has iced my jacket into a frozen cast. During my nightly conversation with my family on the radiotelephone, the battery dies. I hear Judy, but she can't hear me. Probably the battery wasn't sufficiently charged. I turn in early, wondering, "When is the snow ever going to stop?"

For the next three days, I try to make it to Peniel Cabin. I push, strain, and fight the mountains, returning each night to Caribou to sleep. The snow is now up to the handles of the back sled bow and is over the backs of the dogs. They are swimming in snow. The dogs cannot break the trail anymore. Each day, I have to snowshoe in front of the dogs. When the sled gets hung up, I stride back through the snow to the back of the sled to break it loose again. Where is Judy when I need her? It's very slow, and it takes three days to reach Peniel. I get thirsty, so, like the dogs, I lap the snow along the way. Lots of trees have blown down over the year and must be cut down out of the way.

The run into Peniel cabin is mostly a gentle descent. Peniel sits, also dug into the ground, beside an alpine lake. At last, I'm here! The dogs look at me and say, "I need a day off!" And, I say the same.

During the next two days, I put tin, which I'd brought in, on the Peniel Cabin roof, as I'd also done on Schist Creek, to save them from rotting in the summer. After each cabin was built, we equipped it with a necessary thermometer. The next day, the temperature drops to -45° F. I can't snowshoe on the worst, and last leg, into Gilles Creek cabin at these temps. Because I took extra days to break the trail to Peniel cabin, I'm running low on dog food, so I plan to return home on my back trail without going on to Gilles Creek. I bundle up well, but because of the temperature, the dogs are stiff and are barely locomotive. I have to push the sled on level ground until their engines warm up, but finally, they kick in.

I pick up some marten on this leg of the trip. At Caribou Cabin, it is -45° F. upon arrival. I'm really cold and stiff-handed. I have to get a fire going and warm up first.

Next morning, I get up; it's -55° F and I've got to keep going because there's no guarantee it will warm up soon! We take off at a slow start again. As I mush along Caribou Creek, I dread the thought of getting a wolf, which would give added weight to the sled. I look up and notice, "Hey! Where's my snare?!?" The snare was broken off and the trees were churned up, with blood left on the branches. The tale was there; the wolf had chewed the snare free.

During all this return mushing, I have eight inches of fresh snow yet again to buck. The wind is blowing and it's piercingly cold. But when I arrive at Schist Creek, it's only -20° F. I start a fire and warm up before unharnessing the exhausted dogs. As I warm my hands, I notice, out the window, a spark or two falling from the roof. I look up and the roof is on fire! I take melting snow off the stove, and throw it up at the roof. It seems to squelch the fire. After fifteen minutes, I notice more sparks coming down. I shove a stick into it and a lot of sparks fall down. I know the roof is on fire. Due to the new tin roof that I'd put on last year, I can't reach the fire to put it out. I tell myself, "Don't panic. You are going to have to get the fire out or you're going to freeze!" So, I scramble up on the roof and chop a hole in my new tin roof near the stovepipe, to successfully dig the fire out of the sod roof without too much damage to the roof.

As I finally settle down on my bunk, I hear my wife's fourth Trapline Chatter message on KJNP radio; she'll be in to pick me up on the November 13th! Only one more day to go! I know she is worried with no explanation for the cut off radio communication. Outside, Zeb is barking at the wolves howling in the distance.

The next day, the weather is warmer. Due to the deep snow, it takes me an hour to get up Parachute Jump. The rest of the day is normal.

On the thirteenth, the dogs know we are headed home! As I top the crest into Rosa Pass, an A-10 fighter jet spots me. I'm driving primeval transportation, and he has the newest. I wave, and he rocks his wings. He calls over to his buddy in another jet fighter: "Do you see the guy on the dogsled?!" The buddy comes over, and together they give me an aerial ballet of loops, backward flips, and buzzes. After the extravaganza, they wave their wings, "Good-bye," and head north to Fairbanks; I turn south for home.

Thanks, kids.

Reb

154. Reb with offending sled handles.

Chapter Sixty Seven
SLED JOCKEY

uring the thirteen years we lived up the Tanana River, my husband always went to town on Monday. In 1985, he prepared for his routine trip; he hooked up six dogs and, armed with a grocery list, he mushed 4 miles to the Holler to our waiting truck.

From our picture window, we watched him disappear as he and his team sped down the field to the frozen Tanana below. Sarah, knowing it was time for school, pulled her desk over by the wood stove and opened her second-grade reader. Fifteen-year-old Clint climbed the stairs to study his geometry. There was bread to make, laundry that I had washed and sledded in from Delta, yet to fold, baby Ben to change, and a house to clean while I intermittently fielded phonics and math questions.

Since it was December, daylight hours were short. Soon, I was filling lanterns to supplement the kids' 12-volt lights. Twilight-colored, lenticular clouds - omens of wind - drifted like smoke signals over the distant Alaska Range. The wind from Isabel Pass hit the propeller of our wind generator and an awful screeching traveled into the speaker of our citizen's band radio. I turned the squelch knob down, not wanting to wake Ben from his afternoon nap. Vegetables and moose roast were simmering on the stove.

Don Nelson's voice wafted over the radio: "… and now for the evening news…"

Through my kitchen window, I saw in the dark a distinct headlamp skimming up the field. "Dad's home," I stage whispered to Clint upstairs, and Sarah replied, "Ben's awake, Mom."

Clint wrestled into his coat, preparing to help his dad unharness the yapping dogs. Blowing in with the wind, Reb thumped through the door with a heavy pack on his back. Cold air danced off the load as he dropped it to the floor.

"Hi, Dad," pigtailed Sarah grinned, and searched his hands for a treat.

"You know, on the way home," Reb said, "I hit something."

"Yeah?" I asked, puzzled.

"You know Ashby's slough?" he began. "To save on battery juice, I switched off my headlamp before approaching that frozen beaver dam," he continued. "Well, the dogs hit the glare ice and started going fast, when-bam! We hit a tree stump just above the ice. The impact drove the sled handle right into my leg. I flipped over the load and landed on the wheel dog. I sat there in terrible pain, saying, 'It's not broken, maybe it's a charley horse.' Putting my weight on my good leg, I managed to get home."

Then, rubbing his sore leg, he said, "Just don't bump it."

All through the night, he moaned with the throbbing of the charley horse.

At daylight the next morning, he got up briefly, but returned to bed. A half an hour later, he stood up, and then collapsed backwards in a heap.

"What's the matter?" I asked.

Trying to put weight on his right leg again, he fell back on the bed once more. His face was turning gray-yellow, and sweat was on his forehead.

"What's wrong?" I cried. Memories from Sarah's medical evacuation began to run through my mind.

"My leg. My leg," he moaned, seeming to be drifting in and out of consciousness. His forehead was hot.

Across the river, Carol Dufendach, a nurse, was only a radio call away. She confirmed that fevers can sometimes accompany broken bones and called Delta's Dr. Andreasson to get help and medical supplies.

Giving my husband some leftover pain medication from a former surgery, I watched him begin to rest. Following the river's edge alone with his dog team, 15-year-old Clint was sent on a mission.

155. Sled without offending sled handles.

Following a chain of sloughs, he crossed an island, and finally a bridge into the Holler. On the other side of the bridge, he met Carol, who gave him medical supplies and a pair of crutches. Before arriving home, he stopped at our neighbors' home to coordinate medical transport for Reb with Paul Ashby.

The "hero" returned home and found his dad sleeping on the sofa next to the fireplace. Clint handed me casting materials and directions. Dipping into a basin of water, I began moistening dry plaster gauze. I laid the wet strips down the length of Reb's leg, while he promised he would chainsaw the handles off the sled as soon as he was well.

A few days later, when it had warmed up a bit, Paul Ashby came in his canoe with a friend. The two men helped Reb on his crutches and together they slowly worked their way down the hill. But, before going out the door, Reb flashed a smile at me and confided, "Even the best sled jockeys go down..."

Dr. Andreasson confirmed that Reb's femur was indeed cracked. Approving of the cast constructed by an amateur, he sent the man who had saved his AA headlamp batteries home to heal.

As soon as Reb could walk, he marched straight to the offending sled and sawed off the protruding handles.

156. Sarah in tepid bath to cool fever.

Chapter Sixty Eight
MOVING POX

The curse of the pox: itching, sores, fever, seizures, and hallucinations hit four out of five of our family when we least needed it … To further complicate our infirmary, our horses ravaged the grain barrel, causing them to threaten to founder … but the house we were building had to continue! Three weeks remained before the snow flew and we needed a roof over our heads. Clint and Sarah, 15 and 8, were beginning school with other students; we had to have a house.

In 1981, we had lived for one winter on the road system, far from the Tanana. None of us liked the flatlands, powered by gasoline, carpools, and life centering on schedules. When spring came, we quickly sold our house, jumped in our boat, and headed back upriver to the peace of our remote homestead.

But, practicality intervened. I knew I was reaching the end of my home schooling abilities. I insisted on saving the profit from the sale of the house on the road to eventually re-invest in property, located both on the river and the road. Reb added, "The new land also had to have a spring-fed creek."

When I was 39, I gave birth to our third child, Ben. I had forgotten that a new baby is only one step removed from the womb and requires almost constant attention. Clint, our eldest, needed more help with higher math than I could give him. He also needed companions. Further, our second grader, Sarah, needed more customized teaching than I could give her, while also keeping house and baking bread.

Clint had found a school he liked down the river and he was willing to pay the price for commuting. To get to school, he woke at 5 A.M., and in the dark and ice fog, he gripped his lead dog's collar, edged onto the tilting, 4-foot wide ice shelf around the Tanana bluff, while the main current rushed near his feet. In the evening, after the long, mush home, Clint had stacks of homework. It was time to move.

I had heard about land downriver, located on the road. One day, Reb walked the property. Below the land's high bank, next to the Tanana, there was a spring-fed creek. With the previously saved profit, Reb made a down payment.

But, moving back to the conventional 9 to 5 work/school system that most people live, the life of so-called convenience, was intimidating to Reb. He knew it would erode our wilderness life style. So we built a small trap cabin, just an overnighter. When we came to town, we heated the 16-by-18-foot cabin with a venty, 55-gallon barrel, wood stove. During the night, the fire roasted those in the top bunks, while those in the lower bunks froze. We decided to build a two-story log home, but not too big; after all, this was only temporary…

Over the summer of 1986, Clint peeled logs, while the root cellar was dug with a backhoe. When Reb's seasonal job with the Forestry Service was over, a month remained before winter. He and Clint went into over-drive on the building; their stock answer to all distractions was, "No!"

Then one day, I got a CB call. "Everyone at church has chicken pox," the message said. It was not long before the illness struck Ben. Immediately, pox appeared all over both 8-year-old Sarah and 2-year-old Ben. The diaper only incubated Ben's infection, making it worse, so he lay naked on the bed with the sores salved with baking soda.

I thought, "Clint's never had chicken pox… If he and Reb can stay well…" But shortly, Clint was writhing with the pox. At 16 years of age, he hallucinated with high fever and the itching left him inconsolable.

He eased into our galvanized tub and soaked in tepid baths. Afterward, he caked baking soda on his crawling skin, leaving a trail of powder everywhere, but still, he was miserable. When he was only marginally well, he returned to the downriver house to pound nails.

One morning, Reb woke with a mild fever. Forestry called on the CB radio, asking Reb to take an Outside fire assignment. Reb only moaned, "Not today…" Clint continued laying boards while Reb rested.

One morning, after everyone was finally well, I noticed Black was freely coming in and out of the barn where the grain was stored… "Oh, NO!" I cried, "He'll founder!" Never slackening their pace, Reb and Clint, like automatons, marched to the river to drive the boat downriver to continue their work on the house. To Clint, I cried, "But Black is your horse!" "Take care of it," they replied, in unison. On the previous advice of a veterinarian, I tried to purge the horse of the grain, tying his head upwards, and syringing mineral oil down the corner of his mouth. But, he continually knocked my turkey baster to the ground. Finally, to cool his hoofs that were hot with the calories from the excess grain, I tied him off while he stood in our cold creek. He never showed any ill effects, so I assumed perhaps my remedies helped.

In ten days, the snow flew. Finally in the new house downriver, we shut the door against the Blue Norther, and waded through 5 inches of sawdust. Each of us had a mattress against the walls. We climbed a ladder to get upstairs. On a piece of plywood, next to the stove, I made our meals. We hung our clothes on a suspended cord. We had light from Coleman lanterns and brought water up from the well with a bore bucket. Our parlor was a putrid yellow sofa, a thrift shop special. Our first night, separated from our scenic, upriver home, Reb surveyed our new barracks. "This is going to take some getting used to…" he said, and rolled over, and faced the wall. Silently, I agreed, but we had crossed our river; the Tanana was choked with ice.

Chapter Sixty Nine

TRAPLINE FAMILY

When we were rearing Clint and living upriver during the early 1970s, we depended upon the Bush. After Sarah and Ben were born, our life slowly evolved from primitive to convenient. Because there are 7 years between Clint and Sarah, and also between Sarah and Ben, each child lived a very differ-

157. Sarah leading Clancy, loaded with paniers.
Waiting on Reb en route to Gilles Creek, 1993.

ent life. Sarah and Ben never experienced Clint's isolated, subsistence life
in the Bush or knew, as Clint did, who
Reb and I were as young people. On
the other hand, Clint's battles were different from those of Sarah who had to
fight for a life impacted by natal injury
and illness. Clint paved the way for
Sarah by introducing her to a school, a
Christian community, Whitestone
Farms. Whitestone, a community full
of creative, responsible people, worked
hand in hand with Sarah throughout
her developmental years, giving her a
gift beyond price: the tools to meet life
on its own terms. Ben, whose wilderness experience, unlike Clint's, was vol-
untary and recreational, followed his
siblings' footsteps at Whitestone.
During the 1990s and into this new
millennium, dedicated teachers shaped
Ben's wit and elocution into the finely
honed art of forensics. In his first year

158. Clint looking back at Heather en route to Schist Creek, where he cut trail 22 years before. 1993.

of forensics, he placed third in the State of Alaska's Lincoln-Douglas Debate. At the same time as our lives were changing, Alaska also was evolving from classical, old Alaska to a State homogenous with the outside world. Our children had to be prepared for the transition.

However, in 1993, Ben was still a young pup, only 9, and Sarah was 15. Neither of them had experienced the trapline in its depths. Our cabins and trails needed repairs; we saw a chance to let Sarah and Ben experience an essential part of our lives.

Sarah left her friends behind and, to keep in touch, started a journal. Her entries recorded the events of that extensive fall trip.

"Dad and Ben led our draft horse, Clancy. I followed leading Black, and tried to avoid get-ting hit by the panniers - the hard packs on the horse's back. Yellow birch leaves fell on our heads while Mom brought up the rear, riding my mare, Yahna," Sarah wrote.

"After we left our first cabin, swamp stretched before us as Schist Creek wandered through a narrow valley. Leading the horses, we had to step quickly to avoid being trampled by them as they scrambled for their footing. Yahna tripped Ben and ran over him in the moss, but Ben was just a little sore. Crossing a short bog later, Clancy sank up to his flanks." Sarah recorded, "Dad and Mom stripped Clancy's packs and laid brush down for traction. Mom hollered from behind while Dad pulled on the reins. Finally, Clancy lunged out of the goo." From then on, at the creek crossings, we built bridges out of logs for the horses.

The next day was better when we climbed cranberry ridge, passing into grassy meadows and big spruce. Emerging from the woods into a pass, we could see, off to the south, the Shaw Creek drainage and, to the north, the Salcha. Needing pasture for the horses, we camped in a grassy swamp and then continued on the next day to Caribou Creek cabin, one of our dugouts.

Sarah wrote, "There's only room in here for one person moving around at a time, so we widened it by shoveling out the dirt floor to make some space.

"I dug, and handed buckets of dirt to Mom and Ben.

"I wasn't interested in taking an icy plunge, but Mom walked us upstream for a needed bath. Afterwards, she tempted me, saying, 'It was great!' So I tried sudsing my hair, and it numbed my brain. Back at camp, Mom shampooed Ben with campfire-heated water while Dad simmered beans on the side.

"I had a blister forming on the bottom of my foot from all the walking. Mom put a Moleskin patch on my foot to protect it. But several days later, when she ripped the patch off, the adhesive was so strong, that it took a deep wedge out of the skin on the sole of my foot! My boot was coming apart, too, but Dad squirted it with Shoe Goo. That repaired my shoe better than the Moleskin did my foot," Sarah grinned, and closed her journal for the night.

The next day, we went deeper into the wilderness, climbing through a prison of poplar saplings. Sarah frequently read, holding the lead horse of the pack string while we cleared the trail. As evening came on, we quit working. Trying to get to the next cabin before dark, we started crashing through the woods, but the dark and rain forced us to camp in the wet grass. We covered the saddles with a tarp while the horses hunkered down through the dark night of steady rain. While we slept, all wedged together in the tent, condensation formed inside the tent and the ominous, pooling water seeped into our sleeping bags.

Slipping down a seam in the mountain the next day, we followed the trail to an alpine lake and discovered a bear had ransacked our Peniel cabin, but with only minor damage. While we followed the beavers' canals and examined their cache mound, Peniel's lake mirrored the blue of the sky and

159. Judy leading Clancy in Caribou Valley, followed by Sarah and Ben on Jahna, 1993.
Same valley where we cut trail and lost one horse, 22 years before.

160. Judy shampooing Ben's from camp-fire heated water, Caribou Cabin.

the yellow leaves of the trees. Ben followed the beavers' canals, and exclaimed over the chewing marks that were everywhere.

The next night, on the way to Gilles Creek, we camped on the ridge. It was a perfect evening as we sat by our campfire feeling the balmy autumn breeze rustle the canopy of leaves over us. Through the trees, the stars were twinkling, and off to the south, we could see the distant lights of Delta, a sight we had not seen in many days. The following morning, we continued through the mountains. We went single file through moose ruts toward Gilles Creek. Eager for fun, Ben grabbed a willow for a sword and pierced some tiny, hollow stumps to make his sword's handle. He began fencing with Sarah, tripping through deep moss and spruce roots. We paused on the top of a 2,500-foot mountain and quietly surveyed the South Fork of the Salcha River. In ten days, the woods had all slipped from green to yellow, and on one slope, there was a patch of crimson red. We hurried downhill into Gilles valley, to our cabin on a rocky creek.

The next morning, the eerie sound of a babe lost in the woods interrupted our breakfast. The woods erupted with a bull moose thrashing through the brush after a cow. Hunting was not our option, being so far in, so we turned to fixing the cabin's rolling gables and its collapsing roof. That night, we fell asleep smelling fresh sap from a new spruce pole that was jacking up the ridge log.

On the radio, we heard of a weather change, so we saddled up and rode double, leading Black, toward home, trying to outrun a winter storm. Galloping through a mountain pass and into a cold wind, we watched ominous clouds brewing across the sky. Sitting behind Reb, I rode on Clancy's muscled rear as we passed Peniel, trying to outrun the snow. I held on tightly while Reb cantered him across the mountains. Late in the day, the rain caught us and we felt our way through fog, down the trail into Caribou Creek. We dried our gear by the stove in the dugout, and awoke the next morning to snow sifting down over the horses' black hair.

Settling into our cold, rigid saddles, we rode through the mountains able to go fast enough to skip a cabin every day, making two cabins a day. We hunched our necks into our collars while fresh powder cascaded onto our shoulders and legs. Glorious fall had been transformed into winter by 6 inches of white fluff. We were the only blotches of color scooting through the corridor of snow-laden spruce. The weighted branches hung in our faces making the trail no wider regardless of all our earlier trail-cutting work. We arrived at our Campbell's cabin, stiff, hungry, and chilled.

After a hot dinner, Sarah added to her journal, where she had already recorded creek baths, sword fights, and the smell of spruce sap, "Tomorrow I get a real bed, real food, and a hot shower ... tomorrow, I go home."

Chapter Seventy
CARIBOU PLATEAU

161. Sarah, Ben, Reb and the monarch, 1995.

n a beautiful September morning in 1995, we started our seventeenth season hunting caribou from horseback. From our base camp at the Sevenmile Lake Trail, off the Denali Highway, we could see other horsemen on the skyline, scanning the valley for their winter's meat. Reb was impatient to get hunting. He was sure his trophy caribou was lined up in someone else's cross hairs.

Ben swung onto Clancy's back behind his dad. "Let's go!" Reb cried, "It's 10:30!" Sarah sat gazing with her wide-brimmed hat flopped down her back and her rain slicker tied on behind Yahna's saddle. She was intent on the horizon: searching, searching. Her eyes and ears strained for any movement in the brush. Ben had his shotgun slung across his back, ready for any sign of ptarmigan. I was alert for unwanted rain clouds.

We started down the trail keeping our voices low. A third of the way up Boulder Creek, we arrived at a large rock positioned with a sweeping view of the valley. While our turkey loaf and cocoa were heating up on the alcohol stove, we looked around the area through the rifle's scope.

Reb can see a caribou the size of a pin, miles away on the tundra. In his scope, there on a rise just over Boulder Creek, he spotted a most elegant bull. Not only did he have a stately rack, but his cape was snowy white, down to the tufts on his chest - a silver-haired king.

We crossed the creek and climbed a short way. Then, Ben and I held the horses, while Reb and Sarah made the stalk. A flat, far-off bang sounded - seemingly separate from the caribou, but he staggered, and then he was down. We approached this king of the tundra, took pictures, and set to work skinning. There were three inches of clean, white fat that I later rendered for homemade soap. Sarah and I skinned the meat off the ribs and head, not wanting to waste any of it.

The next morning, we headed out to look for two more bulls. The clear, dry weather of the first day took a foreboding turn. We rode up on a high plateau on the south side of Boulder Creek, but descended quickly as there was nothing up there to protect us from the cold, wet wind. That night, we ate hot caribou back straps and fried the ptarmigan Ben had shot. Inside the tent, I was thankful for the propane heater that blasted life back into my chilled cells. I relaxed in the sleeping bag -- that is good to -50° F. -- and, luxuriously laid on my foam-padded cot. Life is rarely so comfortable in our hunting camps.

The next day in the drizzle and the rain, Sarah focused on the hunt. Suddenly, three bulls in a

162. Sarah with her first caribou, shot just before dark. 1995

small band of caribou ran across the tundra; Reb and Sarah took off after them. When Sarah overshot, the whole herd vanished down the valley as if they were ghosts. When we discussed the shot late that night in the kitchen tent, she took the disappointment in stride.

The next morning, I studied the ominous clouds, and thought, "He that observeth the wind shall not sow; and he that regardeth the clouds shall not reap." So, I swung up onto my horse, packed extra clothing, and looked for white tails or sky-lined racks.

By midday, we were hunched in-between wet muskeg, crouched under a blowing tarp tied off to brush. We ate a hot lunch and dozed, curled up as the rain drove into the nylon cover. The horses stood motionless in the wet onslaught. The caribou were safe, obscured from us by a gray haze.

The rain covered the countryside into the next day. We were just one more detail in the landscape of sodden tundra. Then as Reb and I looked through the scope, shafts of wet sunshine suddenly broke out, streaming strangely bright all around us; we were surrounded by wonderful, white rain. As the sun shot through the soaked atmosphere, a rainbow stretched from wall to wall across the valley.

A ptarmigan suddenly broke the grass cover and whirred up on Ben's left. "Boom!" he fired his shotgun. Birds erupted on his right. "Bang!" More birds flushed behind him. "Ka-boom!" A whole covey had been hidden in the grass around us. As the rainbow filled the valley, Ben, with his hands full of ptarmigan, stood with his dad under the full arch.

Ever since Sarah's herd of caribou had disappeared down the valley, I felt they were on the far side, across the creek away from us. But Reb was confident that he could see everything from our side of the valley. The land beyond the water called me. I longed to search those provocative hills.

We had ridden until late afternoon before stopping on a knoll near Boulder Creek. Reb spotted some nice bulls, like distant specks, in the scope. They were north of the creek, up high on the northern plateau. Normally, we would not have headed up that far so late in the day, but we had not seen a decent caribou in five days. We quickly cleared our lunch camp and swung into the saddle.

The creek that had been an invisible boundary for us was filled with slippery rocks, making footing treacherous for the horses. Even more hazardous was the hollow bank on the creek's far side. Our horses scrambled; then, we began climbing, with some trepidation, up the rolling mountainside. An eagle soared high above the creek, winding below like a sinuous ribbon. Above Seven Mile Lake, a fragment of rainbow hung suspended in the cloudy twilight, quieting my anxiety as I memorized the terrain on our way up the mountain.

Far ahead, the bulls were sky-lined on a ridge. They were able to see our approach, but they were feeding. Ben and I waited behind boulders with the horses while Sarah and Reb began their stalk. They could only move while the animals were grazing; they froze when the bulls looked their way.

The minutes ticked by. Ben and I watched a cow and a calf clip nimbly by, enjoying their evening play. A young bull passed by us, leaping down the mountain. We had finally found the long sought caribou pastures.

Forty-five minutes later, Ben and I dared to poke our heads over the boulders, peeking at the progress of the stalk. Instead of two bulls still up ahead, there were five, but they were looking right at Sarah and Reb as they crouched motionless. A distant crack suddenly exploded in the air, followed by two more. Sarah and Reb split up and disappeared over the ridge, along with the caribou. Ben and I approached, mounted on two horses and leading the third. Very carefully, we picked our way across a deep, rocky ravine and crested out onto the vast, unknown plateau.

We were only yards from the clouds that were hanging on the mountain peaks above us. I won-

163. Ben and Reb with Ptarmigan

dered if the fog would hold there or descend over us. It began misting, and worse, the sun had set. It was thirty minutes before dark. I called Reb and Sarah's names. It was strange that Reb had not contacted us. "Well, he could be rushing to gut her caribou before dark," I reasoned.

Ben fired three shots, a sacred family signal for desperate communication. But, there was no response. A picture of my daughter flashed across my mind, of her wandering lost and alone in the foggy night on this high plateau. "Could she accidentally have shot Reb?" I wondered.

We heard a faraway cry. It sounded like it came from downhill, but there, the mountain dropped off. I let my horse choose his way. He continued climbing upward over the ever-unfolding curve of the plateau.

"Don't go up that way, Mom! That's not right!" Ben called.

The plateau gave me no hint; it was as helpful as a silent tomb.

Finally, "Mom!" I heard Sarah's faint call.

"Sarah?!" I yelled. "Are you OK?"

"Yes!" came the muted response.

"Is Dad OK?" I called.

"Yes!" I could hear her say. Joy shot through me and we followed their voices on up the mountain.

As soon as I arrived, and before the gutting went too far, I snapped a picture of Sarah with her caribou. She had really worked for this animal and I was deeply proud of her. We set to work finishing the job and I no longer cared that it was dark, nor was I worried about cold, rain, or fog. We were together and that was all that mattered. We took turns holding a flashlight or a hindquarter, and felt with our knives for the dividing line between hide and flesh.

Reb explained that, because of the deep dusk, he had started gutting as quickly as he could. He had stationed Sarah where he could see her, and yet she could still yell for us. When we never arrived, he shot the .44 pistol, but we never heard it. Finally, Sarah moved farther out, to just within her father's hearing, and called louder for us. It was then that I finally heard her. The plateau tilted toward the heavens and all of our sounds had emptied into, and had been absorbed by, outer space.

The dark sky cleared off, and the stars studded the vast sky over us. I led the way on foot across the ravine and off the mountainside. At the creek, fog hung over the roaring current. Reb carefully searched for a crossing. I rode behind him on Clancy's muscled back, and led Black, who was packing all the meat. The moonlight flashed on the rushing torrent. Following behind, Sarah and Ben rode double on Yahna. We splashed and slid our way through the swift water, over the slippery rocks, and safely to the other side. Once on the old trail leading back to camp, I turned to see the Northern Lights dancing over the mountain peaks in unfolding curtains of quivering color, shimmering above the Big Dipper. By 3 A.M., we saw the dark outline of our horse trailer, and our dog's barking greeted us as we stumbled back into base camp.

The next morning as we broke camp, there was no end to the perfect weather. On our way home, we picked blueberries at Tangle Lakes. The smell of the caribou permeated our packs; the berries stained our hands; and all around us was the crisp perfection of fall.

Chapter Seventy One
ICE FISHING
Secret Lake Spot Yields String of Luck for Pair of Fishermen

164. Ben in tent fishing open holes in the lake ice, 1996.

In March, a man and his boy slept inside a tent, different from the usual ice-fishing huts and campers parked on bigger lakes. Surrounded by hills, they were alone on a secluded lake. Next to their sled, the huskies were sleeping with their noses in their tails. The light of dawn slowly bathed the hills and the tent. A light breeze caused the canvas walls to flap in harmony with the breathing inside.

Reb began to toss and turn with a morning bladder, but there was 2 inches of ice water covering the tent floor. He had to find his boots. All night, a yo-yo reel, anchored to a leg of Reb's cot, had been set in an ice hole.

"Zzzzzzzzzzzz-z-z-z whirr!" Reb was jolted upright! The fishing line was going wild and spinning out of control under the ice. The red bobber was frantically popping up and down in the hole, and then, it disappeared.

Struggling for his bag's zipper, Reb groaned, "Got to grab that fish. Where are those boots? … and I need ta…" With his toes in his boots, Reb leaned over the hole and began cranking the 1950's yo yo reel. To his delight, up through the blue ice, he pulled out an 18-inch rainbow trout, shimmering silver and pink, flipping and wiggling on its hook. Feverishly, with wet, exposed fingers, he re-baited the hooks while glancing side-ways at the holes. The boy, Ben, began to stir in his cot. Reb tossed the fish onto the ice. He told his body he would rebait this one hook and then he would take care of his needs. Mashing the tiny shrimp and the squishy, salmon egg onto the hair-thin hook, he dropped it into the hole, satisfied that it was set.

But, as he headed for the door, he suddenly heard, 'ZZZZZZZZ-Z-Z--WHIRR-RR!" He looked with disbelief at where the bobber had just been, but was … no more. He gingerly retreated back to the submerged line, unhooked the trout, and lobbed it over by the first one. Patiently, he smashed another shrimp onto the same hook and stepped out of the tent door, but was jerked back.

"ZHZ-Z-Z-Z-WHING!" He ripped off the last, great trout, and ran out the door - bait or no bait. Ben was electrified awake. He was scrambling for his boots in the melt water, looking for his own yo-yo reel. Jealously wanting his own prize fish and trembling with adrenalin, Ben prepped for a day of serious ice-hole staring. He was not disappointed.

The fishing was so good that morning that Ben competed to stay one or two fish ahead of his dad. As one hole slowed down, they hand augured another - like prospectors hoping to hit that vein of gold.

While Reb made breakfast over the open fire, Ben tossed fish onto the ice, which turned them instantly into mini frozen logs. The bobbers were bobbing and the reels were zinging as fast as the pegs in a pinball machine. The sun was blinding on the soft snow and glare ice. While a bull moose browsed in the willows along the shoreline, they ripped off their shirts to get the year's first tan.

By afternoon, the lake breeze whipped up, forcing them to put their shirts back on and to retreat into their Arctic Oven tent, protecting two ice holes. They relished that they were no longer exposed as in years past when they had not had a tent.

By evening, as Reb fried trout, a creature-of-the-deep grabbed his hook, and submerged his lightly anchored reel, taking it under the ice to unknown realms. Stung, Ben ran watching from hole to hole, barely eating his crunchy trout.

The chinook-soft breeze of the day stilled into an evening calm. Velvet dark replaced the softness of sunset's delicate pinks and blues. They packed up and harnessed the dogs. Instead of the day's soft snow, ice needles crunched underfoot. Winter had returned with the night, and man and boy zipped their parkas shut against the cold.

A contented boy and his father mushed their team toward home. There were many fish to be cleaned, but as they went, they savored the day together at "the lake, that only we know about."

Chapter Seventy Two
MUSHING GLACIERS

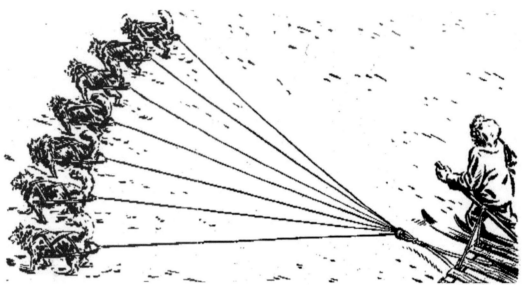

165. War Department Field Manual, Dog Transportation, 1944. Figure 23. Fan Hitch.

Fan hitch design harnessing involves hooking the dog team into one ring that is connected to the sled. Used on open terrain, fan was used where there were no trees. But, without trees, there was no way to anchor the lead and wheel dogs while harnessing the team. Inevitably, they looped back in their traces and became knotted in tangles with their teammates, and then, lunged at each other's throats.

This nightmare unfolded in 1991 as Reb, Sarah, Ben, and I harnessed our teams to mush the Castner Glacier in the Alaska Range. Along with many other people, we were out to enjoy the spring weather. Ben rode with Reb and his team of five dogs, while Sarah was with my four dogs and me. Skiing spectators watched from warming cars. I was desperate to get the dogs moving forward and out of sight. Finally, we clucked, "Let's go! Huh!"

We set out for the higher ice. The sun was warm on our faces, but was very bright when reflecting off the glare of the ice. We fastened our sunglasses and climbed all day, and by 3 P.M., we were in the pass, the threshold to the glacier. We sacked out in our sleds, had sandwiches for lunch, and hot tea.

Reb said the glacier stretched for miles up into the mountains. For us, it was only a weekend trip, so we turned around and headed back to make a camp.

Reb and I threw up the tent while the children watched the teams, but once inside the tent, we had to move carefully. We four were sandwiched in a small, mountaineering tent. As I made dinner, little pans of food and water were heating on the 12-by-6-inch stove, when suddenly I knocked over a teapot, spilling scalding water on my thin long johns. The heat was held in the polypropylene johns, frying my skin. I could not get the pants off quickly. As I stripped them off,

I ran out of the tent and rolled my thigh on the ice, over and over, crying with pain. Reb took one look and packed us up for home. Blisters and open skin covered my entire leg. He packed ice and snow next to my leg, and eased me into my insulated pants. In forty minutes, we were at the truck. He threw the gear into the sleds, and slid them onto the truck's dog box, with my sleeping bag still in the bed of the sled. As we sped down the highway, our finest sleeping bag, a -50° F. Holubar, blew out of the sled into the dark. Not only was I burned, but the loss of my Holubar was like losing my other skin.

When we arrived back in Delta, there was no medical facility open, but I got advice, mainly - endure. I was more comfortable at home, but the pain would not abate. Finally, at 3 A.M., the aspirins began to be effective and I slept.

While my leg healed, Reb posted my sign notifying the public of the lost bag. A Fairbanks skier not only found it, but he even called us. The skier's friend informed him, "Do you know what you have? They don't even make Holubars anymore."

Lying on my sofa, with my leg sticking out of my -50° F. bag, I healed in a few days.

Chapter Seventy Three
BIRCH GIFTS

n 1957, Reb voyaged by canoe through eastern Ontario with the Boy Scouts and with canoe guide and celebrated wildlife photographer, Leonard Lee Rue III. Traveling through the North's birch trees, they paddled to an Algonquin settlement, where birch craft was still part of daily life.

As they pulled up to the village, the boys smelled birchbark burning as the evening fires warmed the cabins. Next to a teepee, there were birch canoes made from overlapping layers of bark.

On a similar trip, twenty-two years later, when Reb, Clint, and I kayaked the Kobuk River, we noticed conspicuous brown bands girdling many of the birch trees. As we paddled our kayaks into the village of Kobuk, we spotted Wilson Ticket, quietly walking the trail along the bank in the sunset. After we landed, he invited us to his home, where his wife, Daisy, was sitting in the soft light stitching a birch-bark lampshade.

She smiled shyly and explained to me that due to the lack of trees near the village, they went, every spring, up the Kobuk to harvest their bark. The next day, Rosie Horner showed us the tiny fist-size, birch berry baskets she made her small daughters.

During the subsequent days while we paddled the Kobuk, my mind was more on feathering my nest than on the river adventure. Five months pregnant with Sarah, I spent my

166. Ben tapping birch trees, 1996.

191

167. Rosie Horner's tiny birchbark berry basket for her daughters. Kiana, on Kobuk River, 1977.

days planning a nursery for her. When we returned from the trip in 1977, Reb surprised me with a beaded birchbark infant carrier, a belated birthday gift. When Sarah was a severely jaundiced newborn, I put her in her birchbark baby carrier by the window to catch the December light.

When Sarah was 12, my friend, Carol Walters, who lives on the Nowitna, a tributary of the Yukon River, came to visit us. Because she has been crafting birch for years, we asked if she might teach us and two of Sarah's teachers how to make birchbark baskets.

As the five of us gathered in my kitchen, Carol explained, "It's best to remove a simple wrap-around cut from the birch trees during late May to early June."

A Delta forester, Steve Joslin, warned, "Only cut into the brown layer and not into the white cambium tissue or you may kill the tree." "Any cut," he added, "will leave a permanent scar. Banded trees are more susceptible to disease, so use the harvest as a thinning tool only in a crowded stand of trees."

"After the bark is gathered," Carol continued, "if you don't use it immediately, store it flat, held down by weights, off the ground and away from rain and sunlight.

"When you're ready, submerge it in water to soak it, and then, lay it on the table to trace your pattern."

We laid our basket pattern on the bark's white side, and then flipped the birch skin to use the contrasting brown side for the trim. We folded and secured the corners with clothespins, trying not to crack the bark. Using moistened, split willow roots for thread, we stitched the basket's rim through holes we punched with an awl.

For Christmas that year, Sarah made Ben a thick, bark, laundry hamper, decorated with wild roses and sealed with varnish. Using a thinner bark, Ben easily folded a small canoe for his dad.

One May afternoon, I called, "Ben!" Getting no reply, I looked behind the house. He was squatting by a birch tree with his father's drill, fitting hard plastic tubing into holes he had just drilled into the birch trees. He had swiped half of my kitchen pots and set them at the base of the trees in his new birch orchard to collect sap. I heard the "drip, drip, drip" of clear, running sap. In a few hours, one tree had chugged out a gallon of barely sweet, water-like liquid. During one week, Ben's six trees trickled twelve gallons. When Ben was finished, he plugged the trees.

The Alaska University Cooperative Extension Service's *Wild Berry Recipe Book* taught, "quick boiling of the syrup will yield a … milder tasting product. Heat it only to 221° F., being careful not to scorch the product." After two days of intermittent boiling, Ben tasted the amber liquid that yielded two pints of tangy-sweet, uniquely birch syrup. Ben's white-barked, gentle giants had produced twelve gallons of sap that rendered down to two small jars of northern ambrosia.

168. *Algonquin elders birchbark canoe, Quebec, 1957. Courtesy of Leonard Lee Rue III.*

Chapter Seventy Four
FERGUSON MEANS FARMER

169.*Ben transplanting in downriver greenhouse, 1996.*

en is not only a hunter, but he is also a farmer, bred in the genes. His grandfather, Rowe Ferguson, came from a North Carolina valley filled with Ferguson farmers, where corn was the mainstay.

Both of our sons always wanted to grow corn, but ... we were in the Sub-Arctic. With a large greenhouse at the upriver house, and a small one downriver, we could cheat the climate. We studied inventions: planter boxes to warm the soil and perforated drip hoses. But, the critical element was timing the transplanting of the corn. The plants had to be started in the greenhouse sufficiently early to maximize the season, but not so early that the plant could not withstand transplanting.

Whether we were living upriver or down, we timed our greenhouse planting thusly: celery, tomatoes, and peppers - February; flowers - March; cole crops - April 1st; and corn, cucumbers, and squash by mid-May.

After the children began school at Whitestone in 1986, I had to wait until they were home in the afternoon to help.

170. Reb, Sarah and Ben taking transplants to the upriver greenhouse, 1996.

While I waited, I dug soil from thawing berm piles, then, sterilized it and mixed it with Pearlite for drainage.

After school, we made an assembly line: perforating cans to convert them into planters, filling the cans with dirt, planting seeds, labeling and covering the cans with plastic wrap until the seeds sprouted. To maximize warmth and condensation, we kept the cans on a high shelf in our warm home to aid germination.

Every day, we peeked to see if any green tendrils had penetrated the dark soil. As soon as they surfaced, we slipped the trays of cans under grow lights. Careful not to douse them, we sprayed the soil with warm water and rotated the planters for uniform growth.

By early April, nighttime temperatures were slowly rising. We could make a fire in the greenhouse's wood stove without the loss of too much energy. Sunlight had become the priority for the tiny plants, so we had to waste some extra wood to get the plants on my overflowing shelves into the greenhouse. We transplanted tomatoes, peppers, and cucumbers directly into the beds, but in between the planted vegetables, we put trays containing crops that would later be planted in the upriver greenhouse or directly into the garden soil. As they grew, I had to separate the starts and plant them in larger cans. By May, the greenhouse was exploding with multiplying containers of transplants. However, we could not easily move them to the upriver greenhouse. In May, access to our upriver homestead was still blocked by a frozen slough. To move the plants, we would have to carry everything, by wheelbarrow, from a sandbar across the ice. We loaded the plants into our riverboat and protected them from the wind and spray under the canopy of the boat. Sarah and Ben were wedged between tomato, pepper, and corn plants, their faces obscured by a green spray on their laps.

As the boat pushed slowly upstream, resting geese on the sandbars began to stir, ruffled their feathers, scattered, and then, swooped in front of us. Rivulets of melting snow trickled from the riverbanks, carrying the smell of fresh earth, while the air was scented with pussy willow sap. The solid ice of the winter was fragmenting into crystallized needles as the mass disintegrated, separating into thawing spikes.

On top of the ice, pools of mushy puddles were forming. We snugged the boat into the sandbar, stuck the anchor into the ice, and tied the boat to driftwood. We threw a plank over the side of the boat, and rolled the wheelbarrow, loaded with plants, onto the sandbar. Sarah and I balanced boxes of green on our heads. Like a botanical parade, we pushed our garden across the sand, over the slough ice onto our still-frozen dog trail, up the bank to the first field, and then, up another shelf to the greenhouse.

Once at the greenhouse, I flung open the Dutch door and memories of years of peace, planting in solitude up the river, washed over me. We set to work. We ripped out last season's dead, paper-dry plants, turned and watered the soil by hand -- carrying buckets of melted snow water from the pond.

"Don't forget to French Trench," I reminded Ben. He dug a shallow basin in the greenhouse bed and laid the tomato plant's stem in horizontally: the more fuzzy hairs that could contact the soil the better the base root would grow. He gently curved the top of the plant to the ceiling, then fertilized, and covered the lower three-quarters of the stem with soil and tamped it solidly.

After planting upriver, I ran the boat up every night to make a fire in the wood stove in the greenhouse. Then, I hurried downriver to tend the week-old chicks that were under lights in our garage. Some of the birds were potential layers to replenish Ben's aging, laying hen program.

Ben and Reb had prepared a winter poultry barn by digging into the hillside by the riverbank. They had lined the earthen walls with plywood and insulated the small building for a chicken shed. Ben had sworn that he would take care of the birds. During the following winter, every day after school, Ben rotated frozen buckets of mucky water from the hen house with fresh ones from our home. He scratched the whorls of opaque, white hoarfrost off the shed's window, and peeked in to see if any hens were yet sitting on a clutch of eggs. The chickens were walking inside their hillside cave, quietly clucking, but the boxes on the walls were empty.

Ben really wanted a hen to hatch a brood of chicks. Several times, he left eggs in a nest for six weeks. When I gathered them, I soaked the eggs in water to loosen the crustacean-hard feces. "Yuk, Ben! It'll be a miracle," I said, "if the eggs aren't green." When a poultry owner later advised us, "Sitting eggs has been bred out of most chickens," I considered getting an incubator to fulfill Ben's dream.

In late July, when Ben's corn was maturing upriver, we bought enriched feed to boost his hens' egg production. By the time of the Delta Fair, Ben had saved matched, brown eggs to enter in the fair, along with several ears of golden, succulent corn. He sold excess eggs at the local store. Grandpa's junior Ferguson had the instinct for farming, sub-arctic, but Ferguson, style!

171. Reb and Clancy in harness with Reb's homemade sleigh, 1996.

Chapter Seventy Five
SQUIRRELLY SLEIGH RIDES

A horse-drawn red sleigh flashed through the trees. Our friend, Irene Mead, was out for a ride in the spring sunshine. The sight rekindled the same fascination Reb had when he watched the Quaker buggies racing to church in Gary Cooper's movie *Friendly Persuasion* or the troika in *Dr. Zhivago*. That day, Reb determined he would have his own horse-drawn sleigh.

After pricing them in a catalog, he decided to build a sleigh himself. He photographed Irene's horse sled from different angles, and then purchased rods and 1-inch flat steel to begin the project. Our blacksmith friend, Ron Tate, invited Reb to work in his shop at Dry Creek. After several days of welding, the carriage and runners stood independently, and the sleigh began to seem fantastically real. Reb cut the sled patterns out of plywood in our garage, fastened them together with bolts, and then painted them a deep red. Now, the conveyance was ready for Clancy, our black gelding.

Clancy was part Percheron, a breed of large, fast-trotting draft horses. When he was nervous, his eyes went wild; he starched his ears straight up and pranced. Looking like a king's stallion, Clancy did not resemble the little colt of his youth that was once mauled by a bear. The day that Reb led him down the driveway pulling the strange, new toy, he was unusually high-strung. Joshua Bos, a teen-age friend of our family, held Clancy while Reb harnessed the agitated horse and fitted him to the sleigh. Reb boarded the sleigh and signaled to Josh to let the horse go. Before he could, Clancy bolted, leaving Joshua running to catch up with him.

Soon, I heard Reb return and call through our front door, "Judy! Come for a ride in the new sleigh!" Because I had not seen the first takeoff, I slipped innocently into my snowsuit while he continued, "We'll pick the kids up at school."

Eagerly, I climbed on board and felt transported into the old West. We shot out of the driveway, narrowly missed the ditch, and began bouncing down the neighborhood road. Reb pulled on the reins, but Clancy took no heed. Since it was not 1861, I was worried that a car might come speeding around the curve at any time.

I calculated the sleigh's speed and the space I needed for a cowboy roll out of the sled and onto the ground. Clancy slowed down and I leaped out and grabbed a rein. But, I noticed a strap dangling from his chin; it was the curb strap used for leverage to stop the horse. With nothing to replace the strap, I trotted along with Clancy, while Reb handled the reins. I spied some baling twine lying in a driveway. As we passed, I snatched it up, tied it under Clancy's chin, and climbed back into the sleigh. Finally, our black gelding began to behave like a gentleman. We started to relax and enjoy the majestic mountains as we clipped along in the spring air.

At school, a crowd gathered around the horse, while our children, Sarah and Ben, got their coats. Reb agreed to a few rides even though the unfamiliar sounds of enthusiastic school children were causing Clancy to become nervous again. The sleigh barely slowed down long enough to allow the excited riders to board. As they jumped in for a ride, they were oblivious to the excitability of the horse. Clancy swung around and bolted, running out of control down the hill. The children were squealing with joy; this was more fun than a carnival ride! An adult passenger bit her lip and squeezed the side of the sled, praying for it to just be over. Finally, Clancy stopped, lathered with sweat and quivering with adrenalin. Reb dismounted and walked over to the horse's head. There, dangling from Clancy's chin was the undone baling twine.

The young men standing around watching the sleigh rides, Jason Underhill, Aaron Seeger, and Seth Baronoski, were impressed. The next day, they asked Reb to teach them to operate a horse-drawn sleigh. Reb saw an old photo of a stone sled - a platform on skis, low to the ground. He decided to build one, making it easy for everyone aboard to abandon ship, if necessary.

The next spring, when Jason Underhill and Lura Blohm decided to get married, Jason asked Reb to drive his new bride and him in the sleigh from the church to their honeymoon car, waiting several miles away. When the time came, I held my breath, hoping the picturesque exit would not turn into a traumatic trip with a runaway horse. After the ceremony, Aaron Seeger held Clancy's head, while Reb, in the sleigh, controlled the reins. The bride and groom trustingly boarded the sleigh and Clancy cantered out over the soft, March snow. Safely, they disappeared over the horizon, blissfully bound for their honeymoon.

Every spring, young men come over to learn from Reb how to work with the horses and sleigh. One day, Aaron was capable enough to dig the stone sled out from the snowbank, harness the horse, and take the outfit down the road. Like the pioneer photo Reb originally found of the stone sled, the sleigh has been a window for teaching yesterday's bygone skills of working with animals to the young.

172. *Charlie Boyd with grizzly-bear Skolai Pass, c 1977.*

Chapter Seventy Six

GUIDE CHARLIE BOYD

A Dall sheep stood sentry over a flock of ewes feeding by the Johnson River Glacier. That day in 1989, Patty Gooley edged her way up the moraine with her eyes on the old man of the slopes, gauging how long she might have before he spotted her.

In her backpack, Patty carried a vial containing the ashes of Charles Anderson Boyd, Jr.

Patty had met Charlie twenty-one years earlier, in 1968, when he was 40 and she was 19. When Patty was only 4, she had lost her father. Widowed with several children, Patty's mother sought help from a children's home to take care of her children. As a result, Patty spent many years in orphanages and in foster care.

When Patty met Charlie, she was not drawn by his good looks, and certainly, not by his youth. In 1999, she mused, "Charlie had a way with animals." She confided, "I was sort of a wild one and he was very good with me."

By the time Patty met Charlie, he was already well established as a professional hunting guide and trapper in Alaska, and he had been alone most of his life. Put up for adoption at birth, Charlie shared this life experience with Patty.

"We had a kinship, as if we had known each other from way back," Patty said. "He always called me 'the Kid;' in turn, I called him 'Dad.'"

Charlie's former assistant guide and now Patty's husband, Dave Davenport, said, "It takes a special kind of person to set up a four star hotel in the wilderness, and Patty did it for years. She was always flown into camp first, where she did everything from improving the airstrip to putting her kitchen wall tent in order. Then, Charlie followed with his hunters."

Charlie's guiding areas, as categorized in the State of Alaska Fish and Game Regulations book, were Unit 20 D/Johnson River; Unit 20/Wood River and Goodpaster; and the Wrangell-St Elias, which he shared with five other guides.

By 1975, Charlie's operation had grown sufficiently to hire young Dave Davenport as a packer, and later, as an assistant guide.

Dave, whose heart exceeded his experience, would routinely scramble up goat cliffs at Boyd's request. Once, looking down from loose shale cliffs, Dave complained to Charlie of the impossibility of retrieving the client's wounded animal.

Boyd quipped, "If a wounded goat got up there, why not you?"

A few days after his clients had gone home, Boyd dropped Dave off to hike across the Johnson River Glacier on his own sheep hunt. Just as he was starting out, a blizzard began to spread across the crevasse-laced slope. As quickly as he walked, Dave's back trail filled with snow.

The next morning, Boyd had not slept, anticipating what had probably happened. Tears filled his eyes, "He was only 22, and I killed him," he moaned, "He trusted me, and I killed him." A few hours later, a frozen, but not dead, Dave, wandered back into camp.

Patty routinely did camp chores while Charlie and Dave guided. From an airplane tire for landing on the tundra and a 55-gallon, oil drum, Charlie had made Patty a Bush wheelbarrow. Every fall for years, Patty removed rocks to smooth the Charlie Boyd airstrip at the Johnson River

"Filling in the holes helped. Charlie was an excellent pilot, but he was hard on equipment. We crashed that airplane at least three times!" Patty laughed.

Once when one of the plane's tires was not only flat, but lacked the tube stem to inflate it, Patty ingeniously removed the stem from their air mattress, pressed it into the gaping tire, and soon, they were on their way.

"Native intelligence!" Boyd said, saluting Patty, who had formal schooling only up to the eighth grade.

"I was his mentor, in a strange way," Patty said, "and he was mine." There were other complications however. Charlie and Patty decided it was best for them to separate. As good friends, Charlie later endorsed Patty's marriage to Dave Davenport.

In 1999, Patty continued her retrospective of Charlie's memory, "Delta's wild buffalo herd was also a part of

173. Patty Gooley and Dall sheep, Johnson River Glacier, 1989.

Charlie. He worked hard to protect Delta's herd that was continually lured from the hardscrabble of foraging in the snow towards the alluring new crops of the recently opened Agricultural Project."

"In 1980, a careless farmer left a stack of fertilizer unguarded. As a result, twenty to thirty buffalo died," Patty recalled.

In between meetings to save the buffalo, Charlie began having other problems. Known for always getting his clients a trophy sheep no matter how difficult the terrain, in the fall of 1980, Charlie began to have trouble just walking across his cabin floor. I heard about Charlie's problem and asked him if I might take him to see a physician.

After I admitted Charlie to the hospital and he was awaiting a diagnosis of his own, he heard the report about the fertilizer and the dead bison. Charlie intoned, "…Well, it's me AND the buffalo…!" That evening, Charlie learned he had brain cancer.

As Charlie passed through the degenerative stages of cancer, Dave and Patty maintained around-the-clock care of Charlie.

On April Fool's Day, 1982, Charlie died in Patty's arms. He had asked for his ashes to be spread across his Goodpaster River trapline and near his mountainous hunting camps. Patty waited to carry his remains to their old Johnson River glacier camp.

Eight years later, Patty, who had never shot a sheep herself, but had packed many, won a Fish and Game Sheep Permit. Dave described the hunt, "I was Patty's guide;" adding warmly, "she was my client."

In 1989, the Dall ram stood sentry over ewes and lambs. Afraid he might spook, Patty risked a long galley shot, and brought the ram down. Choked with grief, she dressed him out and spread Charlie's ashes on the glacier.

"That night," Patty said, "there was a torrential downpour. Boulders crashed all night, and the cauldron below us boiled.

"I should have known," she smiled, "Charlie was not going to let me get away easily."

Chapter Seventy Seven

174. Ben's first caribou, Sevenmile Lake Trail, 1994.

ALERT ON HIS WATCH

From the beginning, Ben was his father's son, always with him, watching and learning. On our annual caribou hunt when Ben was 10, he walked ahead of us following the Sevenmile Lake Trail through the mountains near the Maclaren River. Armed with his .22, his eyes caught anything that flushed. Ptarmigan frequently landed on the trail ahead of us. Riding on horses behind Ben, we froze while Ben got closer to his prey, raised his rifle, and sent a few feathers flying. Ben's eyes had become more alert with every passing year.

We rode the trail all day, made camp, and began looking for caribou. For days, we searched up and down the valley, but the caribou seemed to be up high in cooler air, away from the bugs. Tired and hungry, we took a break. Sarah, her friend, Julia Dufendach, Ben, and I reclined on a sunny slope for lunch. Reb hiked up the hill to a lookout spot, packing his food and setting up his spotting scope. I lay back, soaking up the sun and enjoying the military repast of C-Rations. The girls tittered and talked, but Ben could not eat. Like an electrified wire, he kept straining to see his Dad beyond the knoll. Out of sight, Reb finally called in a loud whisper, "Send Ben up." Ben dropped his uneaten food and leapt up the slope to his father. Reb whispered to Ben, "There are some beautiful bulls above us." Pointing to the tripod, he murmured, "The rifle and scope are set on the best one, just squeeze the trigger." Ben hunkered down, peered through the scope and fired. A monarch was hit, bagged by a 10 year old.

175. Sarah feeding week-old Thunder, 1998.

Chapter Seventy Eight
RAISING A WILD THING

n thirty-six years of wilderness fur trapping, and recently as pet owners, my family and I have observed wolves and wolf hybrids as shy, private, albeit nervous, creatures.

Hybrid wolves, although half dog, are not dogs and must be treated quite differently. But, as with all of life's elements, the issue is not so much the animal itself, but the responsibility of knowledgeable handling of possibly volatile elements. Hybrids offer a special friendship, and our life with Nishka is a story of one such relationship.

In 1998, our Ukrainian friends gave us a 4-day-old wolf pup to raise. With her paws, baby Thunder grasped the bottle Sarah offered her and sucked voraciously. During Thunder's first weeks of life, Sarah rose throughout the night to feed her baby. During the day, if we went anywhere, Thunder was always carried with us, tucked in a basket. Sarah and Ben warmed calf replacer supplement and fed the pup by bottle until she could eat solid food. The little raw-boned baby perceived Sarah and Ben as her moms.

As the pup was growing into a mature female, Sarah left home and began studying in the Lower 48. During the year she was gone, Ben became the exclusive parent. When the time came for Thunder to mate, we picked our Siberian sled dog, Kodiak. By June, when Sarah returned home for vacation, she found Thunder swollen with her own babies. A little apprehensive after their separation, I watched Thunder closely as she greeted Sarah. To our astonishment, Thunder rolled on her back, begging to have her belly stroked. Thunder had forgotten nothing.

A week later, Thunder had her first litter. After a couple of weeks, we separated the pups from the mother, so that we could bond with them and feed them ourselves. From the beginning, a little female caught Reb's attention. Nishka's eyes, one gray and one blue, betokened her vivacious personality.

Every day as we approached the puppy box in our garage, Nishka's head popped up to greet us along with the six other little jack-in-the-boxes. All ears, eyes, and smiling snouts, they greeted us. Each night, Reb carried Nishka into the house for a special feeding and play.

One day when she was only 4 months old, Reb saw her waiting motionless outside our porch. Her eyes were fixed on the mice paths coming from under the house. When a mouse zipped near her, Nishka's paws, in a flash, flattened the rascal.

176. Nishka and Reb watching T.V., 2001.

When winter arrived, Nishka was a skilled huntress. Poised on our snowy riverbank, she stood like a sentinel with her eyes glued to a shallow area of the Tanana. When she spotted life, she tensed her body into a spear. Then, she dive-bombed through the snowy drift to remove any scent and to coat her longer, coarse guard hairs. Thus armed like a seal, she sliced into the river with her mouth wide open. Her teeth locked around a fish, and she climbed out onto the bank, proudly parading her trophy.

When Reb saw her, he ran to keep her from consuming the slime of the fresh fish, which, due to past experiences, we thought could be potentially toxic. He wrestled her catch from her and lobbed it on a snowy cabin roof, figuring it was safely out of reach. Not for Nishka. She climbed a makeshift ladder as easily as any human and retrieved her bounty.

Throughout the short fish run, Nishka passionately fished. When her catch became stiff as boards, she charitably fed them to her canine brethren chained in the dog yard. When the excitement of the salmon run was over, Nishka's attention turned to running with me when I went jogging. She ran not beside me, but loose in the woods, loping along parallel to my tracks. With life on her own terms, Nishka expressed unbridled joy.

In the evenings, as Reb tried to relax, Nishka gave us no peace. She pressed her face and paws against the picture window and demanded entrance, so she might be at Reb's feet. Once inside, she contentedly extended her paw to him, habituated to him stroking it as he watched T.V. As sweetly as the closest friends, they spent hours in complete understanding, unwinding before the tube. Reb said he could never again have just a dog. Yes, a hybrid requires special care. Perhaps, like the wind or the river, they should be enjoyed for the beauty of their sovereignty, but in the sanctuary of a rural environment.

As Archbishop Hudson Stuck said at the beginning of the Twentieth Century, it will be a shame when all the little peoples of the earth are swallowed up and all humanity is the same. Similarly, may we not be cheated of a responsible and intimate relationship with one of nature's most noble creatures, the hybrid, a link to our unbridled earth.

177. Sarah at Peniel, trapping, 1995.

Chapter Seventy Nine

TRAPLINE PARTNERS

When Sarah turned five, we had a special birthday party for her at Gilles Creek, our most remote trap cabin, but as she grew, she was seldom at that far cabin. Sarah was usually with me while our sons were generally off having adventures with Reb. As Sarah grew older, Reb wanted to do more with her, but dolls and schoolwork were not his thing.

After Sarah graduated from high school in 1996, Reb popped a proposal to Sarah, "If you'll go trapping with me, I'll split the profits with you."

178. Partners share rewards: wolf, marten and fox pelts, 1995, downriver home.

Before Sarah could protest, she was signed on, packed up, and ready to go. Knowing what Sarah would face, it was with some trepidation that I said goodbye to her and to Reb. Despite a lingering cold, she was eager to hitch up her dogs and speed off with her dad over the horizon.

Covered by 6 inches of new snow, a base trail wound around sharp curves and down steep mountains. Having a hard time steering, Sarah frequently missed a curve and plowed the sled into deep snow off the trail. She learned the technique of righting the sled: hoist it, edge the outside runner onto the hard packed trail, balance with one foot, while pushing with the other, shove, and plead with the dogs to help. But, when she was back on the path, if her balance was off during a sharp turn, her sled would overshoot the trail, sailing around the wrong side of a spruce tree. Then, she had to wrench the sled backward while the screaming dogs pulled it forward, working against her. She pushed until her wrists ached.

Sarah learned to mush across wobbly muskeg, ramming into bare tussocks, and then, unwedge a stuck sled. She pushed her sled up a 3,500-foot mountain while the dogs' tongues dripped saliva, pausing for short breathers. The trail steepened to a 60° pitch and narrowed into a deep moose rut. The dogs abruptly stopped. They were at the end of their strength. The load was too heavy and they were not yet hardened. It was up to Sarah. Dad was too far ahead. Sarah shoved the heavy sled forward and cried, "Let's go!" The reward came when she was finally on top, when the valley below opened up, ringed by mountains, blue in the distant haze.

That night, as Sarah lay on her pole bed in the cabin, she stared at the ceiling with her joints groaning from all she had endured.

Underneath Reb's bed, in his trapping box, he had packed a surprise package, waiting for December 5th, Sarah's special day. As he drifted toward sleep in the heat of the cabin, his mind began to recall Sarah's fifth birthday at the Gilles Creek cabin, fourteen years earlier.

Sarah's feet had dangled over the rough bench where she sat in that cabin, watching her mom make her birthday cake. Mom had found some cocoa, sugar, and biscuit mix in the cache barrel. Even though it tasted like musty long johns, those were the basics of Sarah's fifth birthday celebration. The cake was baked on top of the barrel stove under an overturned skillet.

As Reb's memories gave way to sleep, and Sarah slept on the other bunk, the outside temperature quietly dropped to -40° F. The next morning, the dogs moved stiffly as they shifted from their cozy, melted nests. Once the dogs were harnessed to the sled, Reb and Sarah trudged deeper into the wilderness, pausing at the top of Gilles Mountain. Before plunging downward, Dad taught Sarah to rough lock her toboggan runners to help control her descent.

As Sarah flew down the mountainside, she watched a plume of snow shooting out from Reb's brake as he zigged and zagged all the way down. Arriving at the bottom, they mushed over a frozen beaver dam, sledded up a little hill and stopped at Gilles Creek cabin.

As Sarah rested in camp the next morning, Reb checked traps. To celebrate that evening, Reb broke open the rum cake. From under his bed, Reb brought out his secret stash, the mysterious package. Smiling curiously at her father, Sarah opened the bright, little boxes. Sarah fingered the cappuccino candy, tea, and chocolate caramels.

At 9:20 P.M., Trapline Chatter, KJNP's Bush messaging, came on the radio, "Going out to Sarah Ferguson and her dad at Gilles Creek. Coming from Julia and Naomi in Delta, 'Have a great birthday, Sarah! I hope you'll be OK without your cold pizza and cocoa on your birthday morning!'" Sarah's face brightened as she strained to hear over the static and the hissing lantern the seventeen messages sent especially to her.

She and her dad mushed toward home a few days later. When the furs were stretched and dried, they went into Delta to see fur buyer, Dean Wilson. Sarah watched Dean grade the furs, judging their size and color. True to his word, Dad shared the rewards.

Many years later, Sarah is thousands of miles away from the trapline, studying nursing in Oklahoma. But she is still taking fur orders for Dad. Oklahoma friends see and want some of Dad's red fox, marten, and wolverine. Sarah has become Dad's long distance fur handler, still his trapline partner.

Chapter Eighty

THE PLUNDERING OF THE LAND

When I came to Anchorage in 1965 to visit my boyfriend, we brushed by a strange, low hulk on tracks lying in the snow. He gestured casually while explaining, "That's the new snowmachines."

In 1965, Reb, Schulz, Trastek, and Arrington used one of those new snowmachines for trapping. They were expensive, big, heavy, and not dependable. Because Russ Trastek worked in construction on the North Slope, he could afford one and for more dependable transportation, he also had a track vehicle, called a Weasel. Russ was like a king compared to us, the more impoverished trappers. During each spring, the Four Renegades rode the Weasel to hunt moose and to supply their trapline cabins.

179. Reb and Judy return to MonteChristo Creek by dogsled on their 25th anniversary, 1993.

At that time, the Bush was generally inaccessible to those who did not have dogs, a riverboat, or a Super Cub airplane. There were no All Terrain Vehicle/Four-wheelers, efficient snowmachines, or airboats. The Alyeska Pipeline opened Alaska to the modern era, increased the population, and greatly improved the economic base. As the urban population grew, they bought the new recreational vehicles to experience the Bush. As a result, rivers, muskeg and sky became filled with these new toys. Additionally, their hunting pressure resulted in great political arguments as to who should be permitted to hunt, and who shaould be defined as subsistence users of the land.

Contrary to public opinion, Alaska does not have unlimited game. Reb has always contended, "The further north a person goes, the less game he will see per square mile than he did in the warmer, more southerly climates." Continuing, Reb illustrated, "Animals, like humans, thrive where the living is easy, not in the rigorous deep freeze." Formerly, it was clear to the average Bush Alaskan that urbanites could buy beef while those dependent on the land needed game for their winter's meat. However, the issue of equal access to wild, renewable resources for rich and poor, urbanite and Bush dweller has become a political football. The subsistence issue was further complicated by some Native arguments that defined subsistence as Native-use only. Snowballing into years of controversy with no solution yet, the management of the state's fish and game subsistence issues has currently defaulted to the judgment of the federal government.

This land can't endure the deep penetration of the efficient new machinery. Both the political issues and men's equipment plunder the rivers and hills that until recently were only used by Natives and by other trappers.

We resisted buying snowmachines until 1997. Now that we have them, we don't have to wrestle dogs into harnesses. A short trip doesn't have to be an expedition. We can hop on the machine and commute like any modern savage, as Reb often calls us.

The change is similar to our shopping. We no longer buy case lots of food for our winter supply at Probert's grocery store. I don't stand with Clint in my parka on my back for hours at -30° F. hitchhiking on the highway to Fairbanks to go shopping. We don't bring the outhouse toilet seat in to warm by the stove. To do the laundry, it is no longer necessary to chain up my dogs, push a stovepipe under the engine of my Datsun, fire up a propane powered weed burner, and shoot the heat through the stovepipe to heat up my car. Similarly, to communicate, I no longer wait weeks to get a reel-to-reel audiocassette tape from my family in Tulsa. Now, I can email them daily. When I was pregnant on the trapline in 1969, I felt as removed from my comfortable youth and from my family as if I had been transported to a distant penal colony. Now living in a home with a telephone, computer and more able to afford an airplane ticket, I feel my family lives only a certain distance away, not on another planet. Today, when I enter K-Mart or Fred Meyer in Fairbanks, I am no different from those around me. But the young people shopping around me know nothing about, nor are they interested in, a life that was common to Bush Alaska not so very long ago. A Tulsa suburbanite stepped into the last of classical Alaska just before it disappeared in a vapor - like a ghost sliding into its own past…

Remembering an epoch only thirty-five years ago, Reb turned to me, "Do you remember when Quartz Lake was really FAR away? Quartz Lake Charlie Glatfelder lived at the lake, and it was very remote. Charlie needed snowshoes and dogs to get in and out, unlike access today by motor home."

I remembered. When I had first arrived in Alaska, I had walked the Cat trail to Quartz Lake for two long hours, barefooted, packing a load, in cold mud up to my calves. It was one of my many initiations into the country.

Chapter Eighty One
A SON'S RETURN

180. Clint's mode of transportation in 1990, Black. Rika's Roadhouse State Park.

n 1971, when Clint was growing up on the trapline, he would sit -- while we worked -- in the trail hollows, in-between the tree roots, pretending he was in a toy car. By the hour. he sat there, making "varoom-m, varoom-m-m" noises as his dad and I cut trail. For play, Reb carved faces for 13-month-old Clint in the tree burls: Mr. Happy, who was all cheeks and Mr. Rabbit, who had blazes for tall ears. During the winter, when we whizzed by on the frozen trail, we always saluted the tree burl men. They were our signposts.

Our life back then was steady and quiet. A sudden whirring on the trail alerted us to a spruce grouse just ahead. In preparation for winter, squirrels stacked dry, crunchy cones in piles under the spruce trees. It was routine every evening that before we descended the hills to a trap cabin, Reb would step off the trail into the deep fluff. He stripped some birchbark off a tree for making the fire in the cabin below. Later, as we relaxed at Campbell's, the sweet odor of birchbark burning mingled with that of the barrel stove's heating metal -- always meant we were back.

181. After a long but successful night's hunt, Clint and Heather with caribou on Black, 1997.

The three of us, Reb, Clint, and I, lived a natural existence and were each other's company. Clint was 7 years old before he had a sibling. He home-schooled alone upriver until he was 16. In the middle of his sophomore year, he entered a school with other children at Whitestone Farms.

In his junior year, Clint met Heather, a girl who was formerly from an East Coast city. He courted her as his father had courted me by riding on his black horse to see her. That spring, after he flunked his driver's test, he asked me, "What's an expressway?" Shortly after, Heather asked me, "What's an outboard …?" I knew we were in for some adjustments.

Always, Reb had maintained that any prospective mate of his children had to first endure the rigors of the trapline. Just after they married, Clint took Heather on the trapline. They each rode a horse. Like Reb had first done to me, Clint did not simply take her to Campbell's Cabin, which was relatively easy to access. Instead, he took her to the cabin that was hardest to get to, Schist Creek. Clint led her on a merry ride up mossy, very steep mountains. Heather clinched her knees as the horse lunged, fighting for his footing in the narrow, deep moose rut bordered by hollow moss cover. Clint had only one weekend free to hunt, but the only complaint Heather made was that Clint had a myopic focus: hunting.

For years, Clint had wanted to see more of the Lower 48 than he had seen during family visits south. In 1995, he and Heather moved to the southern part of Georgia, deciding to build log homes in a growing area. In 1997, we invited them to return home and go hunting with us. I promised Heather that if the going got rough, she and I could take the truck and go home, leaving the hunting to the guys.

Reb's childhood friend, Bill Chmura, also wanted one more hunt, but he would have to go by horseback because his knees were bad. With only three horses for seven people, Ben, Reb, Clint, and Heather hiked. Ben trotted ahead, scouting for ptarmigan as usual. Reb was close behind. Riding the horses, Sarah, Bill, and I packed camping equipment for seven people up to spike camp. Trumpet-like tendrils of white lichen crunched under foot as our parade marched, scanning the horizon for caribou.

The next day, Reb, Bill, and Ben left spike camp and rode to the plateau above the lake. Clint and Heather spotted a grizzly in the opposite direction and riding double, they began working their way toward it. Sarah and I tended camp.

182. Three Ferguson men: Ben on Jahna, Clint on Black, Reb on Clancy, caribou hunting, 1997.

Near the lake, Bill and Reb spotted a snowy-bearded caribou. Just before dark, Bill landed the bull, but it fell in the swampy edge around the lake. They tied the caribou to our horse, Clancy, and slowly edged it out of the water. They butchered and retrieved the meat, and still returned to camp not long after dark. The moon rose as Bill, Reb, and Ben drank cocoa by the fire, but still - Clint and Heather had not returned. Standing on a boulder, like a pinhead in the vast valley, I held our Coleman lantern up, hoping to guide them in, in the deep black. No response. The hours ticked by. I thought of Heather...and of my promise...I stewed; before now, she had never hunted quite so hard.

I finally heard the breathing of a large animal and the sound of canvas panniers brushing against the shrubbery. We ran to greet them. As they entered the circle of the lantern light, caribou horns, the crowning achievement, rode on top of bags of meat hanging off of Black. Clint explained the stalk, that he had shot just before dark and how Heather had helped in every stage of the gutting process. Heather's pants were caked with mud. Her Italian brown eyes were wide with fatigue. Mustering a minx grin, she remembered my promise saying that we could exit if the going got rough. She accused, "You tricked me!" "Yes," I admitted, "I guess I did..."

Clint and Heather returned to base camp the next day leading the horse, loaded with caribou meat to store in the trailer, and also to reward Heather with a hot shower at the nearby lodge. The second day, they rode double bareback, returning from base back up to spike camp. On the way, Clint scoped the brush by the river. He saw a moose rack appear and then, disappear.

To be a legal moose to shoot, the rack had to measure 50 inches across. As a builder, Clint imagined a 48-inch piece of plywood and decided the rack seemed large enough. So, with no saddle or tripod to use to steady his rifle, he shot the moose from 300 feet, stabilizing his rifle only against his shoulder. In recent years, we had only hunted caribou. This was the first moose our family had gotten since the last one Reb and Clint had shot thirteen years before. As if marked how special it was, the moose had a crook in the left palm of his rack, a unique deformation.

With the moose, when Clint re-entered spike camp with yet more meat, his grin spread across his face, "Yeah," he said, "it seems like the game ran down from the hills to welcome me back home."

Chapter Eighty Two
FRESH BREEZE

Riding the Invisible Line, riding on the heights of the earth, speeding past spruce trees, propelling down hills…" Elaine Eads, a new transplant to Delta, wrote these song lyrics after a trip on our trapline in 1990.

Elaine had grown up in southern California, where, every day, she was able to go swimming outside. She had come to Alaska not at all sure about moving to the Alaskan icebox. Although a lover of the outdoors, she had no familiarity with the North.

I, on the other hand, had twenty-five years experience with life in the sub-Arctic.

In the late 1960s, it had been normal in the springtime for Reb and me to fly down 3200-foot high mountains with our dogsleds, singing, "Born Free!" on hills known only to us.

In the dark evenings of those midwinters, we had read *Wilderness Welfare*, a book in which a young couple, like us, lived in the Bush. When the couple turned fifty, the woman no longer enjoyed sitting on the cold, hard earth. When I was 23 years old, I found her attitude incomprehensible.

Yet, when I became 50 and Reb still asked me every spring, "Hey, you want to hitch up a team and go with me out to Campbell's?" I often busied myself with something else. How many times must I wrestle maniac dogs, travel the same moose rut, get wet feet, arrive exhausted and sweat-soaked to sit for a few hours in a sunken cabin, and then, head back?

But, Elaine's outlook had not always been as happy as one in springtime. For one so young, she had experienced a deep valley; a time when she was unsure if spring would ever come again. When it did come, Elaine, a gifted musician, wrote, *The Harvest Has Come*. The song started low in tone and then soared, *"Though the winter may come; you're set to go on; for there will be a spring."* She followed this song by another, *"But you shall ride on the heights of the earth, and taste of things not seen or heard…"* Elaine had an inner eye for riding on blue hills.

That April in 1990, each of us handled a team as we sledded into the wilderness. Elaine mushed behind Reb on his dog sled, and I followed on my sled. That morning, Elaine loaded an overnight bag into her sled and then began pushing the sled slowly up the hills. An hour later, she topped the mountains, sailing along the hard trail. She was overcome by the blue hills unfolding around her, as far as the eye

183. Elaine Eads on Ferguson trapline, 1990.

could see. She sang, *"Wait for the Lord; and you will ride on the heights of the earth."* Softly, she said to me, "but I never expected it to be so soon."

Elaine and I were never ones to learn by rote. If there was a maverick trail, we always tried it. Suddenly, Elaine saw something she liked, stepped off her sled to go see, and immediately sank into snow up to her hips.

"Helpppp!" She called to Reb, her guardian. "Come get me!" she called as she swam in the bog of fluff.

"Can't leave my sled," Reb said with more inertia than needed. "Huh?" Elaine was stupefied.

"Can't leave my sled," Reb reiterated. "My dogs will get away. Judy can't leave hers either. Dog fights."

Understanding well her plight, I coaxed, "Elaine, push against that sapling tree and you can get up."

Back on the trail, Elaine began to discover the invisible line - the one-lane margin of security - our hard-packed trail in the unending white fluff. As we mushed, she began to write a new song *"Riding the invisible line, a trail that's been tested by time..."*

But, the invisible line was narrow. If Elaine didn't cut her runners into the uphill side of the trail, she and her sled caught the softer snow and bottomed out again in the drift. In a most coquettish tone, Elaine again called sweetly, "Rebbbb!"

"Can't leave my sled," Reb replied laconically.

That evening at Campbell's Cabin, Elaine tried to befriend the white, cold fluff. She strapped on snowshoes and pointed her tips forward, but unused to their length, she was soon sprawling again deep in the white morass.

To reward her that evening, after the fire was warming the barrel stove, Reb poured Elaine a cup of cocoa and added a bit of Peppermint Schnapps.

As we relaxed on our individual, spruce-pole bunks, Elaine opened her mysterious overnight bag. Reb and I were wide-eyed as she unloaded perfume, make-up, and dry shampoo, covering a crude shelf in the cabin with cosmetics.

The next morning, like birch sap rising in the spring, Elaine chirped to me, "Good morning, Sunshine," as she pecked me on my cheek.

In the morning light, through my pinched-shut eyes, I could see her combing dry shampoo through her tawny tresses.

That evening, as we drove home in the truck, Elaine was a woman reborn. She sang softly, *"Riding the invisible line, a trail that's been tested by time. A watchman in front and a shepherd behind, riding the invisible line."*

184. A child primed for canoeing, Ben, at end of trip, 2000.

Chapter Eighty Three
THE YUKON AND ALASKA BY CANOE

The Long Way Home…Porcupine River and Beaufort Sea…

Inspired by our friend, Charlie Wolf, who in one summer had canoed the Rat River, portaged to the Bell, and paddled the Porcupine and Yukon Rivers, my family and I began dreaming in the 1970s of someday canoeing that route.

Charlie spent his winters in Fairbanks mapping the Hudson Bay Company's routes. He focused on the corridor that threaded through the Yukon Territory's Bell River, crossing the international boundary on the Porcupine River and over to Alaska's Fort Yukon.

One winter, Charlie described his Rat/Bell/Porcupine trip to us by letter and added, "If you wait a bit, the Canadians will finish the Dempster Highway and you can simply drive to the Eagle River and launch there."

Folding Charlie's onionskin paper that was smudged from his manual typewriter, I tucked the idea away for someday.

Charlie died a few years after the Dempster Highway was completed in 1979. Twenty-one years later, I recalled his river stories as I read a travel brochure that said: "The Dempster, Canada's northernmost highway, 737 kilometers…" Someday had come.

August 6, 2000, Reb, Ben, and I drove the Dempster with two different excursions on our minds. Each of us chose the direction of our adventure. Reb and Ben would canoe from the Eagle River in the Yukon Territory, following the rivers of the Vuntut Gwich'in Natives, west to the Yukon River Bridge in Alaska. They would end their trip where the Yukon River crosses the Dalton Highway. After leaving them at the Eagle River, I planned to drive the truck north on the Dempster, passing through Gwich'in Indian lands to Inuvik and the Inuvialuit Eskimo area of the Beaufort Sea in the Northwest Territories. I would then return to Alaska, and three weeks later pick Reb and Ben up at the end of their trip. Reunited at the Yukon Crossing, we would then return home to Delta.

After driving the Dempster to the Eagle River access, we pulled up to look at the river. In the dark, I stared incredulously at the rivulet in a scrub forest, swarming with bugs, at the end of the Dempster's trail. That was a river?! In the morning, I would be leaving my family there. To offset my feelings of desperation, before going to bed, we celebrated Ben's 16th birthday in a gravel pit where we were camping.

The next morning, in hip boots, Ben waded into the Eagle to finish loading the canoe. Reb snapped down the canoe's nylon splash cover.

"Why don't we just go home?" I asked.

"We are going home," he said with a smile. "You're going one way and we're going the other…"

A little nervously, Ben zipped up his life jacket and eased through the canoe's splash skirt into his seat. When Reb turned the canoe, I could see only 6 inches of freeboard in the rear. They waved as they rounded the curve, disappearing into the Yukon Territory's maze of watersheds.

185. Ben and Reb begin 800 mile canoe trip, Eagle River, Yukon Territory, 2000.

Their trip was chronicled in Ben's journal:

Day One: After two hours of farewells, we headed out for a three-week trip on the Eagle, the Bell, the Porcupine, and the Yukon Rivers: 800 miles total.

Along the river's edge, a tawny head with tufted ears, and marble yellow eyes - a lynx - watched through the wind-parted grasses.

Eagles' nests stood guard over the placid river.

The Eagle River had no banks, but only ropes of soft silt oozing into the creek. Just before another rainstorm hit, Dad got a tent up and built a large campfire.

Day Two: A white wolf watched as Dad and I pulled our loaded canoe through the shallow Eagle. In this forgotten land, we passed another lynx, a moose, and circling peregrine falcons. Some wet moss softened our rocky pallet where we spent the night.

Day Three: The current almost sucked us into a sweeper/cut bank trap. We paddled hard. Finally, the water was deep enough to use the motor.

When we startled the geese and ducks, they didn't fly. Later, in Old Crow, the Gwich'in said to us, "The ducks don't fly in July…because of change in feathers."

Since it was pouring rain, the campfire I made was, to me, a work of art.

Dad added, "We have used 6 gallons of gas so far."

Day Four: After an hour, we hit the Bell, a slightly clearer river. Dad was cutting through 2-foot waves and I was getting soaked. I zipped my splash cover to my chin.

Then, to our surprise, we saw black dots on the shoreline. Ten people were going to a big camp-out where the Bell meets the Porcupine.

At the campout, we met Lenny who was from Washington D.C. He and Heather were leading a bunch of kids from Aklavik, Inuvik, and Fort McPherson, Northwest Territories to protest the proposed drilling in the Arctic National Wildlife Refuge because of concern for the Porcupine caribou herd.

Old Crow resident, Freddy Frost, whose relative, Jack, was mentioned in *Two In the Far North* by Margaret Murie -- her account of their trip to the Porcupine in 1926 -- also greeted us at the confluence.

Freddy had just killed a caribou. He skinned, stretched, and pegged the hide on the ground using sharpened willows pegs to show the kids the elders' way.

Day Five: Bull caribou crowned with horns splashed along the Porcupine's shoreline.

The Northern Pike were a dime a dozen.

Today, I caught a 5-pound Pike and a big Sheefish.

Day Six and Seven: After we were under way, the wind began blowing and driving rain. The waves got really big. We pulled out, set up tarps, made camp, rolled the canoe over, and got a big fire going.

As we worked, a 24-foot riverboat, carrying people huddled under a tarp, pushed through the storm.

Through a very windy night and next day, we were snug reading, *The Mad Trapper of Rat River.* We woke the second day to snow.

Day Eight: The next morning, we saw a boat pass from Old Crow; there was smoke coming out of a tent on the riverboat's deck.

Bull caribou were running in 2 inches of fresh snow.

We arrived in Old Crow, the most remote and northern village in the Yukon Territory."

Road to Inuvik Graveled with Good Intentions

Waving, Reb and Ben slipped from my sight at the Eagle River boat launch, beginning their 800-mile canoe voyage from the Yukon Territory to the Yukon River highway crossing in Alaska.

Alone, I swung into our diesel truck ready for high adventure on the Dempster Highway, a gravel road with a reputation for flat tires and isolation.

Reb was not comfortable with our original plan of me driving alone to Inuvik and had been urging me to return straight home.

But, I wanted to see just around the next bend. I opened both windows, turned up my music, and drove. The North opened up in every direction.

A sign proclaimed "The Arctic Circle," but a rainbow over the endless valleys promised the top of the world. As I drove a little further, the road unfolded one view after another. Suddenly, there was a sign, like an outpost to the hinterlands, saying I was entering the Northwest Territories.

Resembling the mountains of the moon, the country warranted a pause at a highway turnout on a plateau. The fresh air filled my lungs as I strode to the elevated viewing stand. The land dropped away to the Peel River, its floodplains, and the Mackenzie River drainage. When I turned around, I caught my breath. My truck was sitting on a completely flat tire.

For an hour, I had been alone on the highway, but just when I was in need, a car appeared and stopped. An hour later, its occupants were wishing they had never seen me. The tire bolts were one solid mass of dirt and corrosion, inseparable from the rim. I only had a primitive lug wrench, but the patient Good Samaritan from Ontario, although sweating, worked unceasingly on the tire and never swore. Finally, the tire broke free. With his tired eyes twinkling, my roadside helper instructed me to buy a long-handled lug wrench soon - somewhere.

Fort McPherson, on the other side of the Peel River ferry crossing, was my first possibility. As I waited to cross, the town's name brought to mind visions of the radio show of my childhood, *Sergeant Preston of the Yukon* as the Mountie would mush into a French-Canadian fort. After crossing the moderately sized creek on the ferry, I rumbled across the very rocky road and turned into Fort McPherson.

The Dene Indian mechanic's accent was Scottish-Canadian. Using high-speed tools, he checked all my tires and said if I hurried I could get across the last river and buy tools in Inuvik the following day.

Reb, probably knowing the truck only had a primitive lug wrench, had feared for me to drive alone to Inuvik and the Arctic Ocean.

But, "if you hurry," the mechanic said, "you can catch the ferry and get to Inuvik by midnight, where you can get a long-handled lug wrench."

No problem. I hurried to the crossing, and gasped. It was an ocean. What I had thought would be the Arctic Red River was not only that, but was also where the Mackenzie River intersected with the Red. Cutbanks, imposing at a distance, were on the east side of the Mackenzie. The ferry was dwarfed by the broad river intersection. After my truck was loaded, the ferry chugged slowly across the river to the continuation of the Dempster on the far side.

On the ferry, I eased out of the truck and looked back at the church in the village of Tsiigèhtchic glowing white in the midnight sun's slanting rays. The green water was capped with gold. Peace was close…but with a long handled wrench…

The sun began to slide toward the horizon, it was nearly midnight and fatigue slipped over me as, back on the road, I muddled through a construction zone on the east side of the Mackenzie River. The carbuncle gravel, grooves, and ruts slowed me to a crawl. The gravel ribbon that was called a highway was a narrow pad installed above water in the mosquito zone, threading through spongy ground and lakes. Up here on the moon, a dry campsite was almost impossible to find.

I was feeling I had pushed myself too far; the glory of the trip was behind me. But, I was committed. I had to continue forward… The few-and-far-between islands of dry ground beckoned me to stop and rest.

Finally, like a mirage, I could see the Beaufort Sea in the distance. I stopped on the crest of a hill at a hand-painted sign announcing the town of Inuvik. The sign was decorated with paintings of inuksuk - a pile of stones arranged in the likeness of a human being. The town, itself, spread below me.

In a land with few gravel pullouts and no natural, dry ground for camping, there was no choice but to pull into an RV park.

Managing the RV park was a young man, Denn, an Inuvialuit - meaning "real human beings" - which is a branch of the Inuit, "the people." During our conversation, he pointed to the map and told me about Nunavut, the new Canadian territory that was formed April 1, 1999, when the Northwest Territories split into further subdivisions. Nunavut, meaning "our land" in the Inuktitut language, is the largest of the three Canadian territories and came about as the result of more than 30 years of negotiations by the Inuit of the Eastern and Central Arctic.

Dene further explained the strange rock piles, the inuksuk. He told me that prior to modern

186. Tsiigehtchic (pron: "T seh guhchek") formerly Arctic Red River, 2003.

communication, the Inuit left signs on the open tundra, little messages of human existence. Visible for miles, these rocks could simply mean a smile, or they might mark a cache or a previous camp. The inuksuk have become the winsome symbol for the Northwest Territories.

That night, I collapsed on my truck's back seat wondering where I was... And where my family might be.

Angels Found on the Road and in an Igloo

Lying on my back in the backseat of my truck in the RV camp, I awoke trying to grasp the idea that I was at the far end of North America, at least as far as one can drive, in the Northwest Territories, 442 graveled miles into my trip.

With a little coffee inside me, I was ready to see Inuvik, the "Living Place." This community is called home by 3,000 Dene Athabascans, Inuit, and other non-Native Canadians, despite the drawbacks of paying seven dollars per head for lettuce, the restrictions of living at the end of an interminable gravel road, and bills that exceed their income.

The round shape of the Inuit dome on top of the Catholic Church was striking, and beckoned me to investigate. Agnes, the Athabascan caretaker of the Arctic style igloo, promised to give me a tour of the church. Reaching only to my shoulder as we walked side by side, Agnes tilted her face up to mine, peeking out from under her flat sunbonnet. She poured out information with a laugh that rippled like an unsuppressed song. I realized she waited daily in her church, available to any struggling tourist who might simply need to talk.

As we sat in a pew under the elaborately arched igloo ceiling, a Notre Dame in the Arctic, Agnes asked me if I liked to camp.

"I grew up trapping," she said as she remembered her family's nomadic life. "Marten, muskrat

215

187. A Notre Dame in the Arctic, igloo stylized Roman Catholic church, Inuvik, Northwest Territories, 2000.

trapping. I lived in a tent with my family. I had enough of that. Today my husband and I trailer when we travel.

Agnes had scrubbed the floor for the arrival of a church emissary that day, but she had prepared no more urgently for him than she did for any of God's tourists.

I craned my neck to see the ceiling of the church, designed by a French priest with only a third-grade education. But, I had to cut short my fascination with this architectural wonder as I had a mid-afternoon flight to catch.

I wanted to fly over the Mackenzie Delta to the Beaufort Sea village of Tuktoyaktuk and had signed on for a commercial tour. I embraced Agnes and hurried to the floatplane dock.

When I was safely seated with the other five passengers, the six-seater aircraft lifted off the bay, circled over a channel of the Mackenzie River, and headed over the delta's marshy lands. As we flew, the pilot explained that pingos are an Arctic upheaval of land, appearing like pimples on the terrain. Over time, many of them sink and form lakes. As we watched from the windows, the setting sun glinted diamond lasers off the lakes formed from sunken pingos. We flew 137 miles north along high coastal bluffs. Near the edge of the cliffs, an empty reindeer station testified to the Alaskan-Canadian effort of 1935-1964 to raise domesticated reindeer tended by Inuvialuit herders.

We skidded into Kugmallit Bay at Tuktoyaktuk, a picture reminiscent of an Alaska magazine calendar photo. Reds, blues, and ochers echoed in an iridescent vibrancy in the slanting rays of the Midnight Sun. Wearing a thin kuspuk - the Yupik and Inupiaq summer parka - our hostess showed us both her salmon smoking and the baleen from the village's last whale hunt. She pointed out a traditional home made of driftwood, moss, and sod blocks that demonstrated the era before pre-fabricated houses. She showed us a vast, underground tunnel that was used year-round as a natural freezer for the village's fish and meat. Like a microcosm of the coastal village's culture, she, a Caucasian, was married to an Inuvialuit, and they reared their children in the traditional as well as the computer-based cultures. We drove past large oil storage units and then, stepping on the plane's wing, we left behind the pure colors of the Beaufort Sea and returned that evening to Inuvik.

The next morning at a café in Inuvik, Jimmy, an elderly Inuvialuit gentleman climbed the steps of the café and in a deeply human, genuine manner spontaneously and warmly greeted me. We sat next to each other over breakfast while he told me of his days as a reindeer herder. Walking as if he might still be chasing reindeer, Jimmy had worn out his knees chasing the animals.

In a government-sponsored experiment for herding reindeer, he and his partners had lived in a tent as they worked the herd, never using mechanical vehicles. Once, unsuccessfully, they tried riding the reindeer to keep up with the herd. They traveled from water hole to pasture. Eventually, nature ended the experiment as the herd mingled with wild caribou. After all, Tuktoyaktuk means, "resembling a caribou."

After breakfast, I was almost ready to face the Dempster Highway again. At an automotive store, I purchased the long-awaited, long-handled lug wrench. To my new tool kit, I added a wire brush and spray solvent for stubborn tire bolts. Then, I confidently started down the narrow, gravel strip through the Northwest Territories toward home.

As night clamped down as I headed south at 1 A.M. on the late July night, ghostly warnings swept up the highway: belts of heavy fog, omens of the approaching winter. At midnight, I peered through the windshield wipers whipping back and forth, watching the desolate highway unrolling in front of me. Past the mountains and south into Dawson, I finally drove into an RV park at 2 A.M. "Not another mile," I whined and collapsed again on the back seat of the truck.

The next morning, a young man tapped on my truck window, "You have a flat tire," he intoned. What could have been flashed through my mind: me (with my new lug wrench) in the dark and stinging cold at 1 A.M., alone in the mountains, and trying to change a flat. I thanked God for the company of another human and sank into civilization's embrace.

After the young man used my new wrench to fix the tire, I sped home to Delta to begin the long three weeks of waiting before I would meet Reb and Ben at the Yukon River Bridge north of Fairbanks.

Pair of Voyageurs Share Rite of Passage

188. Ben and Reb, Yukon Crossing, 2000.

Reb and Ben were traveling far beyond Ben's familiar world, into the Arctic wilderness, with no safety net.

With Old Crow behind them, they approached new Rampart House. The designation of new had stuck, even though it had been 110 years since it was built. A former Canadian Customs House, and a remnant of the Hudson Bay Company, the new Rampart House was once the focus of an international boundary squabble.

During the gold rush of the late 19th century, it was found that the two-story Canadian Customs House building was actually on American property, necessitating moving the building 30 miles upstream into Canadian territory. In those days the rivers were the highways and new Rampart House was a very busy border crossing. But, as Reb and Ben cruised down the Porcupine River from Canada into the United States, there were no longer any border guards in sight.

The Salmon-Trout, a glass-like river, appeared on their left. Its clear water, moist air, and narrow walls invited the hungry fishermen. As they entered, the cathedral-like rock walls extended like a vault high above them, blocking out the sky. Ben trailed a fishing line in the green stream. Suddenly, he felt a heavy hit. A fish splashed and fought, but in 5 minutes Ben had landed a 15-pound Sheefish safely into the boat.

That night, Ben cooked dinner for Dad in a skillet over an open campfire. In a white spruce and mossy forest, squirrels had stashed mounds of cones in preparation for winter. Reb stretched a tarp between the trees. Raindrops hit the nylon, rolling and funneling into a 5-pound coffee can to be used for their drinking water.

The next day, continuing up the Salmon-Trout River, Reb and Ben hit shallow water forcing them to pull the boat up the narrow canyon. As Ben waded in the river, pulling the boat's bow upstream, he began to get moist from the spray of rolling waves. Hawks flew far above them in the open sky. With migration season nearing, adolescent ducks were practicing their flying. As Reb and Ben turned back downstream, every cast brought a 17-inch grayling; there was no way to keep them all.

For days, Reb and Ben had been breathing slightly smoky air. Forest fires were raging in Alaska and the pollution was drifting into the Yukon Territory. Reb saw dollar bills floating by as he missed weeks of firefighting pay and overtime. It chafed him, and worse, he was getting low on gas. It did not bother Ben; he hoped to remain in fisherman's paradise forever. In the distance, Ben saw a red object bobbing like a life jacket around a bend in the Porcupine.

The next morning, Reb stuck his head out of the tent to see what kind of a day it was. The river level had dropped and, in the night, the river had washed up a sealed can of mixed gas, leaving it stranded high and dry on a rock. Reb tested it, poured it into his outboard, pulled the recoil, and then he was back in business. Ben's shoulders slumped; they would now make better time and he was not ready to go home.

The deep, clear Coleen River appeared, and disappeared, on the right, for Reb was boogying to Fort Yukon. However, they still had a ways to go. At John Heberts Village, they visited Old Simon, a Native guide, who was scorching a porcupine's quills off the meat. With a spruce pole, he rolled the meat over on the rocks and scraped the charred mass. Reb and Simon talked of guns and hunting season, and Simon offered Reb and Ben a hot dinner. Well fed, they thanked their host and left the Porcupine, turning their boat into the mighty Yuke's 5-mile breadth. To stabilize their craft in the turbulent waters of the Yukon River, Reb strapped two inflatable pontoons to either side of the canoe.

Before bed that night, to facilitate an easy fire in the morning, Reb prepped some kindling by scraping sticks backward with a knife. As they tried to sleep in the tent, Reb and Ben heard some teenagers from the village of Venetie inspecting the camp. One said, "Hey! This guy knows what he's doin' 'Fizz sticks! My grandpa used to do that." Reb and Ben unzipped the mosquito netting and greeted their midnight visitors.

During the night, there were more guests. About fifty geese, on their southern migration, had landed and were taking a break for gossip on the sandbar. Later, a panting sound slowly began to creep into Reb's sleep-numbed brain.

"Hey, Ben," he hissed. "There's a wolf outside the tent."

Unable to sleep, Reb stuck both his gun and his Mini Mag Flashlight out the door, but his wolf was actually blowing brush rubbing against the wall of the tent. Relieved, the two men slept. The next morning, they started for Stevens Village; from there, they called for me to come get them.

As they began the last leg of their adventure, the Yukon narrowed into a canyon. Around the bend, the Yukon River Bridge suddenly appeared, an apparition in the wilderness. With the rays of the setting sun reflecting on it, the bridge appeared as a beam of light suspended across the river.

As I drove across the bridge, Reb was waiting on the bank. Next to him, and smiling back at me, Ben stood: tall, tan, and not a boy, but instead a blue-eyed man. A full rainbow framed the bridge as the seasoned father, the grizzled voyageur, loaded their gear into the truck.

With the engine revved at 55 mph, we headed south. Ben cried, "It's so fast! Take me back to Stevens Village!" All the way to Fairbanks, he studied the book *Wild Rivers of Alaska*, excitedly describing each river, pointing out which one they could explore next.

As we pulled up to Fred Meyer's neon-lit diesel pumps, Reb turned to me, "It was the perfect timing," he winked from under three weeks of grime, "for a boy to take a trip he will never forget."

Chapter Eighty Four
BOW LEGEND
'The Great One'

189. Ben, accomplished bow hunter, Brooks Range, 2001.

With his heart pounding, Ben Ferguson, after six days of hunting, had a barren-ground caribou in his bow sights. As the animal came toward him, he only had split seconds to make his shot.

Ben was learning an ultimate hunting challenge: archery in the Brooks Range. While Ben was growing up, Clint had told him stories of bow hunting and of bagging the big one. Many times, Reb had recited to both his sons the story of shooting his first deer with a bow.

While Clint was growing up on our solitary upriver homestead, he played both cowboy and Indian with his small bow and arrows, preparing to later use the real bow that Reb's childhood friend, Bill Chmura, had given him. But not until Clint was grown and living in his own home in South Georgia, did he seriously bow hunt. He got his first deer with a Broadhead point. In his spare time, he watched his 3-year-old son, Hunter, play with his own little bow and arrows.

"There's something special about bow hunting," Clint told me on the phone. "It's the ultimate challenge in hunting. Also, the ambience of the quiet nature of the sport is very satisfying. When the shadows deepen here in the dense vegetation, it's very mysterious."

Once a year, the three Ferguson men hunt the creek bottoms of South Georgia together. In November 2000, Ben, the only Ferguson who had not bagged anything with a bow, was inspired.

In 2001, Reb had one goal in mind. He carefully chose equipment ordered through Cabela's archery catalog. Then, he practiced nightly for a projected big trip to the Brooks Range.

When Reb and Ben were not ordering points, camouflage clothing, arrows, archery tranquilizers, and targets, they were at Alaska Fish and Game's required archery course.

On a foggy August 18, 2001, we started up the Dalton Highway, listening to trucker chat on the Citizens Band radio and hugging our side of the road as semis whizzed past.

Suddenly coming into view, Sukakpak, a jagged mountain, was an explosion of rock.

We crossed Atigun Pass, the highest point on the Dalton Highway, and then left the last tree behind on the south side of the Brooks Range. Descending the Brooks Range on the north side, the mountains were stark, obtrusive, and prehistoric, rising above the undulating tundra.

We had passed through four topographical zones and driven 847 miles in three days. It felt more like two countries than a single State. At mile J353, we turned into the Wyoming Gage Turnout and set up camp.

190. Ben practicing, Brooks Range, 2001.

As the men blew up air mattresses, they were tormented by views of wandering caribou. When the shelter was up, they hurriedly slipped into their leafy camouflage gear and headed for a gully full of brush, the only cover for miles.

Caribou bulls were roaming the hills in twos and fours, drifting south. For the next five days, Reb and Ben walked miles of muskeg, stalked, lost arrows, and fought morning and evening coastal fog. In the evenings, they practiced shooting at targets in camp, adjusting the distance pins of their bow sights from 25, 50 to 75 yards.

On the sixth day, they decided on a different hunting technique.

The day began crystal clear. By 10 A.M., the coastal fog filled every valley. We sat in camp cut off from the world by the pea soup coming in off the Beaufort Sea. Damp disgust settled into

189. Clint, practicing upriver, 1977.

our bones. Tired of wasted time, we began packing to look elsewhere.

By 1 P.M., everything but the tent was loaded in the truck. But now it was suddenly hot. The riveting sunshine had burned off the fog and bulls were roaming tantalizingly across the now visible hills. From time to time, the caribou broke out into a run. Bugs were driving them higher to cooler climes.

Throwing their tree garb back on, the hunters left one more time for the big one. For ninety minutes, they hiked across the muskeg, but then decided to wait, not to chase.

They split up onto two ridges that were separated by a natural caribou corridor. Reb hunkered down on his hill, while Ben scanned from his ridge. The majestic bulls were in no danger; everything

191. Reb, the veteran, Brooks Range, 2001.

192. Sukakpak, border where Inupiaq and Athabaskans historically traded, Brooks Range.

for miles was visible across the unbroken hills. Half dazed by the sun, Ben opened his lunch and began munching.

Abruptly startling him out of his stupor, a medium-sized caribou, driven wild by the warble flies, ran straight for him on the ridge. He ducked behind a bush, but the caribou had spotted him against the horizon.

"Well, that's it," Ben sighed, having carelessly allowed himself to be sky-lined. But the caribou was passing in front of his dad's vantage point, running towards Ben, 200 yards away. Not daring to risk the noise of movement, Ben did not draw his bow then, but let the bull pass, giving him a lead of 50 yards.

Through the sights of his 50-yard pin, Ben moved his bow in sync with the running caribou and aimed just above his back. "Yo!" he yelled. "Hey!" The startled animal turned. Ben let his arrow fly. The arrow, entering the bull's ribs and passing through his lungs in one shot, incredibly, did the job. "We got a downed caribou!" Ben yelled, but his voice drifted out over the open tundra. Hearing something, Reb walked laconically toward his son, sure they were going to stalk another missed caribou. "Well," he said, scanning the horizon. "Where?"

"There's a sleeping bull over there!" Ben said as he pointed, figuring he could fool his dad.

"Where?" his dad asked as he craned his neck to look at something strange.

"There's a sleeping caribou, Dad, only 100 yards out. We can still get him."

"Where?"

"Dad!" Ben exploded, "We got a dead caribou!"

Reb's eyes softened as he cuffed Ben affectionately.

The two packed the meat back to camp as the golden sunset warmed their faces. The 17-year-old Ben, the son of the Trenton hunter had closed the gap. He could sit now by Clint's hearth and tell his older brother's son the story of the great one, the bull Uncle Ben shot in the Brooks Range in 2001.

Chapter Eighty Five
A SOLSTICE NIGHT'S DREAM
Peak of Summer: Celebrating Solstice

When I was a child, summer solstice meant William Shakespeare's *Midsummer Night's Dream*. In Tulsa, Oklahoma, we had no Midnight Sun or mountain wild-flowers, but we had Golden Records. As children in the 1950s, my sister, Marian, my brother, Walter, and I spent hours listening to those records. One was a musical version of the whimsical Midsummer Night's Dream. During the hot days of Tulsa's summers, the stories provided a marvelous land of escape.

When I was 22, I left Tulsa and the ordinary daylight of the Lower 48 realm. As I headed north, I entered a land where the sun shone at a different angle, making deep, intense colors. The first night I was in Fairbanks, I gazed at the houses bathed in midnight gold. I had entered a timeless zone: the magic world of Shakespeare's fairy, Puck, and of Queen Titania. Around me people talked, but an evening reverie washed the grass, the sky, and us. Transformed, I knew I was home. Three days later, I met Reb, my future husband.

For the next thirty-four years of married life, solstice marked a special time in our lives, an anniversary of sorts. During most of those summers, however, Reb was frequently away fighting forest fires. Nevertheless, I celebrated the magic of the Midnight Sun as I took care of our horses, sled dogs, garden, and our three children. I reveled in the wash of gold as I, like most homesteaders, did my midnight chores.

When Sarah was 20 and Ben, 13, my sister, Marian, came to visit us during solstice, 1997. To celebrate, we traveled to Circle City, a Yukon River community, taking the Steese Highway north first to Central and then on to Circle City. As we approached Eagle Summit, the oblique light was bathing the mountaintops. From a high plateau, drifting like smoke signals, colored kites wafted in the evening light, a celebration of time-out. Festivity was quietly circulating through the North.

My sister read in *The Milepost* that wildflowers could be found in nearby alpine pastures. We pulled over and climbed downhill. The undulating mountainside appeared to be only green and brown, but then a glimpse of yellow caught our eyes. At our feet were nuggets of exquisite, delicate species. Patches of tiny wildflowers gently nodded over the rolling tundra as far as our eyes could see.

Ben rolled in the meadows like a young cub. The ground was like a carpet and I tussled with him on the tundra. For the next half hour, Marian and I lay on the ground and snapped photographs of wildflowers from every conceivable angle.

As the chill seeped into our bones, we returned to the car and continued to drive toward Central. In the park near Crabb's Corner in Central, I met Alice Carroll, gathered with her family and friends. Even though it was around midnight, everyone in town was out visiting. Outside, couples were dancing to a live band. Children were everywhere, playing on the swings, hanging on their moms. As we left around 1 A.M., a young man pulled up with a recent kill, a black bear, in the back of his truck. The music faded as we drove out. We passed the old Central Roadhouse, with the Midnight Sun saturating the decaying logs, enriching their color from the distant past.

At 3 A.M., a full moon rose over Circle as the sun still warmed the air.

Years later, my two younger children and I celebrated summer solstice on Delta's high point, Donnelly Dome. Sarah was twenty-four. Ben was 17 and too big for me to tussle with on the tundra. But apparently, I was under the impression I was still 25 and I suggested we climb the dome to celebrate the longest day of the year. For years, our children had wanted to climb what was known as Delta's gateway. It seemed the perfect time. We drove partway up the backside of the mountain and parked.

In a shaded area, we noticed tiny, purple orchids: the uncommon Fairy

193. Judy wresting with Ben, Eagle Summit, 1997.

Slipper. Sarah and Ben began scaling the mountainside. I punched uphill through the soft moss, winding my way through the spring flowers. In the warm sunshine, butterflies flitted around me. Delicate spring beauties swayed in the gentle breeze.

Every so often, I sat to take in the view and catch my breath. Far below, a moose was browsing in the brush beyond the truck. A bear was feeding, working his way toward an alpine lake in the distance.

My children were far ahead of me. They were following a rocky path to the top and it seemed they would disappear into the clouds.

As I neared the summit, I came upon mossy pincushions filled with minute, purple flowers - Moss Campion - perfect bouquets growing in the rock outcrop. Yellow Cinquefoil added color near the boulder where Sarah was sitting at the top of the Dome.

She was eating her sandwich and drinking in the 360° view. Ben ran like a caribou down to the valley and back again. Off in the distance, the Alaska Range crowned the view of the sweeping Delta River that curved from the mountains and down, spilling across the tilted land.

At 9 P.M., on Delta's sentinel landmark, we memorialized the longest day of the year and then started downhill. Sarah and Ben, like happy pups, ran down the mountain; while my rubbery legs braked hard, and I forced myself down the hill, aching as I edged down through a deep, steep moose rut.

Finally in the car, my legs relaxed with the familiar mechanisms of the accelerator. I looked back at the massive cone where we had been. The golden glow was giving way to the pale pink of a midsummer's night. A gloaming, an Alaskan dusk, enclosed us as we drove home.

194. Sarah cooling candles on our downriver snowy porch, 2002.

Chapter Eighty Six

A SPECIAL PLACE IN TIME

Remembering Childhood's Christmas...

We had always been creative in our Christmas gifts. That approach came from being perennially broke trappers, who also preferred making crafts to shopping.

When we were raising our family in our isolated Tanana River home, unfettered by the schedules of others, we celebrated Christmas for an entire month. The winter of 1976, when he was 6 years old, every night Clint chanted his Christmas mantra to me while clinging to my apron: "Fort Apache...$14.92... J. C. Penney, page 119." Barely able to afford the cost of the laundromat, let alone a store bought gift like that, Reb made Clint's fort from split firewood at his workbench in the house. Every night, he and our sandy-haired, woods' boy, together, enjoyed crafting roof shingles for the stockade and glued fence rails. An evolving Fort Apache covered Reb's bench. Reb and Clint worked diligently as the full moon glistened off the glittering snow outside our picture window. Under the table lay a female sled dog quietly nursing her pups. She had had a litter when the temperature was -50° F., so we brought them inside to protect the pups. By the hissing of the Coleman lantern, I painted a trapline scene on birchbark while Jessica, the Husky mom, settled into motherhood near my feet.During the winters of the late 1980s, Ben shaped moistened birchbark into laundry hampers, picture frames, and canoes. He hollowed short, dried saplings, then fashioned them into sewing and fishing kits: one for mom, and one, for dad.

Sarah's birthday is December 5th, so her birthday parties were a challenge. Always, we had to mush Sarah's guests up the frozen Tanana. By contrast, Clint's birthday, April 11th, arrived when boating began, and Ben's on August 7th was easy: the Tanana was at full bank. But, Sarah's birthday occurred in the deep frozen, hibernation time of the Sub-Arctic.

The whole world opened up to us when we moved to the road system in 1986. Sarah's birthday parties became easy; we heralded the Christmas Advent season with her special day. The house was decorated by December 5th when Sarah's guests arrived. From year to year, we alternated making homemade soaps, or best of all - candles. In 1990, the year Sarah turned 13 was a year for making candles. For a month, I had saved juice cans, boxes of crayons, paraffin, wax hardener, wicks, glitter, holly berries, and dried flowers. We gathered a snowman, puppy dog, and honey bear molds; in the store, we eyed Mrs. Butterworth's pancake syrup glass bottle with envy, wondering how we could break the container and save a candle made from her comely shape...

We covered the stove with aluminum foil and the floors with tarps, and began melting wax in a double boiler made from coffee cans.

Ben, only 6 years old, bumped into the legs of fifteen, scrambling girls as he wove his way from the table to the stove for me to pour his mold. I gingerly tipped a tiny bit of black, molten paraffin into his Frosty the Snowman's top hat. Ben scuttled out to the porch, under the Christmas lights, to let Frosty gel in the -20° F. temperatures. There, in the deep freeze under the twinkling lights, wax in varied molds congealed quickly. A constant traffic of girls dribbled paraffin from the kitchen to the porch: blue, green, red, yellow …

Christmas music played softly while Julia, Joy, and Sarah helped Ben pour snowy white wax into

195. Judy, Sarah and Ben, Denali Park 1995.

the round body of his snowman. Julia began cutting poinsettia petals for her candle from thin red wax. As soon as Joy iced white, frothy paraffin onto a candle, Julia glued the poinsettia petals to the cylindrical, snowy taper. Ben slipped Frosty from his rubber form and crayoned in a carrot nose. The girls then began to shift to pizza mode, so we wrapped up papers and assembled rainbow, snow, cocker spaniel, and coke float candles to photograph: a testament of a singular time.

In 2002, Ben is now taller than I am. Many of the girls are married, and some have children. Sarah is studying nursing in Oklahoma. Before returning home this year for Christmas, she telephoned Julia and Joy. "You want to come to my house for a candle making party!?" she asked playfully. "Sure!" they responded, "…but we can't mush the dogs to Oklahoma…" "No," she chirped, "I'm coming home! Save juice cans and crayons!"

December 17th, a young lady stepped off the plane. Her hair was short and she sported three tones. She had left behind her car and apartment, her business and studies, and slipped away for a moment to a life left somewhere in the tricky veil of time.

The sled dogs yelped to see her and soon, on the stove at home, dad was boiling spruce branches to de-humanize the scent of his traps. December 22nd, Julia and Joy re-entered our home. I was finishing a project, but the girls knew exactly what to do. They covered the stove, the counters, and the floor. Excited, they handled the new candle dyes and scents I had purchased. After pouring the molds, once again, we hustled candles onto the cold porch while "Silent Night" played, but this time, they left no rainbow trail of wax. After precious hours in a time locked in childhood, Joy had to return to teaching and Julia to her family's business.

Through the candle glow, I put Sarah on the airplane the next Monday. But she promised, she would come home again…next Christmas, and the one after that…

Chapter Eighty Seven
THE CORRIDOR

Throughout the winter of 2002, Reb dreamed of launching our 21-foot canoe near Fort Simpson, Northwest Territories at the headwaters of the Mackenzie, the second largest river system in North America. The craft could hold a total of 2000 pounds of freight throughout the projected 900-mile trip to the Beaufort Sea. I was the designated driver to deliver Reb and Ben to the headwaters, and then pick them up at the mouth of the river, a driving distance of 4,000 miles. Reb knew the Mackenzie was infamous for its wind, and felt I should not plan on participating in the canoe voyage. But I wanted to be included, so we agreed that I would fly to meet them at some intermediate point.

First, however, we had to drive the Alaska Highway, which neither of us had experienced -- the portion south of Whitehorse -- since initially respectively arriving in Alaska -- in 1962 and 1968.

Past Parallels Present on Highway

In 2002, driving the Alaska Highway was a trip down memory lane, as well as holding serendipitous, new experiences.

The first time Reb came to Alaska was in 1962. When he arrived from New Jersey, and when I later came from Oklahoma, what was then called the Alcan was only 26 years old. At that time, it was a gravel corridor running through a remote wilderness, full of holes, washboard-like areas, and soft spots. Only 18 years old, Reb and his childhood friend, Bill Chmura, originally hitch-hiked all the way from New Jersey.

In 1968, before the advent of today's sleek motor homes, I traveled up the Alcan in a World War II era jeep. Back then, only the brave drove the 1422 miles from Dawson Creek, British Columbia to Delta Junction, Alaska. On our respective trips, Reb and I each met Natives at Lower Post, British Columbia, and enjoyed Whitehorse, Yukon Territory, which at that time was only a small mining settlement where Diamond Tooth Liz's was the main attraction.

In the intervening forty years, we heard that the highway was paved, but it was hard for us to believe. August 3, 2002, we took Ben on a trip for his 18th birthday down the Alaska Highway, through the Yukon Territory, British Columbia, and on to Fort Simpson, Northwest Territories (NT) to begin a canoe trip on the Mackenzie River. I was to deliver the truck to the pick-up point in Inuvik, and then fly to meet them at Tulita, past the mid-point of the river, for the rest of the trip to the mouth.

On our drive down the Alaska Highway, we passed through what is now the metropolis of Whitehorse. With so many miles ahead of us, we did not pause, but continued pressing for the Northwest Territories. As we drove, we flipped the dial of the radio through exotic French programming as well as English. When we entered Muncho Lake Provincial Park, we began seeing caribou and Stone sheep rams .

As he drove, Reb leaned back and began telling Ben of his adventures of, "when Dad was 18." He grinned, thinking of thumbing his way up the Alcan with Bill all those years ago.

"Bill and I were always hungry in those days. Broke, we ate when we could, hitching across country. Near Muncho Lake, a prospector, Jim Orr, wanted to hire us to retrieve mineral samples

196. Ben and Reb forced ashore at Norman Wells by high winds on Mackenzie River, 2002.

from mountain peaks." Reb cackled at the memory. "That morning before climbing the mountain, Bill and I ate on Jim's tab like kings. Then we waited in front of the lodge for Jim. Jim said, 'Good morning, boys! Let's go eat some breakfast.' We didn't tell him we'd already eaten. In the end, he paid for two, full breakfasts for a pair."

Reb was just getting warmed up, "With our bellies satisfied, we met some Dene Indians, the MacDonald family at Muncho Lake. The Indians saddled up a horse pack train. For the next few days, we prospected together."

Forty years later, in that same lodge where Bill and Reb originally breakfasted, Reb, Ben, and I looked at a magazine depicting Reb's original Dene friends, the MacDonald family. In Volume 44 of *Beautiful British Columbia*, the MacDonald family was featured in a story titled "The Last Mountain People." It described Natives who prefer to live in archaic, alpine ways, sleeping on pine boughs rather than on mattresses, and living near their natal lake.

North of Fort Nelson, British Columbia, we left the modern Alaska Highway and found the gravel highway of our memories when we turned off onto the Liard Trail in British Columbia, and then onto the chug hole riven, euphemistically titled, Mackenzie Highway. As we crossed the Liard River on a ferry, Ben's eyes brightened as we neared the island where Fort Simpson, Northwest Territories is located, near the head of the Mackenzie River.

The next morning, Ben's 18th birthday, he and his dad began the 900-mile trip down the Mackenzie River to Inuvik on the Beaufort Sea. Nervously, I watched them prepare, and then leave for the long journey north.

A Second, Solitary Drive Up the Dempster Highway...

After I waved goodbye to them, I started my 1,700-mile drive toward the mouth of the Mackenzie River passing back through British Columbia, the Yukon Territory, and Dawson City on the Alaska Highway, and then turning north onto the Dempster Highway. Locals started telling me it was one of the wettest summers on record in both the Yukon Territory and the Northwest Territories. At Eagle Plains, Yukon Territory, the gravel road turned to slime. The steady downpour of rain had even sent construction crews inside. Behind them, they had left soft berms of dirt in the deeply pockmarked road. Some of the holes were camouflaged craters. As I climbed the summit that marks the boundary between the two territories, the heavens collapsed,

197. *Windbound on Mackenzie, Tulita; full rainbow.*

ripping with lightning, and exploding with thunder. I plunged into a deep hole hidden under the mud. I hit so hard the cooler on the back seat flew forward, splashing dirty water everywhere. The atmosphere was solid rain. My skin crawled. I could not, as planned, climb into a canoe in this weather. The truck was in four-wheel drive. With white-knuckles, I gripped the steering wheel as I made the descent onto the Peel River's plateau. The sodden land stretched on and on toward the Beaufort Sea.

After twelve hours including crossing two rivers on ferries and miles of swamp to Inuvik, I pulled into the parking lot of a Bush airline. The owner had kindly agreed to watch our truck while I flew to join my family at Tulita on the Mackenzie River. Reb had a satellite phone in the canoe. A Delta friend had agreed to be the message relay station. I called our Delta friends; they told me Reb and Ben would be at Tulita in a day and a half. I parked the truck and re-packed my gear into compact portability. Flying to Tulita on Wednesday, I watched the Mackenzie unfurl below me. The airport in Tulita was a small building. A villager, who had come to pick another passenger up, graciously gave me a ride to Tulita's main street. As I described my son and husband to the driver, I glanced over toward the Canadian Government's Band Office. After a separation of eight days, Reb and Ben appeared lean and tan to me as they waited for me, talking with the locals. As they came to meet me, they pulled a baggage cart of empty, outboard gas cans to refill. The day was pleasant with no rain in sight. I changed from tennis shoes to hip waders, and con-verted from truck driver to wilderness woman.

"Wade into the river, balance the canoe's sides with your hoisted weight, and slide one leg at a time into your splash cover portal seat," Reb said the same as he had taught me many years ago.

Following the Aorta of the Northwest Territories

After we slid into the canoe, we pushed off into the Mackenzie. Waves were lapping the bow of the boat; water surrounded us as far as the eye could see. In front of us, there stretched weeks of travel. Ben sat in front. Between us a spray skirt was snapped to the sides of the canoe. In a can-vas hole over the middle seat, I was wedged between my baggage and the freight in the rear. Behind me, Reb guided the 15-horsepower outboard. Protected by a plastic windshield, he navi-gated the Mackenzie River, the fourth largest river discharging into the Arctic Ocean.

A little farther north, where the Great Bear River joins the Mackenzie, we camped in the shel-ter of a rock mountain that is marked by three mineralized circles, called the The Beaver Pelts by the Gwich'in Indians. As I made dinner on a two-burner stove, Reb and Ben planned the next

198. *Great Bear Rock with circles, like beaver pelts.*

day's fishing trip up the reputedly favorable Great Bear River.

The next morning, under moderately cool, light rain, we turned up into the Great Bear River. When the rain increased, we popped up safari-size umbrellas. We were doubly snug due to our tightly snapped, spray-skirt-covered canoe.

Great Northern Pike began breaking water. Ben pulled us ashore, grabbed his pole, and despite pouring rain, waded into the river. With every cast, he caught a Pike, or a white fish called a Conni. He hollered for Reb when a 20-pound Pike bent his pole.

We returned that night to the Mackenzie and set up a new camp further downstream. Reb and Ben stretched a kitchen tarp over a twenty-foot log tripod. They suspended a coffee pot, hung from wrought-iron stakes driven into the sand, over a blazing bonfire. Sitting in my sandy kitchen, I rolled fish in pancake batter, frying the chunks to a butter-soft delicacy.

While I cooked, we listened to the radio weather forecast for Fort Smith, Hay River, Yellowknife, and where we were: the Satoh Region and further, to the Mackenzie Delta. Afterward, the news was broadcast in the Gwich'in language for the 52 % of the population of the Northwest Territories that is aboriginal. I felt wrapped by a Bush neighborhood, spread across the vast outback, connected by the Mackenzie's corridor.

As night settled over the beach, the wind suddenly hit the tarp with a violent stab. It ripped up the umbrellas, blew them down the beach, and yanked the tarp's moorings loose. Waves hammered the canoe, straining its line, and stretching it to the limit. Whap, whap, the waves sloshed over the canoe's open rear where Reb navigated, soaking everything stored on the bottom. Together we strained to pull the heavy boat up high on the beach, safe from the angry, foaming river. I grabbed bags and ran for the tent tucked against a hill on a high shelf. From the relative safety of the tent, I watched Reb and Ben securing camp down by the wind-blown bonfire, pressing against the wind trying to stay rooted. When they finally wiggled into the tent's narrow opening, Ben gasped, "Uh, oh." "What?!" Reb asked, exhausted. Ben warned, "There's a dead tree leaning over our tent. It could kill us while we're sleeping." Reb looked out and decided the tree would miss us.

The next morning, the tree lay exactly where Reb thought it might fall. However, the Mackenzie more closely resembled the ocean, stretching 5 miles from bank to bank, than any river. We were wind-bound. Unbothered by the gale, Ben set burbot lines up and down the bank, bending his face directly into the onslaught. Reb kept a fire going under the kitchen tarp and read. I had not left the technological age behind. When I wasn't cooking, I was in the tent download-

199. Ben and Northern Pike, Mackenzie River

ing my digital camera pictures into my laptop or trying to figure out how to use my new Palm Pilot. In the late afternoon, I read out loud to Reb and Ben from a book about a 1972 Mackenzie canoeing trip called *Ultimate North* by R. D. Mead.

Finally, on the third day, it was calm. As we loaded the canoe, the docile Mackenzie bore no resemblance to its schizoid twin of the previous night. Suddenly, out of the mist, an immense apparition loomed: an enormous barge, carrying semi tractor-trailers. Five minutes after the barge passed, 2-foot waves created by the barge began vigorously rocking our loaded canoe.

Wearing hip boots, we waded out to our boat, gingerly got in, and pushed out. Once during the day, we stopped while Ben walked the beach, considering whether or not to fish. As he strolled, a black bear suddenly broke through the brush onto the beach and rose up on his hind legs. Foregoing confrontation, we decided to continue on toward Norman Wells, knifing through the waves, rather than share a fishing spot with a bear. We camped that evening above, to the south of, Norman Wells, where we could see the lights of the town twinkling downstream. I wanted to push on to the community while the river was displaying its cordial personality, but I was overruled. We went to sleep, trusting we would be in Norman Wells the next day.

But, we woke to the bitterly cold wind hammering our tent, yet again. I knew the routine. To survive the process of relieving myself, I struggled into heavily insulated clothes, raincoat, rainpants, and hat, and then crawled out the narrow, zippered door, flopped like a crippled dog across the high threshold onto the sand and into the teeth of the north wind. Our glorious travel amounted to one step forward and three steps back: helpless and victimized by the elements. It would easily be over two more weeks before we reached the Mackenzie's Delta, instead of the ten days for which we had hoped. And, the Sans Sault Rapids lay ahead followed by 7 miles of canyon walls.

After breakfast, Reb built a windbreak from driftwood on the edge of the sandbar, so we could view Norman Wells with less agony. Inside the driftwood corral, Ben warmed us with a bonfire. I continued reading aloud from *Ultimate North* for a couple of hours, almost forgetting our situation. When my bone marrow was finally saturated with cold wind, I crawled into our only oasis, the tent. I came out to fry a fish dinner and prayed as we went to bed that the wind would abate.

The next morning, as I crawled out of the tent into freezing cold, sheeting rain. I could not refrain from an, "Oh, God...not again." With thirty-five years of experience, I knew the routine. I grabbed my bucket and headed down the beach grateful that Reb had supplied me with a camping trip luxury: a toilet seat that clamped onto a bucket. The gray curtain of driving rain obscured our view of Norman Wells. But regardless of the weather, we decided to try to reach town; the wind was relatively good.

Rather than pack up a mess, we threw our soggy fried fish back into the river, loaded the boat, and headed downstream. In the canoe, I buried my face into my chest and breathed warm air into my jacket. On man-made islands in the middle of the river, Norman Wells' oil pumps churned rhythmically up and down, but I was thinking more of the bitter cold of my fingers whose chill was numbing my mind. We beached, tied up the boat, and walked toward town. Immediately, a warm soul, which is the common denominator of the Northwest Territories, appeared. With genuine hospitality, Murray offered us a ride in his truck.

200. Sarah, Shayna, Kristin, Clara and me
Inuvik Library, 2002.

Norman Wells looked like a twin to Deadhorse, Alaska: restaurants and motels were constructed from trailers like those used for the Alyeska Pipeline. From the 1930s, Norman Wells, deep in Canada, has been partly developed by the American military. During World War II, its oozing oil was the life-support for northern military outposts, supplied by the CANOL (Canadian Oil) pipeline.

We got a room in a motel that night in Norman Wells and settled down for an evening of showers, washing machines, hamburgers, TV, and piped heat. Reb faithfully checked the canoe, night and morning, in the mud and rain. "This is the worst summer we ever had," Mackenzie locals repeatedly told us. "We never had so much rain and cold." Looking out the window at the never-ending mist, I thought about the Sans Sault Rapids ahead of us. Struggling between wanting to endure what my family experienced and also desiring to protect them, I knew I would be a liability; I opted to fly back to Inuvik and wait there for them.

For Reb and Ben, the next days on the river continued the same: high wind, rain, and below-freezing temperatures. Reb telephoned on the satellite telephone saying that the Sans Sault Rapids had turned out to be uneventful and the canyon had actually been majestic. He added, "One day, a Gwich'in man headed south, pointed to us, gestured to his home, and indicated he wanted us to stay there." Reb added, "When we did, we found it was like Alaska used to be. There was a sign that used to be left in all cabins of the north, 'Please use what you need; respect and leave it as clean as you found it.'" Throughout the Northwest Territories, as was so in classical Alaska, cabins were routinely left open with such simple requests.

On the way downstream, Ben caught a whopper Pike that he skinned, and mounted the giant fish head on a stick in the bow, turning it to face the wind like the prow of a Viking ship.

Meantime, in Inuvik, I worked on my laptop in the local public library where Reb called me daily on his satellite phone. After only eight more days, when he and Ben were close to Tsiigèhtchic (Arctic Red River), the village nearest the Dempster Highway, they asked me to come get them.

At Tsiigèhtchic, where the Mackenzie and Arctic Red Rivers intersect, I drove the truck onto the ferry to meet Reb and Ben on the village's side of the confluence. At the town's dock, we unloaded all the freight into the truck, put the canoe on top of the vehicle, and were finally ready to return home. Then, a Gwich'in man drew near, rolled down his car window, and warned us, "The ferry's rudder is broken." The Mackenzie River was on one side of the village and the Arctic Red River was on the other. The Dempster Highway back to Alaska was on the far side of the Mackenzie; we were not going anywhere.

Wanting to find beadwork anyway, I used the time to search for Gwich'in handicrafts. In the village, we were directed to Carol Ansdell. We walked into Carol and Bob Ansdell's yard and immediately discovered we had a common friend, Reb's forestry colleague in Tok. After talking for an hour, we got a call telling us the ferry would be down for the next two days. Bob and Carol opened their home to us, with the amazing hospitality intrinsic to the northern tradition; they treated us better than family.

One evening, Carol described, "My great grandfather taught us, 'If a stranger paddles into our country, he is worthy of respect. Honor him; he is our guest.'"

As she spoke, the breeze blew over the town's high plateau ruffling the isolated Mackenzie. The Northwest Territories reminded me of Alaska in the pre-pipeline era. The next day, we would go back through that invisible door to a more developed world. We left an immense land spreading across the top of the world: the king, the Northwest Territories.

Chapter Ninety
AN IDITAROD HISTORY

When I called 1975 Iditarod champion and record setter, Emmitt Peters, on the phone recently, he summed up his dynamic mother, Mary, in relation to dog mushing and traditional Alaska. Emmitt began, "My parents, Mary and Paul Peters, always kept dog teams for trapping from 1925 and I have continued it until well into the present. When I began mushing in Ruby, I had the third team in the village.

"My mom, Mary, had girl-like energy even in her later years. She always had her own trapline and she trapped with dad." Pausing, he continued, "When I entered the 1975 Iditarod, my mom identified with me throughout the high tension of the race. She didn't understand how, during a race, a serious contender could take a twenty-four hour layover as mandated by the rules of the race. I had planned my rest at home in Ruby. Of course, while I rested everyone passed me. By the time I left at midnight, I was number 26. My mom cried, 'My poor son's been left behind!'

"When I caught up to number 5 position at Unalakleet, my mom was excited. She said to my dad, 'I want to hook the dogs up! Let's go!!' My dad, in his gentle way, would have none of it. Telling a practical lie, he said, 'Emmitt took all the tug lines and harnesses. We have no way to hook up the dogs. No way.'" When Mary continued for twenty-four hours, crying, "Let's get the dogs going…" Paul, like some Athabascan mantra, stoicly intoned, "Too bad. Too bad. Too bad."

To celebrate the new Millenium, twenty-five years after having set the Iditarod record, a 58-year-old Emmitt borrowed a dog team and mushed one more time to Nome. This time, his sons, 18-year-old, Emmitt Junior, and 15-year-old, Emory, rode snowmachines part way to Nome, but when it became impassable, they returned to Ruby. They, and their mother, Edna, flew to welcome Emmitt into Nome, as he, Number 44, crossed the finish line.

Emmitt said, "The 2003 Iditarod has a new problem with this year's warm temperatures and lack of snow. My understanding is they will have to approach Ruby and Nome by starting at

Nenana this year, adding another 100 miles to the course. I predict the winners will finish this year in ten days. That's my prediction."

The 2003 Iditarod wound up beginning its restart on Monday, March 3, 2003, at 10:00 A.M. on the Chena River behind Pike's Landing in Fairbanks. Robert Sorlie was the first musher to cross the finish line in Nome on March 13th after 9 days, 15 hours 47 minutes, and 36 seconds. Emmitt's prediction of 10 days was a good call. Look for further race information at http://www.iditarod.com.

Chapter Ninety One
ONE LIGHT

201. Jerry Isaac, Tanacross Tribal Council President, 2003.

In downtown Anchorage one evening in July 2002, tourists in white tennis shoes drifted between gift shops. Across the street, by the Visitor's Information Center, disoriented Native Alaskans lounged in a pastoral park, unseen by the cash flow passing around them. The tourists had arrived on an Alaska Airlines airplane that was adorned with a logo of a smiling Eskimo. Shoppers drifted in and out of stores seeking aboriginal, authentic handicrafts.

Jerry Isaac, the Tanacross Village Council President pondered, "How can my people find the bridge from the past to the present and orient to a life with new rules?"

There is a great struggle within many Natives today to find a healthy, profitable way to bridge into today's world. Many Natives are not comfortable in the Caucasian workplace. Others can adapt, but are concerned with not losing their cultural uniqueness, their life-style.

One man who has wrestled deeply with these problems is Jerry Isaac. Sitting across the Tanacross Tribal Council table, June 2002, Jerry Isaac explained the challenges of the village, his hurdles while growing up, and his vision for his people. Jerry began, "I want to clarify that improvements in Tanacross have been a result of everyone's efforts. It's been a team effort." He clarified, "In Tanacross, we started out with nothing. We were unskilled Natives. We came from socially, economically, politically-impacted disarray. We had to take what came; we had no choice. Take it and live with it. It resulted in a low self-esteem."

Running his fingers through his long, graying hair, Jerry said, "It's a Catch-22 situation. I can't force employers to hire my people.

"In 1995, Tanacross had 68% unemployment. The Council that is responsible to provide social services, mediate the people's needs, and offer scholarships, had a budget of only $60,000 and one staff person. No accounting was done, or records kept. Additionally," he added, "All of our accounting and reimbursement went through the Tanana Chiefs Conference, costing us 25% of that yearly budget."

Jerry has experienced everything his people have experienced. The nephew of the last traditional chief, Andrew Isaac, Jerry remembered of his high school years, "I was a bad student. I had a hard time learning through the standard, linear teaching method. I couldn't synthesize and condense. My vocabulary was poor; communication was a nightmare. (Due to God and personal relationships, I survived.) But, I had to learn how to learn for myself."

"My thinking was different," Jerry continued, "To me, everything was intra-connected. To us Natives, the sun, the moon, and the hills belonged to us." Jerry continued, "Those, on the other hand, who are trained in the system and have college degrees may not know how to use them. White or Native, if a man is out of touch with himself, his fellow man, and the universe, he is out of sync emotionally, physically, and spiritually. A college degree does not guarantee wisdom."

Jerry remembered, "I finished high school at Chemawa Indian School in Oregon. Because of the Native issues awareness of the school and respect for the spiritual approach of Native Americans, I began to feel proud...I returned home wearing a feather in my hair."

Jerry looked at me seriously, "I fight fires; it doesn't take much knowledge. My spiritual life has been my strength. My only credential has been my concern for my people."

Picking his words like a blind man feels for Braille, Jerry continued, "The fire triangle illustrates the basics a man must also have. For fire, there must be oxygen, fuel, and heat. Conversely, for a man to be a productive citizen, he can't be hungry, or without hope. Employment gives a people a purpose, a reason to improve, and an orientation. However, to create jobs, credit must be available.

"The means of creating jobs: grant applications, negotiating contracts, and legislative lobbying, can, for the unskilled, seem an insurmountable mountain, a negative."

Jerry said, "I knew there was more out there. We had to know how to bring it under our control, and translate it into a holistic approach."

Jerry went to an Anchorage bank who would risk loaning money to a village with no line of credit.

"We had to learn two types of contracting. We began with contract vehicle: contracting monies from the Bureau of Indian Affairs to deliver money to the people. Now, we are still working on general contracting. None of us were qualified."

Jerry's staff members, Adam Martin and Kevin Krauklis, entered the office. Jerry introduced them to me, "Beginning in September 1998, we decided to hire outside professionals. It was a hard choice, but we needed the expertise: Adam became Environmental and Natural Resources Director. Three years later, Kevin became Operations Manager."

Adam Martin began, "Jerry and I brainstormed. We saw general contracting as a village-based industry. Tanacross' traditional use areas and sacred sites were bordered by the potential National Missile Defense system based at Fort Greely. Perhaps, someday, the Alaska Railroad and the proposed natural gas pipeline would go through tribal lands.

"It bothered us," Adam stated, "for billions of dollars to flow past the Upper Tanana people, but still, they might wind up with nothing." Jerry and Adam developed Dihthaad Global Services, (DGS) with five members on the board and two tribal council members. Adam became DGS General Manager.

Adam commented, "After Fort Greely was chosen for the National Missile Defense Program's Ground-based Midcourse Defense-Test Bed (GMDTB) main site, we received over $4 million for the 400 person, Man Camp contract.

"Through Bechtel National, Inc, we were given the GMD Test Bed housekeeping and janitorial work contract. Through Fluor Alaska, Inc., DGS received the million-dollar GMDTB security contract." Jerry pointed out, "We wrote into the construction contract a request for Delta local hire."

He added, "We have other contracts, and more pending."

"Finally," Adam said, "if you want something, you put in time, blood, sweat, and tears. We could lose our shirt, but risk-taking is part of business."

Jerry concluded, "Now, in seven years' time, Tanacross, apart from Dihthaad's budget, is worth over $4.3 million. We operate with a nine-member staff, including four who are Non-Native. We keep all our own records and accounting. Subsequently, village employment has improved by 12%. Certainly, any village can take this option."

"Tanacross has a bright future," Kevin Krauklis smiled, "because they are looking to participate. They understand value given for value received."

Adam summed up, "My goal is the same as the tribe's: to attain 100% employment and to eventually, in 10 years time, become profitable enough to pay meaningful dividends to our tribal members."

Jerry looked at Adam, "As you can see, our staff is racially mixed. I won't discuss, approve, or condone…reverse discrimination. Not on my watch." Jerry added, quietly, "Maybe some day, I'll provide significant employment to Non-Natives: …on the basis of the US Constitution, based on equal opportunities for all. You never know."

202. Jack Stewart, 1998..

Chapter Ninety One
POGO CREEK

Jack Stewart, like his friends: Fred Campbell, R.L Johnson, Charlie Boyd, Fred Cook, Bill Arrington, John Schulz, and Russ Trastek, was adept at making something from nothing. Not having the money for frequent travel to Fairbanks, hotel accommodations and expensive merchandise, each man, typical of classical Alaska, stockpiled spare parts of every variety in caches and storage tents. They knew their piles as well as any storekeeper knew his well organized shelves. Able to do whatever was needed whether welding, mechanical repair, inventing, trapping, mining, big game guiding, well drilling, flying, building or logging, these men's needs for independence exceeded the limitations of the domesticated Lower 48 States. They were the men of whom poet

Robert Service wrote, **The Man Who Didn't Fit In.** *The mindset of these men was shaped by the focus of the Cold War era, magnified near the sites of Alaska's military forts. Knowing that any foreign attack on Alaska could quickly shut down the supply avenue to the north, many Alaskans had enough survival gear for a battalion just in case of Soviet invasion.*

Today, as big mining corporations are gradually replacing the individual miner, Probert's grocery store has long since been replaced by Fred Meyer One-Stop Shopping Center in Fairbanks, Native elders are dying, and a trip to Fairbanks now takes half the time it did, so also the irascible man of Service's poetry is fading as Alaska, too, becomes domesticated.

Back in the 1950s when he was 23 years old, Jack Stewart had a choice to run his own business in Texas or to wed Mary Dolby and travel 4,000 miles north to homestead in Delta Junction, Alaska. He chose marriage and homesteading in Alaska.

Bob Johnson, raised on the Goodpaster River and owner of Delta's Caterpillar rental business, cleared the Stewarts' homestead. Jack soaked in the old Alaska stories that Bob told him during his coffee breaks. Bob, who was raised at Central (Creek), 50 miles up the Goodpaster River, told of hard rock mining at the Goodpaster's Tibbs Creek during the 1930s. That gold vein had lasted only a couple of years, dead-ending at what was probably an old earthquake shear.

In the early years, Jack worked to support his family of eight children by supervising heavy equipment at Fort Greely. In 1974, the homestead that the family had worked so hard to build was cut in half by the new Alyeska pipeline corridor. Maintaining that the pipeline could take a more direct course, rather than dogleg off through his property, Jack sued.

Of his long, but unsatisfying legal battle, Jack said, "My problem wasn't with the pipeline, but with the laws that took, in land and attorney fees, much of what I'd worked for."

The fight exhausted Jack. Finally, after receiving only token compensation for the part of his property that was affected, Jack took his wife and six of their younger children up the Goodpaster River to begin a wilderness lifestyle at Bob Johnson's old home.

For the next five years, with only one-way communication through KJNP radio, the Stewart children: Elvin, Glinda, Sonya, Joyce, David, and Kim began home schooling at Central.

Delta's home correspondence teacher, Dan Beck, frequently radioed the Stewarts and flew in monthly to check on the students. Many winter evenings, Dan and Jack discussed Tibbs Creek's historical mining and the possibilities that might still remain.

Staking a claim on nearby property, Jack thawed ground using a porcupine boiler, which is a 5-gallon bucket of boiling water with pipes welded out its sides, like quills, for warming the earth. Then, mucking the resulting hole out with a simple pick and shovel, Jack went down 46 vertical feet. He did not clarify what he found, but he continued operating on an intuition that the gold was there. During the evenings, he pored over maps, assessed drainages, and considered rock and mineral concentrations. His research drew him to the base of a ridge near an anonymous little creek; Jack resolved to check it out in the early spring.

As soon as it was warm in 1982, he boated upstream to this Goodpaster tributary and began digging. "If I don't try, I'll always wonder," he said, and with his pick he loosened up the first dirt. Shoveling deep over several days, Jack scooped up good color, indicating gold, and called the little stream, "No Name Creek."

Jubilant with his find, and seeking a backer, he thought of his kindly brother-in-law, V.E. Mitch Mitcham, in Texas. Having no phone in his remote Goodpaster home, Jack called him from downstream and appealed to Mitch's gambling instincts, explaining the potential of the Goodpaster discovery. Mitch not only signed on, but also went to a local shoe store in Texas to gear up for a trip to Alaska. Thinking he was prepping for the Alaskan winter, Mitch purchased a pair of Colorado mountain climbing boots.

When he arrived in Alaska, he found Jack assembling essential mining equipment for the Cat train bound for No Name Creek. Mitch, Jack, and the Stewart sons loaded the Go-Devils - sleds pulled by the Cats - with shaker screens, a sand screw, a generator, and 5,000 gallons of fuel at the starting point at Quartz Lake. Taking off on an old winter trail that connected to the former tele-graph route, they traveled seven days, driving a loader and three D7 tractors pulling not only the heavy sleds, but a dump truck as well. Sometimes they slept in the snow at -20° F., and in the morn-ings Mitch crawled out of a damp bag and into the mountain boots that had no insulation. Complaints were of no use; they were cold, but they had been cold before.

Arriving at his 100-acre claims, Jack and the men set up an Army maintenance tent, construct-ed a floor and walls, and covered it with a 16-by-32-foot tin roof. They bulldozed settling ponds and plowed in an airstrip.

For the next several years, Jack dug deep shafts up and down the sides of the mountain. Using ropes and ladders, he lowered himself deep into the earth trying to find the hidden veins of gold. After a long day, he washed the silt off in his makeshift bathtub - a 55-gallon oil drum.

"I didn't need a bathroom mural," he said. "I had God's panorama all around me."

During the long years of solitude, bear skirmishes, and frustration with mining regulations, Jack could easily have quit, agreeing with spectators that the gold really was not there. His old friend, Dan Beck, saw only fine gold come out of the claim. Environmental regulations kept making it harder for the small prospector to survive. Slowed down by threats of large fines if ecologists judged the creeks muddy, Jack backed off and just did assessment work.

"Pretty much, I was just holding the land and keeping my shovel in the ground," Jack explained.

While he stayed on at Faith Claims, Mary, at their Delta homestead, helped the children grad-uate from school and get launched on their own.

But, in March of 1991, others began bringing their bigger shovels to the area. An Anchorage geological consulting company, WGM, Inc., started exploring the forks of the Goodpaster. Through deep drilling, it was estimated the gold was 300 to 500 feet down, much farther than Jack could ever have gone with his equipment. The precious metal was lodged in quartz and would require hard-rock mining techniques to extract it. The exploration company demonstrated its findings by means of graphs at a public meeting in Delta Junction. They shared that a wide, thick vein, with the length as yet undetermined, had been found.

Meanwhile, Jack's claims were surrounded by the mining claims WGM was hired to explore.

Jason Bressler, an employee of WGM, spent time with Jack when he and his drilling crew were Jack's guests at his camp in 1994. "Jack was the epitome of Bush hospitality," Bressler said. "He had an incredible amount of savvy. If anything broke, he could fix it. He was a master welder. When I asked him, 'Do you mind if we call the creek Pogo?' He said, 'No, go for it.'"

Three years later, Jack received an offer for his claims from WGM, but holding the portal prop-erty to the valuable discovery, he rejected the amount and asked Mitch to be his negotiator. In October 1997, transactions began with a Canadian mining and exploration company, Teck Corporation, for them to gain access to the creek. December 1997, Teck gained its needed avenue to Pogo Creek. Jack received $1,066,392, hitting pay dirt at last.

Jack and I spoke in January 1998 at his family's Delta homestead about how he would invest his money. He said he had needed to replace his wilderness hideaway and had purchased a place just beyond Thompson Lake, a few miles past Quartz Lake and not far from our upriver home. Also, needing a new project, he had invested in huge storage tanks to cache, like many an old Alaskan, gear that might just come in handy.

He has also paid his children's bills and is helping them get on with their dreams.

"Jack just wanted to help the family," Dan Beck told me in a telephone conversation. "He wanted Mary and the kids provided for. Particularly due to all those years alone up the Goodpaster, the family is close and takes care of each other."

Beck and Jack visited in 1998 with Jack's daughter, Sonya, at Nick Stepovich's Soapy Smith restaurant in Fairbanks where Sonya worked as a waitress. Dan said he asked Sonya how her life had changed since her dad had shared his wealth.

"I'm out of debt and it's wonderful," she replied. "My sister and I are also starting a business."

As I left Jack and Mary at their homestead in January 1998, it was clear that a million dollars would not change the old miner. Jack smiled ruefully and said, "By the end of January, the money will all be gone and I'll be up at Thompson Lake, just another guy on Social Security." As he waved good-bye, he said, "Life's been good, but I'd never do it over again."

Chapter Ninety One
TRANSITION

203. Aleksandar "Sasha" Nikolic and Martin Buser, 2002.

With increasing global pressure against fur garments, Reb and I could see a possible end of old Alaska's trapping way of life. We began to advertise in Mushing magazine for our new business, Dog Sled Expeditions, a tourist-based, mushing adventure, an opportunity for the hardy to experience the life about which Jack London wrote. Jack London was one of the few western authors whose work was supported in the Warsaw Pact-related nations during the Cold War.

I never suspected that our ad in Mushing or -- that Jack London -- would be a link in reconnecting me with the country of my youth: Yugoslavia.

In 1996, at the age of 51, I decided to learn how to use a computer. For several weeks, I tried desperately, blindly, and without much faith to figure out a language about which I knew nothing: the world of 0s and 1s. By the year 2000, email, Internet usage, and word processing had become a way of life for me. My focus became writing and the world of cyber space. Neither Reb nor I had developed our business, Dog Sled Expeditions, but we had maintained the ad. One day, to my great astonishment, a surprise email appeared in my inbox.

Musher Harnesses Impossible Dream to Sled

A puzzling letter from a stranger in Yugoslavia appeared in my inbox in the spring of 2000. It was from someone asking if he might be our dog handler. I thought it must be a joke. A dog musher from Yugoslavia!? Not likely!

In Yugoslavia, in one decade, wars and international sanctions had reduced the once prosperous nation to third-world status. Eighteen years before the collapse of Yugoslavia, Aleksandar "Sasha" Nikolic was born in the inner city of Belgrade, a city of 2 million people. Fascinated with Jack London, he began writing his own stories when still a child. He imagined a team of huskies, each with their individual personalities, flying across the snow. Once, when he saw a German shepherd in a public park, he naturally climbed on its back. As he grew up, Sasha, unlike many who recite obstacles to their dreams, believed that in the midst of one of Yugoslavia's worst decades, he could become a dog sled driver in the Balkans.

As I read his email, I wondered how could this child, Sasha, house, feed, and transport a team of Huskies? As we became acquainted, I pressed him for his story. He had long dreamed of Siberian husky sled dogs, although the canine focus in Yugoslavia was limited to hunting and show dogs. He said veterinary medicine in Belgrade was so primeval that he was studying to become a veterinarian to right what was wrong.

In the early '90s, Sasha heard about a litter of huskies for sale in Belgrade, but they cost six hundred dollars, half a year's salary. When the owner reduced her price to two hundred dollars, Sasha headed out with the money in hand.

At the seller's house, he carefully observed the litter. The wildest one won his heart and Sasha named him Natas. "I will be a champion," he thought, "if I can make a leader of this dog. Then, I'll know I should train sled dogs the rest of my life."

When he did succeed in training the dog, a famous Czech musher, Ivan Sibrt, congratulated him. Soon, Sasha added two more dogs to his team: Pepper and Narya. But, how was he to train the team? Sasha had no journals, no mentors, and no videos to teach him. But word got around, and soon he was training inexperienced dogs and their owners throughout Serbia.

In 1994, even as his country was imploding, he formed two organizations in Yugoslavia: Polarex Beograd and Siberian Husky. While war in Bosnia was raging, Sasha mapped out a mountain mushing expedition. He struggled in Belgrade throughout the year just to survive, but always his focus was set on the annual expedition. Somehow, he found a van and fuel and obtained food for both man and dog.

When the moment arrived, nothing could stop Sasha and his friends as they rushed for the wilderness. On Kopaonik Mountain, there were no groomed trails. Making his own trails with the dogs, Sasha zigzagged among skiers, across rickety bridges, and uphill into the sweet peace of the mountains.

When Sasha was back in Belgrade, he exercised his dogs daily by mushing to the university. He ordered a sled from Budapest, Hungary, that arrived too late for a scheduled race. Then, promotional videos, the race, and all his plans were put on hold in 1999 as NATO unleashed 78 days of bombing on the Federal Republic of Yugoslavia. The films would never be shown.

Finally, in October 2000, something only dreamed - and thought impossible - happened. Former President Slobodan Milosevic was overthrown. But, it was only a beginning. It was projected that if reforms continued, in 16 years the economy might normalize to a 1989 level. Sasha would then be 45 years old.

Squaring off with his future, Sasha began inquiring by E-mail of North American racers - whether anyone might be interested in the lone musher of Belgrade. After an Oregon kennel owner, Jerry Scdoris, offered an opportunity, Sasha with help from his parents, borrowed the airplane fare to the United States and obtained a visa. By November, Sasha was mushing dogs in the United States. What was previously impossible became routine.

Every morning, he exercised twenty of Jerry's dogs through the snowy Oregon mountains, and from a kennel of one hundred, Sasha made a super leader of a hitherto untrained dog.

Still, on a long day, when the moon was full and wolves howled, Sasha was torn. He thought of three dogs in Belgrade: Natas, Pepper, and Narja, just out of reach. But, equally just out of touch over the Lower 48 border to the north were the Iditarod and the Yukon Quest Races in the Last Frontier. In the spring of 2002, Sasha planned to fulfill an aspect of his dogmushing dream and travel north to meet the mushers of Alaska.

Zurich-to-Belgrade Mushing Connection

After eight months of dog handling in Oregon, Sasha flew north to visit our family in Delta and was also welcomed by the Alaskan dogsled champions, the Dean Seibold family, Gareth Wright, and Martin Buser. Dean and Gareth shared the love of dog training with Sasha. Then, I suggested that Sasha meet Martin Buser, the four-time winner of the Iditarod, and an acquaintance of my husband.

Reb, as Delta's Fire Warden, had helped Martin Buser during the 1996, disastrous, Big Lake fire near Anchorage. Buser, who enjoyed unusual names for his kennel, later named one of his dogs "Reb."

Having heard the story of Martin and the Big Lake fire from Reb many times, I arranged for Sasha to meet the famed musher. We drove to Big Lake to talk with the champ whose 2002 win, following his 2001 loss, had been dubbed, "From Worst, To First."

Early May 13, 2002, Sasha and I pulled up to the home of the Busers, a Swiss castle. Towering on a hill behind the home, I noticed a ski hut wrapped in windowpane glass.

On the door to the castle, there was a note, "I'm on the hill. Come on up." We looked up and saw a figure waving warmly to us from the hilltop.

Martin came down and met us at the house. As we sat talking at his kitchen table, he seemed more the surgeon's son that he is, rather than the typical Alaska dog musher. His flashing blue eyes, vibrantly intelligent countenance, and muscled hands spoke of a man who could have chosen any professional career.

Martin explained his childhood in Switzerland: a life filled with intensive animal husbandry led by his father. Today, Martin duplicates that sensitive care in his kennel. "For my dogs, there is no substitute for sincere, dedicated training," he said. "They produce exactly what they are given." Martin recounted then for Sasha the story of the Big Lake fire. June 6, 1996, Martin fought for a week to save his animals. When 50-knot winds fanned a huge plume of smoke that erupted into the Miller's Reach fire, Martin pushed to reach his home that was in the direct line of the fire.

For several days, Martin and his family cut the trees surrounding their home. When the fire crept close to the Busers' back door, Martin grabbed his best 20 dogs, not knowing whether he would be able to return. After he trucked those dogs to safety, he returned home for another load. When, finally, 60 dogs were straining on lengths of gang chains - cables intersected by individual tie-offs - no more hardware remained. Having no choice for his geriatric dogs and pups, Martin simply transported the old and young to the same island on a nearby lake as he had the previous 60, but the remaining 20 had no chains. "It was better for them to be loose than to burn up," he declared.

At home, the electrical power, the well water, and the phone were no longer working. Martin wired a generator to the well to enable them to pump water day and night. For days, with a crew of friends, the family put out spot fires under and around the house.

As the fire began to lap at the house, the family surrendered the perimeter. Martin said he looked silly standing off Goliath's flames with a garden hose. Even though it could have been a disaster, it worked.

"In the end," Martin summarized to Sasha, "Anyone who stayed with their house didn't lose it."

Before leaving, Sasha politely asked Martin, "May we pose together by your Iditarod trophy for a photo? In my country it is such an accomplishment."

Three days later, Sasha left the land where he had enjoyed more than half a year of mushing to return to Belgrade to train youngsters from the Balkans the joy of dog mushing and to share the interview and photos of Iditarod champ Martin Buser. The hard-pressed musher from Zurich took the time to share with his public, remembering what it was like to cross the globe and break into the world of Alaska's dog mushing.

Chapter Ninety Two

GLOBALIZATION IN DELTA JUNCTION

*204. Denise Lassaw,
Homer, 2002.*

In the late 1990s, the site of Jess Taylor and Charlie Boyd's 1947 sled dog kennel for U.S. War Dogs, today's Fort Greely, was designated for obsolescence. As America downsized its military, transitioning into N.A.T.O.'s global, peacekeeping missions, Fort Greely was moth-balled as were many other such U.S Army installations. Consequently, Delta was on the docket to lose its main source of employment: on-base, U.S. Civil Service jobs. Delta's population was deeply effected; many families had to leave. However in the new millennium, new employment arose as Fort Greely was chosen as a site for the National Missile Defense Program's Ground-based Midcourse Defense (GMD.)

Star Wars at the Top of the World

In 2001, when Reb was in Oregon fighting fire, he happened to catch the evening news on television. He was stunned to hear the commentator say, "Delta Junction, Alaska, the home of Fort Greely, is the projected site for the President's 'Star Wars,' anti-ballistic missile system…"

In 1904, international prospectors en route to the gold fields of Fairbanks founded Big Delta as a supply depot. Today, the greater Delta area, about 3500 persons, is a microcosm of the fast paced transition from classical North to Alaska in the Global Village. Today, at the top of the world, the people's focus has shifted from remote wilderness homesteads to worldwide intra-connectedness.

Hourly, Daily Contact From the Tanana's Banks to Belgrade, Half a World Away…

In 1967, when I considered moving to Yugoslavia, but did not, I shut the door to the Balkans, certain I would never again return. For thirty-one years I was locked in my wilderness life. My Serbian friends lived…somewhere…in my memory.

In 1996, I began writing my family's stories of the Bush as well as portraits of our grass roots characters for the Fairbanks Daily News-Miner.

Subsequently, I published my first book, *Parallel Destinies, An Alaskan Odyssey*. I was promoting it in Homer in 2002 when I ran into Denise Lassaw, my pre-Revolution and Haight-Ashbury friend whom I had not seen in a lifetime. We went to her home on a ridge above Homer on the Kenai Peninsula.

We were both in our mid-50s and chose to disregard the schedules of our busy day to catch up. Working on a book regarding global issues, I interviewed Denise, a veteran of our age. Under the golden lamplight of her kitchen table, Denise's face was mature, brimming with the soft nuances of her rich life. Denise was always a citizen of the world. I explained to her that in the last decade I had transitioned from a lifetime of taking care of children, horses, and sled dogs to becoming re-connected to the Yugoslavia of my youth.

In 1997, I had been asked to write the history of Rika's Roadhouse State Park in Big Delta, built, coincidentally, by John Hajdukovich, a Yugoslavian. I had made my first attempt, using the Internet, to research the name "Hajdukovic" in Montenegro. Dr. Miroslav Konstantinovic had responded to my inquiries, subsequently becoming my new friend, along with his wife and children, through the Internet. In a city of two million people, my new friend, Miro, lived in Belgrade only a block and a half from my original friends. Through personal connections, he found not only the Hajdukovics for me, but also my companions from my 1964 summer in France and Yugoslavia. At the end of fifty years of communism and after a decade of his country's implosion, Miro, in just a few days, re-connected me with my original friends.

The fall of 1998, the Hajdukovics, relatives of the Alaskan John Hajdukovich, invited me to Yugoslavia for research. Shortly after, I began publishing my books in Belgrade, half a globe away.

By a few strokes of the keys from a remote Alaskan town, I had been re-connected to my past: the electronic impulse had shot through my life to thirty-one years earlier.

By contrast, in 1901, a letter from Alaska took a year to arrive Outside.

The Classical Alaska developed by the prospectors, the U.S. Army, the construction workers, and the Native people in the first half of the twentieth century had all but disappeared by the late 1990s. Similarly, a high volume, market-driven society and a sophisticated dogsled race, more homogenous to the global marketplace, has replaced the dogsled race of 1973, when John Schulz and other politically incorrect trappers formed the first Iditarod.

In my thirty-one years of Tanana River somnolence, the world shrank suddenly by the implementation of the Internet; suddenly, distanced friends could daily touch hands. Worldwide communication and trade have defeated the miles of snow and ice; Alaska has come out of its isolation into the greater community.

Removed, and as yet, untouched, our trapline's Blue Hills still shimmer in their distance; while this season, Reb once again readies his dog team to hit the trail. But progress is imminent; a road is projected to slice through the hills around Shaw Creek, continuing just short of Jack Stewart's claim --and, on to Pogo Gold Mine. While the wind blows through the large cottonwoods on our trapline and the marten leap through the snow, I give you *Blue Hills, Alaska's Promised Land,* a trail over the mountains, a life on the heights.

205. Sarah and Ben on Donnelly Dome, south of Delta, Summer Solstice, 2001.

Credits

Articles previously published:

"**Reb Ferguson Lives!**" 1990 11 16, *Whitestone Legacy,* January 10, 1996.
"**Her Trial by Fire Keeps Flame Alive,**" *Fairbanks Daily News-Miner,* January 10, 1996.
"**Mushing 'Spy' Catches Army Off Guard,**" *Fairbanks Daily News-Miner,* February 2, 1996.
"**Boy, Dad Strike it Rich at Ice-Fishing Hole,**" *Fairbanks Daily News-Miner,* March 10, 1996.
"**Time Almost Catches Man With Own Pace,**" *Fairbanks Daily News-Miner,* March 24, 1996.
"**With Hard Work 'Outpost' Becomes Home,**" *Fairbanks Daily News-Miner,* April 28, 1996.
"**Delta Has What It Takes to Ignite, Fight Fires,**" *Fairbanks Daily News-Miner,* May 5, 1996.
"**Trials and Tribulations on the Tanana,**" *Fairbanks Daily News-Miner,* May 26, 1996.
"**Return to the Copper River,**" *Fairbanks Daily News-Miner,* June 16, 1996.
"**A Journey by Horseback into Summer Days,**" *Fairbanks Daily News-Miner,* June 23, 1996.
"**Breaking Trail Leads to Rite of Passage,**" *Fairbanks Daily News-Miner,* July 21, 1996.
"**Friendship Becomes Fruit of the Berry Patch,**" *Fairbanks Daily News-Miner,* Aug. 11, 1996.
"**The Crossing: Where Paths Cross,**" *Fairbanks Daily News-Miner,* August 18, 1996.
"**Self Preservation: Mastering the Pressure of Canning in the Bush,**" *Fairbanks Daily News-Miner,* August 28, 1996.
"**Hunting on the High Ground: Caribou on the High Plateau,**" *Fairbanks Daily News-Miner,* September 8, 1996,.
"**Beaver, with a Side Dish of Rose Hips, Rice,**" *Fairbanks Daily News-Miner,* Sep. 15, 1996.
"**Neighbors Come Through for Bush Family in Crisis,**" *Fairbanks Daily News-Miner,* Oct. 13, 1996.
"**Nulato Crews 'taste' Lower 48 Summer,**" *Northland News,* November 1996.
"**Thanksgiving 'Turkey' Falls into Trappers' Hands,**" *Fairbanks Daily News-Miner,* Nov. 10, 1996.
"**The Proof is in the Fruitcake,**" *Fairbanks Daily News-Miner,* December 8, 1996.
"**'Old Acquaintances' Bring the Spice to Life,**" *Fairbanks Daily News-Miner,* January 12, 1997.
"**Army Arctic Training School: Put to the Test,**" *Fairbanks Daily News-Miner,* January 19, 1997.
"**Trapline Brings Dad, Daughter Closer,**" *Fairbanks Daily News-Miner,* Feb. 9, 1997.
"**Last Musher to Nome,**" *Fairbanks Daily News-Miner,* February 16, 1997.
"**Sleigh Becomes Way to Hand Over Reins,**" *Fairbanks Daily News-Miner,* March 9, 1997.
"**Overflow: Friend and Foe Emerges From River,**" *Fairbanks Daily News-Miner,* Ap. 7, 1997.
"**Pioneering Kellys Settle in Delta Junction: Sam & Chaddie: Saga of the Pioneering Kellys,**" *Fairbanks Daily News-Miner,* April 20, 1997.
"**The Seasons of the Tanana Oasis,**" *Fairbanks Daily News-Miner,* May 4, 1997.
"**Birch Stands Ready to Give its Gifts,**" *Fairbanks Daily News-Miner,* June 1, 1997.
"**Doctor Dunlap the Deliverer of Many of Fairbanks' Children: The Doctor was Always In,**" *Fairbanks Daily News-Miner,* June 15, 1997.
"**Delta Derby Filled With Thrills, Spills, Chills,**" *Fairbanks Daily News-Miner,* June 29, 1997.
"**Accomplishing Something From Nearly Nothing,**" *Fairbanks Daily News-Miner,* Aug. 31, 1997.

"Leaves, Autumn Disappear, But Impressions Remain," *Fairbanks Daily News-Miner*, September 28, 1997.

"Life on the Water: Through the Channels," *Fairbanks Daily News-Miner*, October 19, 1997.

The Longest Mush Home," *Fairbanks Daily News-Miner*, October 26, 1997.

"A Man's Cup of Cocoa," *Fairbanks Daily News-Miner*, November 23, 1997.

"Santa Knows Even the Tanana River," *Fairbanks Daily News-Miner*, December 21, 1997.

"Miner's Faith Pays Off at Pogo Creek," *Fairbanks Daily News-Miner*, January 18, 1998.

"Even the Best Sometimes Need a Leg Up," *Fairbanks Daily News-Miner*, February 15, 1998.

"Outings were Thrill for Isolated Students," *Fairbanks Daily News-Miner*, March 22, 1998.

"Partners Corralled Delta Beef Enterprises," *Fairbanks Daily News-Miner*, April 18, 1999.

"Through the Secret Door to Alaska's Heart," *Fairbanks Daily News-Miner*, May 16, 1999.

"Calling the Old Names of the Yukon," *Fairbanks Daily News-Miner*, June 20, 1999.

"Yukon's Villagers Share Sorrow And Bounty," *Fairbanks Daily News-Miner*, July 18, 1999.

"Before There Was Grayling, There Was Holikachuk," *Fairbanks Daily News-Miner*, Aug. 22, 1999.

"At the Yukon's Confluence of Indian and Eskimo," *Fairbanks Daily News-Miner*, Sep. 19, 1999.

"Under the Guidance of Charlie Boyd," *Fairbanks Daily News-Miner*, October 24, 1999.

"Grand Coincidence Eclipses 'Grand Slam'," *Fairbanks Daily News-Miner*, January 23, 2000.

"Proprietress Was There for Wash and Life Cycles," *Fairbanks Daily News-Miner*, March 19, 2000.

"The Ice Free Corridor into the Arctic," Fairbanks Daily News-Miner, June 16, 2000.

"*A Boy Who Turned into a Caribou;* An Arctic Hobbit: Contradictions of the North," Fairbanks Daily News-Miner, July 16, 2000.

"Clues Found Ashore Along Corridor Into the Past," *Fairbanks Daily News-Miner*, Aug. 20, 2000.

"Site of Hermit's Fortune, Misfortune," *Fairbanks Daily News-Miner*, September 17, 2000.

"Greely School Remains in Students' Stories," *Fairbanks Daily News-Miner*, October 15, 2000.

"Cache-and-Carry System Fueled Bayless & Roberts," *Fairbanks Daily News-Miner*, Mar. 18, 2001.

"Epidemic Survivors Begin Community Anew," *Fairbanks Daily News-Miner*, June 17, 2001.

"Bringing a Dying Village Back to Life," *Fairbanks Daily News-Miner*, July 15, 2001.

"Going Our Separate Ways to Adventure," *Fairbanks Daily News-Miner*, August 26, 2001.

"Road to Inuvik Graveled with Good Intentions," *Fairbanks Daily News-Miner*, Sep. 23, 2001.

"The Making of a Bow Hunter," *Fairbanks Daily News-Miner*, September 23, 2001.

"Angels Found in an Igloo and on the Road," *Fairbanks Daily News-Miner*, October 21, 2001.

"Pair of Voyageurs Share Rite of Passage," *Fairbanks Daily News-Miner*, November 18, 2001.

"Musher Harnesses Impossible Dream to Sled," *Fairbanks Daily News-Miner*, Dec. 30, 2001.

"Raising and Cherishing a Wild Thing," *Fairbanks Daily News-Miner*, February 3, 2002.

"Keeping Goats and Finding Trouble," *Fairbanks Daily News-Miner*, March 17, 2002.

"Meeting Alaska with a Song in her Heart," *Fairbanks Daily News-Miner*, April 28, 2002.

"A Solstice Night's Dream," *Fairbanks Daily News-Miner*, June 16, 2002.

"In Smokey's Footsteps," *Fairbanks Daily News-Miner*, June 23, 2002.

"Thrown Into the Midst of the Mighty," *Fairbanks Daily News-Miner*, July 21, 2002.

"Past Parallels Present on Highway," *Fairbanks Daily News-Miner*, August 18, 2002.

List of Illustrations

34. Quonset hut similar to one in which Lea lived. (Post Exchange at Big Delta's Allen Army Airfield, c. 1948.) Courtesy of John Callahan.
35. Lea, 1979.
36. Reb, John Schulz, Valdez goat hunt, 1966.
37. Russ Trastek, Jake Miller, John Schulz during storm on mountain shelf, Valdez goat hunt, 1966.
38. Fred Campbell, c. 1944, Courtesy Delta Historical Society.
39. Bill Arrington building log home c. 1967. Courtesy Bill Arrington.
40. Hans Seppala, c. 1965, Courtesy James Harrild.
41. Slim and Jolly's homestead, Goodpaster River, c. 1991. Courtesy Marian Sexton.
42. Paul and Margaret Kirsteatter taking wolf hides to market c. 1990, Tanana River. Courtesy Paul Kirsteatter.
43. Charlie coiling copper wire at McCarthy, 1967.
44. Copley News Service article on Reb, "the spy," 1967.
45. Soldiers in harness pulling sled during military maneuvers, c. 1948, U.S. Army Arctic Indoctrination School Annual, 1947, Big Delta Allen Army Airfield. Courtesy of John Callahan.
46. Franklin on the Fortymile River, c. 1905. Courtesy of Alice Roberts Bayless.
47. Howard Bayless, center, Bayless and Roberts Trucking, c. 1957.
48. Charlie Boyd's boat that conquered the Johnson River. Courtesy Dave Davenport and Patty Gooley.
49. Client with full curl ram.
50. Reb packing clients' Dall sheep, 1970.
51. Reb, 1948, Trenton Cowboy.
52. Curly Brant, fire boss, 1967, Fairbanks Daily News Miner.
53. Joe Mead, horse trader, c. 2002. Courtesy Irene Hansen Mead.
54. Reb splitting wood at Peniel, 1982. Courtesy Ed Speer.
55. Putting a new roof on Campbell's Cabin as Clint is learning to whistle, 1976.
56. Sledding a 55-gallon, cache drum down Flat Creek mountain, c. 1972.
57. Reb wraps ropes around toboggan runners, roughlocking, to slow downhill descent, 1982.
58. Reb by Salcha slough and cabin, 1976.
59. Reb, Judy and Clint in front of home cabin, 1970.
60. Judy, Clint on Amigo, 1971.
61. Judy, Schist, 1971.
62. Judy, Clint on Amigo; Reb, Klondike, Sox, 1971.
63. Firefighter waits for steak a la shovel and potatoes.
64. Back-burning to stop progress of Hell's Canyon fire.
65. Clint and spruce pole for bunk, 1971.
66. Reb peeling log, Schist Creek, 1971.
67. Judy skinning bull moose, Campbell's, 1976.
68. Reb the jockey after Delta Derby, 1972.
69. Delta Derby, 1973. Courtesy Mike and Lorry Yates.
70. John, Beau and Diane Hansen, 1972.
71. John Schulz at first Iditarod's Starting Line. Courtesy of John Schulz and Anchorage Times, 1973.
72. Charlie Boyd's dog team: Toby, Kandik, Mike, and Cassandra. Courtesy Dave Davenport and Patty Gooley.
73. John Schulz, Nome, 1973. Winner of the "Blue Lantern." Courtesy John Schulz, the Nome Nugget and the 1973 Iditarod Dogsled Race annual.
74. Bobbie Fowler, Fowler's Dairy Farm, c.1968 at Shaw Creek. Courtesy Julenne Fowler.
75. Charlie Boyd and Julian Fowler, pilots discussing mechanics at Boyd's cabin, c. 1968, Courtesy of Dave Davenport and Patty Gooley.
76. Al Remington, Walt and Wes Keaster en route to Alaska, 1954.

77. Remington Keaster Wagon Train, Great Falls Tribune, 1953. Courtesy Emily Keaster.
78. Doug McCollum, 2001, Delta Junction.
79. First harvested grain in the Clearwater. University of Alaska Extension Service Agent, Virgil Severns and Emily, 1955.
80. Map, Graphic Artist, Diane Folaron.
81. Reb packing 55-gallon, barrel stove uphill to new home, Outpost, 1973.
82. Outpost with wind generator, solar panels; barn; greenhouses and garden, 1980, southern exposure.
83. Reb and Clint haul house logs with Klondike, 1973.
84. Reb's fellow Laborers building Trans-Alaska Oil Pipeline at Shaw Creek, 1975.
85. Rosa Pass, the portal of our trapline, as pipe is both elevated and buried on our sled dog trail for the Trans-Alaska Oil Pipeline, looking south to the Alaska Range, 1976.
86. Clint, a week after dog bite, hunting Easter eggs upriver, 1975.
87. Clint and Reb, MonteChristo, 1974.
88. Clint and Reb, MonteChristo, 1974.
89. Clint, Reb, Judy, 1975, Yukon River trip.
90. Loaded to the gunnels, Yukon River trip.
91. Emmitt Peters, lead dog, Nugget, record-setter for 1975 Iditarod, Melozi.
92. Peters family: Paul, Phillip, Mary, Nina, Timmy at Melozi fish camp, 1975.
93. Fish wheel scooping salmon Tanana River, Chena, Riverboat Discovery.
94. Nulato's historical cemetery, 1975.
95. Judy cutting fish with ulu in Kaltag, 1975.
96. Mosquito blight at Holy Cross, 1975.
97. Reb and Clint on the Innoko River to Shageluk, 1975.
98. Reb with historical Episcopalian church at Kaltag.
99. Albert Carroll piloting the Brainstorm, 1975. Courtesy of Albert Carroll.
100 Charlie and Jack Horner in plank boat leaving us on Upper Kobuk to return to Kiana, 1977.
101. Clint and Judy on Upper Kobuk River sandbar, Brooks Range, 1977.
102. Daisy Ticket of Kobuk village making birchbark basket, 1977.
103. Eva Horner, wearing traditional kuspuk, weaving fish net with shuttle, Kobuk village, 1977.
104. Mark Cleveland, elder and artist, Ambler village, 1977.
105. Mark Cleveland's carved wooden mask bookends, Ambler, 1977.
106. Andrew Garbin and gold nugget watch chain, Kiana, c. 1905.
107. Gertrude Sheldon, Miss Kobuk, Kiana, 1977.
108. Reb and Clint approach Kiana in Folbots, 1977.
109. Three-year-old Sarah on porch near rain barrel, 1980.
110. Three-week-old Sarah in beaded birchbark baby carrier-December sunshine.
111. Ferguson Family on Mount Gilles, cutting trail to Peniel and Gilles Creek, 1978.
112. Reb packing Sarah on his front over hills as Clint leads Klondike to Peniel, 1978.
113. "Good morning, Sarah!" at Gilles Creek cabin site, 1978.
114. Smoke Hole above Peniel. Sarah in Johnny Jump-Up. Reb and Clint warm up by fire, 1978.
115. Ferguson Trapline Map: old and new traplines, Graphic Artist, Diane Folaron.
116. Ridge Mushing.
117. Joe Vogler, Alaskan. Founder of the Alaska Independence Party. Courtesy of AIP website.
118. Ben in Russ Trastek's Alaska Tuxedo.
119. Clint and Laddy, black Labrador friend, 1979.
120. Western bluff obstructs access to our upriver home. The ice shelf has formed a narrow corridor.
121. October: the Tanana is choked with slush but the ice shelf around the bluff is not yet formed, preventing easy access. Sarah, Reb and Clint, 1980.
122. Clint, Laura and Sarah, 1979.

123. Clint, Laura, Lady and B.G. walking on shelf ice around bluff, 1981.
124. Veteran firefighter Hell's Canyon Fire, Ukiah Oregon; Reb in 1995.
125. Sarah and Smokey, Delta Parade, 1999.
126. Clint, Reb and bear that was raiding our dog yard, 1976.
127. Cubby.
128. Alicia and Golden Ashby, 1983.
129. Santa Clint, 1983.
130. Clint's Christmas Cookie Tree.
131. Frozen Tanana with moon; mushing east toward home.
132. Sam and Chaddie Kelly, 1940.
133 Chaddie and Yvonne, 2000.
134. Ben mixing fruit cake ingredients, 1990.
135. Judy mixing fruit cake by lantern glow, upriver, 1981. Courtesy of Ed Speer.
136. Judy with 24 ft riverboat, 35 hp outboard on Tanana River, 1997.
137. Judy with 32 pound King Salmon, Chitina, 1976.
138. Judy Grapengeter with red salmon, Judy and Ben Ferguson--fishing team at Chitina, c. 1994.
139. Vera Pavel Tamela Berezyuk picking blueberries like in Ukraine, c. 1995.
140. Sarah canning peaches at downriver home, c. 1996.
141. Reb rototilling garden at Outpost home, c. 1997.
142. The Tanana at confluence with Delta River, bluff, Alaska Range and Mount Hayes.
143. Caribou Creek overflowed into Caribou Cabin, filled 3/4ths of it with ice and jammed the door shut, 1997.
144. Clint's first Dall sheep ram, on Mount Hayes, 1988.
145. Reb and the buffalo that was shot with a borrowed rifle, 1988.
146. Judy pointing to missed Dall sheep ram, Robertson River Glacier, 1990.
147. Ben, Sarah and Judy upriver, returning horses to winter quarters at Brasiers', 1997.
148. Reb and Clint, successful deer hunt on Kodiak, 1989.
149. Reb flying down hill to Campbell's Cabin, 1981. Courtesy of Ed Speer.
150. Reb relaxing on pole bunk at Caribou Cabin, 1981. Courtesy of Ed Speer.
151. Lynx.
152. Caribou Cabin, 1981. Courtesy of Ed Speer.
153. Marten.
154. Reb with offending sled handles, 1980.
155. Sled without offending sled handles. Courtesy of Ed Speer.
156. Sarah in tepid bath to cool fever.
157. Sarah leading Clancy, loaded with paniers. Waiting on Reb en route to Gilles Creek, 1993.
158. Clint looking back at Heather en route to Schist Creek, where he cut trail 22 years before. 1993.
159. Judy leading Clancy in Caribou Valley. Sarah and Ben on Jahna. 1993.
160. Judy shampooing Ben's head from campfire heated water, Caribou Cabin, 1993.
161. Sarah, Ben, Reb and the monarch at Seven Mile Lake Trail, 1995.
162. Sarah on high plateau with her first caribou, 1995.
163. Ben and Reb with ptarmigan under full rainbow, 1995.
164. Ben in Arctic Oven tent fishing over open holes in the lake.
165. War Department Field Manual, Dog Transportation, Figure 23; Fan Hitch, August 19th, 1944. Courtesy U.S Army Center of Military History, Carlisle, Pennsylvania.
166. Ben tapping birch trees, 1996.
167. Rosie Horner's tiny birchbark berry basket for her daughters, Kiana, on Kobuk River, 1977.
168. Algonquin with elders birchbark canoe, Quebec, 1957. Courtesy of Leonard Lee Rue III.
169. Ben transplanting in downriver greenhouse, 1996.

170. Reb, Sarah and Ben taking transplants to the upriver greenhouse, 1996.
171. Reb and Clancy in harness with Reb's homemade sleigh, 1996.
172. Charlie Boyd with grizzly-bear Skolai Pass, c 1977. Courtesy of Dave Davenport and Patty Gooley.
173. Patty Gooley and Dall sheep, Johnson River Glacier, 1989. Courtesy of Dave Davenport and Patty Gooley.
174. Ben's first caribou, Sevenmile Lake Trail, 1994.
175. Sarah feeding week-old Thunder, 1998.
176. Nishka and Reb watching T.V., 2001.
177. Sarah at Peniel, trapping, '95.
178. Partners share rewards: wolf, marten and fox pelt.s, 1995, downriver home.
179. Reb and Judy return to MonteChristo Creek by dogsled on 25th anniversary, 1993.
180. Clint's mode of transportation in 1990, Black. Rika's Roadhouse State Park.
181. After a long but successful night's hunt, Clint and Heather with caribou on Black, 1997.
182. Three Ferguson men: Ben on Jahna, Clint on Black, Reb on Clancy, caribou hunting, 1997
183. Elaine Eads on Ferguson trapline, 1990.
184. A child primed for canoeing, Ben, at end of trip, 2000.
185. Ben and Reb begin 800 mile canoe trip, Eagle River, Yukon Territory, 2000.
186. Tsiigehtchic (pronounced, "T seh guhchek'") formerly Arctic Red River, 2003.
187. A "Notre Dame in the Arctic," "igloo" stylized Roman Catholic church, Inuvik, Northwest Territories, 2001.
188. Ben and Reb, Yukon Crossing, 2001.
189. Clint, practicing upriver, 1977.
190. Ben practicing, Brooks Range, 2001.
191. Reb, the veteran, Brooks Range, 2001.
192. Sukakpak, border where Inupiaq and Athabaskans historically traded, Brooks Range.
193. Judy wresting with Ben, Eagle Summit, 1997.
194. Sarah cooling candles on our downriver snowy porch, 2002.
195. Judy, Sarah and Ben, Denali Park 1995.
196. Ben and Reb forced ashore at Norman Wells by high winds on Mackenzie River, 2002.
197. Windbound on Mackenzie below Tulita; full rainbow.
198. Great Bear Rock with three mineralized circles called by the Gwitch'in, "beaver pelts," Mackenzie River, 2002.
199. Ben and Northern Pike, Mackenzie River, 2002.
200. Sarah, Shayna, Kristin, Clara and me in Inuvik Centennial Library, Northwest Territory, 2002.
201. Jerry Isaac, Tanacross Tribal Council President, 2003.
202. Jack Stewart, 1998.
203. Aleksandar "Sasha" Nikolic and four-time Iditarod Trail Dog Sled Race champion, Martin Buser, Big Lake, 2002.
204. Denise Lassaw, Homer, 2002.
205. Sarah and Ben on Donnelly Dome, south of Delta, Summer Solstice, 2001.

Alaskan Wild Animal Prints, Courtesy of Alaskuts,
Whitestone Farms, Delta Junction, Alaska

Glossary

Ahkio – in Finland, ahkios were a boat-shaped, wooden sled with a copper bottom, pulled by reindeer. The U.S. Army refashioned the Finnish design into a tough fiberglass body.

Air Tankers – large airplanes, fitted with tanks, provide direct support to firefighters on the ground by dropping up to several thousand gallons of water or chemical retardant ahead of an advancing wildfire.

Army canvas mukluks – designed for use in dry cold conditions down to 0° F. The components of this system include 2 wool felt sole pads, 1 heavy wool bootie and a tall zip up canvas outer shell to seal in the warmth. This boot is super warm and comfy, but not waterproof-dry cold only.

Babiche –an untanned animal hide soaked, cut, and dried that may be used for lacing or patching, and that becomes hard when dry. Traditionally, Reb protected the brush bow of his sled with babiche.

Back Trail – a trapper's main trail, but called this when referring to using it for the return home.

Barrel stove – usually a 30 or a 55-gallon metal oil drum that has been converted into a stove by outfitting it with a stove door and a collar for the stovepipe. It is not airtight, so it is hard to regulate.

Beaufort Sea – the huge body of water north of North America.

Berm pile or Berms –topsoil and trees that are bulldozed into piles during the clearing of land.

Blazo cans and boxes –The wooden boxes in which the 5-gallon cans of white gas were crated served as a trapper's shelving, cupboards, and chest of drawers. A hole was punched on either side of the top of the empty 5-gallon gas can into which a # 9 wire was anchored and bent into a carrying handle. Blazo cans were used to carry water, melt snow, do dishes, wash laundry and make dog food. Old-timers cut the cans open, pounded them flat, laid and overlapped them onto a trap cabin's sod roof to protect the roof from decay and the cabin from subsequent collapse. A cabin with a metal roof might last 50-75 years. Without the tin protection, a structure might collapse in 10 years.

Brake, Dog Sled – Historically a brake was two steel claws attached to the underbelly of the dog sled.

Bulldozers and Tractor Plows (Caterpillars) – Tracked vehicles with plows for clearing vegetation. Mechanized equipment can build a fire line faster and more efficiently than human firefighters.

Break-up – the warm temperatures of spring thaw the land, rivers, and lakes, breaking the ice up and sending it downstream to the sea, sometimes resulting in large ice jams, causing disastrous flooding.

Brushed out – the process of clearing trail, sawing deadfalls, throwing brush aside.

Bug – a candle wedged in a two-pound coffee can, a trapline flashlight.

Bunny Boots – Military made, layered insulation, heavy arctic style rubber boots, officially called Vapor Barrier boots. They protect from immersion in overflow and warm trapped water when needed.

Cache – A cache may be any place where humans, or certainly beaver, store their food, their valuables.

Cache drum – a 30 or a 55-gallon metal drum with a lid and locking ring that was made to store paint. Trapline food, sleeping bags, and clothes are stored in these drums to protect the contents from bears.

Cheechakos –newcomers to Alaska.

Chinook winds – The name of a North American, warm, dry wind on the leeward side of mountains.

Cole crops – Broccoli, cabbage, and cauliflower, vegetables that grow best between 60° and 68° F.

Deadfall – a downed, dead tree also called a windfall.

Devil's Club – a springy Ginseng with a very prickly stem.

Drip Torch – throws a stream of flaming liquid, gasoline and diesel, used to facilitate rapid ignition during burn out operations on a wildland fire or during a prescribed fire operation.

Eyuga – *(Athabaskan Koyukon)* half-dried, smoked salmon strips.

Fan Hitch harnessing – snapping each dog separately into one ring under the sled, used on pack ice so that if one or two dogs fall into a crevasse they won't drag the rest of the team in with them.

Fire Line – A linear fire barrier that is dug into mineral soil to deter the advancement of a wildfire.

Fire Resistant Pants/Shirt – Firefighters' flame resistance clothing known as Nomex.

Fire Shelter – A last resort, aluminized tent that protects by reflecting radiant heat and allowing oxygen in a fire entrapment situation. See http://www.smokeybear.com/tools_fs.asp

Fish wheels – A device in which two paddle-like spokes holding two wire baskets scoop returning adult salmon. The river current pushes the paddles that rotate on a wooden axle. The fish fall live into a holding box. The people cut the fish for drying, providing the Athabaskan people with fish for winter.

Fizz sticks – 4-inch sticks of thin firewood, shaved with an axe against the grain for quick fire ignition.

Founder – lameness in the foot of a horse, occasioned by an inflammation of the laminae of the hoof. A horse that gets into a grain bag and gorges itself may develop founder.

Fred Cook – featured in *Parallel Destinies, An Alaskan Odyssey*, Fred was a miner who drilled the water wells in Delta. Able to make something out of nothing, Fred could jury rig whatever was needed.

Freeze-up – process during October-November in which the Interior is changed into deep winter.

Full Curl –the horn of perhaps an eight year old, male Dall sheep that has grown through 360 degrees.

Gee – The command used to direct the lead dog(s) to go to the right.

Giardia – dubbed "Beaver Fever," is a diarrhea-inducing parasite connected with animal feces.

Grand Slam –a big game term referring to Dall, Stone, Big Horn, and Desert sheep.

Haw – the command used to direct the lead dog(s) to go to the left.

Helicopters in Firefighting – helicopters drop water, foam, or retardant on a fire to prevent its spread.

Helitack – crews trained in helicopter use for fire suppression. Helitack can be rapidly deployed.

Hot Shot crew – a first strike, highly trained firefighting force.

Inuksuk – a pile of stones used as a marker by the Inuit People and made like a human being.

Inupiaq/Inupiat (Ak) –The Inupiat people are the Inuit of Northwestern Alaska, stretching from Norton Sound to the Canadian border. They are part of the broader group from circumpolar lands.

Inuvialuit – the Inuit of western Canadian Arctic called *"Inuvialuit"* or "real human beings." Their homeland extends east to the Canadian Arctic Islands and is bisected by the Mackenzie River Delta.

Kazheem – a communal sweat bath with underground chambers. In Shageluk, originally a square, tapering building with a four-sided skylight. Mask dances were held there during January.

Kicker – a small outboard motor.

Kuspuk – the traditional Inuit, Inupiaq and Yupik summer parka, hooded, long sleeved and to mid-leg.

Kuuvangmiit –two Kobuk River Inupiat societies, the Akunirmiut and the Kuuvaum Kangianirmiut, whose descendants today are the "Kuuvangmiit" of Kiana, Ambler, Kobuk and Shungnak.

Lower 48 – the 48 states of the United States that are contiguous on the North American continent.

Marten cubby – a baited trap walled in with spruce branches.

Muktuk – the fat of a whale – blubber – a delicacy often stored in seal oil.

Muskeg - tussocks of rubbery earth that may grow to two feet high and are often in swamp water. It is not possible to hike on the muskeg but in the tight space in between the tussocks, it is possible to walk.

Neck lines – a short cord that connects from the main tug line to the dog's individual collar to keep the dogs facing forward, the team together and to prevent dog fights.

Needle ice – grouped ice slivers, a few centimeters long, at or immediately below the ground surface.

Nulato-Kaltag stick dance – the Heeyo (Stickdance) Ceremony is a phenomenon unique to the area. The dance centered around a wolverine skin, sacred to the Athabaskans, and held high on a stick.

Number 10 can – a 2-pound size coffee can used for cooking, for "bugs" or for feeding dogs.

Outside – anywhere in the world that is not in Alaska, but generally only refers to the Lower 48 states.

Overflow – water oozing under hydrostatic pressure occurring from a few inches to several feet.

Patents – land deeds from the Federal Government for land previously designated as public lands.

Periglacial – Landforms created by intense freeze-thaw action near an alpine glacier.

Permafrost – permanently frozen subsoil that retains water on the surface. The surface layer thaws in summer and freezes in winter. 82% of Alaska and 50% of Russia and Canada are permafrost soils.

Pingos –conical, ice-cored hills that grow to 50 meters in height and more than 300 meters in diameter.

Pipeline gravel pad or corridor – the graveled road constructed from Prudhoe Bay to Valdez for the construction and maintenance of the Trans-Alaska Oil Pipeline.

Pole bunks and tables – beds and tables made from spruce saplings.

Pole boating – in lieu of an outboard, the act of pushing a boat forward with a long, slender pole.

Porcupine boiler – a 5-gallon bucket of boiling water with pipes welded out its sides, like quills, for warming the earth. Then, the resulting hole is mucked out with a simple pick and shovel.

Portage – one of the north's traditional routes between non-connecting rivers.

Project fire – a huge fire that is attacked using multi-levels of manpower and sophisticated technology. The status "Project Fire" gives the blaze priority for maximum resources.

Pulaski – a combination chopping and trenching tool, a Pulaski combines a single-bitted axe-blade with a narrow adze-like trenching blade fitted to a straight handle. Useful for grubbing or trenching in duff and matted roots, it is also well balanced for chopping.

Quonset hut – a military made, portable building made from a combination of semi-circular metal supports, canvas, and siding. The long, rounded Quonset heats quickly and withstands Arctic winds. The prefabricated buildings became a staple for Alaskan homes and commercial buildings.

Rack or palms – refers to moose horns, while antlers generally refer to caribou horns.

Riffles or thin water – refers to shallow water.

Roofjack – generally a 5-gallon can that has both ends removed to allow the insertion of a stovepipe. After a square has been cut into the roof of a cabin and the poles of the roof have been supported with braces, the can is wedged into the hole in the roof. Inside the cabin, the stovepipe is fitted into the collar of the stove and inserted through the roof via the roofjack to protect the roof from accidental fire.

Rough Lock –Turning the sled onto one side, two-inch rope or chain is woven around the runners to create drag, hence slowing down the sled on a downhill run.

Schist – any metamorphic rock that can be split into thin layers.

Scrub spruce – the thin, stunted, shallow-rooted spruce growing in permafrost soils whose branches are often draped with a black, hairy-looking lichen.

Set steel – to set traps.

Shoepacs –a tall, rubberized bottom with leather upper boot insulated with removable, felt liners.

Shrews – a tiny rodent.

Si-wash – the "Chinook language," a trading vernacular used in frontier days, referred to a Native American. Example: camping without benefit of a tent was called a "si-wash camp."

Sled parts – Stanchion – the sled bed's supports. **Waffle irons** – the metal brackets into which the stanchions are anchored to the sled runner. **Brush bow** – the front bumper made from four steamed, and bent tamarack green poles, bound with babiche cords and sheathed with a square of babiche, sealed with hot pepper and varnish to prevent the dogs from lunching on the brush bow. The brush bow protects the sled's bed and front-runners from impact. **Back bow** – the curved tamarack handle that the musher holds onto. The back bow is connected to the back supports of the sled that are anchored to the rear of the sled's runners.

Slough – a lesser branch of the main river. An inlet from a river – a backwater.

Spike Camp – the higher camps for hunting where supplies are stocked by backpack, or on horse-back.

Stags – low-cut boots that are a trapper's house shoes.

Subsistence – the Alaska National Interest Lands Conservation Act (ANILCA) defines subsistence as "the traditional and customary use by rural Alaska residents of wild, renewable resources for direct personal or family consumption for food, shelter, fuel, clothing, tools or transportation; for the making and selling of handicraft articles out of non-edible by products of fish and wildlife resources taken for personal or family consumption; and for customary trade" (ANILCA Section 803, 1980; Hall et al. 1985).

Sweepers – low-hanging, horizontal trees growing from, and extending from the river bank, dangerous for unaware boaters that are hugging the bank.

Tamarack – a coniferous, deciduous larch whose trunks are tough, supple and resilient. The slender trunk is steamed and bent into sled bows and even into snowshoe frames. Found in wet areas.

Tandem harnessing – the pattern of snapping pairs of sled dogs into the same metal ring in the tug line causing them to pull in tandem.

Trail had set up – when a broken trail in snow has frozen and is hard and dependable for travel.

Trapline Chatter – a program for personal messages, transmitted nightly on KJNP-North Pole radio, a 50,000 watt Christian station, to people who have only one-way communication in the Bush.

Tsiigehtchic (pron: T seh gehchek') – the Native village, formerly called Arctic Red River, at the confluence of the Arctic Red River and the Mackenzie River.

Tug line – the main cord into which the individual dog harnesses are snapped.

Tundra – Treeless plains of northern arctic regions consisting of black mucky soil with a permanently frozen subsoil; supports a dense growth of mosses, lichens, dwarf herbs, shrubs, showy-flowered.

Vuntut Gwich'in – meaning "People of the Lakes". The Gwich'in Nation are in Alaska and the Northwest Territories. "Vuntut Gwitchin:" the people in and around Old Crow.

Walked a Cat – drove a Caterpillar across rough terrain.

Wheel Dog – the dog closest to the sled.

Yukon stove – 2-foot long, 1-foot by 1-foot, sheet metal stove that transported easily on the early prospectors' sleds.

We welcome reader response to **Blue Hills, Alaska's Promised Land.**
Your input is valuable.

Books and Materials by Judy Ferguson

Bridges to Statehood: the Alaska-Yugoslav Connection
ISBN: 978-0-9716044-9-0
Parallel Destinies, An Alaskan Odyssey, ISBN: 0-9716044-0-1

Children's Books
Alaska's Secret Door, ISBN: 978-0-9716044-2-1
Alaska's Little Chief, ISBN: 978-0-9716044-3-8
Alaska's First People, ISBN: 978-0-9716044-4-5

Lesson plans based on state standards available for each book.
Also available: books read aloud on CD, signed notecards and limited edition, signed art prints.

Online store:
http://alaska-highway.org/delta/outpost/alaska-outpost-store.htm
Telephone: 1-907 895 4101
Email: outpost@wildak.net
Address: PO Box 130
Delta Junction, Alaska 99737, U.S.A.

Thank you for your support.

Judy Ferguson
Voice of Alaska Press
Big Delta, Alaska